New Asian Disorder

Studies of the Contemporary Asia Pacific (SCAP)

This series is the flagship publication of the London Asia Pacific Centre for Social Science, based at SOAS, University of London and King's College London. "Peace and prosperity" have underpinned the Asia-Pacific region's rise in the international system since the end of the Cold War. This series seeks to understand the contemporary challenges to "peace and prosperity." In particular, it seeks to understand the origins and dynamics of three issues: the divergence between economic and social development along with the worsening of relative disparities, the global constraints facing the region's export-led growth model, and the persistence of interstate conflicts. Based on these comparative and international guiding themes, this series seeks to publish original monographs and edited volumes on the Asia-Pacific, irrespective of the methodological approach.

Series Editors

Tat Yan Kong (School of Oriental and African Studies, University of London), Ramon Pacheco Pardo (King's College London, University of London)

Editorial Board

Dafydd Fell (School of Oriental and African Studies, University of London), Charlotte Goodburn (King's College London, University of London), Nahee Kang (King's College London, University of London), Costas Lapavitsas (School of Oriental and African Studies, University of London), Andrew Sumner (King's College London, University of London), Ulrich Volz (School of Oriental and African Studies, University of London)

International Advisory Panel

Yin-Wah Chu (Hong Kong Baptist University), Jane Duckett (University of Glasgow), Megan Greene (University of Kansas), Eunmee Kim (Ewha Woman's University), Syaru Shirley Lin (University of Virginia), Danny Quah (National University of Singapore), Jeffrey Reeves (Asia Pacific Foundation of Canada), Joseph Wong (University of Toronto), Meredith Woo (Sweet Briar College), Hosoya Yuichi (Keio University), Ariel Yusuf (Padjhajharan University), Feng Zhang (South China University of Technology)

New Asian Disorder

Rivalries Embroiling the Pacific Century

Edited by Lowell Dittmer

Hong Kong University Press
The University of Hong Kong
Pokfulam Road
Hong Kong
https://hkupress.hku.hk

© 2022 Hong Kong University Press

ISBN 978-988-8754-02-1 (*Hardback*)

All rights reserved. No portion of this publication may be reproduced or transmitted in any form or by any means, electronic or mechanical, including photocopying, recording, or any information storage or retrieval system, without prior permission in writing from the publisher.

British Library Cataloguing-in-Publication Data
A catalogue record for this book is available from the British Library.

Digitally printed

Contents

List of Figures and Tables vii
List of Acronyms ix
List of Contributors xi

1. Disorder under Heaven 1
   Lowell Dittmer

Part A: Identities

2. Assessing China's Public Diplomacy under the Leadership of Xi Jinping in Asia: A Pseudo-panel Analysis 23
   Yun-han Chu, Hsin-Che Wu, and Min-Hua Huang
3. Disorder from Within: How the Chinese Public Has Challenged the State on Foreign Policymaking 55
   Jing Sun
4. Between Two Orders in the Asia-Pacific: Navigating a Treacherous Reef 75
   Jeremy Paltiel

Part B: Strategies

5. China in the Rise and Fall of the "New World Order": Toward New Inter-imperial Rivalry 93
   Ho-fung Hung
6. The Coming of the Economic Warring States? China-USA Rivalry and Asian Disorder in the Age of De-globalization 118
   Guoguang Wu
7. US-China Strategic Rivalry: Great Power Competition in the Post-industrial Age 141
   Timothy R. Heath

Part C: Triangles

8. Bringing the Strategic Triangle Back: The Role of Small and Medium States in US-PRC Rivalry 167
   Yu-Shan Wu

9. Southeast Asia among the Powers 187
   Lowell Dittmer

10. A Moderate Phase Transition from Order to Disorder in Asia: The Political Economy of the US-China-Japan Strategic Triangle 218
    Ming Wan

11. Conclusion 238
    Lowell Dittmer

Index 255

Figures and Tables

Figures

Figure 2.1:	Model estimates of favorable perception of China with the Two-Wave Sample (12 political systems)	39
Figure 2.2:	Model estimates of favorable perception of China with the Three-Wave Sample (6 political systems)	39
Figure 5.1:	Annual percentage change in average hourly earnings of production and nonsupervisory employees in private sector, 1965–2018	96
Figure 5.2:	External balance of goods and services of the US, Germany, Japan, and China, 1960–2016 (in current billion USD)	97
Figure 5.3:	Currency composition of allocated official foreign exchange reserves as of 2017 Q4	99
Figure 5.4:	Net outflow of foreign direct investment of the US, Germany, Japan, and China (in current billion USD)	100
Figure 5.5:	Consumption, currency, and capital as foundations of US-led globalization	101
Figure 5.6:	GDP per capita, household income per capita, and consumption per capita of China, 1978–2016	108
Figure 5.7:	China's holdings of US treasuries, in billion USD and in percentage	110
Figure 5.8:	Top currencies' shares in international payments as of November 2015 based on value	111
Figure 5.9:	Customer-initiated and institutional RMB payments (inbound and outbound traffic) by markets as of November 2015	111
Figure 6.1:	The Chinese Warring States, c. 386 BCE	121
Figure 6.2:	East Asia under PRC-USA Rivalry, c. 2019	123
Figure 6.3:	Bilateral trade connections with East Asian economies: The PRC and the USA in comparison (in billions, US$; 2017)	136
Figure 8.1:	Strategic triangles	171

Figure 8.2: SMC's choices ... 174
Figure 8.3: Strategic fault line in East Asia ... 174
Figure 8.4: Taiwan's overall payoff curve ... 179
Figure 9.1: Dual Southeast Asian triangles ... 205

Tables

Table 2.1: Favorable perception of China's influence in Asia (base models) ... 37
Table 2.2: Results of Two-Wave Panel Regression on favorable perception of China's influence in Asia (12 political systems) ... 42
Table 2.3: Results of Three-Wave Panel Regression on favorable perception of China's influence in Asia (6 political systems) ... 44
Table 2.4: Result summary for both Two-Wave and Three-Wave Panel analyses ... 47
Table 7.1: Indicators for assessing intensity of strategic rivalry ... 145
Table 7.2: Assessment of US-China rivalry indicators ... 151
Table 7.3: Potential effects of demographic and social factors on US-China rivalry ... 155
Table 7.4: Potential effects of economic factors on US-China rivalry ... 157
Table 7.5: Potential effects of civilian technologies on US-China rivalry ... 159
Table 7.6: Potential effects of military technologies on US-China rivalry ... 161
Table 8.1: Taiwan's overall payoff in the mini-triangle ... 178
Table 8.2: Fluctuating strategy by SMCs ... 181

Acronyms

ABS	Asian Barometer Survey
ACFTA	ASEAN-China free trade agreement
ADIZ	Air Defense Identification Zone
ADMM-plus	ASEAN Defense Ministers Meeting Plus (ASEAN plus China and Japan)
AEC	ASEAN Economic Community
AIIB	Asian Infrastructure Investment Bank
APEC	Asia Pacific Economic Cooperation
APT	ASEAN plus three (China, Japan, and Korea)
ARF	ASEAN Regional Forum
ARIA	Asia Reassurance Initiative Act
ASEAN	Association of Southeast Asian Nations
ASEM	ASEAN-EU Annual Meeting
BOP	balance of power
BRI	Belt and Road Initiative
BRICS	Brazil, Russia, India, China, and South Africa
BUILD	Better Utilization of Investment Lending and Development
CCP	Chinese Communist Party
CICA	Conference on International Confidence Building Measures in Asia
COMECON	Committee on Mutual Economic Assistance
CPEC	China Pakistan Economic Corridor
CPTPP	Comprehensive and Progressive Agreement for Trans-Pacific Partnership
DOC	Declaration of Conduct of Parties in the South China Sea
DRV	Democratic Republic of Vietnam
EEZ	exclusive economic zone

FOIP	Free and Open Indo-Pacific Initiative
FONOPs	freedom of navigation operations
FTA	free trade agreement
GFC	Global financial crisis (2008)
ICESR	International Covenant on Economic, Social and Cultural Rights
ICCPR	International Covenant on Civil and Political Rights
IGOs	Intergovernmental organizations
IMF	International Monetary Fund
IPR	intellectual property rights
ITLOS	International Tribunal on the Law of the Sea
IWC	International Whaling Commission
JCPOA	Joint Comprehensive Plan of Action
MSDF	Marine Self-Defense Force
NATO	North Atlantic Treaty Organization
ODA	Official Development Assistance
PLA	People's Liberation Army
RCEP	Regional Comprehensive Economic Partnership
RMB	renminbi
SCO	Shanghai Cooperation Organization
SDR	Special Drawing Rights
SEATO	Southeast Asia Treaty Organization
SOE	state-owned enterprise
TAC	Treaty of Amity and Cooperation
THAAD	Terminal High Altitude Area Defense
TPP	Trans-Pacific Partnership
TTIP	Transatlantic Trade and Investment Partnership
UN	United Nations
UNCLOS	United Nations Convention on the Law of the Sea
UNHCR	UN High Commission for Refugees
UNHRC	UN Human Rights Council
WPO	Warsaw Pact Organization

Contributors

Yun-han Chu is distinguished research fellow of the Institute of Political Science at Academia Sinica and professor of political science at National Taiwan University. He was a visiting associate professor at Columbia University in 1990–1991. He specializes in the politics of Greater China, East Asian political economy, international political economy, and democratization. He co-chairs the Executive Council of Global Barometer Surveys, the world's largest social science survey research network, and has served as coordinator of the Asian Barometer Survey, a regional network of opinion research on democracy, governance, and development covering more than eighteen Asian countries. He is the author, co-author, editor, or co-editor of seventeen books. Recent publications in English include *the Routledge Handbook of Democratization in East Asia* (2017), edited by Tun-jen Cheng and Yun-han Chu, and *Democracy in East Asia: A New Century* (2013). In 2016 he was chosen to be a fellow of the World Academy of Science, having been elected in 2012 to the Academia Sinica, Taiwan's highest scholarly honor.

Lowell Dittmer is professor in the graduate school of the University of California at Berkeley. Recent works include *China's Quest for National Identity* (with Samuel Kim, 1993), *Liu Shaoqi and the Chinese Cultural Revolution* (rev. ed., 1997), *Informal Politics in East Asia* (with Haruhiro Fukui and Peter N. S. Lee, eds.) (2000), and *China's Asia* (2018).

Timothy R. Heath is a senior international defense researcher at the RAND Corporation. He worked for more than sixteen years on the strategic, operational, and tactical levels in the US military and government, specializing on China, Asia, and security topics. Heath has published numerous articles and one book. Fluent in Mandarin Chinese, he has extensive experience analyzing China's national strategy, politics, ideology, and military, as well as Asian regional security developments. He earned an MA in Asian studies from George Washington University and a BA in philosophy from the College of William and Mary. He is currently pursuing a PhD in political science from George Mason University.

Min-hua Huang is professor in the Department of Political Science and director of the Hu Fu Center for East Asia Democratic Studies in the College of Social Sciences at National Taiwan University (NTU). Before joining NTU, he worked at Shanghai Jiaotong University, Texas A&M University, and National Chengchi University. He was also a visiting fellow at the Brookings Institution's Center for East Asia Policy Studies (2014–2015). Recent writings include "Cognitive Explanations of Indian Perceptions of China" with Yongrong Cao and Hsin-Che Wu, *Asian Survey* (2021); "The Internet, Social Capital, and Civic Engagement in Asia" with Taehee Whang and Lei Xuchuan, *Social Indicators Research* (2017); and "The Sway of Geopolitics, Economic Interdependence and Cultural Identity: Why Are Some Asians More Favorable toward China's Rise than Others?" with Yun-han Chu, *Journal of Contemporary China* (2015). His degrees are from the University of Michigan (PhD), National Sun Yat-Sen University (MA), and NTU (BA).

Ho-fung Hung is the Henry M. and Elizabeth P. Wiesenfeld Professor in Political Economy in the Department of Sociology and the Nitze School of Advanced International Studies at Johns Hopkins University. He researches on global capitalist transformation, nationalism, social movements, and Chinese development. He is the author of the award-winning *Protest with Chinese Characteristics* (2011) and *The China Boom: Why China Will Not Rule the World* (2015). His works also appear in *American Sociological Review*, *American Journal of Sociology*, *Review of International Political Economy*, and *Development and Change*, among others.

Jeremy Paltiel is professor of political science at Carleton University in Ottawa, Canada. He has published widely on Canada-China relations, Chinese foreign policy, the Chinese tradition and its impact on China's foreign relations, China and human rights, and on domestic Chinese politics. In 2019 he published "Canada's Middle Power Ambivalence: The Palimpsest of US Power Under the Chinese Shadow" in Justin Massie and Jonathan Paquin, eds., *America's Allies and the Decline of US Hegemony*. Prior to this, in 2018, he published "Facing China: Canada Between Fear and Hope." He is the author of *The Empire's New Clothes: Cultural Particularism and Universality in China's Rise to Global Status* (2007), and in 2015 he co-edited with Huhua Cao *Facing China as a New Global Superpower: Domestic and International Dynamics from a Multidisciplinary Angle*.

Jing Sun is an associate professor in the Department of Political Science at the University of Denver. His areas of expertise are Japanese politics, Chinese politics, and East Asian international relations. He is the author of two books: *Red Chamber, World Dream: Actors, Audience, and Agendas in Chinese Foreign Policy and Beyond* and *Japan and China as Charm Rivals: Soft Power in Regional Diplomacy*.

Ming Wan is professor and associate dean at George Mason University's Schar School of Policy and Government. His most recent book is *The Political Economy of East Asia: Wealth and Power*, 2nd ed. (2020). His current research interests include US-China rivalry, political economy of East Asia security, Sino-Japanese relations, and human rights.

Guoguang Wu, a PhD in politics from Princeton University, is professor of political science, professor of history, and chair in China and Asia-Pacific Relations at the University of Victoria, Canada. His major research interests follow two tracks: Chinese politics and its transition from communism in comparative perspectives, and comparative political economy with the focus on institutional transformation of capitalism in globalization. He is author of four books, including *China's Party Congress: Power, Legitimacy, and Institutional Manipulation* (2015) and *Globalization against Democracy: A Political Economy of Capitalism after Its Global Triumph* (2017); editor/co-editor of six multiple-author volumes, and contributor to journals such as *Asian Survey*, *China Quarterly*, *Comparative Political Studies*, *Journal of Contemporary China*, *Pacific Review*, and *Third World Quarterly*; as well as author or editor of fifteen books in the Chinese language.

Hsin-Che Wu is an associate professor in the School of Political Science and Public Administration, Shandong University. He received his PhD from the University of Durham in 2013. His research interests are China studies and East Asia politics. His publications have appeared in *Journal of Contemporary China*, *Asian Survey*, *Journal of Local Self-Government*, *Comparative Economic & Social Systems*, and *Jiangsu Social Science*.

Yu-Shan Wu is academician and distinguished research fellow at the Institute of Political Science, Academia Sinica. He has been a leading scholar in Taiwan's semi-presidential studies and theorization of cross-Strait relations. His area focuses are Taiwan, mainland China, Eastern Europe, and Russia. He has authored and edited twenty-four books and published more than 150 journal articles and book chapters. His English books include *Semi-Presidentialism and Democracy*, *In Search of China's Development Model: Beyond the Beijing Consensus*, *The Chinese Models of Development: Global, Local and Comparative Perspectives*, and *Semi-presidentialism Across Continents: A Dialogue Between Asia and Europe*.

1
Disorder under Heaven

Lowell Dittmer[1]

> All under heaven is in chaos. The situation is excellent.
> —Mao Zedong, as quoted by Zhou Enlai, July 1971

The twenty-first century has been forecast to become the Asian century, and its performance in the last half of the twentieth attests that this was no idle daydream.[2] To be sure, Asia is a latecomer, emerging post war from colonialism, followed by communist insurgencies, and still by the late 1960s the poorest continent in the world—the pessimism voiced by Gunnar Myrdal in his famous 1968 tome *Asian Drama* was then widespread.[3] But by 2016, Asia accounted for 33.84 percent of world GDP (up from 26 percent in 2000) and over one-third of world trade. Based on high savings and investment, a literate tradition reinforced by strong commitment to education, smart state industrial policies, and export-oriented growth, the East Asian economies have consistently outpaced global GDP growth. And, despite being hit by a disruptive trade war and a global pandemic, Asia is expected to continue to thrive. China is now the world's second-largest economy (and soon no doubt the first), competing with the US on all fronts—economic, technological, and

---

1. We are all grateful to the Institute of East Asian Studies at the University of California, Berkeley, for sponsoring a conference in the spring of 2019, at which preliminary drafts of these chapters were first presented, as well as to the four anonymous reviewers for their careful analyses and valuable criticisms of each of the chapters.
2. Asian Development Bank, *Asia 2050: Realizing the Asian Century* (Metro Manila, Philippines: Asian Development Bank, 2011); Kishore Mahbubani, *The New Asian Hemisphere: The Irresistible Flow of Power to the East* (New York: Public Affairs, 2008); Parag Khanna, *The Future is Asian: Commerce, Conflict and Culture in the 21st Century* (New York: Simon & Schuster, 2019); John West, *Asian Century on a Knife-Edge: A 360-Degree Analysis of Asia's Recent Economic Development* (Singapore: Palgrave-Macmillan, 2018), among others.
3. Gunnar Myrdal, *Asian Drama: An Inquiry into the Poverty of Nations* (New York: Random House, 1968), vols. I, II, and III.

geopolitical.[4] Southeast Asia, with a population of some 650 million, is just behind India, with a GDP of some $2 trillion. Asia has always been the world's largest continent and now has more than half its population, which will likely continue to grow for the next fifty years, from four to five billion from 2000 to 2050.

Although Asia is still poorer than the rest of the world (per capita GDP about $5,800), it is growing faster. Asia raised hundreds of millions from poverty over the past five decades; merchants look forward to an Asian middle class of 1.75 billion by 2020, surpassing the West's (defined by number of households with per capita incomes of $10,000, at 2005 purchasing power parity/PPP). By 2050, the Asian Development Bank (ADB) estimates, three billion Asians may have living standards similar to those of Europeans and contribute half of global GDP. As Asia grows richer, it also becomes more integrated. While the rest of the world ensnarls itself in nationalist trade wars, Asia continues to interlink its economies via trade, investment, and tourism. Intra-Asian trade nearly doubled as a proportion of total Asian trade between 1955 and 2005. Scorned by Trump, the Trans-Pacific Partnership (TPP) (now known as the Comprehensive and Progressive Agreement for Trans-Pacific Partnership, or CPTPP) was revived under Japanese leadership and came into force at the start of 2019. The world's largest trade pact, the Regional Comprehensive Economic Partnership (RCEP), was signed in November 2020 (despite India's withdrawal). In the realm of ideas, China boasts a new, non-Western path to modernization; as Xi Jinping put it in 2017, China "offers a new option for other countries and nations who want to speed up their development while preserving their independence." Not all have opted to follow it, but all Asian emerging economies share a neo-mercantilist developmental pathway emphasizing state industrial policy and export-oriented growth, which has proved remarkably successful for seventy years.

But this coin has two sides. The emergent counter-narrative to the "Asian century" has taken two forms, too often conflated. The first is that the rise is illusory, exaggerated, or has run out of steam.[5] The export-oriented growth model has, along with globalization, reached its expiration point—Japan's lost decade is the new normal. The Asian tigers' recovery from the Asian financial crisis has plateaued, and China's economic model is on a slow glide path toward the slower growth rate of a large industrial economy. Japan underwent a demographic transition decades ago, and China is now following suit, getting old before it gets rich. Over 20 percent of Asians will be elderly by 2050. The global financial crisis (GFC) that erupted in 2008 was overcome by piling on debt, and since then no major economy has cut its leverage, while the biggest two—China and the US—have increased it. China's debt overhang

---

4. "China," "the Chinese Mainland," and "People's Republic of China" are used interchangeably throughout.
5. For example, Michael Auslin, *The End of the Asian Century: War, Stagnation, and the Risks to the World's Most Dynamic Region* (New Haven, CT: Yale University Press, 2017).

(now over 300 percent of GDP) has become a drag on GDP growth. China's Belt and Road Initiative (BRI) has provided generous infrastructure support to many less developed countries.[6] But can China afford it? Li Keqiang revealed in a May 2020 press conference that some 600 million Chinese were still earning less than five dollars a day.[7] Trump's "trade war" and the 2020 coronavirus epidemic are the final nails in the coffin. As regional growth locomotive, China's slowdown will take the region down with it.

The second counterargument is that while Asia's rise has been real enough, the prospect of a smooth, "win-win" East-West functional integration has fallen asunder.[8] China's shift to a mixed market-planned industrialization strategy succeeded in building the world's largest manufacturing and exporting powerhouse, but it then turned against the liberal framework in which the market had been nested, both domestically and abroad.[9] High-tech electronic surveillance and censorship, repression of dissent, coercive resocialization of Uyghurs and other religious minorities, assertive territorial claims in the near abroad, the premature withdrawal of Hong Kong's promised autonomy—the bloom is off the rose. With China's tacit support, much of Southeast Asia has also undergone a "democratic recession."[10] Upset by populists like Thailand's Thaksin Shinawatra, fragile steps toward liberal democracy often retreat to a securitized "hybrid democracy," as in Myanmar under the joint rule of Aung San Suu Kyi and the Tatmadaw, Thailand under a military-royalty

---

6. Take Pakistan, for example. Before 2017, Pakistan's largest infrastructure investment was a $382 million project funded by a loan from the World Bank to develop a bus rapid transit system in the port city of Karachi. In comparison the BRI in Pakistan, termed the China Pakistan Economic Corridor (CPEC), promised to bring in investments of $62 billion over a ten-year period. Though it now seems unlikely the project will meet those transformative expectations, with ca. $25 billion invested by early 2020, it has already achieved a great deal (the energy package alone should add at least 14,000 MW to the national grid). See "Asian Development Bank to Support Bus Rapid Transit System in Pakistan," *World Construction Network*, July 8, 2019, accessed at worldconstructionnetwork.com/news.
7. Reported by Caixin Global, June 6, 2020, accessed at https://www.caixinglobal.com/2020-06-06/opinion-china-has-600-million-people-with-monthly-income-less-than-141-is-that-true-101564071.html.
8. After his early enthusiasm with Chimerica, Niall Ferguson adopted this more pessimistic perspective; see for example his Orient Express chapter in *The War of the World: 20th Century Conflict and the Descent of the West* (New York: Penguin Books, 2006); see also Stein Ringen, *The Perfect Dictatorship: China in the 21st Century* (Hong Kong: University of Hong Kong press, 2016); T. J. Christensen, "Fostering Stability or Creating a Monster? The Rise of China and US Policy toward East Asia," *International Security* 31, no. 1 (Summer 2006): 81–126.
9. See Xu Jilin, "Liweitan de youhun: 2000 nian laide guojia sichao pipan" [The Leviathan specter: A critique of 2000 years of Chinese statism], in *Sixiang*, ed. Qian Yongxiang (Taibei: Taiwan lianjing chubanshe, 2011, no. 12); www1.guancha.cn/XuJiLin/2011_07_10_60973.shtiml; see also "Document 9," as translated in ChinaFile, November 8, 2013, https://www.chinafile.com/document-9-chinafile-translation
10. Cf. Larry Diamond, "Facing Up to the Democratic Recession," *Journal of Democracy* 26, no. 1 (January 2015): 141–55; and Francis Fukuyama, "30 Years of World Politics: What Has Changed?" *Journal of Democracy* 31, no. 1 (January 2020): 11–21. Even hybrid democracies fall well short of the seamless dictatorship to which the Xi regime seems to aspire.

duopoly, the Philippines under Duterte, or the one-party states of Hun Sen in Cambodia, Singapore under the Lees, or Bangladesh under Sheik Hasina's Awami League. And to say Asia is politically fragmented is an understatement: China wants to devour Taiwan; North Korea wants to swallow South Korea; the Koreans hate the Japanese; China has territorial disputes with India, Japan, and several Southeast Asian states; and there are disputes between Cambodia and Thailand, Malaysia and Indonesia, Japan and Russia, Japan and Korea. To cap it all off, bipolarity has returned in the form of the trade dispute between China and the US.[11] In China's view, America's insistence on retaining its "leading role" in the region exacerbates all other disputes. At the least, polarization seems apt to result in scrambling supply chains, forcing an unwelcome choice between economic and political security.

Neither of these Manichaean scenarios is inevitable, yet neither is all wrong. The truth is more complicated, and the purpose of this book is to help make sense of it. Bur first, what do we mean by "disorder"? What is the nature of the order being disordered?

The Cold War Order

The nature of international order has been a perpetual puzzle to international theorists and practitioners, given the lack of a supreme authority capable of enforcing it. Kissinger dates the collapse of such authority and the birth of the new order to the incredibly sanguinary Thirty Years' War and the Peace of Westphalia that ended it. Therewith ended the pretensions of the Holy Roman Empire to universal sovereignty, conferring sovereignty to competing secular nation-states. Westphalian principles—national sovereignty, territorial integrity, legal equality of all states (large or small), noninterference in internal affairs—were then transmitted throughout the world, eventually to be taken up by emerging nation-states to divest themselves of European imperialism.[12] Since that time there have been two forms of order: *defined* order, which, absent any supreme authority, rests on consensual agreement among states as set forth in a treaty, compact, or other international accord; and *emergent* order, which arises from the pattern of interaction among states, typically forming some form of geostrategic power balance.

In collaboration with the victorious allies (primarily Great Britain, in the Atlantic Charter), a relatively undamaged and economically preponderant America created many of the rules of the modern world order and

---

11. See Oystein Tunsjo, *The Return of Bipolarity to World Politics: China, the United States, and Geostrategic Realism* (New York: Columbia University Press, 2018).
12. See Henry Kissinger, *World Order: Reflections on the Character of Nations and the Course of History*; see also G. John Ikenberry, *A World Safe for Democracy: Liberal Internationalism and the Crisis of Global Order* (New Haven, CT: Yale University Press, 2020); and Bertrand Badie, *New Perspectives on the International Order: No Longer Alone in This World* (New York: Palgrave Macmillan, 2017).

implementing institutions in the wake of World War II; i.e., the ideals of open markets and free trade in the economic realm, territorial integrity and national self-determination in the security order. The institutional rulebook was set forth by the International Monetary Fund (IMF), the World Bank, the Marshall Plan, and the United Nations (UN). These rules, however, applied only to the "free" world, specifically the forty-four nations attending the 1944 Bretton Woods Conference. In the ensuing Cold War the Soviet Bloc countries remained a relatively powerless minority in the UN but adopted their own set of rules and institutions to govern "socialist" finance and security, the Committee on Mutual Economic Assistance (COMECON) and the Warsaw Pact Organization (WPO) respectively. China joined neither, bound to the Bloc only by a soon fraying bilateral security alliance with the Soviet Union.

The Asian region entered late into the global order and at a decided disadvantage. Technologically behind, most of Asia had fallen under the sway of nineteenth-century European imperialism (or what the Chinese in their case called "semi-imperialism"), from which it emerged only after the Imperial Japanese bid for hegemony was repulsed in 1945. They were then absorbed into the Westphalian state system, abandoning memories of "all-under-heaven" imperial traditions except occasionally to burnish nationalist credentials. But aside from persisting national, linguistic, and cultural differences, within a few years of the Japanese withdrawal the region was swept by communist "national liberation wars." Hence the Cold War security apparatus erected in the West was quickly replicated in Asia, replete with "bamboo curtain" and divided nations, creating two distinct and self-sufficient socioeconomic systems.

Yet there were also important differences between Western and Asian orders. While Europe saw the establishment of two relatively stable multinational defense alliances (NATO in the West, WPO in the East), Asia was too diverse for a SEATO, so Washington established separate bilateral alliances with Japan, Korea, Thailand, the Philippines, and Australia.[13] Moscow supported the establishment of communist governments in China, North Vietnam, and eventually Vietnam. The communist order, however, soon disintegrated: China split sharply with the Soviet Union after the first decade of their thirty-year alliance (remaining, however, firmly anti-capitalist for the next two), while Pyongyang and Hanoi balanced between Beijing and Moscow. Finally, perhaps due to its greater diversity, the Cold War ended earlier and more ambiguously than in the West. The Sino-Soviet dispute so direly threatened China's security that it invited Richard Nixon to Beijing in February 1972, precipitating a major shift in the global power balance. In return for a promised reduction of Chinese support for the Democratic Republic of Vietnam (DRV),

---

13. See Christopher Hemmer and Peter J. Katzenstein, "Why Is There No NATO in Asia? Collective Identity, Regionalism, and the Origins of Multilateralism," *International Organization* 56, no. 3 (Summer 2002): 575–607.

China got implicit protection from a preemptive Soviet strike on its nascent nuclear capability. A seismic shift indeed, but narrowly limited to the security domain—China maintained its Marxist-Leninist ideology, its command economy, and continued to rail and plot against the "hegemony" of the two superpowers.[14] Not until the rise of Deng Xiaoping at the famous 3rd Plenum of the 11th Party Congress in December 1978 did China begin a more comprehensive reorientation of its economic system and foreign policy.

Order after the Cold War

Only after the Cold War did globalization get underway on a truly global scale, characterized by the emergence of transnational corporations, floating exchange rates, megaregional trade agreements, and transnational supply chains. America again played a lynchpin role, but China was not left out—indeed Washington was eager to elicit China's integration as "responsible stakeholder" in the new international order. China took Taiwan's seat on the Security Council (and the General Assembly) of the UN in 1971. It waited to join the World Bank and the IMF until 1980, after such affiliations became compatible with Deng Xiaoping's new line of "reform and opening up." China also joined in negotiating the UN Convention on the Law of the Sea (UNCLOS) at its outset in 1982 and ratified the convention in 1996. Joining such Western-based institutions posed an implicit dilemma: too little participation and China was a free rider; too much fed suspicion of a hostile takeover. China certainly benefited from participation, for example as the world's leading recipient for many years of subsidized World Bank loans. But at first it was little more than a free rider: China's representatives diligently attended but remained reticent, anticipating Deng's advice to "hide your light and bide your time" (*taoguang yanghui*). Only gradually, as China grew its economy and became more involved in world trade, did it become more interested in running international governmental organizations (IGOs).

It first perforce became engaged in the UN Human Rights Council (UNHRC), which embarrassed Beijing in the 1990 with a critique of its 1989 Tiananmen crackdown. From 1990 to 2005, Chinese diplomats managed to defeat twelve UNHRC resolutions critical of the country's human rights record, in part by providing discreet economic incentives to developing country swing states. Since reentering in 2013 (now a reorganized council, the UNHRC) China advocated "economic, social, and cultural rights" within the limits of national sovereignty and non-interference. In China's view, the most fundamental human right is collective "development," superseding liberal

---

14. For example, Michael J. Berlin, "China Assails Soviets, U.S. in U.N. Speech," *Washington Post*, September 27, 1984, https://www.washingtonpost.com/archive/politics/1984/09/27/china-assails-soviets-us-in-un-speech/a4e2e7fe-1014-42bd-a57f-52ea4ea50e72/.

rights of individual expression (the US left the council in 2019).[15] China otherwise played a relatively passive role on the commission in these early years. As its economy grew, China successfully demanded more influence not only in the UN (where they now chair four of the fifteen specialized agencies)[16] but in the more consequential Bretton Woods organizations. Since the 1990s China has become a member of almost all important IGOs. It now has the third largest voting share in both the IMF and the World Bank, after the US and Japan. In the IMF, China proposed replacing the dollar as the international reserve currency. This was unsuccessful, but in October 2016 it got the renminbi included as the fifth currency in the IMF's Special Drawing Rights (SDR) basket (weighted third after the dollar and the euro), the first currency to be added without being fully exchangeable. It entered the WTO in December 2001, after an arduous accession procedure, quickly taking advantage of its membership to vastly increase exports.

Impatient with a slow climb up the hierarchical pecking order of extant IGOs, China since 2000 also become an IGO entrepreneur, especially among emerging nations. China joined the Group of 20 in 1999, co-founded the Shanghai Cooperation Organization (SCO) in 2001, joined the BRICS group (Brazil, Russia, India, China, South Africa) in 2006, and founded the Asian Infrastructure Investment Bank (AIIB) in 2015, not to mention of course founding and leading the visionary BRI. Although China has tended to focus on economic development in its IGO affiliations, it has recently also included security, as in its active involvement in the Conference on International Confidence Building Measures in Asia (CICA), the ASEAN Defense Ministers Meeting Plus (ADMM-plus), or the Shangri-La Dialogue forum.

Over the next three decades China reoriented its political economic system in a more pragmatic direction. After considerable debate, it adopted elements of market capitalism domestically, including limited private property, equity, and labor markets. It then cautiously opened its market to the world (initially only in Special Economic Zones, gradually expanding to the entire east coast and beyond). In the past few years it has been argued that the Chinese reform experience was a superficial or even deceitful "hide and bide" strategy, but that would be an oversimplification. While it is certainly true that the most

---

15. See Ann Kent, *China, the United Nations, and Human Rights: The Limits of Compliance* (Philadelphia: University of Pennsylvania Press, 2013). While international human rights norms have had little effect on domestic policy, China has been extraordinarily sensitive to criticism on human rights grounds ever since Tiananmen, particularly in the wake of disclosure of its blanket "counterterrorism, deradicalization vocational training policies" (including barbed-wire enclosed internment camps) toward China's Muslim minorities. And it has been remarkably successful at soliciting international support: when twenty-two countries sent a letter to the UNHRC in 2019 criticizing Xi's "comprehensive security" framework, thirty-seven countries wrote a letter defending it.
16. That is to say, the International Civil Aviation Organization, the International Telecommunications Agency, the Food and Agricultural Organization, and the International Industrial Development Organization.

ambitious reforms were always economic, which offered an immediate tangible payoff, there were also cautious forays into political reform as well, reaching perhaps a zenith at the 13th Party Congress in 1987, where Zhao Ziyang detached the party from the government and launched an independent civil service, explaining that China was still at "a primary stage of socialism" that might last one hundred years.[17] True, reform then hit a giant roadblock with the Tiananmen demonstrations and subsequent crackdown in 1989 but was revived by Deng Xiaoping in his "southern tour" (*nanxun*) speeches three years later and given an international stamp of approval via China's admission to the WTO in December 2001. In the following decade, China's GDP growth surpassed 10 percent, based primarily on export-oriented growth.

Thus, although the People's Republic was not "present at the creation" of the liberal rules-based order in the late 1940s, it was certainly included in the post–Cold War "new world order," where it has played an increasingly influential role. Even after the Tiananmen crackdown, which did result in international sanctions, most of these did not last long. So to claim that China has been excluded from the rules-based international order would not be correct. China has been an increasingly active participant in the emerging Asian order, and a highly successful one at that, profiting perhaps more than any other nation from globalization. China is now the second largest contributor to funding UN peacekeeping operations, the third largest contributor to the UN, and contributes more personnel to peacekeeping organizations than does any other permanent member of the Security Council.

During the first three post–Cold War decades, we can perceive a slow but sustained movement toward a rules-based order in East Asia. The rules of this order consisted of a consensually constructed version of Westphalian conventions, including the rule of law, national sovereignty, national self-determination, democratic reform, noninterference in internal affairs, respect for ideological differences, open markets, and a renunciation of the use of force to resolve international disputes. These rules were spelled out in a series of mission statements and joint visions at the end of the Cold War, when the collapse of the Iron Curtain made manifest the need for a new regional architecture, such as ASEAN's Treaty of Amity and Cooperation (TAC). And for some time, regional peace and cooperation held sway despite initial skepticism about inclusion of authoritarian states which had previously supported divergent agendas. The two communist states in Southeast Asia's northern tier, Vietnam and Laos, joined ASEAN in 2005 and 2007 respectively (Myanmar also in 2007) after making democratic pledges.

China, having been ostracized after Tiananmen and almost alone in the world after the wholesale collapse of European communism, launched a "charm campaign" to reassure its Asian neighbors and gain inclusion in the

---

17. See Lowell Dittmer, "Three Visions of Chinese Political Reform," *Journal of Asian and African Studies* 38, no. 4–5 (December 2003): 347–76.

new order. It signed ASEAN's Declaration on Conduct of Parties in the South China Sea (DOC) in 1992, was the first non-ASEAN signatory of TAC in 1993, was included as a "dialogue partner" in 1996, helped set up the ASEAN plus three (APT) forum in 1997, and negotiated the ASEAN-China Free Trade Agreement (ACFTA) in 2000, then the largest multilateral free-trade agreement in the world. For ideological reassurance, China also signed the International Covenant on Economic, Social and Cultural Rights (ICESCR) and the International Covenant on Civil and Political Rights (ICCPR) in 1997 and 1998 respectively, ratifying only the former, however, and accurately translating neither for domestic consumption. The PRC's leading slogans during this period were "peaceful rise/development" and "harmonious world," and China's foreign policies were not noticeably inconsistent. Meanwhile, America remained benignly sidelined from East Asia after its withdrawal from Vietnam in 1975, while Russia was internally preoccupied with a difficult transition from communism. Albeit a "strategic vacuum," the region prospered without great power involvement.

Disorder

As Ikenberry notes, the "new world order" that arose in the wake of the Cold War was wider but shallower than its antecedent.[18] Its new members, no longer united by a common threat, did not share the same cultural heritage and were less wholeheartedly committed to it. The surviving communist states—in Asia, China, Vietnam, Laos, and North Korea—now found it practically expedient to engage the world market but remained ideologically committed to a diverging long-term trajectory. The ideologically tolerant liberal community gamely accepted this, initially purely on security grounds (to counter the greater perceived threat from the Soviet Union), and later because it seemed too economically lucrative an opportunity to pass up. But this difference increasingly manifested itself when China became strong enough to insist on its own values and rules, thereby opening what Rozman calls an "identity gap."[19]

The liberal rules-based regional order did not derail in a sudden train wreck but gradually lost momentum. Certainly there were some very basic structural and ideological differences to digest after the incomplete end to the Cold War, but the Asian order was an open-ended one, giving even greater leeway to national sovereignty than did the Westphalian order. The primary

---

18. Ikenberry, *A World Safe*, 258.
19. Gilbert Rozman, *National Identities and Bilateral Relations: Widening Gaps in East Asia and Chinese Demonization of the United States* (Stanford, CA: Stanford University Press, 2013).

reasons for the impasse were two: the intrusion of great power politics into the region[20] and the intrinsic structural weakness of the liberal order's defense.

The PRC was not solely at fault, but China's rise was a major precipitating factor in the resurgence of great power politics, throwing the system into sudden disequilibrium. That said, China rose through an open door, and it was not initially clear which direction it would take. The political-economic liberalization culminating in the protests at the end of the 1980s was only briefly curtailed by the bloody crackdown and economic reform resumed at Deng Xiaoping's behest. China's growing middle class was advised to stay out of politics and plunge into the sea of commerce (*xia hai*). GDP grew 9.9 percent per annum from 1978 to 2008, and per capita income growth averaged 7.2 percent during the same period. Out of the reform-driven 1980s came the 1990s, energized by the birth of an autonomous civil society. NGOs proliferated; market-oriented media outlets flourished. The rights defense movement was afoot, and the internet created space for online speech. Society demanded political reform, and lawyers fought in court for human rights and against abuses. The GFC (which China survived with a massive stimulus) convinced the Communist Party of China that this was the beginning of the end for the decadent West and a period of "strategic opportunity" for China. China's military officials (and retired officials) began publicly insisting on the need to use force to recover lost territories in the late 2000s.

The first clear sign of a divergent approach to normative rules was the unabashedly brutal crackdown at Tiananmen, but for the realist Asians the crux was Chinese infringement of their own territorial interests.[21] This arose in a sovereignty dispute over the maritime borders of the East and South China Seas, both rich in subsurface hydrocarbon deposits and strategically key to control of the Asian rimland, which China claimed based on exploratory visits to the islands "since ancient times" but without producing empirical evidence other contestants deemed dispositive.

Both cases involve expansive Chinese maritime territorial claims, and both hinge inter alia on different interpretations of international law (UNCLOS) but differ in their particulars. In the East China Sea, China claims the eight tiny Senkaku or Diaoyu islands, based on the natural prolongation of the continental shelf, while Japan (which formally annexed the islands based on terra nullius in the context of the first Sino-Japanese War in 1895 and reoccupied them soon after World War II) claims them as lying within its two hundred nautical mile exclusive economic zone (EEZ). Japan's custody (curiously not its ownership) of the islands was included in the Japan-US mutual defense treaty, which the US promises to honor. While the islands are of little strategic

---

20. The essence of "great power politics" was captured with admirable clarity by Foreign Minister Yang Jiechi at an ASEAN Regional Forum (ARF) in 2010: "China is a big country and you are small countries, and that is a fact."
21. See Andrew S. Erickson and Ryan D. Martinson, eds., *China's Maritime Gray Zone Operations* (Annapolis, MD: Naval Institute Press, 2019).

value per se, their EEZs were in the 1970s found to include vast subsurface hydrocarbon deposits, and in 1995 China indeed discovered the Chunxiao field contained substantial deposits of natural gas just outside Japan's EEZ (as defined by Japan) and has been pumping gas from the field since 2006, over Japanese objections. Negotiations for joint development of the field foundered in 2008 over the sovereignty issue. Bilateral relations spiked in 2010 over a trespassing Chinese fishing boat, and again in 2012, when the Japanese government purchased the islands in a misunderstood attempt to take them out of play. Both sides have since dug in their heels though China almost daily sends naval or air patrols over the islands (and Japan chases them away) to assert de facto sovereignty.

The South China Sea is a region of great economic and geostrategic importance. One-third of the world's maritime shipping passes through it, and huge oil and natural gas reserves are believed to lie beneath its seabed. China's claim rests on a "cows tongue" or eleven-dash (now nine-dash) map sketched by the Nationalist Chinese in 1947, encompassing some 85 to 90 percent of the South China Sea (whether the sea itself or the land features within it remains undefined). China claimed to inherit the claim after defeating the Nationalists in 1949 (who refused to surrender, still making the same claim from Taiwan). But it made no effort to enforce the claim over properties whose value no one yet appreciated, nor did the other claimants, newly emancipated from colonialism and preoccupied with nation-building, contest that claim though some did settle offshore islands. The dispute began to heat up only after a UN research team discovered subsurface hydrocarbon deposits in 1969. In 1974 China had a lethal clash with South Vietnam in the Paracels and another with North Vietnam in 1988, but after signing the DOC in 1992, China avoided lethal violence for the next twenty years, in keeping with Beijing's "smile" campaign. China and five other littoral nations (Taiwan, Vietnam, the Philippines, Malaysia, and Brunei) asserted their legal claims to these subsurface resources shortly after UNCLOS, following its formal ratification in 1996, and set forth guidelines for EEZ claims. While China has always insisted on bilateral negotiations, the four Southeast Asian claimants preferred a multilateral forum because individually they were much weaker, but they found it difficult to do so because each had claims against the others (Vietnam made perhaps the strongest historical claim, producing documents showing it had occupied the islands since the seventeenth century). At China's insistence, the negotiations have remained technically bilateral.

Albeit the preferred forum of the Southeast Asians, ASEAN has proved ineffective as a forum to resolve the issue. ASEAN is a formally anarchic organization: it has a tiny permanent secretariat in Jakarta (the secretary-general rotates every five years), but decisions must be unanimous and the secretariat has no power to enforce them. ASEAN has occasionally been able to rise to the occasion, vociferously protesting, for example, when Vietnam invaded Cambodia in 1979, or when the Burmese junta arrested Aung San

Suu Kyi, but in both cases the target was not yet a member. The need for consensus makes it nearly impossible to make controversial decisions involving member states.[22] China is not an ASEAN member, but it joined and effectively upholds its position in the various ASEAN "plus" forums. And its role has been generally constructive, particularly in the early period when it was eager to dispel the "China threat theory." But on the maritime sovereignty issue this was inviting the fox into the henhouse. Whenever another South China Sea claimant attempted to raise the issue (notably in 2012 and 2015), one of China's clients within the organization would rule it out. It would be realistically impossible to conclude a binding code of conduct in the South China Sea (under negotiation for some twenty years now) without China's consent.

During the peaceful post–Cold War hiatus the dispute remained quiescent. It became more acute around 2010, for two reasons: first, China declared (initially in camera) that the South China Sea was a "core interest," brooking no compromise. And it not only claimed but began to enforce its claims—ramming fishing boats, cutting oil exploration cables, using water cannons. China practiced "salami" tactics, using just enough force to induce compliance but no more, starting with throngs of fishing boats, then maritime militia, and finally the navy. China was now in a strong position to control the ladder of escalation with its smaller neighbors, having built the largest fishing fleet (17,000 vessels at last count), largest coast guard and merchant militia, and indeed now the largest navy in the world.[23]

Beijing undertook further escalation upon the rise of Xi Jinping, outbluffing the Philippines (and the US) to seize de facto control of Scarborough Shoal in 2012. In 2013 it began using giant dredging ships to build artificial islands on the seven reefs it occupied, expanding their size by some 3,200 acres. It then proceeded in 2016 to install "significant" defensive weapons systems on these islands (after promising in 2015 not to do so), including docks, air strips, anti-aircraft artillery, and anti-ship missiles. Having survived the GFC that threw the West into years of recession without a single year of negative growth and now under fresh leadership, China grew more self-confident, determined to seize the territory it had long claimed. "The real strength of global power has shifted," we read in the communique of the 5th Central Committee Plenum of the CPC (October 2020), in the context of "global changes not seen in 100

---

22. ASEAN has, however, more recently shifted from a pledge of "non-interference" with dissidents to one of "frank discussions." The informal, incremental approach to cooperation has been strengthened by adoption of a "retreat framework." The first retreat took place in a gathering of ASEAN foreign ministers in 2020 under the banner of "a cohesive and responsive ASEAN." There have even been suggestions of a resort to the expulsion of dissident members, to enforce ASEAN consensus.
23. Since 2012, and particularly since Xi undertook a sweeping reorganization of the PLA in 2015, the People's Liberation Army Navy (PLAN) has launched a major building campaign. In 2016, eighteen new ships were launched, fourteen in 2017, twenty-one in 2018, and twenty-four in 2019. As of 2020, the PLAN had 300 vessels to 290 in the American fleet, many of which are large, fast, and sophisticated.

years." Yet China did not want to risk a *casus belli* with the US. Beijing seems to have calculated that, given the balance of power, these small countries would yield without a fight. This expectation may have been cynical but was not entirely inaccurate.

The second game changer was, however, that the other great power intervened, much to Beijing's surprise and dismay—after all, America had no territorial claims in the disputed territories and had hitherto stayed out of the dispute, merely urging all sides to settle the matter peaceably. But Hillary Clinton in July 2010 at an ASEAN Regional Forum in Hanoi announced that the US had a "national interest" to uphold "freedom of navigation" in international waters. This changed the correlation of forces and Beijing was furious, correctly surmising that the American intercession would inspire local resistance. After Cambodia blocked raising the issue at a 2012 ASEAN forum, Manila took the dispute to the International Tribunal on the Law of the Sea (ITLOS). Beijing, though it had ratified UNCLOS in 1982, along with all other claimant states, denounced Manila's move and refused to participate. ITLOS nonetheless accepted the case and set up a Permanent Court of Arbitration to decide the dispute. A verdict was rendered in July 2016, and it vindicated most of Manila's claims: the nine-dash line was legally invalid, and none of the small islands was capable of sustaining life and hence not entitled to extended territorial claims. Beijing immediately declared the verdict invalid, a mere scrap of waste paper that it would not recognize, and persuaded as many states as it could to say likewise. The US recognized the verdict but did nothing to enforce it. Freshly elected Philippine President Rodrigo Duterte ignored it, as did most of Southeast Asia; anyone who publicly mentioned it was upbraided by Beijing.

China reverted to charm, launching its trillion-dollar BRI to finance infrastructure construction throughout the region. The US continued to sail warships near China's reclaimed islands, in defiance of its sovereignty claims, while Beijing continued to fortify its islands. Thus Beijing seems to have gotten all that it wanted without war or even too much resistance. But its gains were not legitimate; it had violated international law as defined by UNCLOS, to which all parties had previously agreed, and resentment lingers. This has created a climate of opinion that makes it difficult for China to exploit its gains. For example, when in 2014 China emplaced an oil-drilling rig within Vietnam's EEZ, it touched off violent anti-Chinese demonstrations, protesters burning down Chinese-invested factories and attacking Chinese (and Taiwanese) workers, forcing Beijing to evacuate its citizens.

One interpretation of the confrontation is that China is operating on two legal bases: UNCLOS when convenient and its own "geolocal" legal order, the latter justified by great power politics. But that seems unnecessarily complex: Beijing has never articulated a codified set of laws to commend to its neighbors; it just does not want to comply with the existing set when they contravene its "core interests."[24] That is consonant with one customary line of argument in China: that China has a different, socialist morality, one that values collective over individual rights, discipline over freedom, etc.[25] Every nation is entitled to its own sovereign morality and set of rules. "International democracy" in China's eyes means that all nations should be free to establish their own morality without external interference. Legal relativism is a natural outgrowth of moral relativism. China thus takes issue with the current rules-based order, which was after all constructed by others for their own interests and arbitrarily imposed on China and other developing countries. To claim China wants to *overthrow* the rules-based order would be going too far. China is no longer a revolutionary but a "revisionist" state with a substantial interest in the established order; it merely seeks some ad hoc adjustments to fit its interests.[26] Thus a 2017 White Paper notes that "international . . . rules should be discussed, formulated and observed by all countries rather than dictated by any particular country."[27]

This line of thinking is not new; it is rooted in the communist revolution and has persisted tenaciously despite the economic failures of the Great Leap Forward and the Great Proletarian Cultural Revolution. The unquestionable success of Deng's pragmatic "reform and opening" program inspired many to presume China would continue along liberal reform lines and that perhaps communism and capitalism could ultimately converge, as the former adopted markets and the latter adopted social security and the welfare state. Today, as China builds concentration camps in Xinjiang, "Sinicizes" Hong Kong, and adopts high-tech computerization to erect firewalls and purge its internet, this presumption is often derided as a delusion inspired either by naïve liberal triumphalism in the wake of the collapse of Soviet communism or by the lure of the world's largest consumer market.

But was a host of China scholars and Western politicians so easily fooled? A simpler and more parsimonious explanation would be that China was indeed deeply influenced by marketization but that it then grew alarmed with a market thriving out of all bounds and decided to reassert strict party control. Such a policy reversal may seem surprising in view of the outstanding success of the preceding reform policies, but critics of reform found ammunition not

---

24. Malcolm Jorgensen, "Equilibrium & Fragmentation in the International Rule of Law: The Rising Chinese Geolegal Order," KFG Working Paper Series, No. 21, Berlin Potsdam Research Group. "The International Rule of Law—Rise or Decline?", Berlin, November 2018; see also Lynn Kuok, "How China's Actions in the South China Sea Undermine the Rule of Law," *Global China*, November 2019; and Anthea Roberts, *Is International Law International?* (New York: Oxford University Press, 2017).
25. See the insightful analysis by Thomas Heberer, *Disciplining the Society: Social Discipline and Civilizing Processes in Contemporary China* (Cambridge, MA: Harvard Kennedy School, Ash Center for Democratic Governance and Innovation, August 2020).
26. See Melanie Hart and Blaine Johnson, *Mapping China's Global Governance Ambitions*, Center for American Progress, February 2019.
27. "China's Policies on Asian-Pacific Security Cooperation" (January 2017), Section 1.

only in the Tiananmen crackdown but in the widespread decay of ideological commitment ("crisis of faith"), pervasive corruption, and other symptoms of strain between Leninist discipline and consumer capitalism. Zhu Rongji's "grasp the big and drop the small" (*zhua da fang xiao*) corporate reform at the end of the 1990s has been lauded by economists, but it also spiked widespread urban unemployment and a wave of cadre corruption.

Sometime in the mid- to late 2000s the communist leadership took a hard look at where things were going and decided a course correction was necessary.[28] Since the quiet failure of the ambitious 336-item economic reform program introduced at the 3rd Plenum of the 18th Party Congress in December 2013, China has returned in many respects to a more "neo-Maoist" approach.[29] State-owned enterprises (SOEs) are still privileged with loans and subsidies and implicit credit default insurance, the plan lives on as the leading economic indicator, the "mass line" is back, while the private sector is now closely monitored by the party (some 70 percent of private firms are now co-managed by party committees). Above all, there is strict centralization and personalization of power. As Xi Jinping made clear at the outset of his second term, the Communist Party should command everything: "Government, the military, society and schools, north, south, east and west—the party leads them all."

There is also the nationalist factor, strongly emphasized in all Chinese media since the fall of the USSR. In the wake of the collapse of European communism, the leadership turned from ideology to the mobilization of nationalism in a "patriotic education" campaign, and the "hundred years of humiliation" (*bainian guochi*) myth was revived to stoke it.[30] After all, China's triumphant survival of the GFC, overtaking Japan to become the world's largest trader and largest economy (as calculated in purchasing power parity, or PPP) is attributed not to Western market reform but to the Chinese road to modernization, legitimate credentials for pride for which Xi now commends China's path to other emerging nations. In some ways China's nationalist "rejuvenation" fits the changing zeitgeist. Globalism (which China supports, for other countries) has waned in the world at large. As of early 2020, global growth of trade is zero; this may be partly attributable to COVID-19 and the Sino-American trade war, but global trade growth has declined since the GFC from 7.6 percent average growth before 2008 to 3.5 percent from 2009 to 2018. Investment growth has likewise receded: the average growth rate of global FDI flow since 2000 is 0.8 percent, with a decline of -28 percent in 2018 owing to trade tensions.

---

28. Cf. Carl Walter and Fraser Howie, *Red Capitalism: The Fragile Financial Foundations of China's Extraordinary Rise*, rev. ed. (Singapore: John Wiley, 2012).
29. Nicholas R. Lardy, ed., *The State Strikes Back: The End of Economic Reform in China* (Washington, DC: Peterson Institute for International Economics, 2019); see also Suisheng Zhao, 2016. "Xi Jinping's Maoist Revival," *Journal of Democracy* 27, no. 3 (2016): 83–97.
30. See Zheng Wang, *Never Forget National Humiliation: Historical Memory in Chinese Politics and Foreign Relations* (New York: Columbia University Press, 2014).

China's economic performance made it a growth "locomotive" for the rest of Asia, which rerouted its value trains through the PRC and became economically China-dependent. But no free lunch: Beijing sought to utilize the political leverage inherent in these imbalanced trade ties to extract support for its interests, while China's more assertive territorial claims put other claimants on guard. To the US, China's long-time leading trade partner, the opening provided an influx of low-priced products for American consumers and a cap on price inflation, while American investors viewed the country as the next El Dorado. But though both sides benefited, Americans came to view the relationship according to relative gains. Trade was large and growing but consistently and increasingly imbalanced. American manufacturing "off-shored" to China to take advantage of low labor costs, taking jobs with them (job loss estimates from 2001 to 2010 range from three to four million). China's GDP growth has consistently outpaced America's by three or four times, and arms budgets correlate with GDP. All this indirectly contributed to the upset victory of Donald J. Trump in 2016. Trump's anti-China campaign promises were no novelty, but unlike his predecessors he kept them, waging a high-profile "trade war" for eighteen months, disregarding WTO commitments. China's public favorability rating in the US dropped over twenty points.

The BRI has been widely welcomed by Asian recipients in sore need of infrastructure investment, whose leaders often prefer discreetly negotiating loans "no strings attached" to the IMF's conditionality. But it is no aid program. BRI loans from China's Export-Import Bank or China Development Bank (CDB) typically have higher interest rates (and shorter payback periods) than the World Bank's, and loans are typically tied to no-bid contracts with Chinese SOEs that prefer to use Chinese labor and equipment, with little local spinoff. Borrowers must pledge existing assets as collateral and deposit significant sums in escrow accounts in China. Disputes must be taken to Chinese arbitration courts under the jurisdiction of Chinese law. Although China has signed 190 cooperation agreements with 160 countries and has invested over US$100 billion and pledged nearly $1 trillion so far, the initiative has slowed since its debut for a number of reasons.[31] China has been hit by demands for retrenchment or renegotiation from financially strapped recipients (sc., Sri Lanka, Pakistan, Myanmar, Bangladesh, Malaysia, Seychelles) amid complaints of corruption or environmental externalities. Even in China, pushback is heard about spending abroad what is needed at home; while Chinese policy banks worry about getting their loans repaid (China has suddenly become one of the world's biggest lenders, outstanding claims now exceeding more than 5

---

31. According to the AEI investment tracker, China invested $53 billion in BRI projects in 2018, declining to $21 billion in 2019. China committed to making only two BRI-related loans over US$1 billion in the first half of 2019: US$1.2 billion to Egypt and US$2.5 billion to Pakistan. Altogether, China made forty-six loans of over US$1 billion for overseas investment projects in 2016, dropping to twenty-eight in 2018.

percent of global GDP).[32] But lending from Chinese two big policy banks (the CDB and ExIm Bank) declined from $75 billion in 2016 to $4 billion in 2019 and an estimated $3 billion in 2020; China's outbound investment dropped from US$222 billion in 2016 to around US$50 billion in 2020.

China and Asia's rules-based order is changing, and at the root of the current disorder is the fact that, after an extended period of implicit faith in international convergence, the two seem to be veering in different directions. The rise of Xi Jinping inspired a rebirth of nationalism that hearkens in certain respects back to the Maoist era and in others forward to a high-tech future.[33] Ideologically, Xi was very much concerned with the fate of the USSR, determined to prevent any such "peaceful evolution" in China by launching a massive, sustained anti-corruption campaign, by cracking down on religion and political dissent, and by revitalizing socialist ideology.[34] Though a voluble fan of globalization, one facet of his economic policy (even before the trade war) has been on making the country more self-reliant, both ideologically (the "great firewall") and to some extent economically (boosting red supply chains and high-tech long-term plans—"China 2025," now "Vision 2035"). In the wake of the 2015 stock market crash followed in 2016 by capital flight in overreaction to a modest exchange-rate adjustment, further marketization seems to have stalled.

The return of great power politics to the region in the form of two outsize personalities, Xi Jinping and Donald Trump, has infracted many of the rules, shrunk the room to maneuver for smaller countries, and fractured the region. The US has been far from exemplary in its adherence to the rules it set up and preaches to others. Democratic elections permit sudden wrenching changes in American foreign policy, casting the world into perplexity. Since winning his maiden electoral office in November 2016, Donald Trump has proceeded to implement a boldly unorthodox foreign policy. Near the top of his foreign policy agenda are bilateral trade balances and higher rents from allies holding American bases abroad. Making no secret of disdaining both globalism and multilateral diplomacy, he unilaterally withdrew from the TPP, the JCPOA nuclear nonproliferation deal with Iran, the Paris Climate Accord, UNESCO, NAFTA, and the UNHRC.

---

32. Sebastian Horn, Carmen M. Reinhart, and Christoph Trebesch, "How Much Money Does the World Owe China?" *Harvard Business Review*, February 26, 2020, https://hbr.org/2020/02/how-much-money-does-the-world-owe-china.
33. See Francois Bougon, *Inside the Mind of Xi Jinping* (London: Hurst, 2017).
34. "Why did the Soviet Union disintegrate? Why did the Soviet Communist Party collapse? An important reason was that their ideals and convictions wavered," Mr. Xi said in a speech to the Central Committee made on January 5, 2013 but not published until April 2019. It's a profound lesson for us! To dismiss the history of the Soviet Union and the Soviet Communist Party, to dismiss Lenin and Stalin, and to dismiss everything else is to engage in historic nihilism, and it confuses our thoughts and undermines the party's organizations on all levels." No mention of political reform: "Only socialism can save China."

Trump is not the first American international iconoclast. The US never signed UNCLOS, for example, though it claims to adhere to its rules as customary law and scolds China for violations. There is a long list of alleged or empirically documented cases of American interference in the internal affairs of other countries—U2 spy plane overflights and CIA operations in Tibet in the 1950s.[35] Trump's claim to support free trade (hitherto a Republican shibboleth) is belied by his evisceration of the WTO (continuing Obama's failure to appoint new judges to the appellate council), and, most conspicuously, his revival of tariff protectionism for the first time since the 1930s. The resulting trade dispute with China has not only decimated bilateral trade but thrown the region into disarray. Xi Jinping might in comparison be deemed fairly orthodox (certainly ideologically), standing out mainly in the forcefulness and guile with which he effects China's demands. His position on political-economic reform, civil and human rights, particularly visible in China's periphery (Hong Kong, Tibet, and Xinjiang, China's "near seas"), however represents a significant hardening of the Chinese Communist Party position.

Asia faces tomorrow in the dusk of a trade war and a global pandemic. The US is in electoral transition, retiring one power politician from the scene. Xi Jinping still faces considerable blowback from the developed world, particularly the US. It seems likely at this point that high American tariffs will remain in force.[36] For China, the tech war is even more painful, barring certain strategic technology categorically. As Beijing recalls, the Tiananmen crackdown also provoked international sanctions, and it appears confident that the current chill will soon subside as well. Beijing has launched a new charm campaign, using global warming as leverage. But the world has changed since 1989, not least China itself, which now poses a more formidable challenge to the rules-based order. Should the recent decoupling trend continue, its long-term impact will disperse global value chains from China to willing and

---

35. "The CIA in the 1950s was in its freebooting heyday. It organized the overthrow of governments deemed too pro-communist in Iran in 1953 and Guatemala in 1954, helped install pro-Western governments in Egypt in 1954 and Laos in 1958, tried and failed to overthrow Sukarno in 1958, ran sabotage operations in China from Laos and Burma, plotted assassination attempts against Chou En-lai of China, Patrice Lumumba of the Congo, Fidel Castro of Cuba, and Rafael Trujillo of the Dominican Republic." Walter Isaacson and Evan Thomas, *The Wise Men: Six Friends and the World They Made* (Boston, MA: Faber and Faber, 1986), 574. See also John Glaser, "The Amnesia of the U.S. Foreign Policy Establishment," *The New Republic*, March 15, 2019, https://newrepublic.com/article/153323/amnesia-us-foreign-policy-establishment.
36. The average tariff on Chinese imports rose from 2.6 percent in 2017 to a high of 17.5 percent in September 2019. At the first stage agreement reached in January 2020, tariffs were lowered to an average 16 percent. Meanwhile in the US, five of the six quarters prior to the pandemic saw decreases in the US goods and services deficit. Before COVID-19 hit the economy in February, the US gained more than 500,000 manufacturing jobs, while median household income in 2019 rose 6.8 percent from the year before. See Bloomberg, December 20, 2020, https://www.bloomberg.com/news/articles/2020-12-22/trump-trade-czar-eyes-exit-hailing-tariff-power-his-critics-hate?cmpid=BBD122320_TRADE&utm_medium=email&utm_source=newsletter&utm_term=201223&utm_campaign=trade.

ready FDI recipients such as Japan, Taiwan (both offer to subsidize reshoring), Vietnam, and others. China will strive to prevent that, while also moving toward greater economic self-reliance ("dual circulation").

The economic impact of the COVID-19 pandemic on East Asia has been relatively mild and "multi-speed."[37] The political impact has been to redouble the deglobalizing thrust of the trade war, as nations scramble to regain control of medical supplies, weapon parts manufacture, and other strategic industries. The trade war was not economically sustainable insofar as both disputants suffered losses, but "relative gains" also applies to losses. At first glance the US could be said to have "won" by losing less GDP than China has, both in absolute and proportionate terms.[38] But COVID-19 muddies the verdict considerably: Beijing's more competent management of the pandemic enabled its economy to recover faster, boasting a uniquely positive GDP for the year. Despite this genuine achievement, which Beijing has ardently endeavored to advertise, its initial coverup of the outbreak has inflicted lasting damage on China's international reputation.

Mapping Disorder

We approach East Asia *in medias res*, haunted by the legacy of the Cold War structure, still searching for a consensual order, forging vigorously into a better economic tomorrow. Not for the first time this contentious, dynamic region is in transition, from rancorous disorder to a dimly envisaged new order of peace and sustainable compromise. We seek to illuminate the factors engaged in that transition without necessarily trying to fill out the end state. We contend that three factors in particular will be vital in this dynamic transition process: (1) identities, (2) strategies, and (3) triangles.

Identities—National identity has in political science been considered a core constituent of nation-building, engendering the necessary loyalty to raise revenue and political support for the government to pursue public interests. A political identity may be defined as the collective representation of individual desires, particularly those desires that cannot be fully realized at the individual level. Whose desires? In the East Asian transition process two collectives: the nation-state, and the region. The nation-state has always been the strongest collective identity (at least since Westphalia) because it is the only one having sovereignty. But as economies spill over national borders in the form of international trade, financial flows, transportation, media and so forth, the objective need arises for competencies to manage these transmissions.

---

37. International Monetary Fund, Regional Economic Outlook, Asia and Pacific: *Navigating the Pandemic: A Multispeed Recovery in Asia* (October 2020), https://www.imf.org/en/Publications/REO/APAC/Issues/2020/10/21/regional-economic-outlook-apd.
38. Oxford Economics estimated China's GDP was 0.7 percent smaller than without the trade war. Before decoupling began, they predicted China's GDP would rise 5 percent per annum from 2020 to 2030, projected to decline to 4.5 percent under current tariff rates.

The need for management implies the need for authority, and for authority to function effectively it needs legitimacy. A necessary aspect of legitimacy is identity, because a collective identity is the recipient of the projected aspirations of its constituents, without which there would be no way to generate consensus, save naked coercion.[39] Hence we are perforce dealing here with both national and regional identities, and the envisaged transition of identities from the smaller to the larger to manage the efficient integration of trade, personnel, and investment flows. But as the Europeans have also experienced, identities tend to have deep psycho-political roots.

Strategies—Traditional strategy has involved the movement of troops, planes, and other weaponry to conquer or defend sovereignty. But since the prolific bloodletting of the two world wars, and especially the invention of nuclear weaponry, the prospect of zero-sum war has become so daunting that wars grow more limited. Two of the most savage limited wars since World War II were both fought in East Asia, but war is still quite possible at a handful of hot spots. Vast sums are still spent on sophisticated weaponry though the most advanced and expensive weapons are now more used to deter than to fight, and nations prefer to exchange credible threats rather than bullets or missiles. States still want to make other states do things they have no perceived interest in doing, so other levers of power have been resorted to with increasing frequency, including threats, soft power, and economic statecraft. All are covered in this section.

Triangles—Triangulation involves the manipulation of third parties to facilitate (or inhibit) bilateral conflict resolution. The third party may be deployed to various ends: to balance against a potential aggressor, to bandwagon in support of an offensive, or simply to hedge against unknown contingencies. Though hitherto most frequently applied to great power relations, triangular analysis can also help clarify the realistic options of small or medium powers. As we shall see, asymmetric triangles are quite frequently encountered in East Asia because of the wide disparity in the size and power of the states involved.

---

39. Lowell Dittmer, "In Search of a Theory of National Identity," in *China's Quest for National Identity*, ed. Lowell Dittmer and Samuel S. Kim (Ithaca, NY: Cornell University Press), 1–32.

Part A: Identities

2
Assessing China's Public Diplomacy under the Leadership of Xi Jinping in Asia

A Pseudo-panel Analysis

Yun-han Chu, Hsin-Che Wu, and Min-Hua Huang

Introduction

Soon after Donald Trump took office, the United States began to escalate its strategic confrontation with China. Before the election, Trump accused China of conducting unfair trade and manipulating the exchange rate. One year after the election, in November 2017, Trump denied granting China market economy status. Since then, confrontation between the two powers has worsened, as revealed in two US official documents, the National Security Strategy (2017)[1] and the National Defense Strategy (2018).[2] These reports state that China was intent on changing the status quo and labeled the country, along with Russia, as a major strategic competitor to the US. In particular, the reports explicitly mentioned China's authoritarian system, predatory economic strategy, rising military power, and attempts to exert influence through technology and propaganda. Trump himself has criticized China's intention to replace the US as the top global economic power and harm American interests.[3] As a result, although the major focus has been on trade wars and tariff sanctions, many officials in the Trump administration have also pointed to China as the number one threat to US national security. In 2018, polarization between the two powers heightened rapidly, encompassing areas such as trade, the economy, technology, and intellectual property rights, as well as politics and

---

1. Donald J. Trump, *National Security Strategy of the United States of America*, Executive Office of the President, Washington, DC, 2017, https://www.whitehouse.gov/wp-content/uploads/2017/12/NSS-Final-12-18-2017-0905.pdf.
2. Jim Mattis, *Summary of the 2018 National Defense Strategy of the United States of America*, Department of Defense, Washington, DC, 2018, https://dod.defense.gov/Portals/1/Documents/pubs/2018-National-Defense-Strategy-Summary.pdf.
3. Ajay Mohanty, "China No Longer in Position to Supersede US as Top Economic Power: Trump," *Business Standard*, November 8, 2018, https://www.business-standard.com/article/international/china-no-longer-in-position-to-supersede-us-as-top-economic-power-trump-118110800831_1.html.

the military, and even extended to conflict between democratic and authoritarian values and the future of world order.

Prior to the Xi Jinping era, with the rise of Chinese power there were calls within the country during the "Hu-Wen regime" to change Deng Xiaoping's foreign policy strategy of "bide and hide" as early as 2007.[4] However, the official position was still to keep a low profile in foreign affairs. During the second term of Hu Jintao's presidency, China was discreet in avoiding high-profile international propaganda advocating a greater role in great power politics for itself or promoting an ambitious global agenda. The major focus of China's foreign policy was still centered on its peaceful rise and its willingness to participate in and contribute to the international regimes that consolidate the existing world order. China hoped that, by investing in public diplomacy, the international community would accept China's rise, averting direct strategic confrontation with the US.[5] However, after Xi unveiled the Belt and Road Initiative (BRI) in 2013, while also stressing "the great rejuvenation of the Chinese nation" and calling for a "new type of great power relationship" between China and the US, Xi undoubtedly signaled the end of the foreign policy of "bide and hide" and instead sought a level of influence commensurate with its national strength in international politics. In the minds of Western elites, this signals China's intent to change the international status quo, a fact that cannot be concealed no matter how hard China has tried to cast the beneficiary effects to humanity of its peaceful rise.[6]

Experts generally regard the BRI as a top-down and systematic plan envisaged by Xi Jinping and implemented by the Chinese state, with a vision to inject new impetus into globalization by deepening economic partnership with the Global South and accelerating the integration of the vast Eurasia continent. The BRI is also deployed as a central piece in China's public diplomacy programs at national and local levels.[7] However, at key moments, China's exercise of hard power over geopolitical issues might appear to compromise the aims of its public diplomacy. On the one hand China has upgraded its development assistance program, encouraged its state-owned firms to expand foreign direct investment, and actively carried out cultural diplomacy

---

4. Wu Jin, "China's Public Diplomacy at Crossroads," China.org.cn, March 5, 2012, http://www.china.org.cn/china/NPC_CPPCC_2012/2012-03/05/content_24811109.htm.
5. Yiwei Wang, "Public Diplomacy and the Rise of Chinese Soft Power," *Annals of the American Academy of Political and Social Science* 616, no. 1 (2008): 257–73.
6. Michael D. Swaine, "Chinese Views and Commentary on the 'One Belt, One Road' Initiative," *China Leadership Monitor* 47, no. 2 (2015): 1–24.
7. See, for instance, The National Development and Reform Commission of PRC, the Ministry of Foreign Affairs of PRC, and the Ministry of Commerce of PRC, "Vision and Actions on Jointly Building Silk Road Economic Belt and 21st-Century Maritime Silk Road," March 28, 2015, http://en.ndrc.gov.cn/newsrelease/201503/t20150330_669367.html; China Power Team, "How Will the Belt and Road Initiative Advance China's Interests?" China Power, May 8, 2017, updated May 29, 2019, accessed July 10, 2019, https://chinapower.csis.org/china-belt-and-road-initiative/.

through its Confucius Institutes.[8] On the other hand, when the conflict in the South China Sea intensified in 2015, Sun Jianguo, Deputy Chief of the Joint Staff of the People's Liberation Army, sent by the Chinese Communist Party (CCP) to the Shangri-La Dialogue in Singapore, outlined China's position in the dispute in coarse and unyielding terms.[9] This type of language was repeated in 2016, when the Philippines submitted an arbitration case over the South China Sea, and the international community closely watched China's response. Again, Sun Jianguo's stern posture and remarks to the international media could have set back the CCP's public diplomacy efforts for many years. Clearly, the CCP could have used diplomatic language to reaffirm its position rather than resorting to this more abrasive approach. The fact that Sun Jianguo repeated these remarks in 2016 indicates this was not a one-off aberration but was actually approved by the CCP.[10] Incidents like this raise the question of whether the CCP has carefully coordinated its policies and practices in public diplomacy, or whether China's tough military rhetoric and action will undermine the image of the peaceful rise that it has long carefully crafted.

Over the past two years, faced with Trump's more hostile approach, China has to some extent softened its "Belt and Road" rhetoric and publicly denied its political strategic objectives while continuing its effort to promote large-scale cooperation projects under the BRI.[11] The Western mass media have in the meantime turned overtly hostile toward China, running all kinds of negative reports regarding potential threats of China's advances in science and technology, the People's Liberation Army's (PLA) military buildup in the South China Sea, suppression of minorities' religious freedom and human

---

8. See, for instance, James F. Paradise, "China and International Harmony: The Role of Confucius Institute in Bolstering Beijing's Soft Power," *Asian Survey* 49, no. 4 (2009): 647–69.
9. At the 2015 Shangri-La Dialogue, Sun said that "China and the Chinese military are not afraid of ghosts and do not believe in evil, we believe in reason and not hegemony. Never expect us to yield to evil fallacies and power hegemony. The United States disregards history, law, and facts and blames China for its legal, reasonable, and sensible reef construction. We express our firm opposition to this position."〔中國和中國軍隊歷來不怕鬼、不信邪，服理不服霸、信理不信邪，絕不要指望我們會對歪理邪說和強權霸權屈服。美方無視歷史、法理與事實，對中國合法、合理、合情的島礁建設進行指責，我們對此表示堅決反對。〕
10. The original text of Sun Jianguo's speech in Shangri-La Dialogue in 2016 is "China is firmly opposed to this [referring to freedom of navigation operations]! We do not make trouble, but we are not afraid of trouble. China will not bear the consequences, nor will it allow any infringement on its sovereignty and security interests. We will not sit by and watch a small number of countries throw the South China Sea into chaos."〔中國對此堅決反對（指航行自由計畫）！我們不惹事，也不怕事，中國不會吞下苦果、惡果，不會允許自己的主權和安全利益受到侵犯，不會坐視少數國家在南海揭亂。〕
11. In 2017, an official CCP directive prohibited reference to the BRI as a "strategy." The initiative's official English translation was changed from One Belt, One Road (OBOR) to its present name in mid-2016, due to concerns that the former name may lead to misunderstandings about China's intentions. Official information can be accessed on the Second Belt and Road Forum for International Cooperation (BRF), April 24, 2019, 15 cognitive misunderstandings about the "Belt and Road"(in Chinese), http://www.brfmc2019.cn/201.shtml.

rights in Xinjiang, and the burdening of its loan recipient countries with heavy debt. To some degree, China faces a dilemma, because the fundamental basis for China to pursue a commensurate international status is the continuous development of its hard power, but if China is too successful in this regard it will be very likely perceived as a threat. However, if China sacrifices its future rise in national strength simply to reduce the perceived threat of Chinese hard power, then it has little need to conduct public diplomacy in the international community. Therefore, when Trump clearly stated that China's continued rise threatened the national interest of the US, it effectively limited China's space for public diplomacy. As a result, China has resorted to soft power in order to hide its attempts to elevate its structural position in the hierarchy of the existing world order.

At the current stage, there exists a contradiction for China in respect of the goal to develop hard and soft power simultaneously.[12] As a matter of fact, the harder a rising power pushes for more influence in world affairs, the more incumbent powers will accuse it of revisionism.[13] In contrast, the easiest way for the international community to acknowledge a rising power and its corresponding status is to make everything look like it just has happened naturally.[14]

China, as the message sender in carrying public diplomacy, needs to find a way to frame its intention in seeking world leadership as trustworthy and desirable, but paradoxically, this requires recipient states to perceive China as having little desire to use its hard power for advancing its geopolitical interests and to view China's growing influence as beneficial or at least not threatening. In other words, favorable perceptions of China take time to develop through long-term, seemingly non-deliberate, communicative action, and this effect may be neutralized once the effort is seen as overtly purposeful. From this viewpoint, the subjective impressions of China in the recipient states, regardless of whether they are based on specific facts, may be more important than are the public diplomacy efforts of the Chinese government in shaping people's view of China. Therefore, the purpose of this study is to investigate the various factors that determine how citizens in Asian countries evaluate China's influence during the Xi era. In particular, we will assess whether China's deployment of "hard power" has reinforced or inadvertently compromised or even contradicted its effort to upgrade its "soft power." In addition, we will tease out the relative explanatory power of a variety of hypotheses

---

12. See Joseph Nye, "The Limits of Chinese Soft Power," Project Syndicate July 10, 2015, https://www.project-syndicate.org/commentary/china-civil-society-nationalism-soft-power-by-joseph-s--nye-2015-07?barrier=accesspaylog.
13. See, for instance, Elizabeth C. Economy, "China's Imperial President: Xi Jinping Tightens His Grip," *Foreign Affairs* 93, no. 6 (2014): 80–91.
14. Yun-han Chu, Liu Kang, and Min-hua Huang, "How East Asians View the Rise of China," *Journal of Contemporary China* 24, no. 93 (2015): 398–420.

regarding how subjective perceptions are related to favorable or unfavorable views of China's influence in Asia.

China's Foreign Policy under Xi's Leadership and Its Reception

Foreign policy under Xi's leadership has four major characteristics: more resourceful, more assertive, more ambitious, and more aggressive.[15] First, in resources, China's economy continues to grow at an annual pace of above 6 percent despite widespread expectations of its slowing down. According to the latest economic data, China's GDP in 2018 was about two-thirds that of the US ($13.6 trillion vs. $20.5 trillion).[16] If China and the US maintain annual economic growth of 6 percent and 2 percent respectively,[17] then China's nominal GDP will surpass that of the US in 2027 to become the world's largest economy. According to the IMF, in purchasing power parity GDP, China overtook the US as the world's biggest economy in 2014. China also ranked third globally behind the US and Japan for foreign direct investment (FDI) outflows in 2017[18] and the leading position for international tourism expenditure.[19] Second, China has taken a firmer foreign policy line. This is reflected in efforts to strengthen both hard and soft foreign policy. For example, on the security issue, China has taken a tougher stance on East China Sea, South China Sea, and Taiwan Strait issues; however, on economic and trade issues, it has also emphasized that China will play a leading role in global free trade and shoulder greater leadership responsibility just as the US is abdicating its throne under Trump's radical unilateralism. This indicates that China indeed has a clear vision for the future world order, under which it intends to play a leading role and believes that it is entitled to due recognition.[20]

Third, China actively pursues substantive voice and influence in global affairs by launching new multilateral institutions such as the Asian Infrastructure Investment Bank (AIIB), continuing the expansion of the BRI projects, and enlarging the membership of the Shanghai Cooperation

---

15. See, for instance, Michael D. Swaine, "Perceptions of an Assertive China," *China Leadership Monitor* 32, no. 2 (2010): 1–19. For the counterpoint, see Alastair Iain Johnston, "How New and Assertive Is China's New Assertiveness?" *International Security* 37, no. 4 (2013): 7–48.
16. K. Amadeo, "China's Economy and Its Effect on the U.S. Economy," the balance, October 20, 2020, https://www.thebalance.com/china-economy-facts-effect-on-us-economy-3306345.
17. Zishidanggui, "Is Economic Strength Misjudged? 2018 US GDP Growth Rate Is More Than 2.9% but 5.72%! How Many Years Does China Catch Up?" Diyihuangjinwang, March 5, 2019, http://www.liejin99.com/20190305/c610076153.shtml.
18. UNCTAD, "World Investment Report 2018," UNCTAD, June 6, 2018, https://unctad.org/en/PublicationsLibrary/wir2018_overview_en.pdf.
19. UNTWO, "Guidelines for Success in the Chinese Outbound Tourism Market," UNWTO, 2019, https://www.e-unwto.org/doi/pdf/10.18111/9789284421138.
20. Michael D. Swaine, "Xi Jinping on Chinese Foreign Relations: The Governance of China and Chinese Commentary," *China Leadership Monitor* 48, no. 1 (2015): 1–13; Robert D. Blackwill and Kurt M. Campbell, *Xi Jinping on the Global Stage: Chinese Foreign Policy under a Powerful but Exposed Leader* (Washington, DC: Council on Foreign Relations Press, 2016).

Organization (SCO).[21] Although some BRI projects have been prematurely canceled or terminated,[22] and Chinese investment has been criticized by US senior officials as predatory,[23] with the ultimate political objective of controlling other countries,[24] it is also undeniable that many countries have welcomed this type of partnership and regard China as a future leader in global affairs and international economic cooperation.[25] In 2017, one of the main factors in the successful admission of India and Pakistan into the SCO is that both countries believe that China and its economic partners represent an important opportunity for their future economic development.[26] Finally, China has been more aggressive in expanding its military capability, developing its science and technology capability, and persistently pushing its advantage in ongoing security issues. China has increased its military expenditure threefold in less than a decade and is now ranked second globally in total military expenditure, after the US.[27] China is now focusing on space technology and has recently completed a successful landing on the far side of the moon, demonstrating the advancement of its aerospace capabilities.[28] China is also

---

21. With regard to Chinese increasing participation in multilateral international institutions, for instance, see Scott L. Kastner, Margaret M. Pearson, and Chad Rector, *China's Strategic Multilateralism: Investing in Global Governance* (Cambridge, MA: Cambridge University Press, 2018). For the particular case of AIIB, see Gregory T. Chin, "Asian Infrastructure Investment Bank: Governance Innovation and Prospects," *Global Governance* 2, no. 1 (2016): 11–26.
22. R. Radzi, "Malaysia Takes Back $243M from Chinese Firm over Canceled Pipelines," *Benar News*, July 15, 2019, accessed July 16, 2019, https://www.benarnews.org/english/news/malaysian/money-seized-07152019160641.html.
23. There are many reports on the predatory behavior of Chinese foreign investment from Western media. The classic books in the academic world can be found in D. Brautigam, *The Dragon's Gift: The Real Story of China in Africa* (Oxford: Oxford University Press, 2009).
24. E. C. Economy, "China's New Revolution: The Reign of Xi Jinping," *Foreign Affairs* 97, no. 60 (2018): 60–74.
25. From the development of recent years, developing countries and some European countries hope to welcome China as a partner and hope that China can become a leader in free trade. News can be accessed on: D. Shullman, "Protect the Party: China's Growing Influence in the Developing World," 2019, The Brookings Institution website, accessed June 24, 2019, https://www.brookings.edu/articles/protect-the-party-chinas-growing-influence-in-the-developing-world/; R. Kenneth, "Communist China Is Now the Leader of the 'Free Trade' World," *Forbes*, January 24, 2017, accessed July 15, 2019, https://www.forbes.com/sites/kenrapoza/2017/01/24/communist-china-is-now-the-leader-of-the-free-trade-world/#328bd0a521e0; C. Liu and F. Jianjian, "China-Europe Forum on Reform and Globalization Successfully Held in Madrid," *China Daily*, November 26, 2018, accessed July 8, 2019, http://www.chinadaily.com.cn/a/201811/26/WS5bfad631a310eff30328aea2.html.
26. Z. S. Ahmed, S. Ahmed, and S. Bhatnagar, "Conflict or Cooperation? India and Pakistan in Shanghai Cooperation Organisation," *Pacific Focus* 34, no. 1 (2019): 5–30.
27. China Power Team, "What Does China Really Spend on Its Military?" *China Power*, December 28, 2015, updated June 13, 2019, accessed July 15, 2019, https://chinapower.csis.org/military-spending/.
28. BBC News, "China Moon Mission Lands Chang'e-4 Spacecraft on Far Side," *BBC*, January 3, 2019, https://www.bbc.com/news/science-environment-46724727.

accelerating manufactured island building in the South China Sea and holds regular military operations in the area to assert its sovereignty.[29]

To what extent these changes in foreign policy have had an impact on the effectiveness of China's soft power is ultimately determined by the feelings of the people in recipient political systems toward China's influence. Therefore, how people view a future in which China replaces the US as the defender of free trade and economic globalization can only be determined by empirical analysis. Alternatively, whether China's hard line stance on sovereignty in the South China Sea damages its national image and causes citizens in other countries to view China negatively must also be verified by empirical analysis. If people are aware of these events, they may produce significant changes in perceptions of China and other related attitudes. Multi-wave survey data therefore provide valuable information for researchers to detect and measure people's perceptions and views and draw plausible causal relationships between the actions of the message sender (China) and changes in the views of the message recipients (China's Asian neighbors) toward China.

Aside from perceptions of China as an economic opportunity or a security threat, from the message recipient's viewpoint, there are many other factors that could change people's feelings about China.[30] The previous literature has discussed these factors systematically, and they have appeared in the rhetoric of Trump and other national politicians toward China. The first possible factor is how people perceive their own economic benefits or losses associated with China's influence. For instance, many of China's BRI initiatives in Myanmar, such as oil and gas pipelines, the Myitsone Dam, and illegal Chinese logging in Kachin State, have led to strong local opposition to the BRI in Myanmar and a widespread view of Chinese investment in the country as predatory.[31] Similar sentiments also appeared in Taiwan in 2014, during the Sunflower Movement. Many Taiwanese argued that the proposed Cross-Strait Service Trade Agreement was a form of economic aggression by China against the island.[32] Another example is the amendment of BRI East Coast Rail Link

---

29. B. Blanchard and M. Petty, "China Vows to Protect South China Sea Sovereignty, —Manila Upbeat," July 12, 2016, https://uk.reuters.com/article/uk-southchinasea-ruling-idUKKCN0ZS02P.
30. Related literature can be found in the following articles: Y. H. Chu, K. Liu, and M. H. Huang, "How East Asians View the Rise of China," *Journal of Contemporary China* 24, no. 93(2015): 398–420; Y. H. Chu, M. H. Huang, and J. Lu, "Enter the Dragon: How East Asians View a Rising China," *Global Asia* 10, no. 3: 112–20. Y. H. Chu, T. Xiao, and M. H. Huang, "Co-opetition and the Influence of China and the United States in East Asia: An Empirical Analysis" (in Chinese), *CASS Journal of Political Science*, no. 3: 39–50; 126–27.
31. E. E. T Lwin, "Myitsone Dam Project Poses No Threat to Myanmar-China Ties: Chinese Envoy," *The Myanmar Times*, May 22, 2019, https://www.mmtimes.com/news/myitsone-dam-project-poses-no-threat-myanmar-china-ties-chinese-envoy.html.; C. Brahma, "China's Dam Problem with Myanmar," *Myanmar Times* June 14, 2016, https://www.mmtimes.com/opinion/22517-china-s-dam-problem-with-myanmar.html.
32. M. S. Ho, "Occupy Congress in Taiwan: Political Opportunity, Threat, and the Sunflower Movement," *Journal of East Asian Studies* 15, no. 1 (2015): 69–97; I. Rowen, "Inside Taiwan's

project (viewed as major achievement under the Najib administration) on affordability grounds after the opposition unexpectedly won the Malaysian general election in 2018.[33] These examples show that, if citizens believe that China's influence will have economic benefits, they have more positive views of China. Conversely, they may believe that the downsides of Chinese influence are greater than are the upsides.[34]

The second array of factors is related to regime evaluation in level of democracy. Previous studies have shown that people tend to rate a country more highly in democratic terms if they have a positive perception of it and lower if they have negative perceptions of it.[35] Although China claims to be a democratic country that adheres to socialism with Chinese characteristics, China's system is consistently characterized by international media as authoritarian and in opposition to the Western system of liberal democracy. In fact, the legacy of the totalitarian politics of the early days of the CCP lingers in the minds of many people and is frequently evoked in international news reports about the CCP's violations of freedom, human rights, and the rule of law. Trump also made a speech criticizing China's socialist system[36] and demanding structural reforms to China's state capitalism.[37] At the same time, some American politicians have accused the Chinese authority's effort to infiltrate the country and exert undue influence on domestic politics. These

---

Sunflower Movement: Twenty-Four Days in a Student-Occupied Parliament, and the Future of the Region," *Journal of Asian Studies* 74, no. 1 (2015): 5–21.

33. The Straits Times, "Malaysia's East Coast Rail Link back on track after government signs $14.5b deal with China," *The Straits Times*, April 12, 2019, https://www.straitstimes.com/asia/se-asia/145-bln-deal-signed-with-china-on-malaysias-east-coast-rail-link-mahathirs-office.

34. This line of reasoning views China as an agent of greater trade and more economic globalization and the formation of individual attitudes toward China on the basis of a respondent's economic standing in a global economy. See, for instance, Edward D. Mansfield and Diana C. Mutz, "Support for Free Trade: Self-Interest, Sociotropic Politics, and Out-group Anxiety," *International Organization* 63, no. 3 (2009): 425–57.

35. Democracies (especially developed democracies) are more tolerant of each other, while non-democratic countries are more intolerant. Related literature can be found in: S. Werner and D. Lemke, "Opposites Do Not Attract: The impact of Domestic Institutions, Power, and Prior Commitments on Alignment Choices," *International Studies Quarterly* 41, no. 3 (1997): 529–46; M. Mousseau, "Market Prosperity, Democratic Consolidation, and Democratic Peace," *Journal of Conflict Resolution* 44, no. 4: 472–507; D. Manevich, "People in Less Democratic Countries Are More Likely to Say China and Russia Respect Personal Freedoms," The Pew Research Center, March 12, 2018, https://www.pewresearch.org/fact-tank/2018/03/12/people-in-less-democratic-countries-are-more-likely-to-say-china-and-russia-respect-personal-freedoms/. According to the Manevich's papers, the empirical data from the Pew Research Center also point out that non-democratic countries have better evaluations of non-democratic countries, especially considering their respect for human rights and individual freedoms.

36. Steve Benen, "Trump Seems a Little Too Fond of China's Authoritarian Mode," *MSNBC*, February 26, 2019, http://www.msnbc.com/rachel-maddow-show/trump-seems-little-too-fond-chinas-authoritarian-model.

37. Jenny Leonard, "Trump Says Trade Deal with China Must Include Structural Change," Bloomberg, February 6, 2019, https://www.bloomberg.com/news/articles/2019-02-06/trump-says-trade-deal-with-china-must-include-structural-change.

examples show that positive or negative perceptions of a foreign country are often reflected in their regime evaluation, and therefore citizens may assess China's influence positively or negatively due to their subjective evaluations of China's political system.

Culture in the form of value orientation and political predisposition also matters in how citizens evaluate China's influence.[38] If we apply the spectrum of authoritarian and liberal values which distinguishes between collectivism and hierarchical order versus individualism and freedom and equality, China and the US are widely perceived as societies representing two ends of the scale. Previous studies have shown that the affinity (or lack of affinity) in political culture is a key factor affecting how people evaluate China's influence.[39] People tend to evaluate the familiar more favorably than they do the unfamiliar. If people believe that China's rise threatens the values that they are familiar with, they are likely to be more fearful, leading to more negative evaluations of China. If citizens have authoritarian value orientations, they are less likely to view China's influence negatively, due to analogous value orientations; conversely, citizens with anti-authoritarian values will be more likely to view China negatively because of conflicting values.

Finally, popular perceptions of China's role in the international community as well as past successful economic development experience will also systematically influence their evaluations of China's influence. In social psychology, people tend to regard successful people or things as "role models" and

---

38. See, for instance, P. Norris and R. Inglehart, *Cosmopolitan Communications: Cultural Diversity in a Globalized World* (Cambridge, MA: Cambridge University Press, 2009).
39. T. Shi, *The Cultural Logic of Politics in Mainland China and Taiwan* (Cambridge, MA: Cambridge University Press, 2014). In the seventh chapter of the book, Shi Tianjian emphasizes the influence of cultural norms on how people understand democracy. Shi compared Western democratic concepts with China's folk-based traditions. His data analysis found that modern cultural norms made people more inclined to define democracy as a set of procedural arrangements that restricted political power, while traditional cultural norms made people understand democracy as the governance of benevolent guardians. In addition, Shi used the two orientation concepts of orientation towards authority (OTA) and definition of self-interest (DSI) to explore the influence of culture on political attitudes and behaviors. OTA focuses on the proper relationship between individuals and authority (hierarchy, equivalence), and DSI focuses on the legitimate units of self-interest calculation (egocentric, non-self-centered). It is the conceptualization and operation of OTA and DSI that enables Shi to verify the inherent stability and independence of cultural norms based on survey data, and find that cultural norms as independent variables are not a whole: their different internal components and their different cultural orientations have a significant and different impact on people's political attitudes and behaviors.
Empirical evidence can be found in H. Miao, "American Public's Opinion of China's Economic Competitiveness and China's Exchange Rate Policy" (in Chinese), *Forum of World Economics & Politics*, no. 5 (2016): 42–61, and X. Wang and T. Xiao, "The Image of China in the Eyes of the American People" (in Chinese), *Jiangsu Social Science*, no. 5 (2015): 132–37. The familiarity with Chinese culture can significantly affect the impression or policy evaluation of China.

evaluate them positively.[40] Therefore, when they view China's past, present, or future as a role model for successful development, they are likely to evaluate the country more positively.[41] Contrariwise, if people look to a "role model" that represents contradictory values or experiences to China, they will assess China in more negative terms. In addition, such positive perceptions can be also explained by bandwagoning behavior, in that rational individuals tend to identify themselves with prospective winners.

The six explanations for perceptions of China's influence given above do not exhaust all possible explanatory factors. Socioeconomic background, interest in politics, political efficacy, gender, age, and education are other possible predictors. The Asian Barometer Survey (ABS) has conducted multiple survey waves including all of these possible predictors, enabling us to carry out systematic and rigorous causal analysis on how these factors compete with each other to affect the perceptions of citizens in Asia toward China. In the following sections, we will conduct a statistical analysis using a pseudo-panel method with data from Wave 3 to Wave 5 of the ABS to identify which of the aforementioned factors consistently explain perceptions of China across different social contexts within Asia and the strength of these effects.

Assessing Asian's Perception of China's Influence in Asia

The years 2013 and 2017 were critical junctures for Sino-US relations. In 2013, Xi Jinping formally replaced Hu Jintao as China's head of state (and concurrently taking over the helm of the CCP and the PLA). Subsequently, China adopted a more high-profile foreign policy in both hard and soft power. In December 2013, China began large-scale island building in the South China Sea, to create artificial land for both maritime and military purposes and to assert its sovereignty over this sea. This led to escalating tensions with Vietnam and the Philippines, and the US soon issued a statement formally rejecting China's nine-dash line claim of sovereignty over the South China Sea.[42] The dispute between China and its neighboring countries (including the Philippines, Vietnam, Malaysia, Indonesia, and Brunei) as well as the US

---

40. This is known as "social contagion model" in American politics. See J. Pacheco, "The Social Contagion Model: Exploring the Role of Public Opinion on the Diffusion of Antismoking Legislation Across the American States," *The Journal of Politics* 74, no. 1 (2012): 187–202.
41. D. Shullman, "Protect the Party: China's Growing Influence in the Developing World," The Brookings Institution website, June 24, 2019, https://www.brookings.edu/articles/protect-the-party-chinas-growing-influence-in-the-developing-world/. The author of the article mentioned that the Chinese government trains foreign officials through various cooperation programs, in addition to allowing them to recognize the Chinese model and allowing them to support it.
    At present, Tsinghua University in China also has a similar degree program, attracting officials from developing countries to Tsinghua to learn the Chinese model.
42. Daniel R. Russel, "Maritime Disputes in East Asia," The US State Department website, June 24, 2019, https://2009-2017.state.gov/p/eap/rls/rm/2014/02/221293.htm.

quickly became heated, and global attention was directed toward China's aggressive turn in foreign policy under Xi. The year 2017 was another critical time for Sino-US relations, due to Trump's adoption of a confrontational policy toward China, accusing it of unfair trade practices, manipulating currency, infringing intellectual property rights, and stealing technology, and the allegation that Huawei may have built "backdoors" into its devices that could be used to monitor users. The Trump administration outlined its view to the international community that China and Russia are the prime threats to American global leadership, indicating that the conflict has already expanded from a few hot button issues to all-encompassing strategic competition.

A lack of longitudinal survey data at the individual level has prevented researchers from directly assessing the extent to which shifts in the foreign policy of China or the US affects Asians' perceptions of China's influence as well as the relative importance of hard power- or soft power- related factors in these explanations. The Pew Survey has collected longitudinal survey data in a few Asian countries but only publishes its data at the aggregate level without enough information on covariates for control purposes.[43] The ABS, in contrast, collects country-representative individual-level data through face-to-face interviews. Using cross-sectional data from the ABS accumulated at multiple time points, we can apply a pseudo-panel method to resolve the problem of the lack of individual-level panel data and incorporate time-variant variables at the political system level to test whether critical events generate a large impact by applying a quasi-experimental design where other variables measuring perceptions are controlled. The logic of the pseudo-panel data analysis is to use the demographical variables (gender, age, education) to form fixed cohorts of people and then aggregate cross-sectional survey data into the cohort level for statistical analysis. The number of cohorts defined is inversely related to the precision of cohort level estimates, and there is a tradeoff between the sample size of cohorts and the data quality of cohort-level measurements.[44]

The ABS included a battery of questions regarding the rise of China since Wave 3. Specifically, the ABS included a question asking respondents whether they think China's influence in Asia does "more good than harm" or "more harm than good." We apply this item as our binary measure of favorable/unfavorable perceptions toward China and aggregate it to the cohort level as the dependent variable (a percentage estimate). The formation of the remaining covariates from the ABS survey follows the same aggregate procedure,

---

43. Pew Research Center, "Attitudes toward China in America's Global Image Remains More Positive than China's," Pew Research Center Website, July 18, 2013, http://www.pew-global.org/2013/07/18/chapter-3-attitudes-toward-china/.
44. There are twelve cohort observations excluded from analysis because their sample size is under three. The criterion applied here is that eligible cohort observations should have a sample size three or above.

except for the political system level, time point, or entity variables.[45] The definition of cohorts comprises three demographic variables: male/female for gender, youth/adult/senior for age, and below college/college for education, by which each county sample can be subgrouped into twelve cohorts. The fieldwork for the three waves of the ABS used in the present study was conducted between 2010 and 2012 (ABS 3), 2014 and 2016 (ABS 4), and 2018 and June 2019 (ABS 5). For Waves 3 and 4, twelve macro samples (political systems) are included in the analysis, and China and Myanmar are excluded as not applicable and due to data unavailability respectively.[46] Wave 5 of the ABS is currently still in the field. However, surveys in six political systems were completed before June 2019, providing additional data time points to incorporate the possible effects of Trump's presidency into our analysis. The detailed information regarding pseudo-panel formation and methodological issues can be found in Appendix I.

Our analytical purpose is to evaluate four groups of factors that possibly account for popular perceptions of China's influence across Asia. The first group is time-variant variables that capture the temporal junction of critical events associated with Sino-US relations, such as Xi's foreign policy shift or Trump's confrontational strategy. The second group includes cohort and societal-level covariates included for control purposes. Specifically, they comprise perceptional variables (political interest, political efficacy) and entity variables (dummies that represent the demographic information of the cohorts). The last two groups are composed of the major competing explanatory variables. One is the treatment variable for hard-power incidents, specifically the political systems involved in the East China Sea disputes (Japan, Korea, and Taiwan from Waves 3 to 5) and the South China Sea disputes (the Philippines, Taiwan, Indonesia, Vietnam, and Malaysia from Waves 4 to 5).[47] In the East China Sea dispute, there have been sporadic but continuing conflicts between Japan, Korea, China, and Taiwan. Therefore, the cohort observations in Japan, Korea, and Taiwan are coded as a treatment group without the before or after distinction. However, in the case of the South China Sea dispute, a sudden escalation occurred in December 2013, when China launched large-scale island building and subsequent military escalation.[48] Therefore, we code the cohort observations for the five sovereign claimants as the treatment group, and the before-

---

45. Entity variable refers to the demographic variables that are used to defined and form the cohort observation. In this study, the entity variables are coded as binary group dummies.
46. China is not the recipient of soft power, and Myanmar was not included in Wave 3 of the ABS.
47. US Department of State, "China: Maritime Claims in the South China Sea, Limits in the Seas Series Report No. 143," US Department of State website, https://www.state.gov/documents/organization/234936.pdf.
48. Reuters, "China's Land Reclamation in South China Sea Grows: Pentagon Report," Reuters, August 21, 2015, https://www.reuters.com/article/us-southchinasea-china-pentagon/chinas-land-reclamation-in-south-china-sea-grows-pentagon-report-idUSKCN-0QQ0S920150821.

after distinction is defined at Wave 3 (2010–2012, pre-treatment) and Waves 4 and 5 (2014–2016, 2018–present, after treatment). Such a quasi-experimental design is made possible due to the coincidence of a survey timeline matching the timing of the breakout of the South China Sea disputes.

In addition to hard-power incidents, we include five groups of major explanatory variables corresponding to the potential reasons discussed in the last section: *globalization, socioeconomic perception, regime evaluation, liberal values,* and *international relations.* All the variables in this group are formed from aggregation of survey data, and each group is composed of three indicators, with a stepwise method applied to select stronger predictors in the final model, in which we only select two explanatory predictors for each group of predictors. In this way, we can compare the competing statistical power of all theoretical explanations in the final model. It should be noted that panel-data analysis requires a missing-at-random (MAR) hypothesis to analyze unbalanced data (missing observations in repeated measures), but the six unavailable macro datasets of Wave 5 means this condition is not met. Therefore, we split the overall cohort observations and regroup them into two separate datasets: one with Wave 3 and Wave 4 including twelve macro cases (abbreviated "two-wave sample"); the other with Wave 3, Wave 4, and Wave 5 including six macro cases (abbreviated "three-wave sample"). The former two-wave sample is better representative of the Asia-Pacific region but provides shorter temporal coverage. The latter three-wave sample has an extra survey point but with a limited number of countries, and hence the generalizability of its analysis is more restricted, and qualifications need to be made when interpreting results.

Changing Perceptions of China's Influence in Asia

In this and the next sections, we present the findings of the pseudo-panel analysis for the two-wave and three-wave samples. The major restriction when interpreting the two samples is that the two-wave sample does not cover Trump's presidency, and its inference only covers the first part of Xi's first term (before 2017). Conversely, the three-wave sample has only six political systems available, creating potential collinearity issues. For example, only one claimant in the East China Sea disputes is included (Taiwan). We therefore drop the variable of East China Sea claimant when analyzing the three-wave sample, due to its collinearity with the macro-level dummy.

Before we specify the full model, it is necessary to conduct a preliminary test on the entity dummies to see whether the demographic variables composing the cohorts are actually strong predictors of the dependent variable. If they are strong predictors, then the way we categorize the cohorts will matter a lot in the model estimation, producing a further complication with regard to model specification. In this preliminary test, we include four groups of predictors in the basic model, aside from the five major groups of explanatory variables. Here, we also include the macro dummies but do not report its coefficient or the constant; instead, we estimate the mean of each political system's predicted percentage in favoring China's influence. As Table 2.1 shows, the dependent variable is the percentage of respondents with positive views of China's influence in Asia, and the first two columns report the result of the basic model using the two-wave sample and the third using the three-wave sample. The reason we run the basic model twice with and without Japan's cohorts for the two-wave sample is that, by examining the descriptive statistics, we found that Japan's cohorts have an extremely low percentage of favorable views toward China in both waves (mostly below 20 percent in Wave 3 and below 15 percent in Wave 4). We suspect that the estimate of the East China Sea claimants might be mostly driven by Japan's cohort observations and therefore conduct a robustness check by running the regression with and without Japan.

If we examine the left two columns in Table 2.1 together, we find that the magnitude of the effect for East China Sea claimants is reduced sharply when Japan is excluded. Nevertheless, we find both factors in the hard-power category (South China Sea claimants and East China Sea claimants) have a significant negative impact of similar magnitude (–17 percent and –13 percent, respectively) as shown in the second column. This indicates that the hard-power exercises do indeed hurt China's favorability in both the South and East China Sea disputes. Regarding the time-variant predictor, we do not find a significant difference before and after Xi took office in 2013, which suggests the foreign policy shift under Xi either had not been perceived or had been perceived but did not cause any damage to China's favorability. For the entity dummies, none of the demographical variables shows a significant result, indicating that the way cohorts are defined does not influence the estimate of the dependent variable, suggesting that there is no need to change the cohort specification. Lastly, political interest is found to be positively associated with favorable perceptions of China, indicating that greater news coverage actually benefited China's image despite many negative reports in the media about China. These results temporally apply from 2010 to 2016.

Much interest has been focused on Trump's confrontational policy toward China, and therefore the analysis needs to cover all three waves through the end of 2018. As shown in the third column, we find if only six macro cases are selected (Mongolia, the Philippines, Taiwan, Thailand, Vietnam, and Malaysia), the South China Sea conflict still contributes negatively and significantly (about 30 percent) in reducing China's favorability. However, the East China claimants (actually only referring to Taiwan) instead contribute positively and significantly (41 percent). We should bear in mind that such a large estimate does not solely mean the effect of being a claimant in the East China Sea dispute but instead refers to the fact that Taiwan has a more positive perception of China in comparison with Mongolia, the Philippines, and Vietnam,

Table 2.1: Favorable perception of China's influence in Asia (base models)

Independent Variable	Waves 3–4 (12 macro cases)	Waves 3–4 (without Japan)	Waves 3–5 (6 macro cases)	Waves 3–5 (without Taiwan)
Hard Power				
South China Sea Claimants	–.16(.03)**	–.17(.04)**	–.29(.04)**	–.31(.04)**
East China Sea Claimants	–.75(.05)**	–.13(.05)**	.41(.04)**	–
Time Variant Dummy				
Xi Period	.02(.02)	.04(.03)	.12(.03)**	.12(.03)**
Trump Period			.18(.03)**	.19(.03)**
Entity Dummy				
Male (ref: Female)	–.00(.02)	–.01(.02)	–.05(.02)**	–.06(.02)**
Youth (ref: Adult)	.01(.02)	.00(.02)	.02(.02)	.02(.02)
Senior (ref: Adult)	.01(.02)	.01(.02)	–.02(.02)	–.02(.02)
College (ref: Below College)	–.01(.02)	–.01(.02)	–.04(.02)*	–.04(.02)*
Cohort Controls				
Political Interest	.14(.06)*	.15(.07)*	.25(.07)**	.28(.07)**
Political Efficacy	.03(.07)	.04(.08)	.21(.06)**	.20(.07)**
Model Fit				
R-square (within cohort)	23.3%	24.1%	49.4%	53.3%
R-square (between cohort)	85.9%	76.6%	89.6%	91.1%
R-square (overall)	72.4%	60.4%	76.8%	79.4%
N	276	252	209	173

Note: Entry is unstandardized coefficient and figures in parentheses are unstandardized errors.
Level of Significance: *$p \leq 0.05$, **$p \leq 0.01$, estimated by Stata (xtreg with random effect). Country dummies and the constant will be presented by predicted values in country means in Figures 2.1 and 2.2.
Data Source: ABS 3 (2010–2012), ABS 4 (2014–2016), ABS 5 (2018–June 2019)

all of which have a historical enmity toward China. For this reason, we drop the case of Taiwan and rerun the three-wave dataset and find little change in the result of all other covariates. This suggests that the actual effect of East China claimants can only be evaluated when Japan and Korea cases are available in Wave 5.

The most striking result for the analysis of the three-wave dataset is the positive and significant estimates of the time-variant factors, for the Xi Period and Trump Period respectively. They are about 12 percent and 18 percent (or 19 percent) more favorable respectively, provided other variables are held constant. This indicates that, while Xi and Trump both turned to a more hardline foreign policy, China's favorability has not fallen, at least among the six Asian political systems that are adjacent to and have security issues with China. This result might be explained away when other explanatory variables are included in the model, but it shows that common-sense intuition is not self-evident when public opinion attitudes are empirically assessed. For the entity variables, male and higher-educated citizens tend to be less favorable in evaluating China's influence, but the magnitude is very marginal (4 percent to 6 percent).[49] Lastly, regarding cohort controls, both the predictors of political interest and political efficacy are significantly positive. This signals that those who have more interest in politics or believe their political participation is more meaningful tend to be positive about the impact of China's influence in the region, suggesting China is not perceived in the negative terms described by Trump, at least in these six political systems.

With the results represented in Table 2.1, we can present the model estimate of the political system means based on cohort observations for both Wave 3 and Wave 4. As Figure 2.1 illustrates, most of the favorability estimates are stable, except for those for South China Sea claimants, such as the Philippines (dropping from 61 percent to 44 percent), Taiwan (dropping from 65 percent to 51 percent), Indonesia (dropping from 73 percent to 59 percent), Vietnam (dropping from 51 percent to 30 percent), and Malaysia (dropping from 87 percent to 73 percent). The margin of difference for the estimate of the remaining countries is never larger than 2 percent. This result once again reverberates with the fact that the land reclamation incidents in December 2013 deeply hurt China's positive image among people in the societies involved in the dispute. We can extend the analysis to cover the period until 2018, as Figure 2.2 illustrates. The results can be summarized into two trends. One is a U-shaped trend: Favorable perception of China drops from Wave 3 to Wave 4 but bounces back from Wave 4 to Wave 5 (the Philippines, Taiwan, Vietnam, Malaysia), and the other is the continuing rise of favorable perception (Mongolia and Thailand). The two patterns coincide with whether the

---

49. Although this result might suggest that cohort categorization itself might have significant effects, the result based on the two-wave sample is more credible due to its complete coverage of all macro cases.

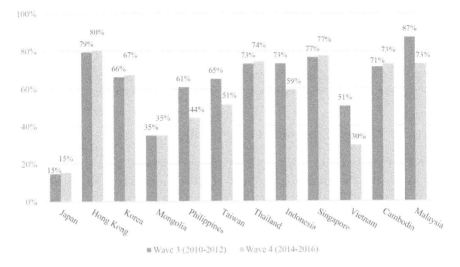

Figure 2.1: Model estimates of favorable perception of China with the Two-Wave Sample (12 political systems)

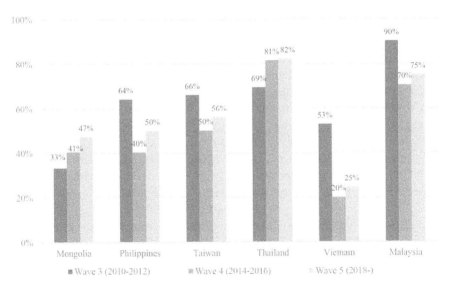

Figure 2.2: Model estimates of favorable perception of China with the Three-Wave Sample (6 political systems)

countries are parties of South China Sea claimants. If they are, the favorable rating drops sharply from Wave 3 to Wave 4 and then bounds back slightly in Wave 5. Otherwise, China's favorable rating has continued to climb in the past decade. Overall, the South China Sea dispute was likely to cause a major setback in China's public diplomacy, and the result is confirmed regardless of whether the two-wave or three-wave datasets are applied in the analysis.

Security Threat, Economic Opportunity, and Value Conflict

In this section, we focus on the comparison of relative power between the five explanatory accounts as well as the hard-power event, the South China Sea dispute. We simplify the model by excluding the entity variables, given their trivial explanatory power. In consideration of distinct outlier cases such as Japan, we also report the coefficient results for two hard-power factors of the two-wave regression without Japan's cohort observations (in square brackets). For each group of explanatory accounts, we select three indicators that fall into the general concept but differ somewhat in nuance. For example, under the concept of globalization, we chose three indicators that are generally associated with different aspects of globalization: *Following Foreign News* (information acquisition), *Learning More from Other Countries* (social globalization), and *Doing More Trade with Other Countries* (economic globalization). The same practice applies to the selection of the other four groups of variables. The rationale for choosing each indicator is explained in Appendix II. Information related to variable formation can be found in Appendix III.

As shown in Table 2.2, Models 1.1 to 1.5 present the results of each group of explanatory accounts. We chose the two best predictors for each group and specify them in the full model. The focus of the analysis is whether the hard-power factor remains significant and which account performs relatively better in explaining favorable perceptions of China. As Model 1.1 shows, all three globalization measures have significant results: those who follow foreign news more often and those who agree we should learn more from other countries tend to have more negative perceptions of China, while those who support more trade with other countries have more positive perceptions. This indicates, even under the general concept of globalization, social globalization and economic globalization have divergent impacts on how people evaluate China's rise. China is perceived more positively if the economic dimension of globalization is stressed but more negatively if the social dimension is stressed. The same heterogeneous findings also appear for socioeconomic perception. As Model 1.2 makes evident, those who are satisfied with their household income tend to view China's influence positively, while those who have higher subjective social status tend to view China negatively. The two findings indicate the potentially divergent effects of socioeconomic factors. For the remaining three groups of variables (from Models 1.3 to 1.5), we find significant results matching our expectations. First, respondents tend to favor China's influence if they rank China higher or the US lower in evaluation of level of democracy. Second, people with stronger liberal democratic orientations tend to have less favorable perceptions of China's influence. Third, those who think that China will be the most influential country in the future or identify China as a model for future development tend to show more favorable perceptions.

Model 1.6 presents the full model for the two-wave panel regression, in which the two best predictors for each explanatory account are included. As expected, favorable perceptions of China for South China Sea claimants drop significantly by 16 percent or 18 percent, depending on whether Japan is included or excluded. However, the effect of East China Sea claimants is not consistent with or without the Japanese case. This suggests that more waves of the dataset are required to unravel its real effect. The time-variant predictor, Xi Period, and the two cohort control predictors (political interest, political efficacy) repeat exactly the same result as shown in the left two columns of Table 2.1. It is noteworthy that, in the five groups of explanatory accounts, each has significant predictors when the model is fully specified. In particular, we found that economic globalization, income satisfaction, and viewing China as the most influential country in the future or the model of future development are all positively related to more favorable perceptions of China, which signals rational thinking among respondents, either in optimism about economic opportunities associated with China or bandwagoning with China for its prospective status. However, we also find factors of regime evaluation and liberal values have significant explanatory power: respondents who view China as more democratic or the US as less democratic or express more authoritarian value orientations tend to perceive China's influence in a positive way. This suggests that value conflict still plays a significant role in explaining how Asians view the rise of China. In sum, the result of the two-wave panel regression indicates that security threat, economic opportunity, and value conflict are the essential causes that drive people to view China's influence positively or negatively.

We apply the same stepwise procedure and conduct the analysis with the three-wave dataset as shown in Table 2.3. Models 2.1 to 2.5 produce fewer significant findings, and in fact only three predictors are significant: those who rate the US as less democratic, have less liberal democratic values, or view China as their model of future development tend to perceive China's influence more positively. When the same full model (Model 2.6) is tested, the result differs slightly from what we found in the two columns on the right of Table 2.1: both the effects of the Xi Period and Trump Period become insignificant. What remains strong is the hard-power factor regarding the South China Sea claimants, accounting for 20 percent less favorable rating of China's influence. For significant results in five explanatory accounts, a similar pattern emerges, showing that, in addition to security threat, economic opportunity

Table 2.2: Results of Two-Wave Panel Regression on favorable perception of China's influence in Asia (12 political systems)

Independent Variable	Model 1.1	Model 1.2	Model 1.3	Model 1.4	Model 1.5	Model 1.6
Hard Power						
South China Sea Claimants	-.18(.03)**	-.16(.03)**	-.13(.03)**	-.16(.03)**	-.18(.03)**	-.16(.03)**
East China Sea Claimants	-.72(.05)**	-.84(.06)**	-.53(.06)**	-.58(.07)**	-.72(.05)**	-.57(.07)**
[South China Sea Claimants] (if Japan excluded)	[-.19 (.03)**]	[-.17(.03)**]	[-.14(.03)**]	[-.17(.03)**]	[-.20(.03)**]	[-.18(.03)**]
[East China Sea Claimants)] (if Japan excluded)	[-.02 (.05)]	[-.11(.05)*]	[-.07(.05)]	[-.15(.04)**]	[-.10(.04)*]	[.02(.05)]
Time Variant Dummy						
Xi Period	.04(.02)	.01(.02)	.02(.02)	.02(.02)	.03(.02)	.03(.02)
Cohort Controls						
Political Interest	.20(.06)**	.12(.05)*	.17(.05)**	.18(.05)**	.08(.05)	.12(.05)**
Political Efficacy	.01(.06)	-.01(.06)	.06(.06)	.16(.07)*	-.02(.06)	.05(.06)
Globalization						
Following Foreign News	-.06(.03)*					
Learning More from Other Countries	-.17(.05)**					-.01(.04)
Doing More Trade with Other Countries	.17(.05)**					.10(.04)*
Socioeconomic Perception						
Income Satisfaction		.16(.04)**				.15(.04)**
Subjective Social Status		-.05(.02)**				-.02(.02)
Economic Evaluation		-.03(.04)				

Table 2.2 Cont'd

Independent Variable	Model 1.1	Model 1.2	Model 1.3	Model 1.4	Model 1.5	Model 1.6
Regime Evaluation						
Assessment of Own Democracy			.06(.05)			
China's Level of Democracy			.05(.01)**			.03(.01)*
US's Level of Democracy			−.06(.02)**			−.06(.02)**
Liberal Values						
Liberal Democratic Attitude				−.23(.07)**		−.22(.06)**
Preferability of Democracy				−.13(.08)		−.11(.07)
Priority of Democracy over Economic Development				−.16(.09)		
International Relations						
China is the Most Influential Country in Future					.31(.07)**	.32(.07)**
China is Our Model of Future Development					.36(.11)**	.21(.10)*
US is Our Model of Future Development					−.03(.10)	
R-square (overall)	74.7%	73.8%	75.8%	74.7%	76.0%	81.2%

Note: Entry is unstandardized coefficient and figures in parentheses are unstandardized errors. N=276 (N=252 if Japan is dropped). Country dummies and the constant are specified but omitted. Level of Significance: *p≦0.05, **p≦0.01, estimated by Stata (xtreg with random effect). Data Source: ABS 3 (2010–2012), ABS 4 (2014–2016).

Table 2.3: Results of Three-Wave Panel Regression on favorable perception of China's influence in Asia (6 political systems)

Independent Variable	Model 2.1	Model 2.2	Model 2.3	Model 2.4	Model 2.5	Model 2.6
Hard Power						
South China Sea Claimants	-.27(.04)**	-.28(.04)**	-.26(.04)**	-.27(.04)**	-.28(.04)**	-.20(.04)**
Time Variant Dummy						
Xi Period	.08(.03)**	.10(.03)**	.07(.03)*	.08(.03)**	.10(.03)**	.03(.03)
Trump Period	.13(.04)**	.16(.03)**	.12(.03)**	.15(.03)**	.14(.03)**	.03(.04)
Cohort Controls						
Political Interest	.13(.05)**	.15(.05)**	.09(.05)*	.17(.05)**	.06(.05)	.06(.05)
Political Efficacy	.16(.06)**	.18(.06)**	.20(.05)**	.24(.06)**	.15(.06)**	.19(.06)**
Globalization						
Following Foreign News (unavailable in Wave 5)	–					
Learning More from Other Countries	.02(.04)					.08(.04)
Doing More Trade with Other Countries	.04(.04)					.08(.04)*
Socioeconomic Perception						
Income Satisfaction		-.02(.02)				.05(.04)
Subjective Social Status		-.02(.02)				-.01(.02)
Economic Evaluation		-.03(.04)				
Regime Evaluation						
Assessment of Own Democracy			-.04(.05)			
China's Level of Democracy			.01(.01)			.00(.01)
US's Level of Democracy			-.08(.01)**			-.07(.01)**

Table 2.3 Cont'd

Independent Variable	Model 2.1	Model 2.2	Model 2.3	Model 2.4	Model 2.5	Model 2.6
Liberal Values						
Liberal Democratic Attitude				-.18(.07)**		-.15(.07)*
Preferability of Democracy				-.04(.08)		.03(.07)
Priority of Democracy over Economic Development				-.10(.08)		
International Relations						
China is the Most Influential Country in Future					.06(.07)	.07(.07)
China is Our Model of Future Development					.46(.11)**	.34(.11)**
US is Our Model of Future Development					-.13(.09)	
R-square (overall)	75.7%	75.9%	79.4%	76.7%	78.7%	82.5%

Note: Entry is unstandardized coefficient and figures in parentheses are unstandardized errors. Country dummies and the constant are specified but omitted. N=209.
Level of Significance: *p ≦ 0.05, **p ≦ 0.01, estimated by Stata (xtreg with random effect). Data Source: ABS 3 (2010–2012), ABS 4 (2014–2016), ABS 5 (2018–June 2019)

and value conflict explain how Asians perceive China's influence. The former is manifested in those who show favorable perception toward China and a supportive attitude toward economic globalization or the China model for future development. The latter, however, indicates that when citizens depart from Western values (rating the US as less democratic or holding less liberal democratic values), they hold more positive views of China's influence. Taking these results together, we can conclude that the dynamics of the causal relationship among the six countries with three data points is largely consistent with what we found in all twelve countries with two data points. Security threat, economic opportunity, and value conflict succinctly summarize the three key factors that determine how people perceive China's influence.

Vulnerability of Soft Power When Issues of Hard Power Are at Stake

Due to the data restriction, many results of our analysis are not stable because of limited period or coverage. Nonetheless, we can find some consistent results that are fairly robust regardless of spatiotemporal restriction. A summary of the results is presented in Table 2.4, showing five findings that are consistently significant: citizens of countries that are South China Sea claimants are at least 16 percent less favorable to China's influence; citizens who support economic globalization are at least 8 percent percent more favorable (per unit) to China; citizens who perceive the US as less democratic have a more positive view of China's influence (6 percent less favorable per unit); citizens who show greater liberal democratic orientations tend to have a less favorable view of China (15 percent less per unit); and citizens who identify China as their model of future development tend to have favorable views of China (21 percent more per unit). All the above five findings vividly encapsulate China's efforts in public diplomacy over the past decade, especially related to how China reacts to hard-power competition, as well as how it plays the leading role in economic globalization while holding to its communist ideology that opposes the Western liberal democratic tradition.

Undeniably, to some degree China has successfully shaped an embedded image in the minds of Asians regarding its leading role in advancing global economic growth, a result associated with China's consistent and strong economic performance rather than as a result of short-term propaganda. This perception is one of the most solid achievements that China has cultivated over the years, irrespective of its ambitious and even aggressive behavior. This revealing finding provides Chinese policy makers a clear message that the most effective practice of public diplomacy is to demonstrate to the world that China is capable of serving and is willing to serve a leading role in the global economy for the long term, despite Trump's latest efforts to contain China.

Table 2.4: Result summary for both Two-Wave and Three-Wave Panel analyses (based on Table 2.1, Models 1.6 and 2.6)

Predictors	Estimate Consistent or Not? (Marginal Effect to China's Favorability)
Hard Power	
South China Sea Claimants	Consistent (at least −16%)
East China Sea Claimants	Not Consistent
Time Variant Dummy	
Xi Period	Not Consistent
Trump Period	Not Consistent
Globalization	
Learning More from Other Countries	Consistent (non-significant)
Doing More Trade with Other Countries	Consistent (at least 8%)
Socioeconomic Perception	
Income Satisfaction	Not Consistent
Subjective Social Status	Consistent (non-significant)
Regime Evaluation	
China's Level of Democracy	Not Consistent
US Level of Democracy	Consistent (at least −6%)
Liberal Value	
Liberal Democratic Attitude	Consistent (at least −15%)
Preferability of Democracy	Consistent (non-significant)
International Relations	
China Most Influential in Future	Not Consistent
China Model of Future Development	Consistent (at least 21%)

However, the toughest challenge is that China's long-term strenuous efforts in contributing to the global economy could be significantly compromised by hard-power exercises, such as the ongoing land reclamation and military buildup in the South China Sea since 2013. While the Chinese government's actions may have been aimed at a domestic audience, as this was the beginning of Xi's first term and he needed to consolidate his political power inside the party, China's abrasive rhetoric and aggressive behavior during this period has caused serious damage to China's image in Asia. Our estimates show that the resulting favorable perceptions of China may be 16 percent lower, even five years after it launched this dramatic move. In this context, any deliberate attempt to preach China's peaceful rise to the world may be futile or even work to harm China's image. This shows that China's soft power can be significantly neutralized when strategic competitors threaten its core national interests, and China is left with no room for ambiguity, particularly when a new leader has not fully secured his power base or political legitimacy domestically.

Value conflict is another issue area which might quickly rise in prominence as we get closer to Trump's possible reelection. Our analysis shows that evaluation of the level of democracy in the US does consistently influence respondents' perception, one score (on a 1 to 10 scale) higher on the scale of perceived level of democracy in the US producing at least a 6 percent decrease in favorability toward China. The consistent and negative effects related to the level of liberal democratic attitudes and favorable views of China also reconfirm the nature of the Sino-US competition. But even so, China for now remains on the inside of the global world order and has reiterated its intention to stay there despite growing questions about its domestic affairs and its willingness to carry out "structural reforms" requested by Trump in the trade negotiations between the two countries.

Despite the non-significant result of the two period dummies (Xi Period and Trump Period) in the full model (Model 2.6, Table 2.3), both predictors show positive and significant effects when only a partial set of explanatory variables is included. This suggests that the growing Chinese influence over the region did not abate, and the explanation of such impact requires a more sophisticated exploration of how various factors co-vary to affect Asians' perception of China. In fact, the effect of Trump's China policy was not simply whether Asians would choose to side with the US or with China, but rather how fragile soft power could be overwhelmed by a series of deliberate confrontational policies when people's attention is mobilized and diverted to such policies. The implication is not restricted to Trump or his administration alone and applies to all leaders of great powers who want to unilaterally change the structure of international relations. Overall, public diplomacy matters, not just for identity construction and selling a vision of international relations (such the peaceful rise of China), but is also important for a country to defend its position when challenges occur.

Conclusion

China's public diplomacy faces many daunting challenges. First of all, it is almost impossible to shed the image of being a revisionist power in the eyes of the great majority of American policy makers, because by definition China's ascendance will inevitably alter the existing pecking order in the international system and dilute if not erode the power foundation of US hegemony. While US allies in Western Europe and East Asia might embrace China as a hedge against Trumpism, they still harbor lingering doubts about China's long-term strategic objectives, are not fully convinced by China's open pledge to uphold existing multilateralism, and view the rising popularity of the BRI as well as the Chinese development model in the developing world as an antithesis to their long-held core values and beliefs. It is also difficult for Beijing to win over the hearts of many of its Asian neighbors, especially in countries where suspicion toward China runs deep due to historical grievance or present-day territorial disputes. While in most Asian countries some segments of the population might benefit from expanding economic ties with China, the distribution of risks and benefits has been very uneven. There are always losers in the game of globalization and economic integration. Only under the most favorable condition, such as the absence of geopolitical conflict or ideological barriers, might China's charm offense be able to run its full course and steadily build up its image as a trustworthy rising superpower and desirable economic partner, most notably in the case of Thailand, Malaysia, and Cambodia, and potentially in Myanmar and Indonesia. Under less favorable conditions, China's public diplomacy and its deployment of economic leverage can be significantly compromised or nullified by the eruption of disruptive events such as the heightening of the territorial dispute over the South China Sea or China's strong objection to the deployment of Terminal High Altitude Area Defense (THAAD) in its vicinity. The ensuing damage to China's international standing can be substantial and last for a long while.

For the near term, China might be able to persuade its Asian neighbors not to take sides in the escalation of strategic confrontation with the US, but it will be difficult to convince most of its neighbors that China is a credible successor to the US in the region. China might be motivated to place more emphasis on three credentials that could enhance the effectiveness of its public diplomacy. First, China is poised to be a new provider of regional and global public goods in establishing new multilateral institutions, opening up its domestic market for trading partners, and being a major source of development assistance and development-related soft loans. Second, China commits itself to supporting the existing multilateral arrangements that are vital to the stability and vitality of the global economy. China makes it clear that it advocates incremental reform in the prevailing international economic order and mechanisms of global governance, rather than radical changes and much less their undoing. Third, China can and will play the role of the locomotive of world economy by sustaining its own growth momentum through reform and innovation for the foreseeable future. These benevolent aspects of China's rise may work to some extent to reduce apprehension about potential Chinese security threats to the region, meet the expectation of the economic opportunities brought about by China as it charts the course of future globalization, and most importantly, soften opposition due to the clash of civilizations.

Appendix I: Information of Pseudo-panel Observation and Related Methodological Issues

The pseudo-panel data is generated by taking aggregate means of twelve groups in each ABS sample. The unit of analysis is a group, which is defined as a cohort categorized by three demographic variables: gender (male/female), age (youth/adult/senior), and education (below college/college). To avoid poor estimates of the cohort statistics, we exclude cohorts that have two or fewer observations in any single wave of surveys. In this study, we have two pseudo-panel samples for analysis. The two-wave sample ideally should have 288 observations (12 cohorts × 12 countries × 2 waves) but actually only had 276 qualified observations. The excluded samples contain seven cohorts, mostly groups of seniors with college education (male or female) in Indonesia (one), Vietnam (one), Cambodia (four, due to the lack of college-educated respondents in the adult and senior groups), and Malaysia (one). The three-wave sample only contains six countries (Mongolia, the Philippines, Taiwan, Thailand, Vietnam, and Malaysia) for Wave 3 to Wave 5. There are also four cohorts containing seven ineligible observations. The actual sample size is 209. The average cohort size is 112 for the two-wave sample and 105 for the three-wave sample.

The assumption of the pseudo-panel method is that those cohorts resemble to the very same unit if our estimates of cohort means are correct. Given the fact that time varies in different waves of surveys, our cohort definition has to be adjusted in accordance to the time of field work. The age variable is adjusted as follows: youth/adult/senior is defined as "below 36/36–55/above 55" in Wave 3, "below 40/40–59/above 59" in Wave 4, and "below 44/44–63/above 63" in Wave 5. The other assumption is that the variables defining the cohorts (called entity variables) should not significantly relate to the dependent variables; otherwise, different categorization could lead to very different outcome of the dependent variable, which requires more complex analysis to deal with. In this study, as shown in the left-hand two columns of Table 2.1, none of the entity variables is significant in the Wave 2 sample that covers all macro cases of the ABS survey. This suggests that the composition of the cohort makes little difference if we change the way we categorize the three entity variables.

Appendix II: Selection of Indicators for Five Groups of Explanatory Accounts

In Tables 2.2 and 2.3, five groups of explanatory accounts are tested, and each of them included three indicators in analysis. Below, we explain the rationale for each of the indicators chosen.

Globalization

There are many aspects of globalization; for example, social and economic globalization might associate with different concepts differently. However, the hypothesis assumed here is that people who support a greater level of globalization might be more likely to favor China's influence, given its indispensable role in the global economy. Here, we also include indicators of information acquisition regarding foreign news, which is a neutral behavioral indicator measuring the respondent's level of globalization in an objective sense.

Socioeconomic perception

The most straightforward rationale to favor China's influence is economic benefits. However, whether people with a better socioeconomic situation would positively evaluate China is an empirical question. We include three indicators to capture different dimensions of socioeconomic perception: respondent's income satisfaction, subjective social status, and evaluation of the political system's economy.

Regime evaluation

The premise in this group of variables is that people generally know what the democratic level of China and the US should be (China much lower and the US much higher). If someone rates China much higher in democracy, this means he or she appreciates China's system and therefore should favor its influence. If he or she rates the US higher, we expect the opposite outcome. Similar logic also applies to the indicator of assessing respondents' own political system. If they rate their political system higher in democracy, they should favor China less, due to its authoritarian regime.

Liberal values

This group captures ideological values related to liberalism and democracy. The chosen indicators include the measure of liberal democratic attitudes, whether the respondents prefer only democracy as a system of government, and whether they put the value of democracy ahead of economic development. The assumption is that respondents who hold greater liberal and democratic orientations will evaluate China less favorably due to its collectivism, hierarchical order, and illiberal norms.

International relations

The debate between the Beijing Consensus and the Washington Consensus is usually understood as the China model versus the US model, which essentially is about which developmental path people prefer. Therefore, the inclusion of the China model and the US model aims to test this preference: respondents who think the China model is better should perceive China more favorably, and those who identify with the US model should tend to evaluate China less favorably. Regarding the prospective evaluation of China's influence, it is easily understood that people normally want to side with the winner, and therefore China should be perceived more favorably if people believe it will be the most influential country in Asia in the future.

Appendix III: Information of Variable Formation

Variable	Questionnaire	Range
Favorability of China's Regional Influence	Does China do more good or more harm to the region?	(0,1)
South China Sea Claimants	Country involved with the South China Sea dispute (after Dec 2013)	(0,1)
East China Sea Claimants	Country involved with the East China Sea dispute	(0,1)
Xi Period	Sample collected after 2013	(0,1)
Trump Period	Sample collected after 2017	(0,1)
Political Interest (mean score)	How interested would you say you are in politics? How often do you follow news about politics and government? When you get together with your family members or friends, how often do you discuss political matters? (all recoded on a scale of 1 to 3)	(1–3)
Political Efficacy (mean score)	I think I have the ability to participate in politics. Disagree that sometimes politics and government seem so complicated that a person like me can't really understand what is going on. Disagree that people like me don't have any influence over what the government does. (all recoded on a scale of 1 to 4)	(1–4)
Following Foreign News	How closely do you follow major events in foreign countries/the world?	(1–4)
Learning More from Other Countries	Agree that our country should do more to learn more from other countries.	(1–4)
Doing More Trade with Other Countries	Agree that our country should do more trade with other countries.	(1–4)
Income Satisfaction	Does the total income of your household allow you to cover your needs?	(1–3)
Subjective Social Status	Subjective social status	(1–10)
Economic Evaluation (mean score)	How would you rate the overall economic condition of your country today? How would you describe the change in the economic condition of your country over the last few years? What do you think will be the state of our country's economic condition a few years from now? (all recoded on a scale of 1 to 5)	(1–5)

Variable	Questionnaire	Range
Assessment of Own Democracy	In your opinion how much of a democracy is your country?	(1–4)
China's Level of Democracy	Where would you place China today on this scale (of democracy)?	(1–10)
U.S.'s Level of Democracy	Where would you place the US today on this scale (of democracy)?	(1–10)
Liberal Democratic Attitude (mean score)	Disagree that government leaders are like the head of a family; we should all follow their decisions. Disagree that the government should decide whether certain ideas should be allowed to be discussed in society. Disagree that harmony of the community will be disrupted if people organize lots of groups. Disagree that when judges decide important cases, they should accept the view of the executive branch. Disagree that if the government is constantly checked by the legislature, it cannot possibly accomplish great things. Disagree that if we have political leaders who are morally upright, we can let them decide everything. Disagree that if people have too many different ways of thinking, society will be chaotic. (all recoded on a scale of 1 to 4)	(1–4)
Preferability of Democracy	Democracy is always preferable to any other kind of government.	(0,1)
Priority of Democracy over Economic Development	Democracy is more important than economic development.	(1–5)
China Most Influential Country in Future	China will be the most influential country in Asia in the future.	(0,1)
China Is Our Model of Future Development	Which country should be a model for our own country's future development?	(0,1)
US Is Our Model of Future Development	Which country should be a model for our own country's future development?	(0,1)

3
Disorder from Within

How the Chinese Public Has Challenged the State on Foreign Policymaking

Jing Sun

Introduction

John F. Kennedy was a fan of the Chinese word *weiji* (crisis). In a speech in 1959, he remarked: "When written in Chinese, the word 'crisis' is composed of two characters—one represents danger, and one represents opportunity. The danger signs are all around us . . . along with danger, crisis is represented by opportunity."[1] Kennedy's interpretation has been challenged as a linguistic myth. Victor Mair, Professor of Chinese language and literature at the University of Pennsylvania, argued that the character *ji* that was thought to mean "opportunity" actually means "critical moment."[2] But such clarifying efforts were paled by luminaries like Richard Nixon, Barack Obama, Al Gore, and Condoleezza Rice, among others, who continued to use the word in their speeches. The popularity of the Western misunderstanding reveals the Chinese word's philosophical allure, however mistakenly construed. Having faith in blessings-in-disguise is not unique to the West.

Political crisis management in China also seems to lend credibility to the Western misconstruing of the word *weiji*. One recent example of turning a danger into an opportunity could be China's battling with the COVID-19 pandemic. The first cases emerged from the Chinese city of Wuhan in January 2020 or even earlier than that. But as time went on, the pandemic that the US President Donald Trump labeled the "China Virus" has become very much a Western failure. In America alone, more than 13.4 million cases and approximately 266,000 deaths had been registered by late November 2020. On the other

---

1. John F. Kennedy, "Remarks at the Convocation of the United Negro College Fund," Indianapolis, Indiana, April 12, 1959; John F. Kennedy Presidential Library and Museum online archive, accessed December 20, 2020, https://www.jfklibrary.org/archives/other-resources/john-f-kennedy-speeches/indianapolis-in-19590412.
2. Victor Mair, "How a Misunderstanding about Chinese Characters Has Led Many Astray," accessed December 20, 2020, http://www.pinyin.info/chinese/crisis.html.

side of the Pacific, though, the Chinese government held a grand ceremony in the Great Hall of the People on September 8, celebrating its "successful victory" over COVID-19. In fact, Chinese self-confidence was soaring so high that a pro-government scholar by the name of Li Yi proudly proclaimed at a public forum in Shenzhen that compared with the death number in America, the death rate and the transmission rate in China are basically equivalent to zero. Li went on to say that, in a sense, no one in China has died of COVID-19.[3]

Li Yi's words proved one step too far in glorifying an otherwise horrifying experience to the Chinese public. Chinese social media were inundated by public outcries to punish the said scholar for losing any basic sense of humanity. They also quipped that Li's words were simply an extension of the Chinese government's effort to "turn a funeral into a wedding"—that is, to repackage a failure as if it were a triumph. Facing a tsunami of public anger, Li first doubled down. In a video rant, he angrily pointed to the screen and shouted "how dare you" to the reporter of *Xinjingbao* who first wrote the critical piece. He also demanded to know "who's behind you" for the publication of the piece. The very next day, however, Li was all smiles. He mentioned the reporter's name in a soft voice and asked him for a get-together. Professor Li said to the camera he wanted bygones to be bygones.[4]

What happened in twenty-four hours that led to such an embarrassing climb-down? Professor Li was right after all when he demanded to know "who's behind you." The newspaper *Xinjingbao* is associated with the Communist Party Committee of Beijing Municipality. Apparently, *someone* talked to him. Meanwhile, though, supporters of Li continued to praise the professor for shaming America, even when that meant denying the dignity of more than four thousand lost lives in China.

I chose this episode as the start of my chapter examining the increasingly complicated interplays between the Chinese state and the public on sensitive issues. Underneath all the brouhaha to this incident, one may detect an increasingly diversified army of societal actors, all trying to use the media to promote their own agendas. Relations between the Chinese state and society used to be decidedly one-sided, the state imposing its will on the society. Now, the Chinese government is finding it harder and harder to maintain a top-down "united front" as it tries to handle sensitive political issues, especially those with international ramifications. The public could be knowledgeable, internationalist; but it could also recruit actors that are nationalistic, militant, and even chauvinistic. Furthermore, there is the media that act as go-betweens, pleasing the public by chasing their tensions in sensational terms before they succumb to the government's political dictate, which orders everyone to shut up.

---

3. The *World Journal*, accessed November 29, 2020, https://www.worldjournal.com/wj/story/121474/5041731.
4. The videos remain accessible at https://www.youtube.com/watch?v=rgcYdmdwfpY, as of December 20, 2020.

Outside China, there has been much discussion on the emergence of an assertive China and how this China may wreak havoc on regional peace and stability. This chapter attempts to open the black box and examine the disorder from within. China's rise could indeed bring great chaos—not because "China" as a unitary actor is getting coherently aggressive. Rather, it could be the result of the Chinese public, once a latent force, experiencing its own stratification. The state is ill equipped to manage tensions within the Chinese public. Spillovers from such internal strains have a destabilizing effect beyond China's borders. In other words, China's threat comes not only from its calculation but also from its confusion and insecurity.

"Many Hands Make Our Job Easy"

Dismissing the Chinese public's role in foreign policymaking has historical roots. After all, the country's founding father, Mao Zedong, saw his own people as droplets in massive human waves and saw himself as the wave maker. Mao and his comrades had an unmistakably top-down perspective in viewing their relations with the masses. The people's importance lay in large numbers, not in individuals.

People's numerical importance was put to good use to serve Mao's interventionist foreign policy. The masses were regularly mobilized to serve purely ceremonial purposes. Foreign guests visiting Beijing during Mao's era were often greeted by tens of thousands of people pouring into Chang'an Avenue—the city's main thoroughfare—and eagerly waving their country's red flag. The masses could also be used as first-responder reserves: The city government of Beijing mobilized over half a million people to sweep snow from downtown all the way to the Great Wall in preparation for Richard Nixon's trip.[5] In this regard, many hands could indeed make jobs easier. It was a time when the government could solely manufacture the public display of any emotion by the masses: celebration, indignation, or hostility. The numerous Beijingers that swept the whole city overnight for the American president in 1972 may well have participated in massive anti-America protests not long before.

Serving the chairman did not stop at the ceremonial level. China sent not only money but also personnel in the tens of thousands to Africa, Southeast Asia, and Latin America, fulfilling Mao's call of aiding the Third World's struggle against both American and Soviet evil forces. The number of Chinese headed overseas could go up to more than 300,000 for one mission.[6] Their tasks ranged from combat to infrastructure building—fighting Americans in

---
5. The *Phoenix News*, "Stories behind Premier Zhao's 1000-Kilogram Abalone Dinner for Nixon," November 23, 2011, accessed on May 23, 2018, http://news.ifeng.com/history/vp/detail_2011_11/23/10843077_1.shtml.
6. Reuters, "China Admits 320,000 Troops Fought in Vietnam," May 16, 1989, accessed May 23, 2018, https://news.google.com/newspapers?nid=1350&dat=19890516&id=HkRPAAAAIBAJ&sjid=_gIEAAAAIBAJ&pg=3769,1925460.

Vietnam and building railroads in Africa. But their missions served the same purpose: To use Mao's metaphor, they were the sparks to start prairie fires around the globe.

Mao's foreign policy paradigm had a second component: resisting foreign intervention. The masses were equally useful for their immense numbers. This is one realm where the boundaries between domestic and international issues blurred. In the name of achieving self-sufficiency and self-reliance, Mao employed the human wave strategy to launch consecutive mass mobilization movements. Some were economic, others political; some were bizarre, like the one aimed at killing sparrows; others cruel as they aimed at killing people. What is not ambiguous, though, was the result: Domestically, such never-ending mass movements pushed the country's economy to the edge of collapse; internationally, fanatical Maoist crusaders eager to spread the chairman's glory contributed to a local distrust so deep that it would take future leaders of China decades to dispel. Meanwhile, overseas spinoffs like Pol Pot of Cambodia and the Sendero Luminoso (Shining Path) of Peru sealed Maoism's international reputation as a militant ideology associated with genocide and terrorism.

In his *Little Red Book*, Mao was quoted as hailing the masses as the real heroes in history. However, some other comments he made about the masses, nowhere to be found in his book, exposed other calculations that guided his assessment of the people's importance. In meeting with a Yugoslav delegation, Mao dismissed the atomic bomb as a paper tiger: "We have a very large territory and a big population. Atomic bombs could not kill all of us. What if they killed 300 million of us? We would still have many people left."[7] In the chairman's eyes, number was what made the masses important. Number was also what made each individual member of the masses petty.

New Paradox and Old Habit

Mao's eventual successor, Deng Xiaoping, abandoned his revolutionary fanaticism for cool-headed pragmatism. Deng also replaced Mao's pursuit of self-sufficiency and self-reliance, which in practice led to delinking China from the global economy, with reform and open-door policies. As China rejoined the global community, the Chinese public paradoxically experienced a shrinking presence in the country's foreign policy. Family-based reunions were sporadic and tended to be confined to coastal provinces. The majority of Chinese families did not have any foreign relatives. As Deng opened the country, exposure to the outside world became a more elitist privilege.

---

7. UPI, "Mao's Theory on Atomic Bomb: They Can't Kill Us All," October 17, 1964, accessed May 24, 2018, https://www.upi.com/Archives/1964/10/17/Maos-theory-on-atomic-bomb-They-cant-kill-us-all/1653831424805/.

The 1980s was a period full of contradictions. As China opened its doors, its people realized their country was no human paradise. The experience was both eye-opening and humbling. Deng warned his people if they did not catch up, China's membership on the globe would be stripped from them (*kaichu qiuji*).[8] Amid a sense of crisis, a national drive for catching up arose. This veering toward domestic, internal development at both macro and micro levels offered foreign policy elites a shielded arena. Practically, most Chinese who could travel internationally at the time were either diplomats or other officials in the "foreign-oriented system" (*duiwai xitong*). Some were experts and intellectuals on government-sponsored trips. Their destinations were almost always countries in the First World. The non-elite majority were no longer needed for fighting or building the Third World. The opening brought the world beyond China visually closer but substantively more distant.

Access to materialistic privileges also contributed to the elitism associated with having foreign contacts. Special Friendship Stores stocked with hard-to-acquire commodities, household electronic appliances in particular, were only available to "foreign-bound personnel" (*chuguo renyuan*). In practice, government officials, particularly diplomats and other officials in the foreign-oriented system, would be their core consumers. Meanwhile, a special currency in the form of Bank of China Foreign Exchange Certificate (*waihui quan*) was only available to foreigners in China. The special currency would allow these privileged customers to purchase commodities denied to ordinary Chinese. Needless to say, black markets flourished. Corruption and crime, in turn, proved how closely guarded the playing field of China's foreign-oriented system was. Officials who occupied these positions became the choke points for controlling a vast country's contacts with the world. Some did not hesitate to profit from being in the right place at the right time.

The initial phase of China opening to the world was thus characterized by contrasts. Contacts were established but in heavily restricted ways. The government's restrictions made the process of having international contacts selective, elitist, and prone to corruption. All the constraints, policy and monetary, created an envious aura to those who were allowed to be "in" the game of talking and going to the world on behalf of China. For the overwhelming majority, though, the door to this game was shut. As television programs, movies, songs, and other media presentations brought lives in America, Europe, and Japan closer to ordinary Chinese, it also added a sense of inaccessibility. To most people, the prospect that one day they could travel internationally for personal pleasure was beyond their wildest dreams.

Mass mobilization for achieving international purposes did not totally die out. However, the scene of a whole city turning out to welcome foreign guests

---

8. An Yan and Handong Yan, "How the Chinese Nation Completely Got Rid of the Danger of Being Expelled from Football," *People's Daily*, http://theory.people.com.cn/n1/2016/0801/c40531-28599851.html.

was gone. Now mass mobilization is to serve more specific, smaller-scale missions. To name one example, students and retirees are routinely mobilized to pick up trash and monitor neighborhood safety during major international sporting events and conferences. The world got a glimpse of China's human wave strategy by watching the opening ceremony of the Beijing Olympics in 2008, when tens of thousands of performers, mostly soldiers, moved in perfect synchronization. The Chinese government proclaimed that the opening ceremony was to celebrate the theme of peace and friendship. If this was the true intention, the Western reception must have been disappointing. As a *USA Today* reviewer described it, the ceremony was "sort of Albert Speer meets Star Wars. As memorable and impressive as that opening, pounding, screaming drum corps may have been, it was also the least welcoming 'welcome' ever recorded—and having the drummers smile during it just made it seem odder and a bit chilling."[9]

Western criticism notwithstanding, mass mobilization remains a popular political tactic for the Chinese leadership. Occasionally, this old habit could put on a new face—mass immobilization. This practice even gave birth to a new phrase: APEC Blue. Before Beijing's hosting of the Asian Pacific Economic Cooperation (APEC) summit in 2014, the government delivered a strong dose of immobilization to sedate the entire city. Measures included temporarily shutting down factories and keeping vehicles and people off the road. Even restaurants were told to refrain from offering barbequed items on their menus. Thanks to cooperating weather, the result was impressive, as azure sky appeared in Beijing for the duration of the summit. Smog quickly returned as Obama's Air Force One departed. Beijing residents woke up to their old normal.

The current Chinese president, Xi Jinping, framed the mass campaign tradition metaphorically: "As everyone collects firewood, the flame will go higher and higher."[10] The APEC experience, though, revealed that sometimes the government would also need its people to put out the fire, literally. Either way, Chinese leaders have a dilemma on their hands: the public's passion does not always blow in the direction the leadership wishes. The flame of the masses' emotions, once stirred up, can turn back and lick the government. Driven by a potent combination of knowledge, wealth, and emotions, the Chinese public has become a new disrupter to the governing elites as the latter seek to maintain their fading monopoly over foreign policymaking.

---

9. Jason Athanasiadis, "Westerners and Chinese Alike Criticize Beijing Opening Ceremonies," *World Politics Review*, https://www.worldpoliticsreview.com/articles/2569/westerners-and-chinese-alike-criticize-beijing-opening-cermonies.
10. The *People's Daily*, "As Everyone Collects Firewood, Flame Will Rise Higher and Higher," January 16, 2018, accessed May 26, 2018, http://cpc.people.com.cn/n/2013/0116/c78779-20213599.html.

Ignorant Officials, Informed Citizens

New challenges keep emerging to complicate relations between the people and the state. More and more Chinese citizens have become connected with the world in all kinds of ways. At the same time, the Chinese officials dwell in a top-down mentality vis-à-vis the masses, viewing them not as people and as not to be served. Rather, they are resources to be utilized and troubles to be tamed. While the public is expecting officials to provide service, officials' self-identification does not include the word "servant." Given this disjuncture of expectations, policy blunders are bound to occur. Purely administrative issues can turn into a political circus, the authorities becoming the clowns.

The latest example attesting to this point is the Shanghai municipal government's flip-flop on evoking *hukou*—household registration—for Shanghai-based Chinese citizens having permanent residence overseas. China does not recognize dual citizenship. But for a long time, some Chinese emigrants who changed citizenship have continued to hold onto their Chinese *hukou*, as such household registration is tied to access to social welfare and local schools. Apparently in an attempt to crack down on these hidden dual citizens, the Shanghai police authorities announced on March 8, 2018 that all Shanghai-based Chinese citizens who have "settled abroad or obtained other nationalities" need to report to the police and have their household registration revoked. The authorities also encouraged people to report on those they knew who maintained their *hukou* despite obtaining permanent residence in other countries. The authorities further warned those who refused to comply that their *hukou* would be forcibly terminated.

There was only one problem: Shanghai is allegedly mainland China's most international city. Yet, public security authorities were apparently unaware of the difference between foreign permanent residence and foreign citizenship. While it is legally sound to crack down on dual citizenship, stripping Chinese citizens of *hukou* when they have foreign permanent residence is a wholly different matter. China does not recognize the usage of Chinese passports inside the country. By stripping Chinese citizens of their *hukou* and annulling their Chinese ID cards, the Shanghai municipal government would effectively make these people citizens of nowhere.

Predictably, the proposal was met with waves of criticism. Many people questioned on what grounds a city government could take away one's Chinese citizenship. The government first doubled down. On March 22, it issued a statement insisting the policy was not new, only that this time the government was serious about implementing it. Then, four days later, just as abruptly, the Shanghai government made a U-turn by posting a midnight announcement, saying it would not revoke residents' *hukou* after all. The announcement made an unusual *mea culpa* plea. The government admitted it had no legal definition of "settling abroad" and was thus unable to implement the policy it had announced.[11] The Shanghai citizens won.

Policy blunders like this are not just embarrassing. They are revealing: policymakers are so detached from reality that they are clueless about the conundrums their policies could inflict on their citizens. As one Chinese netizen commented on a popular online forum, policies are often made by leaders "tapping their foreheads" (*paipai naodai*)—Chinese slang for impulsive policymaking. As a result, they are sporadic, confusing, self-conflicting, and have no consideration of long-term consequences. Fortunately, in the Shanghai case, the more knowledgeable masses offered a legal lesson to the government. On March 8, the government publicized a policy to whip those it thought were cheating on the system, unaware of all the complexities associated with the global flow of population. It did not take long for the whip to swing back and slap the whipper's face.

Wag the Dog: Rise of Patriotic Vigilantes

If the Shanghai *hukou* incident was a result of the officials' top-down perspective hitting the wall of reality, the interplay between the public and the state on the issue of Taiwan would present another kind of power dynamism: wagging the dog. Letting the public run a public display of anti-Taiwan independence could add a popular, non-official narrative to the government's agenda. However, once the masses are given a role to play, they could become emboldened to run their own scripts. Mass actors may end up manipulating the director.

The Mainlanders' popular attitude toward Taiwan has undergone several waves of changes. During Mao's era, state-run media portrayed Taiwanese as compatriots in poverty and agony, hungry for the dawn of liberation to shine on them. Even after Mao died, the opening toward Taiwan was markedly later than was China's opening to other countries. Up to the mid-1980s, during Chinese New Year, school students in Beijing were still asked to use their meager pocket money to purchase candies and other gifts later to be balloon-lifted and dropped to feed the starving children on the other side of the Taiwan Strait—or so they were told.

Chinese leaders knew better about the wealth gap between the Mainland and Taiwan, and who should be dropping candies to whom. The Taiwanese authorities were also confident in their island's superiority over the Mainland. In fact, the gap was one reason that persuaded then-Taiwanese President Chiang Ching-kuo to allow family visits to the Mainland to start in 1987. As Wu Po-hsiung, then-Minister of the Interior, recalls, resuming contact with

---

11. *South China Morning Post*, "China U-Turn after Outcry over Revoking Residency Rights," March 26, 2018, http://www.scmp.com/news/china/society/article/2138916/shanghai-u-turn-after-outcry-over-revoking-residency-rights.

the Mainland would add pressure to the communists and allow Mainlanders to realize who led a better life—they or the Taiwanese they were supposed to save.[12] Singapore's paramount leader, Lee Kuan-yew, arrived at a similar calculation. After visiting China in 1976, Lee returned to Singapore feeling relieved. One accompanying official reported that Lee was "happy" to see how backward China was and decided to encourage Singaporean youth to visit China and see for themselves the real China.[13] In other words, China became a "bad teacher" that could help Singaporeans better value their own country's path. Chiang Ching-kuo would probably agree—after all, it was Chiang who encouraged Lee, a personal friend, to go and visit mainland China.[14]

As people-to-people exchanges commenced, Mainlanders came to realize the saviors had been left far behind by those they were supposed to save. Meanwhile, Taiwanese popular culture also began to permeate China's young minds. Songs, movies, and TV dramas had an ever-growing army of clandestine followers—part of the reason that led party elders to launch their mid-1980s campaign to crack down on "spiritual pollution."

The Mainland public's admiring and even envious attitude toward the Taiwanese began to change as the Chinese economy took off after 1992. In the city of Shanghai, the derogatory term *taibaozi* (hicks from Taiwan) became a popular reference to the Taiwanese. Beijingers have their own crude name for the Taiwanese, calling them Taiwan *tubie* (ground beetle from Taiwan). It took many urban Mainlanders only two decades to reoccupy their commanding height of cultural superiority, viewing the Taiwanese as their hillbilly cousins.

In the first decade of the twenty-first century, there were also occasionally movements to boycott allegedly pro-independence Taiwanese celebrities. The public's attitudinal shift and spontaneous boycotting inspired their leaders in Beijing. Taiwan has become the new Japan—a target to be constantly harassed, humiliated, and mocked. The Chinese government uses popular opinion as a cloak to shield its own agenda of isolating and punishing the island. One recent example is the ongoing so-called public campaign of urging foreign companies to comply with Beijing's "One China Policy." The *Global Times*, a subsidiary of the *People's Daily* known for its chauvinist tones, summed up the calculation well:

> In order to make multinational corporations refer to Taiwan, Hong Kong, and Macau in ways acceptable to China, as a tactic, we should let societal forces take charge. The government could assist them if necessary. This is because whatever the society may demand, no one can blame such outcries as excessive. In addition, such popular opinions send a strong message of

---

12. The *China Times*, "Three Decades of Allowing Cross-Strait Family Reunion: Chiang Ching-Kuo's Personal Decision," September 13, 2017, http://www.chinatimes.com/cn/realtimenews/20170913000922-260407.
13. Jiachang Chen, *LKY whom I Knew* (Singapore: Linzi Chuanmei, 2015), 449–50.
14. Chen, *LKY whom I Knew*, 445.

whom the Chinese market welcomes and whom it rejects. As a result, it is particularly intimidating.[15]

This tactic seems to be taken directly from Mao's piece on guerilla warfare—though now the warriors are Chinese consumers. In early April 2018, a Chinese student in South Korea protested against Jeju Air for listing Hong Kong and Taiwan along with China, Japan, and Vietnam on travel posters as destinations. She viewed the poster as an insult to Chinese unity and told the company representative that "Hong Kong people and Taiwanese are all Chinese," so they did not deserve to be listed as equals next to China. She also notified the Chinese embassy in Seoul of this "violation" and threatened to tear down the poster on her campus. The airline's first response was to fight back, stating the poster was non-political and that it was quite natural for South Koreans to use terms like "Hong Kong people" and "Taiwanese." The company also warned the female student that it would report her to the school authorities if she damaged even one poster. The student retorted by stating "as a Chinese, it is my responsibility to protect China."[16]

A storm in a teacup was thus born. Before long, Chinese netizens began calling for boycotting Jeju Air. On April 20, the company representative issued an apology, admitting it made a "grave error" (*zhongda cuowu*) and that it had corrected the problem to address the student's concern.[17] By doing so, Jeju Air joined an ever-growing list of multinational corporations like Gap, Zara, Marriott, and Mercedes Benz, among others. All of them had to apologize to Chinese consumers for violating the One China Policy or, in the case of Mercedes Benz, quoting the Dalai Lama in its commercial poster: "Look at situations from all angles, and you will become more open," the Tibetan spiritual leader allegedly said. Mercedes Benz would later apologize for "hurting the feelings" of the people of China for its Zen-style post. Of the foreign enterprises China's patriotic vigilantes terrorized, the German luxury carmaker sounded particularly contrite, announcing that the post "published extremely incorrect information, for this we are sincerely sorry . . . (w)e have immediately taken real action to deepen our understanding of Chinese culture and values, including among our colleagues abroad, and in this way regulate our behavior."[18]

---

15. The *Global Times*, "The White House's Groundless Criticism on China Bullying Foreign Countries," May 16, 2018.
16. *Liberty Times Net* (Taiwan), "Jeju Air Lists Taiwan Next to China," April 16, 2018, accessed May 25, 2018, http://news.ltn.com.tw/news/world/breakingnews/2396729.
17. *Huanqiu* (Xinhua News Agency), "Jeju Air Apologizes for Listing Taiwan Next to China," April 20, 2018, accessed May 25, 2018, http://world.huanqiu.com/exclusive/2018-04/11892498.html.
18. The *Telegraph*, "Mercedes Apologises to China after Quoting Dalai Lama," accessed May 31, 2018, https://www.telegraph.co.uk/news/2018/02/07/mercedes-apologises-china-quoting-dalai-lama/.

The anti-Taiwan online guerilla warfare was elevated to a new level in May 2018, when China's aviation bureau, citing "public complaints," demanded thirty-six foreign air carriers remove references on their websites or in other materials that listed Taiwan, Hong Kong, and Macau as part of countries independent of China.[19] The list later would be expanded to forty-four. Although the Trump administration denounced Beijing's threat as "Orwellian nonsense," eighteen of the forty-four air carriers chose to comply by May 25, the remaining twenty-six pledging to fix the problem by July 25. Of course, this could become a whack-a-mole game for China: there is always a violator out there waiting to be smashed. On the day its media announced victoriously the compliance of foreign airliners, Tesla was singled out for using "Taiwan time" in its online post to Taiwanese owners that there may be a signal outage at noon and that they should keep their car keys with them. The media complained that Taiwan does not deserve to have its own time. There is only "Beijing Time."[20]

Beijing's catch-them-if-you-can battle cry to the masses could come back and exhaust itself. Different branches of its bureaucracy are getting busier and busier policing the One China Policy in the commercial world. Not only that—it could create unintended consequences that embarrass the government. Some companies and individuals see an opportunity of using this name-and-shame tactic to drive out competitors or achieve personal vendettas. In December 2017, a Taiwanese TV drama titled *My Boy* starring celebrity actress Ruby Lin was taken off the network in mainland China. The reason? Two Chinese netizens notified the broadcasting bureau that the drama received funding from the Ministry of Culture of Taiwan. Such a depth of knowledge of a specific TV drama's production was curious: the Taiwanese media later revealed that other TV dramas receiving similar funding had no problem entering the Mainland market. The union leader of the Taiwanese TV Drama Production Federation suggested that there was a commercial dispute between Ruby Lin and investors. This led to the latter's blackmailing of Lin by utilizing Beijing's sensitivity to Taiwanese independence. In other words, it was a commercial infight among the Taiwanese that spilled over into China. One side decided to use politics to punish the other.[21] In an effort of damage control, Lin chose to overcompensate: she stated not only that she always sees herself as Chinese but even that she supports China's sovereignty over the

---

19. Reuters, "US Condemns China for 'Orwellian Nonsense; over Airline Websites," https://www.reuters.com/article/us-usa-airlines-china-exclusive/u-s-condemns-china-for-orwellian-nonsense-over-airline-websites-idUSKBN1I60NL.
20. Sohu Auto News, "Soon after 44 Airlines Corrected Mistakes, Tesla Makes Mistake," May 28, 2018, http://www.sohu.com/a/233365466_519108.
21. Guanchazhe Net, "Taiwanese Media: Ruby Lin's Accusations Stem from Taiwanese due to Business Dispute," January 19, 2018, http:// m.guancha.cn/local/2018_01_09_442399.shtml.

entire South China Sea. Eighteen days later, the TV drama returned to the screen.

A more extreme example lies in the case of Michael Huang (Chinese name Huang An)—a fifty-six-year-old Taiwanese singer now residing mostly in Beijing. Huang's heyday was in the early 1990s for singing *New Dream of Butterfly Lovers* in a mega-hit TV series, *Justice Pao*. In recent years, though, Huang rekindled his fame as "the most hated man in Taiwan"—as one foreign correspondent put it.[22] Huang took great pride in becoming an open and vocal informant to the Chinese government on reporting pro-independence Taiwanese entertainers. His most famous, though many would say notorious, case happened in January 2016, when Huang took on a sixteen-year-old girl celebrity, Chou Tsu-yu. Huang accused the young Taiwanese pop star of advocating Taiwan independence because Chou was seen holding a Taiwanese national flag on a South Korean TV program. Soon after Huang announced his accusation, Chou's performances in China were cancelled. On January 15, JYP Entertainment, a company Chou was affiliated with, released a video of Chou visibly shaken and tearfully apologizing:

> There is only one China. The cross-straits territories are one in the same, and I am proud to consider myself thoroughly Chinese . . . as a Chinese, when performing in a foreign country, I hurt my company and the feelings of netizens on both sides of the Strait by my erroneous words and actions. I am very, very sorry.[23]

Chou ended her speech with another deep bow. To many, watching the video was a distressing experience. If anything, the teen pop star's apology, delivered the night before election day, drove younger Taiwanese voters in hordes to Tsai Ying-wen, the candidate from the pro-independence Democratic Progressive Party (DPP).[24] Huang also sealed his reputation among many in Taiwan as a pro-China thug who would bully a young girl though many in the DPP may have thanked him secretly for being the party's most effective campaign manager.

The infamy that Huang received in Taiwan did not necessarily transform into endorsement on the Mainland. Huang's never-ending reporting on pro-independence activities rendered the Taiwan Affairs Office his personal tool for achieving petty vengeance. The Chou incident became the last straw: the Taiwan Affairs Office issued a statement, warning people to "stay highly vigilant" to "some Taiwanese political forces that attempt to instigate

---

22. Josh Horwitz, "Why a Washed-Up Pop Star Is Suddenly the Most Hated Man in Taiwan," January 20, 2016, accessed May 26, 2018, https://qz.com/597272/why-a-washed-up-pop-star-is-suddenly-the-most-hated-man-in-taiwan/.
23. "Zhou Ziyu publicly apologizes," video clip at https://www.youtube.com/watch?time_continue=55&v=t57URqSp5Ew.
24. *South China Morning Post*, "Teen Pop Star Chou Tzu-u's Apology for Waving Taiwan Flag Swayed Young Voters for DPP," January 17, 2016.

confrontations between people on both sides of the Strait by manipulating individual incidents."[25] It did not take long for netizens to find videos of Huang himself waving the Taiwanese national flag on TV programs. Though living in Beijing, two months after the Chou incident Huang flew back to Taiwan in a private jet to receive medical treatment. Pictures of Huang lying on a gurney, wearing sunglasses and a surgical face mask, and covered in a blanket, received little public sympathy. Huang's second spring of fame was transient. However, with the Chinese government subcontracting the job of policing the One China Policy to the masses, similar figures will pop up. Such dramas will continue to create personal agony for the individuals involved, causing embarrassment to Beijing, while at the same time further distancing relations between Taiwan and China.

Crotch Bomb Actress and Economics of Hating Japan

Incidents surrounding Michael Huang and Ruby Lin suggest the rise of a new kind of power interplay between political and non-political issues. In both cases, political agendas were no longer the ends. Rather, politics became a tool utilized by related actors to achieve non-political goals: either to regain fame for a washed-up star or to expose an economic dispute between investors and producers. Economics is the motive, while politics becomes the means.

Nowhere is the economic dimension of foreign-related issues more pronounced than the flooding of so-called *kangri shenju* (farcical anti-Japan TV series) in China. One notorious example of the *kangri shenju* stars an actress named Ge Tian. In the TV series *Together We Fight the Devils*, a TV drama about resisting the Japanese invaders, Ge plays "Sister Yin"—the lover of an imprisoned communist. Ge visits her hero in his jail cell, where he is seen bruised and bloodied, apparently due to torture by the Japanese captors. Ge puts her lover's hand inside her red blouse and lets him fondle her breasts. The two begin kissing each other as a Japanese military officer and his Chinese interpreter stand by. A very sexually suggestive conversation ensues. Among many crude lines, Ge tells her lover: "Earlier, the little Japanese wanted to touch my groin. How can I let them? That place only belongs to you. Come—touch it!" The jailed communist pulls his hand from underneath her dress and is shown holding a grenade. He shouts: "Let's have another great time!" and detonates the grenade, killing everyone in the cell.[26]

The TV series was broadcast by Sichuan TV in 2015, at a time when the marital status of Ge and Liu Xiang, the country's celebrated hurdler, became the talk of the nation. Many viewers were stunned at seeing the wife of China's

---

25. "Chou Tzu-yu Incident: Responses from China's Taiwan Affairs Office and Taiwan's Mainland Affairs Office," http://www.bbc.com/zhongwen/simp/china/2016/01/160116_taiwan_chou_tzu_yu_reax.
26. The video can be viewed at https://www.youtube.com/watch?v=CKxUeE24MEk.

national sports hero in such a scene. Comments on social media were overwhelmingly negative. "The outlandish drama is horrifying. The authorities have banned foreign shows—only to let us see this?" one user wrote. Others felt it bizarre and lewd.[27] The TV series was quickly taken off the network. The remaining episodes were never shown.

As outlandish as the plot is, it probably would not have attracted intense public opinions had the female character not been played by Ge Tian—allegedly China's most famous divorcee at the time. Without her celebrity face, *Together We Fight the Devils* was simply one of numerous similar war dramas that inundated all TV channels. Screenwriters seemed to be competing with one another to see who could conjure up a more ridiculous feat—tearing a Japanese soldier in half with bare hands, shaking a pistol while firing to make the bullet path curve, bombing enemy trains with firecrackers, or letting Japanese soldiers charge by riding pigs. This is a league where the crotch bomb heroine would meet ample superhuman matches. Had this role been played by someone lesser known than Liu Xiang's ex-wife, it would have been buried for its mediocrity.

It is true that the Chinese government intensified nationalistic education after the 1989 Tiananmen Massacre. It is also true that nationalism is all about "we-they" feeling, and that, in Chinese collective memory, Japan would be the easiest target as the "bad guy." Since then, however, hating Japan and, to a lesser degree, cursing America, has become an institution that has acquired a life of its own. It is no longer purely a government-manipulated campaign. Rather, it has earned its own economic logic and evolved into a billion-yuan patriotic industry that the Chinese comically refer to as *hu you* (fool-you). The deluging *kangri shenju* simply constituted a pillar of this lucrative industry. To borrow a *Godfather* quote—there's nothing personal about hating Japan or cursing America. It's strictly business.

So—who is fishing for fame and money in this flourishing business? One can identify publicity profiteers at all levels. At the individual level, there are the patriotic talking heads—celebrity pro-government intellectuals and top brass military officers. We have already met one in Rear Admiral Zhang Zhaozhong, at the beginning episode of this chapter. Two other admirals known for their hawkish remarks are Luo Yuan and Zhu Chenghu. Admiral Luo openly questioned whether Okinawa should be a part of Japan. In his speeches, he used the island's ancient name, Liu Qiu (Ryukyu), and claimed 75 percent of the islanders wanted to restore their relations with China. As Admiral Luo saw it, China should not be satisfied with demanding the Diaoyu/Senkaku Islands. China needs to talk to Japan about who should own the entire Okinawa chain.[28] Admiral Zhu once warned that China would not

---

27. The *South China Morning Post*, "'Crotch Bomb' Scene in Anti-Japan War Drama Is Blasted by Chinese Online Users as 'Lewd, Bizarre'," May 19, 2015.
28. Yuan Luo, "Strategic competition over Diaoyu Islands," http://news.ifeng.com/opinion/phjd/sjdjt/detail_2012_08/27/17117673_0.shtml.

abide by its pledge of not using nuclear weapons first in case of self-defense and that the country is ready to sacrifice all major cities east of Xi'an in a nuclear showdown with America—a remark hauntingly similar to Mao's casual prediction of an atomic bomb wiping out 300 million Chinese. Indeed, Zhu's remarks led China's most famous political dissident and the Nobel Peace Prize laureate Liu Xiaobo to quip that Zhu was a miniature Mao.[29]

On the civilian side, there are intellectuals like Professor Jin Canrong of Chinese Renmin University and Professor Zhang Weiwei of Fudan University. They make frequent media appearances, both domestic and international, and they use their professorial rhetoric to deliver strictly pro-government messages. This is not to deny their popularity—their public lectures are often standing room only. But a reading of Professor Jin's speeches on Chinese diplomacy over the past four years, for example, reveals a high degree of rhetorical consistency: Chinese diplomacy has been invariably described by Professor Jin as "stable" (*wending*) and other parts of the world as "unstable." In 2018, Jin went so far as to argue that the entire world is unstable "except China."[30] The key evidence the professor cited of China's success was, in his words, "a significant increase in political stability"—a euphemism for Xi's tightening political control. Professor Zhang has been actively promoting this "unique-China" argument. He contends that China has "unique language, unique politics, unique society, and unique economy." His tautological conclusion, then, is that "Chinese politics is unique and the country can only govern by using its own method." Professor Zhang further proclaims that the Chinese Dream is much more amazing than the American Dream is.[31]

These publicity hunters, the media, and the masses together form a commercial ecosystem. Exactly because their messages are uniformly pro-government, patriotic public intellectuals and military top brass have paradoxically gained a higher degree of immunity from governmental monitoring. The media, domestic and international, love reaching out to them, particularly those in uniform, because they know there is a good chance they will say something scary and sensational. Their rank could further offer a façade of justification for them to represent China. However, big-mouthed Chinese military officers tend to have similar institutional affiliations: Zhang Zhaozhong, Luo Yuan, Zhu Chenghu, and Jin Yinan were all "theorists" working at military academies. None of them are from the People's Liberation Army's (PLA) core units, whose personnel tend to keep a much lower public profile. Their marginal position in the military's hierarchy offers them more rhetorical freedom as armchair strategists. One institute, the PLA Military Academy, is

---

29. Boxun News, "Liu Xiaobo: Zhu Chenghu Merely a Miniature of Mao Zedong," September 1, 2005, accessed August 24, 2018, https://www.boxun.com/news/gb/pubvp/2005/09/200509010336.shtml.
30. Jin Canrong, "Uncertainty and Challenges for Chinese Diplomacy in 2018," taped speech viewable at https://www.youtube.com/watch?v=BQJ3Yqq0SeY.
31. Zhang Weiwei, "My View of China," http://www.aisixiang.com/data/78189.html.

known not only as a base for talkative admirals but also a nursing home of princelings. Rear admiral Mao Xinyu, the grandson of Chairman Mao, is constantly mocked by Chinese netizens for his girth, his intellect, his handwriting (in contrast to his grandfather's famous calligraphy), and his career.[32]

To media practitioners and people in the entertainment industry, to be patriotic simply means good business. In 2012, for instance, the government approved 303 new TV shows. More than half had a "revolutionary" theme, and of those the vast majority depicted anti-Japanese war.[33] For producers, then, any show about fighting the Japanese would be a bullet-proof license application. Production was also fast and cheap—the Japanese, after all, are an Asian race. Directors could simply hire an army of Chinese temporary actors to pretend to be Japanese, most of whom were from rural areas lured by a salary of $7 per day.[34] To be fair, there was at least one incident of viewers finding a Black actor playing a Japanese soldier, which created a déjà vu of racial diversity during World War II.

Whether the Chinese peasant actors could deliver a convincing performance as Japanese soldiers would be of little importance. Almost none of the Japanese military officer speak any Japanese in these war dramas. Instead, they speak flawless Chinese. Minowa Yasufumi, a Japanese actor, reported the experience of volunteering to play a Japanese military officer in one such TV show. He wanted to add a dose of authenticity to it. The director simply told Minowa to say whatever he wanted to say when the camera started rolling—because "nobody cares." Minowa was disappointed and turned down the role, because he wanted to play a convincing "Japanese devil."[35]

Many such shows are broadcast in the daytime. It is thus reasonable to assume that a key group of viewers they want to attract are retirees or those in rural areas. As corroborative evidence, such shows are often sponsored by companies selling herbal medicine or promoting alternative therapies. Such shows could also be visual fast food: in one episode, viewers could see martial arts, weapons, explosions, high-speed chases, an astronomical amount of blood, and a Chinese victory. With so many striking images and a guaranteed victory, who cares about the plot? Another reason, as one observer pointed out, is that many stories feature females who are sexually assaulted or, in the

---

32. CBS News, "Chairman Mao's Grandson: China's Most-Mocked Man," https://www.cbsnews.com/news/chairman-maos-grandson-chinas-most-mocked-man/.
33. Hao Jian, "Why Are TV Shows about the War against Japan So Popular in China," *China Buzz*, March 29, 2013, accessed May 24, 2018, http://www.eeo.com.cn/ens/2013/0329/241916.shtml.
34. Sohu Business News, "Paid at 40 Yuan for Eight Hours, Salary for Amateur Actors Lower Than Waiters," July 18, 2013, http://business.sohu.com/20130718/n382011942.shtml.
35. The *Global Times*, "Japanese Actor Refuses to Play Japanese Devil," April 25, 2018, http://wemedia.ifeng.com/57948544/wemedia.shtml.

case of Ge Tian, sexually seductive. They thus have an alluring effect on male viewers.[36] To put it another way, even pornography can become patriotic.

Local governments are one more group benefiting from this booming patriotic fool-you industry. Hengdian, a small town in Dongyang City, Zhejiang Province, has become a giant studio that generated 16.5 billion yuan of tourism revenue in 2016.[37] The town advertises itself as the "Oriental Hollywood." As one journalist reported, during the Chinese New Year break in 2013, staff were still working overtime in town to produce nineteen TV shows, ten of which were about fighting the Japanese.[38] On an annual basis, studios in Hengdian alone churn out close to fifty TV shows featuring the war against Japan. Shi Zhongpeng, one of the many temporary actors, told a reporter that on his busiest day he reported to eight different shows featuring the war—and he died eight times that day as a Japanese devil.[39]

Patriotic Chinese Are Also Irritable Chinese

On shaping the ways China interacts with the world, the delicate dance between the state and society continues to evolve. Who is leading whom remains dynamic. What Professor Jin Canrong touted as China's biggest success—the country's tilt toward one-man rule—looks like political retrogression to many others. Among Chinese intellectuals, there is a growing fear of political taboos becoming institutionalized. In 2013, several Chinese scholars revealed to foreign media a new regulation from the "top." The regulation is informally termed the "seven do-not-talks," as it orders college teachers not to talk about seven issues in their teaching:[40]

1. Do not talk about universal values.
2. Do not talk about press freedom.
3. Do not talk about civil society.
4. Do not talk about citizen rights.
5. Do not talk about past mistakes of the Communist Party.
6. Do not talk about privileged capitalist class.
7. Do not talk about judicial independence.

---

36. Hao Jian, "Why Are TV Shows about the War Against Japan So Popular in China?" *China Buzz*, March 29, 2013, http://www.eeo.com.cn/ens/2013/0329/241916.shtml.
37. *Jiemian* (China), "How Small-Town Hengdian Has Evolved to Host 18 Million Visits per Year," accessed August 24, 2018, https://www.jiemian.com/article/1696725.html.
38. The QQ News, "Ten 'Anti-Japanese Devil' Dramas in Production at Hengdian during Chinese New Year," February 17, 2013, http://wxn.qq.com/cmsid/ENT2013021700011600.
39. The *People's Daily Net*, "One Mature Actor 'Killed' Eight Times in One Day," February 23, 2013, accessed May 21, 2018, http://culture.people.com.cn/n/2013/0203/c22219-20416620.html.
40. Duowei News, "Elevation of Zeitgeist Propaganda: 'Seven-Do-Not-Talks' Ensuing 'Five-Do-Not-Adopts'," accessed August 24, 2018, http://www.dw.com/zh/主旋律升级五不搞后迎来七不讲/a-16802727?&zhongwen=simp.

The "seven do-not-talks" is an elaboration of an earlier, shorter list of "five do-not-adopts" laid out by then-National People's Congress speaker Wu Bangguo. In 2011, Wu stated in his report that China would not adopt the following five concepts: a multiparty alternation system, diversity in leading theory, three branches of government and a bicameral legislature, federalism, and privatization.[41]

Wu's "five do-not-adopts" was a public speech. The "seven do-not-talks," by contrast, has been shrouded in secrecy. A search of the term in Chinese on the country's top search engine, *Baidu*, in May 2018 generated only eleven results, almost none related to the seven demands listed on overseas sites. The only one entry that touched upon it was from an article in a party journal, *Red Flag*. Even there, the reference was transient and murky. It neither admitted nor denied the existence of these seven do-nots.[42] My own conversations with several China-based scholars, though, show that all of them are aware of this policy. An identical search on Google generated results in the tens of thousands. Though the contrast is by no means scientific, there is no doubt that eleven entries on China's top search engine are artificially low. Space for voicing alternative thought is definitely shrinking in China. When so many topics have been disallowed, what is left to be allowed? Only aggressive talk from armchair admirals that pass as entertaining jokes and propagandist lectures from establishment intellectuals that pass as scholarship.

Chinese scholars and students traveling overseas have also become emboldened at organizing themselves. Setting up an overseas Communist Party branch is nothing new—state-owned Chinese companies have been doing this for decades. What is different this time, though, is voluntary organizing by private Chinese citizens in foreign countries. In November 2017, several Chinese visiting scholars at the University of California, Davis stirred up a controversy by establishing a Communist Party cell on campus. A few days later, the cell was dissolved, as the leader learned the organization did not comply with the US Foreign Agents Registration Act, which would require all individuals and groups acting under the direction or control of a foreign government or political party to register with the Department of Justice in advance and regularly report their activities.[43]

---

41. The *People's Daily Net*, "What Messages Are Embedded in Wu Bangguo's 'Five-Do-Not-Adopts'?" March 11, 2011, accessed August 24, 2018, http://cpc.people.com.cn/GB/64093/64103/14120049.html.
42. Nianfeng Zhu, Liping Zheng, and Xueling Wang, "Hot Topics in Theoretical Construction in 2013," *Red Flag*, January 13, 2018, http://theory.people.com.cn/n/2014/0113/c143843-24096298.html.
43. The *South China Morning Post*, "Why a Chinese Communist Party Branch at the University of California, Davis, Was Disbanded," November 20, 2017.

Similar requests have also been made by Chinese students and scholars at the University of Illinois and Chiba University in Japan.[44] Local media viewed these stories alarmingly. They took it as evidence of China aggressively promoting its values. Beijing is launching a new round of ideological crusades around the globe. However, it should be noted that such proposals are invariably raised by short-term Chinese visitors. There has been no report of permanent residents of Chinese origin attempting to establish party cells. This nuance is important: —for those who will return to China, the experience of setting up and participating in party cell activities even when overseas could add loyalty perks to their portfolios. After all, the UC Davis party cell only became known because the cell leader notified his Chinese home institution, which gladly announced it on its website. Compared with the assumption that they were trying to spread communism, it is more reasonable to assume that the cell leader and other participants were simply trying to kiss up to their bosses at home. Preaching communism to Americans and Japanese was not their priority.

In the world of recreational or commercial cultivation of patriotism, farcical anti-Japan TV shows are receding. The notoriety of the crotch bomb hero played a role in the genre's demise. Even the party mouthpiece opined that depicting the Japanese as idiots was a cruel act of belittling the Chinese people that underwent all the atrocities and sacrifices during the war.[45] If the Japanese invasion was round one of hurting the Chinese, now more and more people are wondering if these shows are doing the second round of hurting and insulting—only this time done by the Chinese to the generations of their grandparents and great-grandparents.

Although ridiculous anti-Japan war TV dramas are retreating, war-related stories with patriotic themes remain popular. In fact, the trend is now turning to big-budget, big-screen productions. In 2017, the Chinese action movie *Wolf Warrior 2* broke numerous box office records—it yielded the biggest single-day gross for a Chinese movie. With a total gross of $874 million, *Wolf Warrior 2* became the second highest-grossing movie of all time in a single market, behind only *Star Wars: The Force Awakens*.[46] The story features Leng Feng, a Chinese veteran who travels around the globe and punishes those who offend China. Its movie poster makes this point very clear, as it displays the sentence: "No matter how far away, whoever offends China shall be wiped

---

44. UIUC Party cell information at https://www.peacehall.com/news/gb/china/2018/04/201804231939.shtml; Chiba Party cell information at http://blog.sina.com.cn/s/blog_79e6bfad0100q1ha.html.
45. The *People's Daily*, "Do Not Let 'Farcical Dramas' Consume History," May 2, 2018, accessed August 24, 2018, http://paper.people.com.cn/rmrb/html/2018-05/02/nw.D110000renmrb_20180502_5-05.htm.
46. Box Office Mojo: "All time box office," http://www.boxofficemojo.com/alltime/domestic.htm.

out" (*fanwozhonghuazhe, suiyuanbizhu*). In the movie, the story ends with a shot of the cover of a Chinese passport and an accompanying message:

> Citizens of the People's Republic of China—when you encounter danger in a foreign land, do not give up! Please remember: at your back stands a strong motherland.[47]

The massive commercial success of a story about a Chinese Rambo shows the lucrative potential of commercial patriotism. In 2018, another patriotic big production, *Operation Red Sea*, grossed $579 million, becoming the second highest-grossing movie in China, only behind its even more successful predecessor, *Wolf Warrior 2*. *Wolf Warrior 3* will come to a cinema near every Chinese in 2019. Unlike cheap anti-Japan TV shows, these movies are of significantly higher quality in every aspect: from acting to cinematography, from costume design to original score, from screenplay to visual effects. Another noticeable change is thematic. Both *Wolf Warrior 2* and *Operation Red Sea* are no longer about a historical China during its so-called Century of Humiliation. They are about China today and China in an imagined future. The message is no longer about grievance. It is about taking revenge.

An unintended consequence ensues as a result of the success of patriotic blockbusters. People have invited drama into reality. At airports and seaports in Tehran, Bangkok, Tokyo, and Nagasaki, among other places, people have witnessed odd scenes of angry Chinese passengers singing the Chinese national anthem and clashing with local police. They were not protesting against violation of the One China Policy or South China Sea. Rather, they were stranded tourists facing flight and cruise delays. Thanks to movies like *Wolf Warrior 2* and its heart-warming ending message, many Chinese tourists now see any experience of being inconvenienced as offending their national pride.

China's state broadcaster reprimanded its embarrassing travelers: "By putting on a 'Wolf Warrior' style of patriotism improperly and shouting 'China!' whenever you feel like it, you won't gain sympathy from either staff at foreign airports or your domestic compatriots," a Xinhua News Agency commentary said.[48] That is right—one *Wolf Warrior* is good. Millions of *Wolf Warriors* bring national disgrace. Yet, with the rise of a freer, affluent, and diverse army of societal actors, and with profit-driven media utilizing every schism between the state and society to make money, the Chinese government's headache with managing its public is only beginning.

---

47. The *China Daily*, "'Wolf Warrior 2' Promotes How China Will Always Protect Its Nationals," http://www.chinadaily.com.cn/culture/2017-08/02/content_30332014.htm.
48. Xinhua News Agency, "Three Chinese Embassies Warn That Airports Are No Place for Wolf-Warrior Style Patriotism," February 1, 2018, http://www.xinhuanet.com/2018-02/01/c_1122351291.htm.

4
Between Two Orders in the Asia-Pacific

Navigating a Treacherous Reef

Jeremy Paltiel

The Asia-Pacific is poised between two orders: the Postwar Order, defined by the United States and the alliances formed during the Cold War, and the "Great National Rejuvenation" of China, which takes as its premise the norm of China's centrality in the Asian Order prior to the Opium Wars. The US and its allies see the role of the US as essential to order in the Asia-Pacific (now revamped as the Indo-Pacific), while China demurs. The US claims that it welcomes China's rise so long as it acts within the rules and norms. China proclaims that the Pacific is big enough to contain both China and the US and favors a "new great power relationship" that is win-win. Each side claims deference to its own version of order: the US places first importance on its alliances and the security guarantees contained within them, and China looks to "respect for its core interests" and insists that smaller powers "should not take sides." The lines of friction between these normative orders run through the South China Sea and the First Island Chain running south from Japan's home island. Interest in the security of the Korean peninsula involves overlapping and contrasting views over the survival of the Democratic People's Republic of Korea. Is it possible for the US and China to agree to an inclusive vision of order satisfactory to each and attractive to smaller regional powers? Whereas both sides loudly affirm commitment to "Openness," can China dispel suspicion that its identity implies regional domination, and can the US persuade China that its role in the Asia-Pacific is not aimed at "containment" of China's rise? Taking the position that identities are fluid, adaptive selves that must contend with the recalcitrant reality of the Other that can neither be assimilated nor annihilated, this chapter will seek to delineate which elements in each vision of order are adaptive and flexible and which elements are rigid and competitive. The aim will be to show possibilities of negotiating pragmatic consensus in the face of contrasting identities.

This chapter addresses the evolution of identity in the Asia-Pacific and its contingent role in the dynamics of the power shift globally and regionally. While the author affirms that identities are not fixed, the dialectical construction of self and other can influence second-order notions of security and threat. The chapter begins by addressing the creation of the Asia-Pacific as a form of indigenizing the US role in East Asia with the tension occasioned by China's rise. It goes on to discuss how US allies in the Asia-Pacific, Canada, Australia, and New Zealand have struggled to redefine both their identities and their strategic focus in light of growing tension between the US and China. China's effort to promote a benign orbit of "harmony without sameness" will be increasingly strained by doubts concerning its self-regarding politics in the absence of a robust rules-based order.

Identities are interactive; they are the product of self-other relations and not an independent explainer of behavior.[1] Therefore, when we look at the Asia-Pacific (or the Indo-Pacific—a neologism that instantiates the interactive basis of identity), we are mainly looking at the factors that inform identity, not the roots of an identity.

The Asia-Pacific is the product of the rise of European power and most specifically the rise of the US from the turn of the twentieth century and most particularly the alliance systems that grew up in the wake of US victory over Imperial Japan in the Pacific War. Throughout the Cold War and extending into the contemporary era, US power has shaped the security environment of East Asia and through a complex of economic political and even cultural changes come to see itself, and be seen, as an intrinsic factor in the dynamics of East and Southeast Asia, and dominating energy flows through the Indian Ocean to East Asian energy markets.

However, by the early twenty-first century, the terms of US engagement had radically shifted with the rise of China. Trade flows now determined that China became the principal trading partner of all East Asian states, putting in place what John Ikenberry called a "dual hierarchy" of economic and security orders in the Asia-Pacific.[2] By the second decade of the twenty-first century, the terms of the US role had decisively changed, from ensuring regional order in the name of common prosperity to balancing Chinese power in a search to preserve US preeminence in the global order.

China strenuously dissents from the proposition that US primacy is either necessary or essential to the global order, and even presents itself as a potential guarantor to the multilateral trading order.[3] The US for its part, under President Donald Trump, had retreated from its role as alliance leader and

---

1. Peter J. Burke, "Identities and Social Structure: The 2003 Cooley-Mead Award Address," *Social Psychology Quarterly* 67, no. 1 (March 2004): 5–15.
2. G. John Ikenberry, "Between the Eagle and the Dragon: America, China and Middle State Strategies in Asia," *Political Science Quarterly* 131, no. 1: 9–43.
3. Xi Jinping Speech at Davos, January 17, 2017, https://www.weforum.org/agenda/2017/01/full-text-of-xi-jinping-keynote-at-the-world-economic-forum/. Xi Jinping reiterated

guarantor of the multilateral rules-based order in favor of a more narrowly based focus on power and primacy. This has left many US allies confused and bewildered. The reason why Xi Jinping's offer of guarantor to the multilateral trading order had few takers is largely that Western nations have little confidence in China's standing as a rules-based order or rule of law country, due to the dominant role of the Chinese Communist Party (CCP) in domestic governance and complete lack of trust that the rule of law was embedded in China's domestic institutions. This gave rise to a peculiar configuration. The US demurred and in some cases dissented from the rules-based order on policy grounds, but foreign governments, particularly Western governments, continue to put trust in US domestic institutions. While China loudly proclaims its readiness to assume a greater global role, this continues to be viewed with deep suspicion.

Part of the reason for this is the confused rhetoric of China's global aspirations. In asserting its global role, China deploys three distinct discourses in overlapping fashion, each strand of which may lead to distinctive policy outcomes. The primary discourse deployed to domestic audiences and boldly proclaimed as the fundamental commitment of the CCP is the Great Rejuvenation of the Chinese Nation.[4] This commitment is wholly self-regarding, and prima facie precludes normative participation or negotiation with external actors except under the premise of respecting China's own self-defined "core interests" and a vague, though oft-mentioned, return to the ideals of the Chinese cultural sphere in the dynastic age, whereby China pursued a policy of benevolence and tolerance and eschewed hegemony and expansionism. The second thread of Chinese discourse involves the "democratization" of international relations, multipolarity, and opposition to hegemonism. This would tend to suggest some form of revisionism except for the third discursive thread, which emphasizes global order, stability, the United Nations system, and the multilateral trading order. China bundles this view together with the foreign policy discourse developed under Zhou Enlai, which emphasized the "five principles of peaceful coexistence": noninterference in each other's internal affairs, sovereignty, mutual respect, mutual benefit, and the equality of countries large and small. Naturally, all three discourses are rarely deployed with regard to the same issue. However, they are deployed simultaneously and without apparent contradiction. China also deploys another two subsets of discourses with regard to its own identity with international ramifications: China's identity as a socialist state with its adherence to Marxism-Leninism and according to Xi Jinping the continuity of its "excellent

---

China's role as a guarantor of multilateralism in his speech at the 75th anniversary meeting of the UN General Assembly, September 23, 2020 (accessed October 1, 2020).
4. 习近平在参观《复兴之路》展览时的讲话（2012年11月29日，《人民日报》2012年11月30日 (simplified Chinese characters will be used throughout as the original text uses these).

cultural tradition" with its roots in Confucianism and traditional thought.[5] Xi Jinping explicitly denies any contradiction among these various strands. One may also add one other new strand, the "new great power relationship." This view apparently acknowledges the differences between Great Powers and smaller powers and seeks to put China on a basis of equality with the US by reason of recognizing each other's "core interests."

China sees multilateral engagement as a way of stabilizing and securing relations. The aim of multilateralism in this vision is not stabilizing interests and distributing resources and values according to transparent rules but rather securing "harmony" though emphasizing win-win combinations.[6] Shallow agreements are favored over deep and intrusive commitments. There is no thoroughgoing commitment to common norms but rather deference to differentiated interests. China prefers and expects partners to refrain from pressing claims that produce outcomes with clear winners and losers. The norm of "harmony" requires deference to "core interests" and no one entitled to assert that its claims constitute "universal value." According to Xi Jinping:

> The Asia-Pacific dream is about acting in the spirit of the Asia-Pacific community and out of a sense of shared destinies, following the trend of peace, development and mutually beneficial cooperation, and jointly working for the prosperity and progress of the region.
>
> To realize the Asia-Pacific dream, the region should redouble efforts to forge a partnership of mutual trust, inclusiveness and win-win cooperation and jointly build an open economy.[7]

In this vision, institutions form the framework for relationships rather than a system of rules and roles that distributes resources impersonally. Status matters, and the logic of appropriateness prevails over the logic of consequences. Xi's vision is a continuation and development of Hu Jintao's vision of a neo-Mencian "Harmonious World."[8] The difference, and the harder edge in Xi Jinping's "Asia-Pacific Dream," is the more explicit effort to preempt an Asia-Pacific that is explicitly liberal in its normative orientation.

Xi's vision is sharply at odds with the views of Michael Mastanduno and the logic of the US "pivot" or "rebalancing" enunciated by President Obama. In Xi's eyes, "In the final analysis, it is for the people of Asia to run the affairs of Asia, solve the problems of Asia and uphold the security of Asia. The people

---

5. Gilbert Rozman "Invocations of Chinese Traditions in International Relations," *Chinese Journal of Political Science* 17, no. 2 (June 2012): 111–24.
6. See Jeremy Paltiel, "China's Regionalization Policies: Illiberal Internationalism or Neo-Mencian Benevolence?", in *China and the Global Politics of Regionalization*, ed. Emilian Kavalski (London: Ashgate, 2009), 47–62.
7. Xinhua, "Chinese President Proposes Asia-Pacific Dream," https://www.chinadaily.com.cn/china/2014-11/09/content_18889698.htm (accessed November 2, 2020).
8. See Paltiel, "China's Regionalization Policies."

of Asia have the capability and wisdom to achieve peace and stability in the region through enhanced cooperation."[9]

In this respect, the Asia-Pacific and its institutionalization represents a modification of the two versions of international society that Barry Buzan outlines in his discourses on the English School:[10] China pursues a vision of international society that is BOTH pluralistic AND solidary. Sovereignty is paramount but status also counts. Norms are correlative rather than absolute, and status is distributed outside the norms that establish the institution. As the Chinese Foreign Minister riposted to his Singapore counterpart in the presence of the US: "China is a big country and other countries are small countries and that is just a fact."[11] China formalized this attitude in a somewhat more palatable fashion in its White Paper on the Asia-Pacific: in the sphere of great power relations "smaller states should not take sides."[12]

Foreign policy discourses develop in response to interests and are framed in ways that advance interests while drawing from ideological and cultural frames that elaborate policy stances into a coherent and finely articulated worldview. Cultural resources are neither determinative nor are they strictly instrumental. Cultural and ideological resources must be woven together in ways that allow diverse audiences and practitioners of foreign policy discourse to make sense of the policy and guide their own actions and responses. In this regard, Xi Jinping and his close advisors (Wang Huning appears to be the most prominent of his brain-trusters) have made an effort to frame China's Great Power assertiveness in a manner that tries to normalize it rather than emphasize its revisionism, by tying it both to the existing world order and its primary institutions, most prominently the UN, as well as an evocation of a Chinese cultural tradition reputed or claimed to be peaceful, non-threatening, and readily accepted by China's neighbors. Alongside this, Xi appeals to socialism ("with Chinese characteristics") to assert the inviolable primacy of the communist regime with its embedded authority of Marxism-Leninism. The appeal to socialism is almost invariably an appeal to the regime's domestic political base and is rarely (except in the case of the few remaining socialist neighbors and Cuba) intended to provide a broad appeal to like-minded ideological practitioners interested in the universal appeal of socialist humanism. The Chinese exception trumps the socialist universalism.

---

9. 习近平在亚信第四次峰会上作主旨发言(全文),"New Asian Security Concept for New Progress in Security Cooperation" (Remarks at the Fourth Summit of the Conference on Interaction and Confidence Building Measures in Asia, Shanghai, May 21, 2014), http://www.china.org.cn/world/2014-05/28/content_32511846.htm (accessed February 21, 2020).
10. Barry Buzan, "The English School: An Underexploited Resource in IR," *Review of International Studies* 27 (2001): 471–88.
11. "The US Takes Tougher Tone with China," The *Washington Post*, July 30, 2010.
12. China White Paper on Security Cooperation in the Asia-Pacific, January 2017, http://english.gov.cn/archive/white_paper/2017/01/11/content_281475539078636.htm (accessed December 15, 2020).

Altogether, while the tripartite nature of Chinese discourse is intended to allay fears and prepare the ground for friendship and mutually beneficial interaction, it is carefully designed to reduce commitments and expectations that may entangle the Chinese states in unwanted commitments. China offers global public goods in a distinct manner through "complex bilateralism." This is designed to prevent the formation of institutionalized claims and entitlements embedded in a multilateral framework. Where China is both the responsible power and numerically inferior minority actor, it sets up asymmetric bilateral agreements where it maintains discretionary power. In settings where multilateral governance is inevitable, China prefers decision-making by consensus where it retains a veto.[13]

The initial framing of "socialism with Chinese characteristics" was designed by Deng Xiaoping (Hu Qiaomu) as a firebreak that insulated the Chinese regime both from ideological expectations derived from Marxism and from the liberal hegemony of the West. "Socialism" kept China insulated from liberal ideology, and "Chinese characteristics" enabled its leaders to interpret Marxism-Leninism in a particularistic manner. The ambiguities surrounding both sides of this dialectic enabled Deng and his regime to engage instrumentally and productively with the West, without convergence or assimilation. It also allowed the regime to creatively interpret which aspects of "socialism" or "the Chinese tradition" they wished to deploy to distinguish themselves from "the other" while managing the goal expectations attendant on any particular ideological stance. Thus, in the wake of the Tiananmen protests and repression, Deng could both emphasize political distance and themes of struggle with the West while continuing with reform, even going so far as to urge his party comrades to proclaim a moratorium on whether any sort of enterprise is surnamed "socialist" or "capitalist" in his Southern Tour of 1991–1992 that followed the collapse of the Soviet Union. This, after the hiatus engendered by Tiananmen, ushered in the heyday of "linking rails to the world" (向世界接轨) that ultimately ushered China's entry into the World Trade Organization. Following this, in the golden age of the "End of History," the Jiang Zemin and Hu Jintao regimes both attempted to carve an identity distinct from liberalism increasingly rooted in the Chinese tradition, exemplified in Hu Jintao's call to "build a harmonious world." China's response to liberal human rights universalism was far more rooted in Chinese cultural particularism than in ideology.

The particularist strain in Chinese ideological discourse reached its cyclical apogee around the Beijing Olympics with the historical pageant enacted by Zhang Yimou in Ai Weiwei's birds' nest. The Great Recession that engulfed the world around this time occasioned a new turn, reaching a new zenith with the ascension of Xi Jinping as General Secretary of the CCP. His

---

13. Alastair Iain Johnston, "Socialization in International Institutions: The ASEAN Way and International Relations Theory," in *International Relations Theory and the Asia-Pacific*, ed. G. John Ikenberry and Michael Mastanduno (New York: Columbia University Press, 2003), 107–62.

proclamation of the Great Rejuvenation of the Chinese Nation, and the Twin Centenaries, promoted a new spirit of assertiveness that gave rise to the Belt and Road Initiative and the "Chinese Solution" (中国方案) in a "community of common destiny" (人类命运共同体).[14] This notion was originally deployed regionally in China's periphery and then extended to the world as a whole.[15] To assert China's contribution to the global commons, Xi Jinping inevitably had to appeal to universals and cast Chinese identity in universalistic terms that could be understood distinctively from liberal universal values. In this, he came to dramatically reinforce the "socialist" aspect of China's identity, both for domestic purposes (poverty elimination) and internationally through the provision of global public goods and the notion of "shared prosperity." Xi could thereby take advantage of the tarnished legitimacy of global capitalism that followed the collapse of Lehmann Brothers, at the same time that he recast globalization in more inclusive terms.

However, in making space for a revived China on the global stage, Xi had both to confront the implied threat to China's smaller neighbors and the relativization of the US, whose global role since the collapse of the Soviet Union had been unrivalled. The attempt to forge a "new great power relationship" sought to reframe China's relationship with the US on a more equal footing while reassuring Washington that China's new global role did not engender a zero-sum game for influence in the world. The pervasive language of "win-win" was a near-desperate effort to frame China's rise in positive sum terms.

While Xi at Sunnylands received a respectful but skeptical hearing from President Obama,[16] Obama's "rebalancing" or "pivot" proved that the US would hedge its bets and maneuver to retain "full-spectrum primacy" in the Asia-Pacific. Following on this, the Trump Administration has recast foreign relations pervasively in zero-sum terms and begun a historic pushback on China's rise. This pushback is premised on the notion that China's rise is predatory and that US superiority must be clawed back. This has led Xi and his regime in turn to conclude that the US is bent on throttling China's rise.[17] It is therefore not surprising to see Chinese officials recast relations with Western countries in racialized terms, casting a postcolonial tinge on China's relations with the West.

---

14. Full text of Xi Jinping's report at the 19th CPC National Congress, http://www.xinhuanet.com/english/special/2017-11/03/c_136725942.htm (accessed December 15, 2020).
15. 习近平在周边外交工作座谈会上发表重要讲话, http://www.xinhuanet.com/politics/2013-10/25/c_117878897.htm (accessed December 15, 2020).
16. Richard Bush, "Xi and Obama at Sunnylands: A Good Start," https://www.brookings.edu/blog/up-front/2013/06/10/obama-and-xi-at-sunnylands-a-good-start/ (accessed December 15, 2020).
17. "美国挑起贸易战实质是什么", 人民日报, 2018年8月9日, http://politics.people.com.cn/n1/2018/0809/c1001-30220090.html (accessed December 15, 2020).

The CCP has ensnared itself in a net of its own making, as Deng Yuwen has insightfully pointed out.[18] Deng traces Xi Jinping's rise to the fear that China's integration into a liberal global political economy was inducing a hollowing out of the ideological basis of the CCP and the foundations of its regime. Therefore, taking advantage of the diminished standing of Western liberalism in the wake of the Great Recession of 2008, Xi waged an offensive, doubling down on the party's tradition and ideological foundation and tracing a line of continuity between Chinese traditional culture and Maoism, with the core concept that the party leads everywhere.

The Asia-Pacific is, in truth, a concept Made in the USA, built on the Pacific War and its Cold War dénouement that established the US as the security guarantor of Maritime East Asia through its hub-and-spoke series of alliances. This structure promoted the rise of the East Asian economies and made the US the offshore anchor of regional integration. China is challenging that US role less through direct confrontation than by chipping away at its premises, by posing itself as the center of trade and investment in the region, and by asserting its own security priorities in its own neighborhood. China directly questions the need for American hegemony to underwrite the prosperity and security of the region but at the same time does not question American presence in the region. China is more assertive than confrontational. The perception of challenge and competition lies more with the US and its closest allies, reinforced by the growing technical capacity of the People's Liberation Army and its acquisition of AAAD (anti-access, area denial) technologies. However, these war-fighting strategies should not be casually translated into real-time political objectives without careful thinking.

Asian countries obviously do not want to face China alone yet do not perceive the US role in the same way as Americans do. While they would like the US to hedge China, they do not perceive the US as indispensable as the US perceives itself. They want to have the US onside but prefer to deal with China themselves as far as possible rather than through Washington. The US self-imagined role of its own indispensable hegemony[19] sits uncomfortably for Asians who wish to project their own identity autonomously on the global stage. Yet the role of the US in the region is also emblematic of Asian modernity and inseparable from Asia's emergence in global society. America provokes deep ambivalence. The China that the Asians fear is the China they know. The US is loved but mistrusted. Diffident admiration pervades perceptions of both great powers.

China's Community of Common Destiny is like the Greater East Asia Co-Prosperity Sphere without racialized hierarchy and murderous expansion.

---

18. "习太阳"是怎么升起的，能照多久？, https://cn.nytimes.com/opinion/20181030/how-xi-sun-rose-shine/?utm_source=top-2018-stories (accessed December 15, 2020).
19. Michael Mastanduno, "Incomplete Hegemony and Security Order in the Asia-Pacific," in *America Unrivalled: The Future of the Balance of Power*, ed. G. John Ikenberry (Ithaca, NY: Cornell University Press, 2002), 181–210.

It is Asia for the Asians with China as its beneficent sponsor and genial host. America is excluded by default, not by design. Each Great Power pursues its own version of open regionalism—China through the ASEAN + system and the Regional Comprehensive Economic Partnership (RCEP) and the US through its more exclusive Trans-Pacific Partnership (TPP)—until Trump abandoned it. Each effort is ultimately self-regarding and defensive, designed to preserve space for each one's version of globalization. China's is state-led and anchored in sovereignty, and the US is rules-based and anchored in the legal interests of the multinational corporation.

There is mutual construction in the identity of a liberal order and the Chinese construction of a multilateral rules-based order that is pluralistic.[20]

Both China and the US have constructed self-regarding narratives of identity that identify the nation as a World-historic Great Power second to none. While Trump's Make America Great Again (MAGA) may be especially particularistic in its global exceptionalism, the universalistic core of America "the indispensable power" that animated a more liberal manifest destiny anchored in the values of the Declaration of Independence and the US Constitution continues to legitimate America's global role and its presence in the Asia-Pacific. China, for its part, has welded together a national historical narrative that combines the centrality of the Chinese empire in the *tianxia* of Asia's past with the narrative of resistance to imperialism and hegemony. The Chinese narrative tries to legitimate a flattened view of national self-determination and sovereignty that corresponds to the twenty-five years of decolonization following the founding of the UN and glosses over the multi-ethnic and heterogenous governance strategies that characterized the Qing empire (outside the Han core of the eighteen provinces of the Ming empire) in the name of a uniform *Zhonghua Minzu*.[21] These narratives clearly come into conflict around the periphery of China in the Asia-Pacific.

China's narrative of a peaceful rise is poorly understood, even by its authors. China's leaders are at pains to explain that they have no claims on anyone else, only on what is rightfully theirs, and have no ambitions to subordinate and dominate, nor to export their own version of governance. In this they are sincere even though the sphere of "rightfully theirs" may include zones and territories historically claimed and occupied by neighboring countries. Furthermore, China has repeatedly proclaimed its desire for "joint development" in the disputed zones as a demonstration of its benevolent magnanimity. This, however, comes at a price—recognition of the legitimacy of the Chinese claim. The second protestation is aimed directly at the US and the liberal West. China's leaders contrast their own community of common destiny in a spirit of "harmony without sameness" (和而不同) with

---

20. Yongjin Zhang, "China and Liberal Hierarchies in Global International Society," *International Affairs* 92, no. 4 (July 2016): 795–816; Jinghan Zeng and Shaun Breslin, "A G2 with Chinese Characteristics?", *International Affairs* 92, no. 4: 773–94.
21. See Henrietta Harrison, *China: Inventing the Nation* (London: Arnold, 2001).

the universalizing claims and missionary zeal of a US-led liberal world. China appears at pains to understand how its own behavior should be viewed as threatening. Its leaders fail to understand, or are willfully blind to, the sense in which the West sees derogation from the Western liberal rules-based order as a threat and a challenge. The Chinese challenge, if legitimated, is a challenge to the universality of the liberal order and, by implication, threatens its legitimacy. Thus, the thrust of the Asia Society report on managing China's challenge directly instantiates that challenge and that conflict.[22] The very fact of China's (re)new(ed) identity is the basis of the coming conflict which may lead us down the road of a new Cold War (with twenty-first-century characteristics). There is a mutual obtuseness to this dialogue of the deaf. Chinese cannot see how their self-regarding claim to their legitimacy at home threatens anyone else, while the liberal West, led by the US, cannot see liberal universality challenged as anything but a threat to their legitimacy and the legitimacy of the global order.

This at base is a conflict rooted in concepts of Justice rooted in divine law, against a concept of harmony based on respectful relations. The failure of Xi Jinping's "new great power relationship" comes down to this: China is perfectly willing to adjust its relations to accommodate mutual interests between the US and China. The US, however, cannot sacrifice allies with whom it shares values and principles, nor is it willing to give up its principles for the sake of accommodating mutual interests. For this reason, the transactional President Donald Trump is in many ways a more congenial partner than is the principled President Barack Obama. However, because Trump sees American primacy as an irreducible norm, any mutual compromise must leave America on top.

Australia, New Zealand, Canada, and the Rise of China

These three members of the British Commonwealth and US allies have long seen their interests align with the rise of China and, in the case of Australia and New Zealand, have strongly tied their economic strategy to growing demand from the Chinese market, particularly for resources, energy, and agricultural commodities. Their national strategies were built on the integration of China within the liberal order. Growing conflict between the US and China and the growing call within the US to cast the US-China relationship in zero-sum terms[23] has thrown their national strategies into disarray. These three countries are particularly significant, given the values shared with the

---

22. Asia Society, *Course Correction: Towards an Effective and Sustainable China Policy* (February 12, 2019), https://asiasociety.org/center-us-china-relations/events/course-correction-toward-effective-and-sustainable-china-policy (accessed December 15, 2020).
23. Secretary of State Pompeo's Speech at the Nixon Library, July 23, 2020, "Communist China and the Free World's Future," https://www.state.gov/communist-china-and-the-free-worlds-future/ (accessed October 1, 2020).

US and the liberal West and their longstanding and growing engagement with China. The case of Australia is particularly instructive. Australia, since the 1990s but more particularly since the beginning of the current millennium, has tied its prosperity and development to the Asia-Pacific generally and to China in particular. As a symbol of its commitment it issued a wide-ranging White Paper in 2013.[24] At the same time, Australia has proactively strengthened its alliance with the US and made itself an anchor of US security policy in the Asia-Pacific.[25] In a country with highly polarized and evenly divided political camps, this Janus-like policy has been a matter of bipartisan consensus.[26] And yet, in recent years tensions have begun to rise both in Australia and New Zealand due to alleged Chinese interference in domestic politics and influence peddling connected to Chinese ideal and material interests.[27]

In the Canadian case, economic integration with the US is both more important and, in some sense, also constitutes a barrier to more effective economic engagement of China. Yet, for years, Canada has been keen to engage China. This began to shift as China rose, both because some Canadians became wary of a growing Chinese footprint in our resource economy and because of the anxieties shared or imported from the South. Despite this, our current Prime Minister Justin Trudeau, son of the prime minister who initially established diplomatic relations with the People's Republic of China in October 1970, came into office determined to improve our strategic partnership with China that had suffered ups and downs during the administration of the previous Prime Minister, Stephen Harper.[28] Successive shocks have now set back Sino-Canadian relations to a level not seen since Tiananmen. The first shock was the failure to launch free trade negotiations on the occasion of Prime Minister Trudeau's last official visit to China in December 2017. The second was the Canadian government's rejection of the bid by China's state-owned China Communications Construction Corporation International (CCCI) to buy Aecon Construction, one of Canada's largest infrastructure construction companies.[29] The third was the inclusion in the draft USMCA (the successor to NAFTA) of clause 10A, allowing the US (or other signatories) to withdraw from the agreement on six months' notice, should any member initiate free

---

24. http://www.defence.gov.au/whitepaper/2013/docs/australia_in_the_asian_century_white_paper.pdf (accessed December 15, 2020).
25. http://www.defence.gov.au/WhitePaper/Docs/2016-Defence-White-Paper.pdf.
26. Nick Bisley, "Australia's Engagement with China: From Fear to Greed and Back Again," *International Journal* 73, no. 3: 379–98.
27. John Garnaut, "How China Interferes in Australia: How Democracies Can Fight Back," *Foreign Affairs*, March 8, 2018.
28. See Jeremy Paltiel, "Facing China: Canada Between Fear and Hope," *International Journal* 73, no. 3: 343–63.
29. "Federal Government Blocks Sale of Construction Giant Aecon to Chinese Interests," https://www.cbc.ca/news/politics/canada-blocks-aecon-sale-china-1.4675353 (accessed December 15, 2020).

trade negotiations with a "non-market economy."[30] The final and most serious shock occurred in the wake of Canada's detention on December 1, 2018 of Ms. Meng Wanzhou, CFO of Huawei Corporation, at the request of the US, for extradition on bank fraud charges.[31] This precipitated the tit-for-tat arrest of a Canadian diplomat on leave working for the International Crisis Group, Michael Kovrig, and another Canadian, Michael Spavor. Tension has caused the resignation of Canada's ambassador to China and an unprecedented series of attacks on Canada in Chinese media.[32] In the wake of the arrests, public opinion has turned sharply against China.[33]

New Zealand is one of the first Western countries to have signed a free trade deal with China, dating to 2008. It became a major dairy supplier to China, and in the decade since the signing of the free trade deal, New Zealand trade with China more than tripled, New Zealand enjoying an enviable surplus in trade.[34] Despite that, New Zealand's relations with China took a nosedive towards the end of 2018, culminating in the abrupt cancellation of an official visit by the New Zealand prime minister in 2018.[35] This followed months of accusations of Chinese interference in New Zealand politics and charges of foreign influence and espionage, notably documented by the New Zealand China researcher Anne-Marie Brady.[36] Relations with China continued to fray through early 2019, following New Zealand's decision to ban Huawei equipment from New Zealand's telecommunications infrastructure.[37]

This brief survey shows that US allies, even those who made calculated bets on economic engagement with China, have found it difficult to reconcile their economic ties with their security relations with the US, and find themselves hostage to the ebb and flow of Sino-American rivalry in the Asia-Pacific (or Indo-Pacific). None of these countries has sought to balance or bandwagon

---

30. https://ustr.gov/trade-agreements/free-trade-agreements/united-states-mexico-canada-agreement/agreement-between (accessed December 20, 2020).
31. "Huawei Exec Faces Long and Costly Extradition Battle," *The Vancouver Sun*, December 13, 2018, https://vancouversun.com/news/local-news/huawei-exec-faces-long-and-costly-extradition-battle; https://www.theglobeandmail.com/canada/article-huawei-canada-china-5g-network-explainer/; https://www.theglobeandmail.com/opinion/article-how-the-huawei-crisis-has-exploded-trudeaus-china-policy/ (accessed December 20, 2020).
32. "China Is Prepared to Respond to Canada if Extradition of Meng Wanzhou Materializes," *The Global Times*, http://www.globaltimes.cn/content/1135212.shtml.
33. Paul Evans, "Canada Caught in the Vortex of US-China Techno-nationalism," *East Asia Forum*, https://www.eastasiaforum.org/2019/02/26/canada-caught-in-the-vortex-of-us-china-techno-nationalism/.
34. https://www.stats.govt.nz/news/new-zealands-two-way-trade-with-china-more-than-triples-over-the-decade.
35. "Cracks Appear in the New Zealand China Relationship," *The Diplomat*, https://thediplomat.com/2019/01/cracks-appear-in-the-new-zealand-china-relationship/.
36. See Anne-Marie Brady, "China in Xi's 'New Era': New Zealand and the CCP's 'Magic Weapons,'" *Journal of Democracy* 29, no. 2 (April 2018): 68–75.
37. "New Zealand Fears Fraying Ties with China Its Biggest Customer," *The New York Times*, February 14, 2019, https://www.nytimes.com/2019/02/14/world/asia/new-zealand-china-huawei-tensions.html.

China's rise, and all three countries are deeply committed to open trade in the Asia-Pacific through the TPP (now rechristened the Comprehensive and Progressive Trans Pacific Partnership—in deference to the progressive trade agenda of Canada's Justin Trudeau) but have found it hard to reconcile their free trade ideals with the self-regarding thrust of China's rise. Of course, this has now been matched by Donald Trump's MAGA-style transactional bilateralism that gives US allies relatively little room to maneuver. Therefore, the premise of the room to maneuver in G. John Ikenberry's *Middle Powers and China's Rise* appears to have dramatically shrunk.

ASEAN: In the Vice, or Occupying Middle Ground?

It would seem that ASEAN would be the cockpit of Sino-American rivalry in the Asia-Pacific, and in some sense, the South China Sea has been spotlighted as the terrain of friction. Six ASEAN countries maintain territorial claims that impinge on China's claims within the "nine-dash line." At the same time, the US proclaims freedom of navigation against China's own claim to control passage in what it regards as its Exclusive Economic Zone. Some ASEAN countries have been seen to hedge Chinese power both by joining the TPP and, in the case of the Philippines and Singapore, maintaining defense relations with the US, with pragmatic assent of Vietnam in a low-key hedging posture. Yet China maintains a fruitful and productive relationship with ASEAN as a whole, with which China maintains a robust trade and investment relationship.[38] On the economic side this was cemented by the completion of RCEP on November 15, 2020.[39] Politically , Singapore has led the way in calling for a truce in US-China confrontation.[40]

Tentative Conclusions: The Future of the Asia-Pacific (Indo-Pacific) in a Zero-Sum World

The rise of Chinese assertiveness, with increased tensions in the South China Sea, along the Sino-Indian border, and with Taiwan, are offset by the increased attention of Xi Jinping to "peripheral diplomacy."[41] Chinese policymakers make relations with ASEAN a consistent priority and make frequent and regular visits on a head-of-government or head-of-state level. China's own

---

38. Min-hua Chiang, "China-ASEAN Economic Relations after the Establishment of a Free Trade Area," *The Pacific Review 2018*.
39. "ASEAN Hits Historic Milestone with RCEP Signing," https://asean.org/asean-hits-historic-milestone-signing-rcep/ (accessed December 15, 2020).
40. "Singapore PM Calls for US China 'Truce' after Tumultuous Years," Bloomberg, November 16, 2020, https://www.bloomberg.com/news/articles/2020-11-17/singapore-pm-calls-for-u-s-china-truce-after-tumultuous-years (accessed December 15, 2020).
41. Stephen N. Smith, "Harmonizing the Periphery: China's Neighborhood Strategy under Xi Jinping," *The Pacific Review 2019*, https://doi.org/10.1080/09512748.2019.1651383.

preferred foreign policy outlook meshes well with the ASEAN way, with its emphasis on consensus and consultation, non-interference, and respect for sovereignty.[42] ASEAN countries will remain China's partners for reasons that transcend economic partnership and are unlikely to join in any potential renewed "containment" strategy towards China, such as the one suggested in Vice-President Pence's speech at the Hudson Institute.[43]

The policy preference of Mr. Trump's democratic opponents that seems to be embedded in the recent Asia Society report entitled "Course Correction: Toward an effective and sustainable China Policy" does not effectively provide more room though it does recognize and valorize the role played by US allies in hedging China's rise.[44] Regardless of who is in power in Washington, the assertiveness embedded in Xi Jinping's Chinese Dream and the new era, alongside stiffening resistance to China's assertion of a global role in Washington, is bound to shrink the terrain for an Asia-Pacific community of common destiny or otherwise. Instead, the Asia-Pacific appears destined for contestation. Both liberal and neo-Confucian varieties of toleration are capable of inciting controversy while allowing room to de-escalate confrontation in the interest of maintaining cooperative relations and interdependence. We appear to be doomed to stretch the limits of a networked web of Confucian-style relationships coupled with a rules-based order of rules and roles, neither side fully able to exclude the other or arrive at a joint understanding that legitimates the claims of each.

There is a paradox at the heart of each of the rival concepts of order championed by China and the US. China promotes "inclusiveness, tolerance, and win-win" within an open order even as it pursues an increasingly hierarchic, closed, and autocratic order at home with an order centered on the CCP and the CCP centered on the person of Xi Jinping at its apex. On the other side of the Pacific, the US is torn between the multilateral rules-based order that it helped to create and its own eroding leadership. The US can either champion its offspring while coming to terms with its own capacity to shape particular outcomes, or deploy its still potent and as yet unrivalled capacity to shape particular outcomes at the cost of commitment to a shared rules-based order with its allies. These allies are unlikely to be lulled into alignment with China, unless direct pressure from the US threatens their fundamental interests but are more likely to accommodate themselves to China's rise, so long as China refrains from pressing local advantages to pursue territorial claims and

---

42. Zha Daojiong, "For China, ASEAN Is Far More Important Than a 'Talking Shop'," *South China Morning Post*, January 3, 2019.
43. "Vice President Mike Pence's Remarks on the Administration's Policy Towards China," https://www.hudson.org/events/1610-vice-president-mike-pence-s-remarks-on-the-administration-s-policy-towards-china102018.
44. https://asiasociety.org/sites/default/files/2019-02/Course%20Correction%20Toward%20an%20Effective%20and%20Sustainable%20China%20Policy.pdf.

acquiescence to its ideological preferences. Each side is best placed to maintain prestige when it allows smaller powers the space to choose their own destiny.

On May 15, 2019, Xi Jinping staked claim to the Asian identity in a speech to the Conference on Dialogue of Asian Civilizations that he convened in Beijing. While reaffirming tolerance, inclusiveness, openness, and diversity, he asserted an *ASIAN* Community of common destiny that was in some sense prior to the community of shared destiny for humankind. In this, Xi appears to implicitly reject a single scale of universal values that unites all and provides a common template for value judgment. Instead, Xi insists on placing the values of different civilizations on an equal footing:

> 每一种文明都扎根于自己的生存土壤，凝聚着一个国家、一个民族的非凡智慧和精神追求，都有自己存在的价值。人类只有肤色语言之别，文明只有姹紫嫣红之别，但绝无高低优劣之分。认为自己的人种和文明高人一等，执意改造甚至取代其他文明，在认识上是愚蠢的，在做法上是灾难性的！如果人类文明变得只有一个色调、一个模式了，那这个世界就太单调了，也太无趣了！我们应该秉持平等和尊重，摒弃傲慢和偏见，加深对自身文明和其他文明差异性的认知，推动不同文明交流对话、和谐共生。

> Every civilization is rooted in the soil of its own survival, and integrates the extraordinary wisdom and spiritual aspirations of a single state and nation. Each maintains the value of its own survival. Humanity has only differences of skin hue and language and civilizations likewise have only differences of colour variety but no distinction of high or low or better or worse. To consider one's own race or civilization as first class and to willfully seek to transform or replace other civilizations is epistemologically foolish and operationally disastrous! Should human civilization become monochromatic and unimodal then the world would become too uniform, and too uninteresting! We must maintain equality and respect and put aside arrogance and prejudice, to deepen our understanding of the differences between our own and other civilizations and promote the exchange and dialog between different civilizations along with their harmonious coexistence.[15]

Xi lays claim to an Asian identity constructed in dissent from liberal internationalism, a kind of illiberal internationalism built on mutual respect and deference along sovereign national political lines. Here, China plays a central role in benign indifference to value differences that do not spill over national boundaries. However, this leaves open the value foundation of a rules-based order. Some practical implications of this distinct value orientation can be seen in this argument by Su Hao:

> The Confucian culture stresses the role and efficiency of governments' management and the importance of morality in the administration of the government. It means governing is not only about following the rule of law, but also about the pursuit of high moral standards.

---

45. Xi Jinping, 深化文明交流互鉴 共建亚洲命运共同体 [Deepen intercultural exchange and comparison, build a shared Asian destiny], http://politics.people.com.cn/n1/2019/0515/c1024-31086589.html.

> The Western administration system is based on individualism. Social management consists of two ways: One is bottom-up, another is top-down. The two characters need to work together to reach an effective governance. The West's absolute bottom-up approach often brings about problems, such as populism and selfishness. Take the anti-globalization sentiment in the US. It only focuses on the interests of the US, while causing harms to other countries' interests.
>
> Although the West's governance has its advantages, people need to be aware of its drawbacks.
>
> Many Asian countries have developed at a considerable speed. The top-down management system stemming from the Confucian culture is efficient. The West's criticism of the East is prejudice of civilization.[46]

Note that this quotation anticipated Chinese celebration of its superior governance in tackling the COVID-19 virus. China increasingly juxtaposes effective governance with Western liberal celebration of rights and liberties. The situation in the Asia-Pacific shows increasing tendencies towards polarization alongside the rising tensions between China and the US. The middle powers of the Asia-Pacific are torn, but pragmatic cooperation across the two orders is possible. Nonetheless, flare-ups over questions of value and principle as well as fundamental interest are inevitable. China has yet to convince its neighbors, let alone its global rivals, that it has a viable normative system that can protect their interests while advancing its own. However, its effective governance in the face of looming threats in global health and the environment, as well as the global economy, will convince most countries to hedge. China's proven capacity to shape its own future provides powerful incentives to shape a future alongside it. Traditional US allies like Canada, Australia, and New Zealand, as well as Japan, will coordinate more closely with Washington, but they are unlikely to pursue a sharp "decoupling" and rally to the US in a new Cold War. China's appeal will continue to be largely interest- and transaction-based under a thin veneer of Asian identity. The US can continue to be a firm anchor of the Indo-Pacific if it harmonizes its liberal values with firm material support to its Asian allies. It is fair to say that China has so far failed to shape a discourse that will tie its periphery to its own identity. At the same time, the credibility of the US as a credible guarantor of a liberal order has eroded. Regional identity remains fractured amid growing confrontation. The future of the Asia-Pacific will be written by the power that can convince lesser powers that their interests will be preserved under its umbrella.

---

46. Sharing improves Asian governance, http://www.globaltimes.cn/content/1149852.shtml (accessed December 15, 2020).

Part B: Strategies

5
China in the Rise and Fall of the "New World Order"

Toward New Inter-imperial Rivalry

Ho-fung Hung

Introduction

Globalism and democracy are now in retreat amid the rise of right-wing populism across the globe. Recent discussions lamenting the retreat of globalization and democracy treat both as a natural process, neglecting the historical origins of the recent rise of globalization-democratization as a political project and its internal contradictions since its inception.

In this chapter, I trace the origins of the globalization- and democratization-promotion projects that the United States has undertaken since the Reagan administration. I argue that these twin projects can be traced to the profitability crisis of capitalism among advanced capitalist states, as well as the crisis of US hegemony in the 1970s. These crises motivated the US state to open new markets for US capital exports as a way to revive profits by taming domestic organized labor. In the meantime, the US started the democracy-promotion project, with the intended or unintended consequence of neutralizing the protectionist resistance of authoritarian states, including America's own Cold War allies in the developing world.

After the end of Cold War, this globalization-democratization project marched on in full force under US leadership. This brought forth a unipolar global imperial moment of the US at the turn of the twenty-first century. The resulting "New World Order," which George H. W. Bush used to refer to the post–Cold War world order in a 1990 speech, hinged on US aggressive intervention to ameliorate recurrent financial crises triggered by both free flow of capital on the one hand and on US military power as the means to topple authoritarian regimes and promote democracy. This new era is marked by the US Treasury's involvement in the bailout of Mexico amid the 1994 peso crisis, its bailout of several Asian countries during the 1997–1998 Asian financial crisis, the NATO bombing of Belgrade in 1999, and the Second Persian Gulf War.

I also delineate how this imperial world order is grounded on the US's quasi-alliance with authoritarian and state-capitalist China. This alliance helped cement the US-centered global circuit of finance and trade and warranted the global supremacy of the US military. The contradictions between US capital and China's state capitalism, China's newfound capability of sustaining its authoritarian regime abroad, and the explosive inequalities within core countries have been eroding the political legitimacy of the globalization-democracy project in the Global North and South, precipitating the current crisis of these twin projects. We will see toward the end of this chapter that, with the unraveling of the globalization and democratization project and the failing of the US global empire, the world is confronted with an emergent inter-imperial rivalry that could lead to world war among great powers.

Crisis of the US Hegemony in the 1970s

In the aftermath of World War II, the US came to become the hegemonic power among all other advanced capitalist countries. With the horror of the Great Depression and World War II that were attributable to an untamed free market and too low a labor share of income, leading to underconsumption and an overproduction crisis, the US led the Western industrialized world to adopt Keynesian and social democratic policies of government intervention, welfare state, full employment, high wages, and incorporation of organized labor into mainstream politics. These policies were also regarded as necessary for preventing the spread of communism to war-torn Europe.[1]

This paradigm of activist government and working-class power seemed to work well in the context of the long postwar boom of most Western capitalist countries, which were experiencing uninterrupted industrial expansion amid reconstruction from World War II.[2] The long postwar boom ended in the late 1960s. The full recovery of Europe and Japan led to an oversupply of manufactured products and hence increasing competition among industrialized powers. At the same time, prolonged empowerment of organized labor and the resulting long rise in wages fomented a wage-price spiral and curtailed profit.[3]

Over the 1970s, manufacturing profits fell in most industrialized economies,[4] while the 1973 oil crisis aggravated the downturn. Throughout the 1970s, the US and other advanced capitalist countries experienced frequent

---

1. Giovanni Arrighi, *The Long Twentieth Century: Money, Power, and Origins of Our Times* (London: Verso, 1994); Beverly Silver, *Forces of Labor: Workers' Movement and Globalization Since 1870* (New York: Cambridge University Press, 2003).
2. Robert Brenner, *The Boom and the Bubble: The US and the World Economy* (London: Verso, 2003).
3. Giovanni Arrighi, *Adam Smith in Beijing: Lineages of the Twenty-First Century* (London: Verso, 2007), Ch. 3–4.
4. Brenner, *The Boom and the Bubble*, 7–47.

and ever more severe recessions. A fiscal crisis of the state unfolded, which was worsened in the US by the failed, costly Vietnam War.[5]

The postwar economic boom and containment of communism, both led by the US, had hegemonic status across the capitalist camp of the Cold War, leading to a profitability crisis in most advanced capitalist countries. Meanwhile, the US defeat in Vietnam, and the Nixon administration's abandoning the gold standard amid a deteriorating fiscal crisis and gold outflow from the US, brought the US hegemonic status into serious doubt. As an attempt to revive capitalist profitability and restore US leadership in the world, Washington devised the globalization project, followed by the democratization project, in the 1980s.[6]

The Globalization-Democratization Project and the "New World Order"

As one of the primary sources of capitalist decline in advanced capitalist countries is a wage-price spiral driven by increasing wage demands of organized labor, the solution to the crisis has to involve the taming of organized labor. This is done through reorienting the state's domestic and foreign policy at the same time. Domestically, Thatcher and Reagan, who took power in 1979 and 1980 respectively, launched a direct attack on the unions.

Another key tactic the US power elite employed to discipline labor was a radical monetary tightening campaign in the name of stifling high inflation and rescuing the international credibility of the dollar under Paul Volcker as chair of the Federal Reserve, with the backing of Ronald Reagan as president. Recent research does show that beating back the wage demands of workers was the real and concealed motivation of the monetary-tightening campaign, as it could lead to the bankruptcy of enterprises, layoff of workers, and rising unemployment, dampening the bargaining power of organized labor.[7]

Besides this domestic-oriented tactic, another key means for the US state since Reagan to break the back of organized labor is to take advantage of the rise of low-cost export-oriented economies in the developing world under the "New International Division of Labor" in the 1970s to pursue a globalization project. The anti-labor policy plus globalization led to the massive exodus of

---

5. James O'Connor, *The Fiscal Crisis of the State* (New Brunswick, NJ: Transaction Publisher, 1979).
6. David Harvey, *A Brief History of Neoliberalism* (Oxford: Oxford University Press, 2007). See also Arrighi, *Adam Smith in Beijing*, Ch. 4–6; Giovanni Arrighi and Beverly Silver, *Chaos and Governance in the Modern World System* (Minneapolis: University of Minnesota Press, 1999), Ch. 3.
7. Ho-fung Hung and Daniel Thompson, "Money Supply, Class Power, and Inflation: Monetarism Reassessed," *American Sociological Review* 81, no. 3 (June 2016): 447–66, https://doi.org/10.1177/0003122416639609; Ho-fung Hung, "Global Capitalism in the Age of Trump", *Context* 17, no. 3 (Summer 2018): 40–45, https://doi.org/10.1177/1536504218792525.

manufacturing establishments from the US to low-wage countries like Mexico and East Asian newly industrializing economies. The rapid disappearance of manufacturing jobs amid a drastic capital outflow and importation of low-cost foreign manufactured products destroyed manufacturing employment and eroded the foundation of unions and other labor organizations. Wage growth fell off a cliff after 1980, as shown in Figure 5.1. The wage-price spiral as the root cause of the capitalist profitability crisis in the 1970s dissipated.

Since the 1980s, the US has been leading the world into globalization by opening its own market for foreign manufactured exports in exchange for its trading partners' openness to US investment. In the decades of globalization, the US has been running the largest trade deficit with the world, while every other major economy (Europe, China, Japan, etc.) has been running surpluses of different sizes. The result is a massive exodus of US manufacturers to low-wage countries like Mexico and China, manufacturing consumer goods there, and exporting them back to the US. This is how the global supply chain network, the bedrock of globalization, was born.

Under the global supply chain, export-oriented economies like Japan and China imported raw materials and components from around the world, and then turned these ingredients into final consumer products to be sent to the US and other consumer markets. The US is always "the consumer of last resort" for the global economy. Without US consumers, there would be no

Figure 5.1: Annual percentage change in average hourly earnings of production and nonsupervisory employees in private sector, 1965–2018

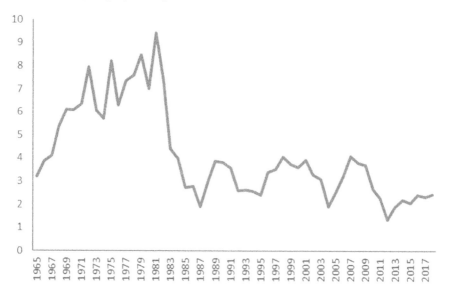

Source: Federal Reserve Bank of St Louis.

globalization. Lowering tariffs for exports from other economies entering the US market is a major tool that the US harnesses to lure other countries into the game of globalization. As Figure 5.2 shows, of the world biggest economies, the US is the only one with a big trade deficit, while all other export-oriented economies ran a large trade surplus. Subtracting the US from the equation, the circuit of global trade would simply unravel. As such, access to the US consumer market has been one of the biggest bargaining leverages the US possessed in multilateral or bilateral negotiations promoting trade globalization.

This special role of the US consumer market in the global economy is not accidental. It is the outcome of two historical developments dating decades or even a century ago. First, American political economy has been unique compared with other advanced capitalist economies since the turn of the twentieth century. The US tax system promotes consumption and represses savings through the absence of heavy federal-level sales tax and the presence of myriad tax deductions for specific kinds of consumption. In contrast, tax systems in France, Germany, and Japan, among others, have been promoting savings and export and repressing consumption through heavy value-added taxes. This uniqueness of US fiscal structure can be traced to its late nineteenth-century high agricultural productivity, which led to an overproduction problem that urged the federal government to remedy it through consumption-encouraging

Figure 5.2: External balance of goods and services of the US, Germany, Japan, and China, 1960–2016 (in current billion USD)

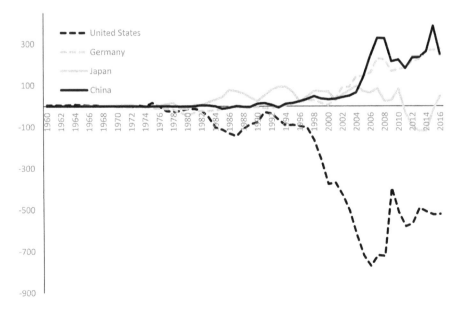

Source: World Bank.

policy. The state's responsiveness to this agricultural economic problem was in part a result of the importance of the Midwestern agricultural states' voters in the political process.[8]

While American capitalism has been uniquely biased toward consumerism, the role of the US dollar as the global reserve currency since 1945 allows and necessitates the US to run a large current account deficit with the world. To maintain the dollar's grip on the world economy as the default currency of international transaction and denominator of foreign exchange reserves in most countries, the US has to provide the world with sufficient liquidity through a massive outflow of its money. This is achieved through massive US capital exports and its equally massive import of goods from around the world. Despite the talk of the collapse of the dollar dominance since Nixon's abolition of the dollar's gold convertibility in 1971, the US dollar is still the dominant currency as an international transaction medium and foreign exchange reserve around the world today, and the euro ranks a distant second (see Figure 5.3).

This global dollar standard and the large demand for US dollars (USD) in the world economy allow the US to sell its debt internationally in its own currency at low interest rates. This is dubbed an "exorbitant privilege" of the US.[9] The establishment of the global dollar standard in the aftermath of WWII and its survival after Nixon's abolition of the gold standard in the 1971 has been grounded largely on US global military domination.[10]

The global dollar standard and US global military supremacy also facilitated the export of US capital to the world, another foundation of US leadership in globalization.[11] Ever since the end of WWII, the US has been the largest

8. Monica Prasad, *The Land of Too Much: American Abundance and the Paradox of Poverty* (Cambridge, MA: Harvard University Press, 2012).
9. Barry Eichengreen, *Exorbitant Privilege: The Rise and Fall of the Dollar and the Future of the International Monetary System* (Oxford: Oxford University Press, 2011).
10. David J. Katz, 2013, "Waging Financial War," *Parameters* 43, no. 4 (Winter 2013–14): 77–85, https://ufdcimages.uflib.ufl.edu/AA/00/06/26/77/00004/Winter-2013.pdf; Francis J. Gavin, "Ideas, Power, and the Politics of America's International Monetary Policy during the 1960s," in *Monetary Orders: Ambiguous Economics, Ubiquitous Politics*, ed. Jonathan Krishner (Ithaca, NY: Cornell University Press, 2003). See also Eichengreen, *Exorbitant Privilege*, 71; Susan Strange, "Germany and the World Monetary System," in *West Germany: An European Global Power*, ed. Wilfrid Kohl and Giorgio Basevi (Lexington, KY: Lexington Books, 1980), 45–62; Andrea Wong, "The Untold Story Behind Saudi Arabia's 41-Year U.S. Debt Secret," *Bloomberg*, May 30, 2016, https://www.bloomberg.com/news/features/2016-05-30/the-untold-story-behind-saudi-arabia-s-41-year-u-s-debt-secret; Adam S. Posen, "Why the Euro Will Not Rival the Dollar," *International Finance* 11, no. 1 (May 2008): 75–100, https://doi.org/10.1111/j.1468-2362.2008.00215.x; Jonathan Krishner, "Dollar Primacy and American Power: What's at Stake?" *Review of International Political Economy* 15, no. 3 (May 2008): 418–38, https://doi.org/10.1080/09692290801928798; Ho-fung Hung, "Cold War and China in the (Un)making of the Global Dollar Standard," *Political Power and Social Theory* 26 (2014): 53–80, https://doi.org/10.1108/S0198-8719(2014)0000026003.
11. Leo Panitch and Sam Gindin, *The Making of Global Capitalism: The Political Economy of American Empire* (New York: Verso, 2013).

Figure 5.3: Currency composition of allocated official foreign exchange reserves as of 2017 Q4

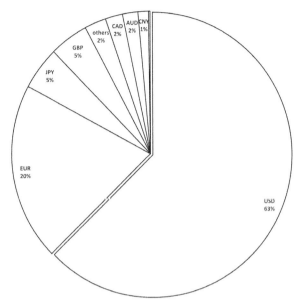

Source: IMF.

capital exporter in the world, shaping different economies across the globe after the image of its transnational corporations. US capital outflow accelerated after the 1980s and helped drive the globalization process, as shown in Figure 5.4. Such massive outflow was enabled by the privileged status of the USD, in which US capital is denominated. Such capital outflow was also sustained by the protection that the US military offered to US investors abroad. To a large extent, US rising capital exports and rising trade deficit are two sides of the same coin that complete the circuit of globalization. Consumption and capital export are like the positive and negative poles of a battery that drives the electric current to circulate the global economic circuit.

In sum, US leadership in the globalization project has been grounded on the US role as the largest consumer market of the world, the USD's hegemonic status in the global economy, the US role as the largest capital exporter of the world, and the supremacy of US military and geopolitical power. All these foundations of a US-led globalization interlocked with and reinforced one another, as shown in Figure 5.5.

US-led globalization was indeed a spatial fix of the crisis of capitalist profitability among advanced capitalist economies in the 1970s. Once the global free trade order was established, manufacturing outsourcing to low-wage countries became a core-wide trend. This, in conjunction with other measures to check the power of organized labor, successfully beat back wage growth

Figure 5.4: Net outflow of foreign direct investment of the US, Germany, Japan, and China (in current billion USD)

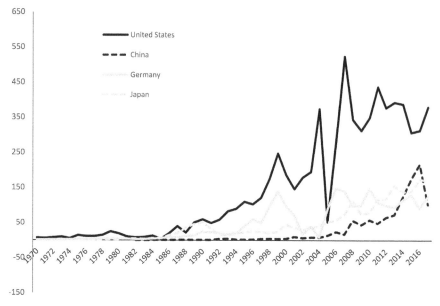

Source: World Bank.

and inflation. It did not restore profitability to the golden age level in the 1950s and 1960s, but it did arrest the fall of profit rate. Many developing countries, either ruled by leftwing, pro-Soviet regimes or even pro-US rightwing regimes, were initially resistant to this emerging global free trade order. Throughout the Cold War period, the dominant paradigm of development in the Global South was import-substitution industrialization. Many of the authoritarian regimes in the developing world jealously guarded their domestic market and restricted entry of foreign capital, leaving the biggest prizes of the economy to the politically well-connected monopolistic local enterprises, many of which lived off generous subsidies from the state.

To draw these developing countries into this game of US-led globalization, the US resorted to two main policy means. One is to take advantage of the international debt crisis since the 1980s to push through free market structural reforms of the heavily indebted countries via the policy loans offered by the IMF and the World Bank. The other is the democracy promotion project that started in the Reagan era.

These two paths went hand in hand in many times. When interest rates on the USD peaked to double digits under Volcker's tightening campaign in the early 1980s, many developing countries and three Eastern European countries that borrowed heavily to finance their development and consumption in the

Figure 5.5: Consumption, currency, and capital as foundations of US-led globalization

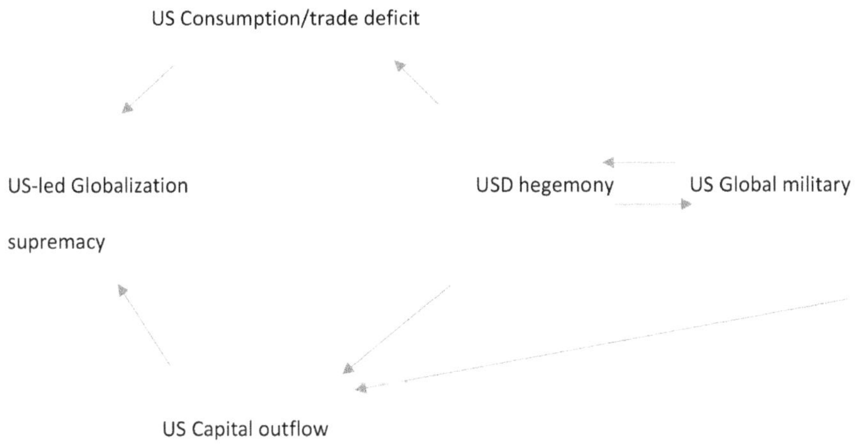

```
                    US Consumption/trade deficit

US-led Globalization            USD hegemony      US Global military
supremacy

                    US Capital outflow
```

1970s "Golden Age of development" under low interest rates and abundant USD credit suddenly became broke. The IMF and the World Bank stepped in to offer emergency loans to these countries to keep them afloat, but on the condition of pursuing structural adjustment reform, that is, to privatize state enterprises, open up their economy for foreign capital, and boost export. These policies came together as a vehicle to push these countries into the global circuit of free trade and free flow of capital.[12]

Going hand in hand with this push for market reform is the democracy-promotion agenda devised by the Reagan administration. Under this agenda, the US would no longer defend its traditional authoritarian allies in the developing world and would not back their crackdown on their people, should they face the challenges of a democratic revolution. The US would actively sponsor social forces in countries with regimes that were unfriendly and were not facing democratic challenge from within, to help these social forces grow and develop democratic movements against the government. Documentation research does illustrate this democracy-promotion agenda has been connected to the free market and the free trade promotion agenda of the 1980s.[13]

In the first instance, many US authoritarian allies have seen their power base weakened by the structural adjustment reform, and this erosion of their power base led to blossoming of democratic movements seeking liberalization and democratization. In stark contrast to the US policy in previous decades,

---

12. Manfred Bienefeld, "Structural Adjustment: Debt Collection Device or Development Policy?" *Review: Fernand Braudel Center* 23, no. 4 (Winter 2000): 533–82, https://www.jstor.org/stable/40241499.
13. William I. Robinson, *Promoting Polyarchy: Globalization, US Intervention, and Hegemony* (New York: Cambridge University Press, 1996).

when any democratic challenge to US authoritarian allies would be declared as infiltrated by communist influences and crushed with the backing of the US, Washington from the 1980s on adopted a hands-off policy to let many of these movements sweep away Washington's authoritarian allies, while cultivating a US-friendly post-transition leadership. The People's Revolution that toppled Marcos, a long- time Cold War ally of the US in 1986, is a case in point. In other cases when the authoritarian regime was not friendly to the US and held up well despite the erosion of their capability because of the debt crisis, the US, through such vehicles as the National Endowment for Democracy, actively supported and nurtured democratic opposition, armed or peaceful, within their societies, with an aim to topple the regime. The US support of the Contras that rebelled against the Sandinista regime in Nicaragua and the US support of Solidarity in Poland are cases in point.[14]

In either path, the resulting wave of democratization in the developing world and socialist bloc opened up a large group of countries for free trade and foreign investment, as the resulting democratic governments coming from this wave of democratization were invariably neoliberal, supporting their countries' incorporation into the US-led free trade order. This embrace of globalization is not only due to the pressure of structural adjustment reform from the IMF and the World Bank and of the anxiety to warrant US support of the new regime. It is also due to of the inherent affinity between democratic regimes and the support of free trade. Empirical analyses have confirmed that democratic regimes in developing countries are more likely to adopt an open economic policy than authoritarian ones are, as they need to warrant the popularity of their government through jobs creation, which could be done by participation into the global trading system and opening to foreign capital, taking advantage of abundant low-cost labor in these countries. And democratic regimes do not have the networks of politically well-connected state enterprises and monopolistic enterprises to protect them, as in the cases of the previous import-substitution-industrialization authoritarian regimes.[15]

As such, the globalization project and democratization project that the US has been pursuing since the 1980s were intertwined projects underlined by the effort to restore capitalist profitability and US global standing from the financial crisis of the 1970s. While the twin projects faced resistance from within the US—traditional industries and residual power of organized labor that fought against free trade—and outside the US—the constraint of the Cold War had not yet gone totally as the Soviet Union was still around—it marched on more vigorously after the collapse of the socialist bloc and the Soviet Union itself in the late 1980s and early 1990s, fostering the "New World Order" of US unipolar imperial domination in the 1990s. This globalization-democratization

---

14. Robinson, *Promoting Polyarchy*.
15. Helen V. Milner and Keiko Kubota, "Why the Move to Free Trade? Democracy and Trade Policy in the Developing Countries," *International Organization*. 59, no. 1 (January 2005): 107–43, https://doi.org/10.1017/S002081830505006X.

project reached its peak in the first decade of the twenty-first century before it unraveled under the weight of its own contradictions.

The Coming of the American Empire in the 2000s

In the aftermath of the collapse of the Soviet Union, two interpretations appeared of how the world order would become dominated by the US and the Western intellectual world. One is Francis Fukuyama's hyper-optimistic "end of history" thesis, as laid out in his book *The End of History and the Last Man*, published in 1992.[16] The other is Huntington's "clash of civilizations" thesis formulated first in his article published in *Foreign Affairs* in 1993 and elaborated in his 1996 book, *Clash of Civilizations*.[17] Despite divergent assumptions and analyses, the two theses in fact converge on the policy (either as explicit advocacy or implicit call) of scaling back the US's activism on the world stage, a shared advocacy that many overlooked.

For Fukuyama, the long history of competition between free market democratic capitalism and statist, autarkic communism had ended with the collapse of the Soviet Union. Humanity had finally reached the consensus that liberal democracy and free markets are the most effective form of organizing political and economic affairs, and little debate would ensue. With this new consensus, the world has already reached a liberal nirvana, or is on the way to reaching it. The implication is that, with any other alternative to liberal capitalism and liberal democracy discredited and defeated, there is little the US state was left to do other than just enjoy the peace dividend. Globalization and democracy no longer need to be promoted, as the world would naturally converge on this new consensual system and norm.

For Huntington, the collapse of the Soviet Union marks the end of the "civil war within the West," as both capitalism and communism stem from Western intellectual tradition. What came after the end of the Cold War is not the liberal nirvana that Fukuyama predicted but a return of more malign conflicts between civilizational-religious values that had defined world history for millennia, until they were suppressed under the rivalry between capitalism and communism. While capitalism and communism both originated from the Western Enlightenment and shared a lot of fundamental values such as progress, secularism, and material well-being of humanity, different civilizational-religious systems of values diverged fundamentally from one another. It follows that geopolitical conflict originating from civilizational rivalry would be more deadly and more difficult to contain. Further, Huntington thinks that democracy and free markets are grounded on Western civilization and are

---

16. Francis Fukuyama, *The End of History and the Last Man* (New York: Free Press, 1992).
17. Samuel Huntington, "The Clash of Civilizations?" *Foreign Affairs* 72, no. 3 (Summer 1993): 22–49; Samuel Huntington, *The Clash of Civilizations and the Remaking of World Order* (New York: Simon and Schuster, 1996).

inherently incompatible with many other world civilizations like Islam and Confucianism that are hostile to individualism. Huntington therefore argued that the US/Western project of promoting globalization and democracy is doomed to fail in the world regions that reverted to their traditional civilizational roots after the end of the Cold War. He therefore suggested that the US state should give up the illusionary project of promoting a free market and democracy to those regions but rather stay away from them and uphold the internal purity of an Anglo-Saxon culture by fending off immigrants from unfriendly civilizations—a theme that is elaborated in his controversial 2004 book, *Who Are We?*, that was deemed xenophobic and nativist.[18]

The post–Cold War world order and the US response to it turned out to be very different from what Fukuyama and Huntington foresaw and advocated. First of all, it was far from a liberal nirvana in which the world automatically converged to liberal democracy and free trade and required no active intervention by the US. The world did look this way in the early Clinton administration, Russia and Eastern Europe seemingly democratizing and opening to free trade and foreign investment, the end of apartheid in South Africa, and sweeping democratization and economic liberalization of Latin America, and so on. In the early 1990s, the Fukuyama excitement about the "end of history" prevailed. But as the 1990s moved on, malicious conflicts emerged and got out of control in different parts of the world in the aftermath of the dissolution of Soviet competition, threatening the democratic and free trade order of the post–Cold War world. The Rwanda genocide of 1994 and the breakup and then bloodshed in former Yugoslavia, on top of the rise of Al-Qaeda and escalating terrorist attacks targeting the West in general and the US in particular—including the World Trade Center bombing of 1993 and its bombing of two US embassies in Africa—urged the Clinton administration to become ever more interventionist in foreign policy, to stifle the rising chaos jeopardizing the stability of the free trade and democratic new world order. The escalating chaos in different parts of the world and pressure on the US to respond eventually moved the Clinton government to develop the doctrine of "humanitarian intervention," culminating in the US-led NATO bombing of Serbia over the genocide in Kosovo in 1999.

The global free trade economic order did not sail on smoothly either. What followed the expanding freedom of movement of capital in the world economy was the increasingly severe and frequent financial crises that threatened to become a generalized global financial crisis: first the Mexican peso crisis of 1994; then the Asian financial crisis of 1997–1998; followed by a series of similar crises in Turkey, Argentina, and Russia in 1999–2001. These crises that jeopardized capital from the US and other advanced capitalist countries having invested in different parts of the world in the end pushed the US to

---

18. Samuel Huntington, *Who Are We? The Challenges to America's National Identity* (New York: Simon and Schuster, 2004).

adopt an active bailout policy to prevent the contagion of each of these crises. In the bailout operation, Washington mobilized vast fiscal resources to rescue the economies struck by the crisis, either through the direct intervention by the US Treasury or indirectly through the IMF.

By the end of the Clinton administration, it became clear that the post–Cold War order based on democracy and free trade would not maintain and stabilize itself but rather depend a lot on US commitment of its fiscal resources to uphold it through military intervention and financial rescue operations. Far from a liberal nirvana, the unipolar, US-centered empire imagery emerged in conceptualizing the contour of the world order, as represented by Hardt and Negri's *Empire* (2000).

Just as the empire talk was taking off, the 9/11 terrorist attack shocked the world. At first, it looked like Huntington's clash of civilization thesis was being vindicated. But rather than following Huntington's advice of staying away from the "intolerant" Islamic civilizations inherently incompatible with liberal democracy, the Bush administration, having been taken over by neoconservatives advocating democracy promotion through military means, started the Afghanistan and Iraq wars in response to the attack, turbo-charging the democracy promotion project by committing large and enduring military forces to carry out regime change missions in both countries. The American empire talk then came to dictate most of the international relations discussion as the new foundation of global order.[19]

Just when the US military was still stuck in Iraq and Afghanistan, upholding their fragile democracy erected by the US marines, the 2008 financial crisis hit. It unfolded like many other earlier financial crises since the 1994 Mexican peso crisis—dubbed the first financial crisis of the twenty-first century—except that this time the epicenter of the crisis was Wall Street instead of outside the US. But the US response to the 2008 crisis is just a replay of its response to the earlier crises since the 1990s, that is, to adopt an active bailout policy by employing massive fiscal resources. With this hyper- intervention of the American state, the fragile global economy did hold up and recover somewhat from the crisis ten years on.

In retrospect, the globalization-democratization project that emerged in the 1980s continued into the 2000s and was perpetuated by the increasing fiscal and military commitment of the US. The democratic and free trade global order after the end of Cold War was increasingly founded upon a global imperial order centered on Washington. What enabled Washington to commit that many resources into maintaining its interventionist posture necessary for upholding the global democratic and free trade order, ironically, was Washington's quasi-alliance with China, a rising capitalist giant that denies

---

19. G. John Ikenberry, "Illusions of Empire: Defining the New American Order," *Foreign Affairs* 83, no. 2 (March/April 2004): 144–54.

and defies democratization and jealously guards its bureaucratically managed and protectionist state capitalist system.

Chimerica as the Foundation of the "New World Order"

China's reincorporation into the global economy started in 1972, when Nixon visited China and established a quasi-alliance relation with Beijing in the US struggle against Soviet expansion. This move was part of Washington's strategy to manage its defeat in Vietnam, recruiting China's help to contain Soviet influence in Vietnam, and to prevent the fall of dominos in Southeast Asia. In return for assisting the US in achieving this geopolitical goal, China effectively broke away from the trade embargo that had been placed on it since the Korean War. China's trade with capitalist countries, particularly trade via British Hong Kong, soared with the increasing importation of Western capital goods. China also obtained a lot of economic assistance in the form of grants and concessionary loans from Japan in the 1970s.[20]

While the actual incorporation of China into the global capitalist system was still precluded by Maoist ideological orthodoxy in the 1970s, China's capitalist transformation accelerated out in the open after Deng Xiaoping consolidated his power and China established formal diplomatic relations with the US in 1979. In the same year, the US started granting Most Favored Nation status to China, allowing Chinese goods to enter the US market at low tariffs.

China's capitalist transformation under Deng started with the decollectivization and restoration of a peasant economy in the countryside in the early 1980s, followed by the urban state enterprise reform and price reform in the late 1980s. In the 1990s, state-owned enterprise reform accelerated, and some of the biggest state enterprises were transformed into state-controlled profit-oriented transnational corporations. Through these stages, the main thrust of the reform is to decentralize the authority of economic planning and regulation and to open up the economy, first to Chinese diasporic capital in Asia and then to transnational capital from all over the world. Allured by the opportunities for profiteering activities, local governments with different preexisting resource endowments devised different strategies of capital accumulation. Lacking technical and management know-how as well as marketing networks in overseas markets, most local developmental or entrepreneurial states depend heavily on labor-seeking transnational capital to jump-start and sustain local economic growth.[21]

After a temporary setback following the revolt and its suppression in 1989, market reform accelerated again in 1992, after Deng dictated that faster

---

20. Ho-fung Hung, *The China Boom: Why China Will Not Rule the World* (New York: Columbia University Press, 2016), Chapter 2.
21. Ho-fung Hung, "Rise of China and the Global Accumulation Crisis," *Review of International Political Economy* 15, no. 2 (April 2008): 149–79, https://doi.org/10.1080/09692290701869654.

integration with the global economy is the way to prevent a Soviet-style breakdown of the communist regime. In the 1990s, Beijing pursued an aggressive neoliberal economic agenda throughout the 1990s, following the advice of US financial capital conscientiously. This approach provided the cover and incentive to the Clinton administration to set aside all doubts about the Communist Party of China (CCP) regime in the aftermath of Tiananmen and to adopt an engagement policy toward China in the name of promoting human rights improvement through enhancing economic freedom and openness.

In the 1990s, export-oriented manufacturing started to roar in China. Though the export sector had emerged in the 1980s, thanks to the beginning of the inflow of Hong Kong manufacturing capital, it did not go far, as most surplus labor in the countryside was retained in the rural collective enterprises (known as township and village enterprises, or TVEs) and the booming agricultural sector. The one-off devaluation of the renminbi (RMB, the Chinese currency) against the dollar by more than 30 percent in 1994, followed by a peg to the dollar, was a boost to China's export manufacturing in the 1990s. The Clinton administration's 1994 decision to delink trade relations with China from human rights considerations, to the dismay of organized labor and human rights activists in the US, opened the door of the US market to Chinese exports. China's eventual accession to the World Trade Organization (WTO) in 2001 integrated China fully into the US-led global free trade circuit as a formidable export engine.

One key advantage enabling China's export-oriented success was the protracted low wage of Chinese manufacturing, given China's "unlimited supply" of rural surplus labor. China's wage level had been much lower than that of other East Asian exporters in their comparable phase of development, even with the recent wage increase in coastal cities. The low wage regime results in low household income growth compared to GDP growth and therefore a low consumption share of the economy (see Figure 5.6).

As China's productive capacity kept growing and its consumption growth did not keep up, China relied heavily on the global market to consume its products. The US constituted the single most important market of China's exports, only to be surpassed recently by the EU as a whole. The rapid expansion of China's export-oriented industries has already made China the biggest exporter to the US of all Asian exporters.[22]

With China's huge army of reserve labor—which was not only unparalleled by other developing countries in number but was marked by its good health and high level of literacy, both legacies of socialized health care and education in the Mao era—China became the primary destination of US manufacturing off-shoring in the 1990s and 2000s. As Acemoglu et al. point out, China's accession to the WTO and China's free trade with the US accounted for the loss of more than two million manufacturing jobs in the US from 1999

---

22. Hung, *The China Boom*, Table 3.6.

Figure 5.6: GDP per capita, household income per capita, and consumption per capita of China, 1978–2016

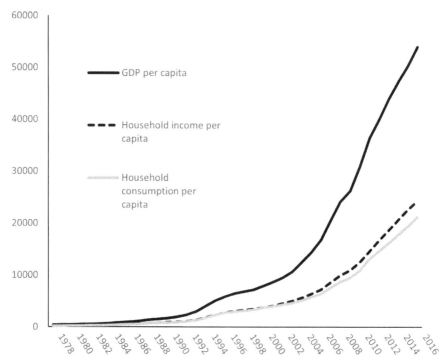

Source: China's National Bureau of Statistics.

to 2011.[23] If the globalization project was primarily a project to disempower organized labor by destroying jobs through manufacturing outsourcing, then the US effort to recruit China into the global circuit of free trade by offering Chinese goods low-tariff access to the US market since 1979 and helping its accession into the WTO in 2001 was a policy that hit the jackpot.

Besides the export sector, China's fixed asset investment including infrastructure construction and housing construction undertaken mostly by the state sector also play an important role in driving the Chinese economy. But most of the fixed asset investment in the Chinese economy was financed by bank lending enabled by expanding the RMB supply. A large portion of RMB liquidity in the banking system was backed up by expanding foreign exchange

---

23. Daron Acemoglu, David Autor, David Dorn, Gordon H. Hanson, and Brendan Price, "Import Competition and the Great Employment Sag of the 2000s," *Journal of Labor Economics* 34, S1 part 2 (January 2016): S141–98, https://doi.org/10.1086/682384; Robert E. Scott and Zane Mokhiber, "The China Toll Deepens: Growth in the Bilateral Trade Deficit between 2001 and 2017 Cost 3.4 Million U.S. Jobs, with Losses in Every State and Congressional District," Economic Policy Institute, Washington, DC, October 23, 2018, https://www.epi.org/files/pdf/156645.pdf.

reserves, mainly in USD, originating mostly from the trade surplus and export sector. Without the backup of growing foreign exchange reserves, the aggressive expansion of the money supply in RMB would have caused depreciation and capital flight that would have destabilized China's financial system, like what many Southeast Asia economies encountered on the eve of the 1997–1998 Asian financial crisis. The twin engine of investment and exports in China's economic boom is, therefore, a single engine of export. It is not exaggerating to say China's export sector is the mother of its economic boom.[24] In other words, the China boom has been driven by China's inclusion into the global circuit of free trade, which is in turn driven largely by US consumption. Private consumption has been surely rising in China. But the increase in production capacity outpaces the increase in consumption, bringing forth a chronic excess capacity that has been digested by deficit countries, most importantly the US as the consumer of last resort.

The Chinese economy has relied heavily on exports as its main source of dynamism, and the overwhelming majority of its exports have been invoiced in USD. The chronic trade surplus therefore helped China rake in increasing amounts of USD that denominate most of its expanding foreign exchange reserves. With the expanding holding of USD, China's central bank had little choice other than investing nearly all of it in US Treasuries as the safest and most liquid USD-denominated asset in the world market, helping finance the expanding US fiscal deficit. Figure 5.7 shows that China's holdings of US Treasuries increased rapidly with the expansion of China's foreign exchange reserves since 2001, becoming the world's largest foreign holder of US Treasuries. In the decade after the 2008 financial crisis, China's holding of US Treasuries effectively doubled.

As such, China not only helped the US achieve its goal of trade globalization by offering its abundant low-cost labor to suck in manufacturing capital from the US and around the world, but it also actively supported the consolidation of the US global empire by financing Washington's expanding budget deficit essential to its foreign military intervention and bailout policy that maintains the stability of the global economy amid recurrent systemic financial crises. This US-China symbiosis, dubbed "Chimerica" by Nial Ferguson,[25] is the foundation of the US global empire.

One of the most important glues that holds Chimerica and the global economy together is the global dollar standard. With a global dollar standard, the US Federal Reserve creates money that is used to pay for Chinese manufactures. The Chinese exporters, after earning their USD, surrender their USD holdings to China's central bank, which in turn invests the USD in US Treasury bonds. In such an arrangement, the US Federal Reserve prints money to pay

---

24. Hung, *The China Boom*, Chapter 3.
25. Niall Ferguson and Moritz Schularick, "'Chimerica' and the Global Asset Market Boom," *International Finance* 10, no. 3 (Winter 2007): 215–39, https://doi.org/10.1111/j.1468-2362.2007.00210.x.

Figure 5.7: China's holdings of US treasuries, in billion USD and in percentage

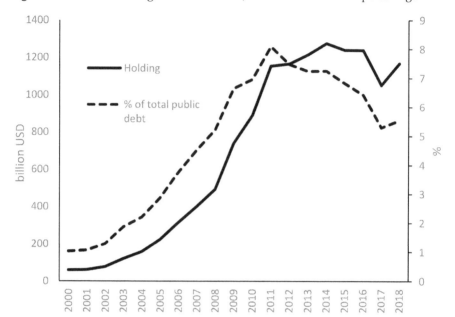

Source: US Treasuries and Federal Reserve of St. Louis.

for the expanding bill of the US state, due to China raking in consumer goods manufactured in China along the way. China also spends a large portion of its USD earnings to acquire raw materials and parts of manufactured products from other parts of the world, pumping the USD back into the global circuit of trade and hence enhancing its use as an international transaction currency.

There has been some effort on the part of China to rid Chinese economic dependence on the USD by promoting the international status of RMB. It is exactly what the Chinese government has claimed to aim at in its effort to internationalize the use of the RMB in recent years. Between 2011 and 2015, the ranking of the use of the RMB in international payments has shot up from below the top fifteen currencies to the fifth as of November 2015, trailing behind the USD, the euro, the pound sterling, and the yen. This appears to be an impressive achievement. But a more careful look into the data shows that the fifth rank of RMB represents only 2.28 percent of all international payments, still far below 42.7 percent for USD and 29.5 percent for the euro, as shown in Figure 5.8.

More importantly, of the 2.28 percent of international payments carried out in RMB, 70.5 percent are transactions done in Hong Kong—a former British colony that became an offshore market under Chinese sovereignty with its own USD-pegged currency and a façade of autonomy despite Beijing's increasing control of its financial sector, as shown in Figure 5.9.

Figure 5.8: Top currencies' shares in international payments as of November 2015 based on value

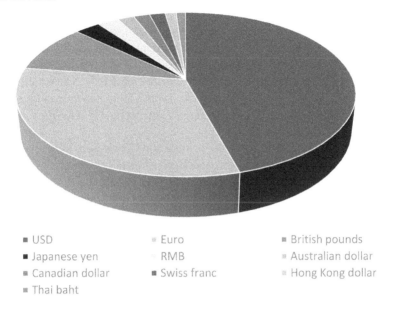

- USD
- Japanese yen
- Canadian dollar
- Thai baht
- Euro
- RMB
- Swiss franc
- British pounds
- Australian dollar
- Hong Kong dollar

Source: SWIFT.

Figure 5.9: Customer-initiated and institutional RMB payments (inbound and outbound traffic) by markets as of November 2015

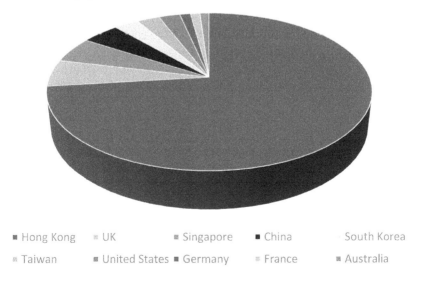

- Hong Kong
- Taiwan
- UK
- United States
- Singapore
- Germany
- China
- France
- South Korea
- Australia

Source: SWIFT.

After 2015, partly because of the heavy-handed crackdown on capital flight following the stock market rout and drastic depreciation of RMB in the summer of 2015, the ranking of the international use of RMB fell, and as of spring 2018, its share of international payments slipped to 1 percent, while 70 percent of those international payments were still conducted in Hong Kong. Insofar as the CCP is not yet confident enough to liberalize its financial system and open up its capital account, RMB will not be freely convertible and its international use will remain limited. As such, China's export engine and its economy at large will continue to be dependent on the USD for the foreseeable future.

The Chimerica formation as the foundation of the globalization-democratization project undertaken by the American empire is ironic. First, China has been maintaining its state capitalist system and even many of its mercantilist policies despite its stated commitment to global free trade. Also, China has been an authoritarian country and its authoritarian regime has manifested stark resilience. The most ironic part of this irony is that China's state capitalist system and its authoritarian regime managed to sustain through all the challenges in the 1990s and 2000s because of China's high-speed economic growth, which is largely attributable to the US policy of incorporating China into the global trading system despite its authoritarian state capitalist system, a policy choice that the US made in the 1990s.

Unraveling of the Globalization-Democratization Project

Just as the globalization project of the American empire toward the end of the 1990s reached its zenith with the integration of China into the world trading system as the biggest prize, the project encountered a legitimacy crisis in the US.

While the globalization project is to revive capitalist profitability of the advanced capitalist economies and has succeeded in achieving this by effectively beating back organized labor and disciplining the working class in those economies, politicians pursuing globalization have always obtained political legitimacy in the electoral process in the Global North through the promise of "trickling down"; that is, globalization would benefit the corporate sector first through restoring viability of the capitalist economy, and the benefits would eventually spread downward and benefit everyone. However, now it is very well known through Milanovic's elephant curve that this trickling down never happens. While income and the living standard of the global elite from advanced capitalist countries and the vast population of the emerging world, most notably China, saw significant growth amid globalization from 1988 to 2008, the living standard of the working class and middle class in the Global North saw no improvement and even a decline in real terms.[26]

---

26. Branko Milanovic, *Global Inequality: A New Approach for the Age of Globalization Cambridge* (Cambridge, MA: Harvard University Press, 2016).

With China's vast army of reserve labor—which was not only unparalleled by other developing countries in number but was marked by its good health and a high level of literacy, both legacies of socialized health care and education in the Mao era—China became the primary destination of US manufacturing off-shoring in the 1990s and 2000s. As Acemoglu et al. point out, China's accession to the WTO and China's free trade with the US had accounted for the loss of more than two million manufacturing jobs in the US from 1999 to 2011.[27] If the globalization project was primarily a project to disempower organized labor by destroying jobs through manufacturing outsourcing, then US effort in recruiting China into the global circuit of free trade by offering Chinese goods low-tariff access to the US market since 1979 and helping its accession into the WTO in 2001 is one that hits the jackpot.

But with the hemorrhage of manufacturing employments—which had been a stable source of income in many working-class communities across the US—popular backlash against globalization has been gathering speed in the US, first signaled by the massive and violent anti-WTO protests in Seattle in 1999. In the 2000s, many early promoters of the globalization project, from financier George Soros to Clinton-era economic advisors like Joseph Stiglitz and Lawrence Summer, have been warning about eroding popular support for the globalization project and warned that if no redistributive policies—like employment insurance that compensates workers who lose their jobs owing to globalization and paid by beneficiaries of globalization—are put in place, globalization will finally lose its political support and will sooner or later be rejected by voters.[28] While this worry has been very well taken, this discussion has failed to bring any meaningful policy change, and the losers of globalization continue to lose.

The prophecy about the breakdown of political legitimacy for the globalization project in the Global North became a reality with the Brexit referendum and the election of Donald Trump in the US in 2016. These two instances, together with rising rightwing populist parties across Europe, cast a long shadow over the future of the globalization project.

This populist politics hit the US during its 2016 presidential election. In the Democratic primary election, centrist candidate Hilary Clinton, whose husband's presidency was tied to the policy of free trade globalization and embracing China into the global trading system, was surprisingly pressed by Bernie Sanders, who had been strong in Midwestern rustbelt states among

---

27. Acemoglu et al., "Import Competition and the Great Employment Sag of the 2000s," 141–93; Scott and Mokhiber, "The China Toll Deepens," https://files.epi.org/pdf/156645.pdf.
28. George Soros, *The Crisis Of Global Capitalism: Open Society Endangered* (New York: Public Affairs, 1998); Joseph Stiglitz, *Globalization and Its Discontents* (New York: W. W. Norton, 2002); David Leonhardt, "Larry Summer's Evolution," *New York Times Magazine*, June 10, 2007, https://www.nytimes.com/2007/06/10/magazine/10wwln-summers-t.html; Dani Rodrik, *The Globalization Paradox: Democracy and the Future of the World Economy* (New York: W. W. Norton), 2012.

union and working-class voters. Sanders's record of anti-globalization in the US Congress since 1990 has been consistent. As we have seen in the last chapter, in 1994, when most of the Democratic Party had been swayed toward giving up on human rights conditions on Chinese exports' low-tariff access to US market, Sanders was among the very few still adamantly advocating ending China's low-tariff access to the US market once and for all. In 2016, it appeared that his long-time rejection of free trade with China had been right, and his campaign platform of protecting American jobs by raising tariffs became popular in the rustbelt states.

In the end, Sanders lost the primaries to Clinton, who moved on to compete with the Republican candidate, Donald Trump, who had a similar anti-free trade stance as Bernie Sanders despite their vast differences on immigration, climate change, and most other issues. In the end, Trump won marginally in the traditionally Democratic strongholds of Wisconsin, Michigan, and Pennsylvania. Surveys show that Trump's upset victory there was grounded in the votes from blue-collar workers and union families, some of whom voted for Sanders in the primary and Trump in the general election. It was the first time an anti-globalization candidate, who has been advocating the use of heavy tariffs to pressure China on all kinds of issues, won an election and became the president.

In Trump's four years in office, Washington reversed the continuous march for globalization by withdrawing the US from trade agreements in negotiations, most notably the Trans-Pacific Partnership (TPP) and the Transatlantic Trade and Investment Partnership (TTIP). They are the multilateral free trade pacts that the Obama administration had been negotiating with Asian countries and the European Union respectively. When the Trump administration declared the end of US participation in those trade agreements, anti-trade leftists on the Democratic side like Bernie Sanders hailed the move as the right one. The Trump administration also started trade wars with other major trading partners. His campaign to raise tariffs covers US rivals (China) and allies (such as South Korea, EU, and Canada) alike.

Trump's four years in the White House is the personalization of the popular backlash against globalization in the US. Largely attributable to Washington's mishandling of the COVID-19 pandemic in an election year, Trump lost the 2020 presidential election, marginally in a number of key battleground states. Though Joseph Biden, a centrist Democrat in support of globalization throughout his political career, won the presidency, the political terrain regarding trade in the US has shifted fundamentally. It is expected that he will be very cautious not to hastily restart the push for free trade globalization.

While the US is turning against free trade globalization, China continues to be mercantilist in its economic policies seventeen years after its accession to the WTO. Its economy has never been as open to foreign capital as promised. And after attaining the status of the second-largest economy poised to overtake the US, the Communist Party-state was starting to use its advantage of size relative to marginalized private enterprises and foreign corporations in its domestic economy and allow its state-owned companies to dominate. It has also been accused of aggressively dumping its surplus capacity, under generous state subsidies, to markets around the world. The emergence of such a mercantilist power in defiance of the stated principles of open markets and free trade has eroded the legitimacy of multilateral organizations and trade agreements grounded on such principles. While there have been discussions about China replacing the US as the new leader of globalization, this is no more than wishful thinking. As a surplus country that needs to export its spare capacity and surplus goods, China can never replace the US's unique role as the world's consumer of last resort.

In tandem with the crisis of the globalization project is the crisis of the democratization project, and it is largely attributable to the rise of authoritarian China. As we have seen, the democracy- promotion project led by the US has been dependent on the activism of the US state, from humanitarian intervention to neoconservative regime change, on top of the modest aid that the US state provided to the democratic political forces it meant to cultivate across the globe. Authoritarian China, with its massive purchase of US Treasuries, ironically helped provide the financial resources for this project.

But as China's global economic weight grows, its ambition of extending its geopolitical clout to the developing world also grows. Over the last decade, China has been diverting an ever larger part of its foreign exchange reserves to providing loans and aid to its authoritarian allies in the Global South, from Zimbabwe to Iran and Venezuela and North Korea. As a result, many of these regimes could now break the US-led sanction regime and find an alternative source of finance for their development. While this China agenda of expanding its influence in the developing world was piecemeal in the 2000s, by the 2010s, it had become an all-out strategy to carve out China's sphere of influence at the expense of US influence, particularly after Xi Jinping's rise to power in 2012. As many authoritarian regimes in the Global South now receive increasing support from China in one form or other, the wave of democratization starting in the 1990s faded out and has been replaced by authoritarian resilience and a wave of authoritarian comebacks.

Conclusion: From "New World Order" to New Inter-imperial Rivalry

In the unipolar-imperial moment at the end of the Cold War, the US restored capitalist profitability and its leadership in the global system through its globalization-democratization projects. But the resulting "New World Order" is far from stable. Globalization of capital brings about financial crises that break out every once in a while in different parts of the world, starting with the

Mexican peso crisis of 1994 and culminating in the Wall Street meltdown in 2008. These crises in the end require Washington's active intervention and vast financial resources to contain. Forces hostile to Western domination unleashed in the aftermath of the Cold War in the developing world also led to the rise of regional dictators and terrorist groups in defiance of the West in general and the US in particular. These forces also require massive resources of the US to contain and beat them back. This led to the increasing militarization of the US democracy-promotion project, peaking in the neoconservative regime change project in the 2000s.

The vast fiscal and financial resources required by such activist intervention by Washington in maintaining the world order grounded on globalism and democracy is, ironically, provided in large part by state capitalist and authoritarian China, whose growth into a capitalist giant was made possible by US support of its Communist Party-state's quest for reincorporation into the global capitalist system since the 1980s. While supporting the US global empire building and its globalization-democratization project, China also started to become an emerging, competing imperial power of its own, increasingly capable of exporting its capital and projecting its political influence to the developing world at the expense of the US.

In 2009–2010, the Chinese government redoubled state bank lending to boost fixed asset investment of the state sector to stimulate the Chinese economy out of the fallout of the global financial crisis that made China's export engine stall. In the aftermath of the stimulus, the Chinese economy, the state sector in particular, was left with a high level of indebtedness, excess capacity, and shrinking room for profitability in the domestic market. Pronounced slowdown of the economy ensued, underlying the financial and currency crash in the summer of 2015. The domestic economic crisis of China created an urge for China's state enterprises to accelerate their expansion overseas as a way to export their excess capacity. This is an important impetus behind China's Belt and Road Initiative, which was inaugurated in 2013 to offer developmental finance to infrastructure construction projects in Central Asian, Southeast Asian, and South Asian countries, which in turn hired Chinese companies as contractors or procured Chinese materials. China's increasing capital exports to the developing world urged Beijing to experiment on different ways to project its military and political powers afar, to protect its foreign investment, leading China to carve out its own sphere of influence in competition with the US security umbrella in the Indo-Pacific region.[29]

With China rising as an alternative source of financial, political, and military support, authoritarian or semi-authoritarian powers in the developing

---

29. Ho-fung Hung, "China and the Global South," in *Fateful Decisions: Choices That Will Shape China's Future*, ed. Thomas Fingar and Jean Oi (Palo Alto, CA: Stanford University Press, 2020).

world hostile to the US gain ample new room for consolidation and expansion. This, in combination with the working-class revolt against globalization in the US that led to the domination of anti-trade politics, as manifested in multi-front trade wars initiated by the Trump administration after 2016, significantly undermined the globalization-democratization project of the US. While US global domination fades and China is starting to build its sphere of influence in parts of the developing world, China is not yet ready to take on the role of a new global leader capable of constructing a stable new world order. This results in a fragmentation of global political-economic power. The rise of China as an alternative source of financial and political support outside the US-led bloc enables the survival and empowerment of a group of large powers despite US sanctions. Russia and Iran are the two prominent examples. With the lifeline from China, these giant powers, together with a number of smaller states, from North Korea to Venezuela, equally reliant on Chinese resources to perpetuate their regime survival, actively expand their geopolitical influence over their neighbors, eroding US influence.

Given this new development, the US Pentagon's National Defense White Paper published in the spring of 2018 suggests that the US should devote less effort to combating terrorist groups and more resources to counteract the rising "revisionist powers," most notably China and Russia, plus Iran, as the highest priority.[30] With the unraveling of Chimerica and the globalization-democracy project, the world order is descending into competition between conflicting spheres of influence dominated by rival powers. This leads to a situation resembling the competition of a few Great Powers—the UK, France, Germany, Russia, the US, Japan, etc.—after the British empire weakened as a global hegemon at the turn of the twentieth century. Back in the early twentieth century, this inter-imperial rivalry moved from economic competition to geopolitical contest to world war. The incipient inter-imperial rivalry of today could well lead to a new form of stable, multipolar global governance based on a plurality of democratic and authoritarian regimes, as the efforts in building the G-20 as the new core of global governance in the aftermath of the 2008 global financial crisis showcased. This rivalry could also bring escalating conflict among different empires and power blocs resembling the early twentieth century rivalry, paving the way to world wars. Which trajectory will prevail is still too early to tell. This is a time of great uncertainty, when choices and actions of states, corporations, and social movements matter most.

---

30. Department of Defense, United States of America. *National Defense Strategy of The United States of America*, January 19, 2018, https://dod.defense.gov/Portals/1/Documents/pubs/2018-National-Defense-Strategy-Summary.pdf.

6
The Coming of the Economic Warring States?

China-USA Rivalry and Asian Disorder in the Age of De-globalization

Guoguang Wu

Introduction

This chapter takes a historical comparative perspective to analyze the shaping of the East Asian international political-economic order with the emergence of the China-USA rivalry.[1] First of all, it attempts to draw an analogy between current East Asian international relations by political economy and inter-state politics of wars during the ancient Chinese Warring States period. Some prominent similarities will be compared, to set a framework focusing on when a powerful state arises and is perceived as the major threat to other states in the existing order, how pertinent states respond with options between two basic strategies, *hezong* (合縱), or a multilateral coalition against the rising threat, and *lianheng* (連橫), the rising-power centered bilateral coalitions with each of the other states.[2] Different from the ancient Chinese Warring States when their concerns were preoccupied by state survival and territorial safety, the emerging China-USA rivalry and current East Asian regional international relations are primarily understood in this chapter with emphasis on the economic realm though geopolitical and traditional security will not be excluded from the background of analysis.

---

1. The author would like to thank Yuesheng Xu for her research assistance in making the figures in the chapter.
2. The Chinese Warring States (*zhanguo*, or 戰國) occurred in the historical period of 475–221 BCE. What must be highlighted here is that, although the Warring States period lasted for more than two hundred years, during which huge changes took place in inter-state relations, this historical period is often remembered as a prolonged process of the rise of Qin and marked by the situation of *hezong* versus *lianheng*. It is in this sense that this chapter compares it with current East Asian international relations, in which China is on rise and international strategies similar to *hezong* (or multilateralism, in a contemporary sense) and *lianheng* (or bilateralism) are confronting one another. Some more historical information will be provided and discussed later.

This focus on geo-economics is not only for convenience of analysis nor totally due to the author's limited expertise but a logical extension of a theory of the economic state that highlights state transformation with globalization toward the direction of "economics as politics."[3] In fact, this article attributes the deep cause of the recent emergence of the China-USA rivalry to the rise of the economic state in both nations, especially in the United States, where globalization has greatly undermined democracy, increased elites' economic cooperation with and dependence on effective authoritarian regimes in countries such as China, and jeopardized American national interest as an existing hegemon in international relations. The Trump administration's turn to policies of de-globalization to remedy the problem, however, further drives forward the long-term institutional turn toward the economic state in the US. It is at such a juncture of globalization intertwining with de-globalization that arises in the China-USA rivalry, which has so far (as of this writing) primarily and prominently emerged in the economic realm.

East Asia in general and the People's Republic of China in particular have greatly benefitted from their involvement in globalization; deep economic interdependence has grown among the countries of the region (except North Korea) and their connections with the US. Such interdependence, however, is combined with an asymmetry in each of these states' economic relationships with China in advantaging the latter, and they are more vulnerable than is China in their bilateral partnerships with the rising economic giant.[4] It is especially so if measured with trade connections, as this chapter will show. This structural element, the chapter will argue, greatly constrains the strategic options for at least five pertinent states (or state-like entities of international relations) in the region: South Korea, Japan, Taiwan, ASEAN (the Association of South East Asian Nations, viewed as one entity in this chapter), and the US itself in dealing with China. The de-globalization inclination the US now takes, furthermore, offers no option similar to *hezong* for the other four states, while China's aggressive pursuit of *lianheng* provides both lures and duress to the pertinent states. We know that the ancient Chinese Warring States period concluded with the success of the *lianheng* strategy adopted by Qin, the rising power that, though making a "friendship" with each of the six states, eventually conquered all of them for the establishment of the Qin empire. This chapter would not predict the success of China in gaining East Asian states' cooperation against the US, but it seems truly difficult for the US with its de-globalization inclination to gain these states' support in its rivalry with China, at least not their cooperation against China in the economic realm.

---

3. Guoguang Wu, *Globalization against Democracy: A Political Economy of Capitalism after Its Global Triumph* (Cambridge: Cambridge University Press, 2017).
4. For an analysis of symmetry/asymmetry and vulnerability in the interdependence relationship, see Robert O. Keohane and Joseph S. Nye, *Power and Interdependence*, 2nd ed. (New York: Harper Collins, 1989).

The economy is not everything, of course, even with the rise of the economic state. When the security concerns of East Asian states are also taken into consideration, the likely picture would be these states vacillating in choosing sides and being ineffective in coordinating their security alliances with the US and their economic cooperation with the PRC. To this chapter, the prevalence of the dilemma among these states will create disorder in East Asia.

East Asia under the China-USA Rivalry: How Does It Resemble the Warring States?

This chapter draws an analogy between the Chinese Warring States in the historical period 475–221 BCE and current East Asia international relations under China-USA rivalry in political economy. It is a bit unorthodox to make such a comparison, as there is a tremendous gap of time spanning more than two thousand years between the two cases, and, with such a gap, profound differences exist, and fundamental changes have taken place that have almost entirely reshaped human life. One may immediately notice the obvious dissimilarity between the geographic scope the Chinese Warring States covered and the international nature of the East Asian political economy plus its involvement of the US in regional geo-economics with globalization. Experts of history and international relations, however, have pointed out how the ancient Chinese Warring States formed an international system in the sense that multiple states interacted with each other without the existence of a central authority.[5] This has provided the basis for the comparison.

Fully aware of the various fundamental limitations of the analogy, this chapter puts its emphasis of the historical comparison on the analysis of how the differences within a framework of similarities can possibly help deepen the understanding of the political economy emerging in current East Asia. For this purpose, it will first look at what similarities there might be between the Chinese Warring States and current East Asia. The sketch map of the Chinese Warring States in Figure 6.1 may help to make some basic sense of what this chapter is going to suggest concerning the analogy.

Of the major seven states shown on the sketch map, Qin was a rising power that posed a great threat to others. Two major different strategies, therefore, were proposed for either resisting the rise of Qin or making an alliance with Qin, which are known as *hezong* and *lianheng*, respectively.[6] Roughly, *hezong*

---

5. Richard L. Walker, *The Multi-State System of Ancient China* (Hamden, CT: The Shoe String Press, 1953); Victoria Tin-bor Hui, *War and State Formation in Ancient China and Early Modern Europe* (New York: Cambridge University Press, 2005).
6. Hui defines *hezong* and *lianheng* in the following way: "The *hezong* strategy followed the rationale of the balance of power by calling for uniting of weaker states to resist the strongest"; *lianheng* "sought to forestall and break up *hezong* alliances by playing off the various states against one another with threats and bribes, and then marshalling overwhelming

Figure 6.1: The Chinese Warring States, c. 386 BCE

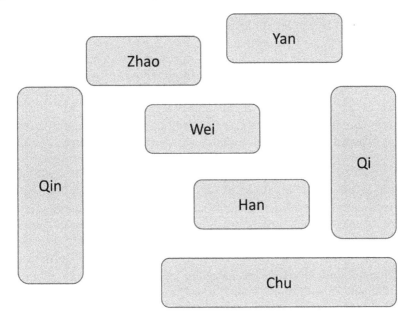

Source: Author. For relevant historical and geographic information, see Tan Qixiang, ed., *Jianming Zhongguo lishi ditu ji* (譚其驤主編,《簡明中國歷史地圖集》) [Concise historical atlas of China] (Beijing: Zhongguo ditu chubanshe, 1991), 13–14; and Yang Kuan, *Zhanguo shi* (楊寬,《戰國史》) [A history of the Warring States] (Shanghai: Shanghai renmin chubanshe, 1961). In the Chinese language, these seven states are: 秦, 趙, 魏, 韓, 楚, 燕, 齊.

highlights multilateral coalitions among the six states against Qin, while *lianheng* counters it by making a bilateral coalition between Qin and each of the six states. The latter strategy, as a matter of fact, wins the contest for Qin, resulting in their conquering of all other states to establish the Qin empire in 221 BCE. During the approximately 150 years before 221 BCE, however, the six states were often swinging between the two strategies. Neither the traditional hegemon state, Qi, nor another existing power, Chu, were exceptions from such a vacillation in dealing with Qin; in fact, Chu was the first of the six to build a bilateral coalition with Qin in hope of self-protection. And Qi made such a choice, which allowed Qin to first conquer those neighboring states and, in the process, to become stronger and stronger, eventually to the extent

---

force to conquer them seriatim." She highlights that they were "based on the geographical locations of the major states." Hui, *War and State Formation*, 67–68. Here, I formulate my own interpretation and definitions of *hezong* and *lianheng* to highlight their confrontation according to multilateralism excluding Qin versus Qin-centered bilateralism.

that it was impossible for Qi, the last of the six states to be conquered by Qin, to resist.[7]

Now let us turn to a sketch map of East Asia in the current stage of international relations with the emergence of the China-USA rivalry (Figure 6.2).

The similarities of the second sketch map to the Chinese Warring States are striking, of which three should be highlighted. First, similar to Qin in Figure 6.1, China in Figure 6.2 is rising as a great power, and it has the potential and strong inclination to threaten the other six states (or state-like entities in international relations; this point will not be repeated) though mostly not in the form of territorial annexation, which the next section will discuss. As we are talking about this issue in 2020, most countries depicted here are partially aware of China's threat. Second, the US, roughly in the position of Qi as in Figure 6.1, while being similar to the historical Qi as the traditional superpower and declining hegemon, is locked in interdependence with China so deeply that various advocates of further China-USA cooperation such as "Chinamerica" had been fairly common for many years until very recently.[8] Third, there are, as in the first map, also seven state entities on the second sketch map,[9] and, besides China and the US, most of those smaller entities, with the sole exception of North Korea, have traditionally since the end of the World War II been allies of the US. But China has also developed strong connections with them since the end of the Cold War, especially in economic terms, if not in security, as also took place between Qin and each of the six states on the first map.

---

7. The classic account of the history of the Warring States is *Zhanguo ce* 戰國策 [Stratagems of the Warring States], for which see, for example, He Jianzhang, *Zhanguo ce zhushi* 戰國策註釋 [Annotated stratagems of the Warring States] (Beijing: Zhonghua shuju, 1990), 3 vols. For various narratives of the history, see, for instance, Fan Wenlan, *Zhongguo tongshi* [A general history of China] (Beijing: Renmin chubanshe, 1978), vol. 1, ch. 5; Lü Simian, *Xianqin shi* [A pre-Qin history] (Hong Kong: Taiping shuju, 1980), ch. 9; Qian Mu, *Guoshi dagang* [An outline of Chinese history] (Hong Kong: Shangwu yinshuguan, 1995), vol. 1, ch. 5; Yang Kuan, *Zhanguo shi* (Shanghai: Shanghai renmin chubanshe, 1998).
8. For a recent volume on the relationship, see Jean-Marc F. Blanchard and Simon Shen, eds., *Conflict and Cooperation in Sino-US Relations: Change and Continuity, Causes and Cures* (London: Routledge, 2015). Also, Handel Jones, *Chinamerica: The Uneasy Partnership that Will Change the World* (New York: McGraw-Hill Education, 2010).
9. The case of Taiwan should not be really controversial, as it is listed here among the seven due to its de facto separation from the PRC and its sovereign power to rule its own territory and citizens independent from any other states, let alone its status as an economic entity with sovereign governance, which is the focus of this chapter's analysis. Hong Kong does not appear on the map simply because it has no sovereign power though its economy is separate from the PRC's. In any sense, it is impossible for the Hong Kong SAR to adopt an international strategy against the PRC, as, according to the Basic Law that governs Hong Kong, Beijing manages Hong Kong's foreign policy. ASEAN is a difficult case here; there is a certain convenience of analysis to regarding it as one entity that is definitely supported by many things in reality, including the economic engagement of ASEAN as a whole, rather than member by member, with China through their free trade zone and similar arrangements.

Figure 6.2: East Asia under PRC-USA rivalry, c. 2019

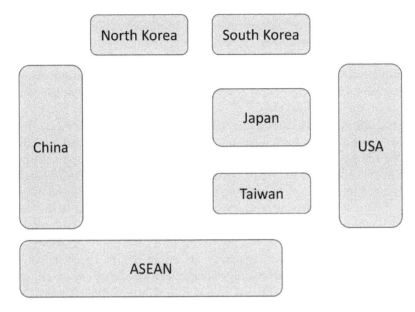

Source: Author.

These three similarities of Figure 6.2 to Figure 6.1—the rise of a powerful challenger, the ambiguous rather than confrontational relationship between the challenger and the traditional hegemon, and the swings of smaller states between two superpowers—are not all of the similarities one may find in comparing them. They are significant, however, and, this chapter would suggest, sufficient for establishing a structure or framework within which further comparisons can be made for analyzing the current East Asian order with the emergence of the China-US rivalry.

Geo-economics at the Center: Globalization and the Rise of the Economic State in East Asia, China, and the USA

Fundamental differences between international relations in current East Asia and the ancient Chinese Warring States exist, of course; they are often vital. One of the most significant differences, quite obviously, lies in the issue of state survival: the Warring States fought to conquer each other, but it is highly unlikely that a state in today's East Asia, as in many other parts of the world, would conquer other countries in terms of territory in order to turn them into parts of its own sovereign nation-state. For China this is also the case, except its relationship with and stance on Taiwan. Everybody knows that the PRC insists Taiwan is a breakaway province of China and never tries to hide its intention to extend its de facto sovereignty to Taiwan despite the fact that the PRC claimed de jure sovereignty over Taiwan is historically and legally rooted in its inheritance from (though through a revolution and the overthrow of) the Republic of China that also currently rules Taiwan.[10] The two Koreas could be another difficult case limiting the emergent norm of not conquering each other's land and people, but it is very unlikely with the current international and domestic situations they will do so with military or any other coercive means. Still, a caveat comes with the wide existence of territorial disputes in the region of East Asia, particularly and prominently maritime territorial disputes between China and Japan, and China and other pertinent nations over the South China Sea.[11] But the nature of such disputes is fundamentally different from what one can observe from the Warring States period, when territorial demands from a neighboring state are unsatisfiable until the targeted state's territory is totally occupied. It can be roughly concluded, therefore, that in the East Asia of the early twenty-first century inter-state relations are not dominated by the so-called "constant war" mode in which each state's fundamental security of state survival, specifically in sovereignty over existing territory, is threatened by any other states, including not by those powerful states and by a rising power. Security concerns seem still strong for the states listed in Figure 6.2, but not as much as for those in Figure 6.1, and not so strong to the extent of dominating those states' behavior.

Instead, the economic concerns of the states in Figure 6.2 are not only very strong but also keep growing; they have already reached the degree at which state security is often redefined with the inclusion of so-called "economic security" into the conception of the national security of the state. Furthermore, economic elements are also considered in a comprehensive way that can refresh the concept of the state's economic strength as so-called "comprehensive strengths" in international competition. In comparisons with many other regions in today's world, East Asia in general is a region with many flashpoints of security concern and potential military conflict, and China in particular often stands at the hub of this friction. From north to south in the region, the Korean Peninsula, the East China Sea, the Taiwan Strait, and the South China Sea are all dangerous places. In most of them, China is a major contender involved in the dispute, even though China's threat, or relevant countries' perceived threat from China, does not primarily concern military security but rather economic and comprehensive competition or economy-centered and the economy-backed elements in widely defined areas of security. Curiously enough, a similar perception has also been increasingly accepted in Taiwan,

---

10. For a recent review of China-Taiwan relations including China's stance, see Lowell Dittmer, ed., *Taiwan and China: Fateful Embrace* (Berkeley, CA: University of California Press, 2017).
11. Monika Chansoria, *China, Japan, and Senkaku Islands: Conflict in the East China Sea amid an American Shadow* (London: Routledge, 2018); Bill Hayton, *The South China Sea: The Struggle for Power in Asia* (New Haven, CT: Yale University Press, 2014).

as exemplified by the popularity in recent elections of political figures like Ko Wen-je and Han Kuo-yu, who mostly disregard any potential security threat from China to Taiwan but gain voters' enthusiastic support by highlighting the economic disadvantages of Taiwan in comparison with China and their own determination and capability to catch up.[12] China downplays security but highlights the economy. China prefers to develop its economy-centered comprehensive capabilities, and with such capabilities, as deemed necessary, to solve the security issues.[13]

This phenomenon of economy-predominance in inter-state relations and regional international politics is not totally new in human history, but it becomes sweeping in the current period of the region of East Asia, as well as in many other regions of the world, which must be attributed to the tremendous wave of post–Cold War globalization. This author elsewhere defines this round of globalization as virtually all the states in the world having accepted the market as the primary mechanism of economic activities,[14] which has institutionally paved the way for the increasingly intensive global flows of capital, labor, consumer goods, technologies, information, and so on, in which globalization is materially and dynamically embedded.[15] As the state and the market have had such ideological conciliation, institutional collaboration, and operational cooperation, the state-market nexus emerges to provide the institutional framework in which capitalism comes to the global stage, and the state has undergone a profound institutional transformation with globalization. The rise of the economic state could be regarded the most prominent change driven by globalization regarding fundamental state institutions and the inherent features of the state: "As the state is primarily occupied by concern over its economic performance, attempting to function in either positive (statist) or negative (neoliberal) ways to promote economic development, and increasingly lays its legitimacy and institutional foundations on the delivery of material or other economy-related benefits to its population rather than on the protection and provision of public goods, it has become, this author suggests, the economic state."[16]

Capitalist East Asia during the Cold War era was where the pre-globalization capitalist state once developed to its height as the economic state, notably in the form of the developmental state as that was observed in post–WWII

---

12. See, for example, Lawrence Chung, "Beijing Warms Up to Taipei's mayor," *South China Morning Post*, July 3, 2017; Lawrence Chung, "From Rank Outsider to Mayor of Kaohsiung," *South China Morning Post*, November 25, 2018.
13. Dittmer, *Taiwan and China*, Conclusion.
14. The obvious exceptions could be North Korea and Cuba. Even these two states, however, have recently also experimented with economic liberalization programs. See Richard Feinberg, *Open for Business: Building the New Cuban Economy* (Washington, DC: Brookings Institution Press, 2016); and Hazel Smith, *North Korea: Markets and Military Rule* (New York: Cambridge University Press, 2015).
15. Wu, *Globalization against Democracy*, passim.
16. Wu, *Globalization against Democracy*, 45.

Japan and, later, in most newly industrialized countries such as South Korea and Taiwan.[17] As I have discussed in a political economy of globalization,[18] this trend of increasing state functions in the economy also occurred during the Cold War in the European market economies,[19] roughly and inversely corresponding to the introduction of the market mechanism into the formerly state-planning economies of the communist world.[20] These different trends, I

---

17. See for example, Chalmers Johnson, *MITI and the Japanese Miracle: The Growth of Industrial Policy, 1925–1975* (Stanford, CA: Stanford University Press, 1982); Frederic C. Deyo, ed., *The Political Economy of the New Asian Industrialism* (Ithaca, NY: Cornell University Press, 1987); Gary Gereffi and Donald L. Wyman, eds., *Manufacturing Miracles: Paths of Industrialization in Latin America and East Asia* (Princeton, NJ: Princeton University Press, 1990); Stephan Haggard, *Pathways from the Periphery: The Politics of Growth in the Newly Industrialized Countries* (Ithaca, NY: Cornell University Press, 1990); Robert Wade, *Governing the Market: Economic Theory and the Role of Government in East Asian Industrialization* (Princeton, NJ: Princeton University Press, 1990); Alice H. Amsden, *Asia's Next Giant: South Korea and Late Industrialization* (New York: Oxford University Press, 1992); Meredith Woo-Cumings, ed., *The Developmental State* (Ithaca, NY: Cornell University Press, 1999).
18. Wu, *Globalization against Democracy*, ch. 2.
19. Peter Evans, Dietrich Rueschemeyer, and Theda Skocpol, eds., *Bringing the State Back In* (New York: Cambridge University Press, 1985); Peter Gourevitch, *Politics in Hard Times: Comparative Responses to International Economic Crises* (Ithaca, NY: Cornell University Press, 1986); Peter A. Hall, *Governing the Economy: The Politics of State Intervention in Britain and France* (New York: Oxford University Press, 1986); Mark Robinson and Gordon White, eds., *The Democratic Developmental State: Politics and Institutional Design* (Oxford: Oxford University Press, 1998).
20. For marketization reform in the Soviet Union, post–Soviet Russia, and Eastern European countries, see, for example, Stephen White, *Gorbachev in Power* (New York: Cambridge University Press, 1990); Anders Aslund, *Gorbachev's Struggle for Economic Reform* (Ithaca, NY: Cornell University Press, 1991); János Mátyás Kovács and Márton Tardos, eds., *Reform and Transformation in Eastern Europe: Soviet-Type Economics on the Threshold of Change* (London: Routledge, 1992); Walter Adams and James W. Brock, *Adam Smith Goes to Moscow* (Princeton, NJ: Princeton University Press, 1993); James Leitzel, *Russian Economic Reform* (London: Routledge, 1995); Jerry F. Hough, *The Logic of Economic Reform in Russia* (Washington, DC: Brookings Institution Press, 2001); Oleh Havrylyshyn and Saleh M. Nsouli, eds., *A Decade of Transition: Achievements and Challenges* (Washington, DC: IMF Institute, 2001); Vladimir Gel'man, Otar Marganiya, and Dmitry Travin, *Reexamining Economic and Political Reforms in Russia, 1985–2000: Generations, Ideas, and Changes* (Lanham, MD: Lexington Books, 2014). For that in China, see, for instance, Harry Harding, *China's Second Revolution: Reform After Mao* (Washington, DC: Brookings Institution, 1987); Sheng Hua, Xuejun Zhang, and Xiaopeng Luo, *China: From Revolution to Reform* (London: Macmillan, 1993); Barry Naughton, *Growing Out of the Plan: Chinese Economic Reform, 1978–1993* (New York: Cambridge University Press, 1995); Jonathan Story, *China: The Race to Market* (London: Prentice Hall, 2003); Scott Kennedy, *China's Capitalist Transformation* (Stanford, CA: Stanford University Press, 2011); Nicholas R. Lardy, *Markets over Mao: The Rise of Private Business in China* (Washington, DC: PIIE Press, 2014). For Asian communist countries' acceptance of market, see, for instance, Sujian Guo, *The Political Economy of Asian Transition from Communism* (Aldershot, UK: Ashgate, 2006); Janos Kornai and Yingyi Qian, eds., *Market and Socialism: In the Light of the Experiences of China and Vietnam* (New York: Palgrave Macmillan, 2009.) For some comparative studies, see, for example, Bernard Chavance, Charles Hauss, and Mark Selden, *The Transformation of Communist Systems: Economic Reform Since the 1950s* (Boulder, CO: Westview, 1994); Minxin Pei, *From Reform to Revolution: The Demise of Communism in China and the Soviet Union* (Cambridge, MA: Harvard University Press, 1994).

have tried to suggest, as the world coming into the post–Cold War era, eventually converged to a fundamental reconfiguration of the state: the rise of the economic state.

China is quite obviously the exemplary economic state of the globalization age, where its authoritarian regime with strong state capacity remarkably promotes economic prosperity through comprehensive involvement in, penetration into, and supervision of market activities. The US, traditionally with little role of the state in the economy, is nevertheless not immune to the worldwide prevalence of the economic state. In another piece on the economic state, this author has compared these two economic superpowers of the current world against six features that the economic state possesses, and found that, despite the very different economic, political, and social-cultural contexts the state operates in the two countries, both the PRC and the US have some basic, significant inclinations in accordance with the rise of the economic state.[21] These six features of the economic state are: the state's increasing economic concerns, the state's extending authority into economic domains, the frequent involvement of state coercion in economic affairs, the shift of sources of state legitimacy to economic performance, the state's declining supply of public goods, and the prevalence of power-money exchange relationships in governmental ethics.[22] The post–Cold War PRC is, comparatively speaking, a fully developed case to meet all of the parameters in both extension and strength, while the US has since the 1990s experienced a gradual, spasmodic, often ineffective, but discernible transformation toward the rise of the economic state.[23] As examples, they help to demonstrate how the economic state arises worldwide across a wide range of countries in very different political, economic, social, and cultural circumstances.

USA-China Rivalry from the Perspective of the Economic State: From Interdependent Chinamerica to Sino-American Trade Wars

As post–Cold War globalization explains this global common trend of the rise of the economic state, including such institutionally distant cases as those of the PRC and the US, here this chapter will extend the propositions concerning the economic state and its connections to globalization with two further arguments in regard to comprehending the latest emergence of China-USA rivalry. The first argument concerns how the wave of de-globalization is institutionally and politically economically intertwined with the continuous

---

21. Guoguang Wu, "Globalization and the Rise of the Economic State: PRC and USA in Comparison," in *Challenges of Globalization and Prospects for an Inter-civilizational World Order*, ed. Ino Rossi (New York: Springer, 2020), 241–59.
22. Wu, "Globalization and the Rise of the Economic State," 241–59.
23. Wu, "Globalization and the Rise of the Economic State," 241–59.

rise of the economic state in the democratic countries, especially in the US. As everybody knows, the US founders did not include much economic consideration in the principles of the new nation; their concerns were human dignity and civil rights of citizens, for the protection and promotion of which the government was established as an agent of public life. Economic concerns belonged mostly to the private sphere, where individuals were to make their own efforts to strive for prosperity. The state, under this logic, simply safeguards the circumstances for citizens to do so. This approach has been under change over time, especially since the end of the Cold War. In industrialized democracies, the disappearance of political, military, and ideological confrontations between democracy and communism with the collapse of the Soviet Bloc greatly promoted an economy-centered mentality among voters, as epitomized in Bill Clinton's first campaign phrase, "It's the economy, stupid!"[24] The Clinton years are, accordingly, remembered and celebrated for their economic achievements, a time of unprecedented wealth, of breathtaking progress in technology, and, therefore, a "golden age" in which American society was "so favored as it entered a new millennium that its people could be excused for believing they were experiencing their very best of times."[25] It is its economic performance that has since then increasingly become the central concern of the American state for both politicians and voters; people who are not aware of this centrality of economic concerns are simply scorned "stupid."[26]

The rise of Donald Trump in American politics further demonstrates that this evolution of the US toward the economic state is well beyond partisan politics and instead is a roughly continuous acceleration through the 1990s to the 2010s. Trump's campaign slogan, "Make America Great Again," clearly signals the upgrading of the Clinton "it's-the-economy-stupid" cognizance in at least two aspects: First, national economic performance, which sits at the center of this Trump slogan, is upgraded to the degree that the greatness of the US is embedded; and second, the state's action, as indicated in the word "make," is regarded as necessary and perhaps inevitable for improving national economic performance, in contrast to Clinton's vague expression concerning the economy that connotes the necessity of politicians' awareness of voters' economic concerns. These campaign slogans might be deemed superficial signals, but they are doubtlessly emblematic; they have clearly shown how economic concerns have more and more dominated the US political agenda.

The position of the US in this latest wave of globalization, however, is increasingly becoming awkward. This wave of globalization, by and large,

---

24. For the phrase and its background, see, for example, Wikipedia, https://en.wikipedia.org/wiki/It's_the_economy,_stupid, accessed February 15, 2019.
25. Haynes Johnson, *The Best of Times: America in the Clinton Years* (New York: Harcourt, 2001), 1.
26. For an in-depth study of such a phenomenon, see Raymond M. Duch and Randolph T. Stevenson, *The Economic Vote: How Political and Economic Institutions Condition Election Results* (Cambridge: Cambridge University Press, 2008).

originated from the US, with the prevalence of neoliberalism.[27] As neoliberal policies successfully drove post–Cold War globalization and helped to shift state concerns to geo-economic competition, things become awkward for the leading industrial democracies, particularly the US. Globalization intensifies global competition in such a way that not only private firms but also states are involved; but the neoliberal policies of the US, while facilitating the global flow of capital, have, in return, undermined the American economy as well as American democracy in many ways.[28] Manufacturers have moved out to countries, including China, where capital finds cheaper labor to make greater profits; thus jobs for US workers have evaporated; immigrants have come in to take lower-paying job opportunities in the service sector; economic polarization, like elsewhere in the world of globalization, has arisen to such a severe degree that it nurtures hatred, crime, and sociopolitical splits.[29] Trump's rise clearly indicates the discontent of American voters on these problems; such discontent has now amassed to the degree that a majority of citizens have turned to the state for a stronger economic capacity for remedies. Traditionally, the US state was often criticized for its lack of an industrial policy. The rise of the economic state, however, implies that the US state pays increasing attention to various economic policies, primarily including trade policy, research and development policy, and industrial policy. The Trump administration has further expanded the domains of the state's economic governance into infrastructure and greatly enhanced state efforts in promoting growth and creating jobs though how effectively it has done so is debatable.

This turn from neoliberal to somehow statist economic policies, to this author, does not challenge the assumption of the rise of the economic state,[30] but it is obviously a change of the form the American economic state takes. In my interpretation, following the positive-negative distinction suggested by Isaiah Berlin, this Trumpist turn indicates that, while the market power of the US in managing globalization, with its neoliberal and "negative" nature, has been undermined by various elements, especially by the rise of the

---

27. David Harvey, *A Brief History of Neoliberalism* (New York: Oxford University Press, 2005).
28. Wu, *Globalization against Democracy*.
29. Nolan McCarty, Keith T. Poole, and Howard Rosenthal, *Polarized America: The Dance of Ideology and Unequal Riches* (Cambridge, MA: MIT Press, 2008); François Bourguignon, *The Globalization of Inequality* (Princeton, NJ: Princeton University Press, 2015); Joseph E. Stiglitz, *The Great Divide: Unequal Societies and What We Can Do About Them* (New York: W. W. Norton, 2015).
30. Different from the prevailing interpretation of neoliberalism as the reducer of state roles in the economy, this author has argued elsewhere that the neoliberal state is by virtue a type of the economic state, based on a conceptual distinction between the state's "positive" and "negative" interventions of economic activities and, furthermore, on the fact that the neoliberal state only reduces "positive" interventions for increasing state-market collaboration. See Wu, *Globalization against Democracy*, 49. The positive-negative distinction follows, of course, the concepts suggested by Isaiah Berlin in discussing these two kinds of freedom, as in Isaiah Berlin, *Four Essays on Liberty* (Oxford: Oxford University Press, [1959]1969), 118–72. This distinction is further discussed immediately below.

"positive" economic state as that is represented by China, the US also attempts to strengthen its state's positive roles in the economy. It is expressed as an inclination to de-globalization,[31] a remarkable reversal of the globalization tide awash since the end of the Cold War.

The state, according to Max Weber's classic definition, is a political organization with a legitimate monopoly of coercive power.[32] The rise of the economic state, therefore, inevitably implies that the coercive power of the state is increasingly mobilized and employed to make economic benefits. This coercion-for-benefits phenomenon is not entirely new, of course, to one who has sufficient knowledge of the origins and developments of the modern state.[33] But, it is still new in the current contexts of globalization and de-globalization at least in two senses. First, in the sense of perception: many perspectives of modern social science that emphasize the state-market dichotomy have chosen to ignore this important dimension of historical reality; now the candid or shameless application of state coercion for gaining economic benefits can refresh people's viewpoint of public power. The theory of the economic state, indeed, can help in this regard. Second, in the sense of historical change: during the Cold War era, in confronting the anti-market communist state, the capitalist West often claimed itself the "free world" by highlighting a free market that operated the economy while the state was portrayed with little involvement in or exercise of its coercive power over economic affairs. The post–Cold War rise of the economic state is therefore new when viewed against this historical background.[34] The exercise of state coercion for economic purposes and in economic affairs is now often extended to the degree at which the state can be turned from an agent of public power to a coercive machine for profit making.

The Chinese state never shies away from mobilizing state coercion for ensuring its program of economic development at least since the late 1970s. In 1989, the Chinese government sent tanks to the Beijing streets and opened machine gun fire on university students and citizens who protested against corruption and requested a transition to democracy.[35] The Chinese party-state justified this brutal massacre straightforwardly by claiming the "necessity"

---

31. It seems that the Trump administration is also trying to push some further neoliberalization in global political economy, as its suggestion to reduce trade tariffs with some countries, e.g. EU, to the degree of zero has indicated. See, for instance, David Smith and Dominic Rushe, "Trump and EU Officials Agree to Work toward 'Zero Tariff' Deal," *The Guardian*, July 25, 2018.
32. Max Weber, *Economy and Society*, ed. Guenther Roth and Claus Wittich (Berkeley, CA: University of California Press, 1978), 314.
33. Joseph R. Strayer, *On the Medieval Origins of the Modern State* (Princeton, NJ: Princeton University Press, 1970); Charles Tilly, ed., *The Formation of National States in Western Europe* (Princeton, NJ: Princeton University Press, 1975); Gianfranco Poggi, *The Development of the Modern State: A Sociological Introduction* (Stanford, CA: Stanford University Press, 1978).
34. Wu, "Globalization and the Rise of the Economic State," 241–59.
35. Timothy Brook, *Quelling the People: The Military Suppression of the Beijing Democracy Movement* (Stanford, CA: Stanford University Press, 1992).

of the crackdown for maintaining a "stable" social environment that favored economic development. Moreover, the Chinese state has since then strived to institutionalize the coercion-for-economic-prosperity mechanism, mainly by building up the so-called "stability maintenance" (*weiwen*, 維穩) system, with the help of a tremendous state fiscal budget, for safeguarding the Chinese Communist Party's monopoly of state power and fending off social discontent against socioeconomic inequalities, social injustice, and governmental corruption.[36]

Does the US economic state also exercise coercive means for promoting economic interests? Yes, though not in the same way as that in the PRC, nor to such an extent. Democracy is of course a major institutional factor that could direct state coercion primarily and emphatically outward, namely, in the US's dealing with other countries, rather than inward, as in the case of China with its authoritarian state dealing with its own citizens. This means that state coercive measures for economic purposes are employed mainly in the international realm, that is, global competition. The Trump administration seems especially consciously to be doing so, as it has initiated and fought a series of trade wars with China and many other countries. Yes, trade war is nothing new for states in general and for the US in particular, but it is still not so usual for the American state to do it with such high frequency and great priority at such a central position on the state agenda.

It is exactly with the intensification of trade wars between the US and China that people are now talking about the emergence of China-USA rivalry.[37] Applying the concept of the economic state to the analysis of the China-USA rivalry and its comparative/international political economic implications, especially to the region of East Asia, here this chapter maintains, in the first aspect, that, with China taking the lead, the economic state prevails not only with globalization but also with de-globalization, and that the US, now a leading nation in playing de-globalization under the Trump administration, is in fact a further transformation toward the economic state in the hope of winning competition against China. This helps to explain why China-USA rivalry has recently arisen against the previous trend of Chinamerica.

Hezong versus *Lianheng*: American De-globalization versus China-Led Globalization in Shaping East Asian Disorder

Now let's return to the historical analogy between the Chinese Warring States and current East Asia international relations, to refresh the relevant interpretations in the light of the above discussion of globalization, de-globalization,

---

36. Guoguang Wu, "Repressive Capitalism as the Institutional Crystallization of China's Transition," in *China's Transition from Communism—New Perspectives*, ed. Guoguang Wu and Helen Lansdowne (London: Routledge, 2016), 188–210.
37. "The Rivals," *The Economist*, October 20, 2018, 21–24.

and the economic state. The refreshment mainly concerns the point that it is in the sense of the prevalence of the economic state in the current period, not in the classic sense of Warring States centered on security concerns, state survival, and the attempts at the conquering of land, that this chapter draws significant parallels between China's Warring States period and current East Asia under the shadow of China-USA rivalry. In other words, this chapter compares the international political economy of East Asia in the years around 2020 with the inter-state politics of security and war among Chinese Warring States in the century before 221 BCE. The contents of confrontation, conflict, and battles among states in the two cases are different, as the substantial focus of the current structure is on geo-economics, rather than simply geopolitics, which was the overwhelming consideration for the Chinese Warring States. The structures, however, are similar to each other in those features outlined in the first section of this chapter and sketched in the analogy between Figures 6.1 and 6.2. This section, therefore, will be devoted to an analysis of what the Warring-States-like but geopolitical-economic framework implies to the seven states on the current map and, emphatically, how the pertinent states, especially China and the US as the two major parties involved in rivalry and dominating inter-state competition, conduct different strategies in the face of a rising power's challenge.

Hezong and *lianheng*, as pointed out, are the two contending strategies that dominated the options of the states involved in the Warring States struggle. Here, we use these terms with a refreshed emphasis on their economic contents. That is to say, *hezong* can mean a strategy of all other states except the rising power that is perceived as the threat attempt to promote economic cooperation with each other against the economic threat from the state in a position parallel to ancient Qin, and the traditional, existing hegemon in the economic sense would be especially enthusiastic about doing so to coordinate smaller economies for the purpose. By contrast, *lianheng* is the rising economic power's strategy that emphasizes and promotes its own closer economic connections with each of other six states for the ultimate aim of becoming the new hegemon to which all these states have to bend. The *lianheng* strategy in this context, therefore, also implies reducing those states' multilateral coordination, primarily to reduce the traditional, existing hegemonic power's economic connections with each and all of them.

Though the perception of China's economic threat among the six (or five, except North Korea, as will be explained) states, primarily in the US, may become strong only recently as the mainstream awareness, the rise of China's economic power, is not what happened last night. Here, the chapter, therefore, through taking 2020 as a reference point, discusses the issues with some historical depth. Roughly speaking, the rise of China's economic power has taken place since the 1990s, along with the rise of globalization and, accordingly,

China's embrace of globalization.[38] The sketch map of Figure 6.2, therefore, should not be viewed as static but an indication of the dynamic process of the seven economies' increasing interdependence through globalization and, very recently, their difficult choices with the rise of the US de-globalization strategy and the China-USA rivalry.

Over the decade or two, the US strategy in East Asia regional international economic relations can be roughly divided into two phases: the phase prior to the Trump administration coming into power, and the phase of the Trump administration. The pre-Trump US was, generally speaking, interested in multilateral mechanisms in East Asia and made some effort in building up regional international economic cooperation regimes, as exemplified by Asia-Pacific Economic Cooperation (APEC) and the Trans-Pacific Partnership (TPP). The strategy of the US during this period is to a superficial extent similar to *hezong*, as it promotes coordination among states in the pertinent (sub)system of international political economy. But a fundamental and vital difference exists if such multilateral cooperation is compared with the classic *hezong* strategy practiced during the Chinese Warring States period, which concerns the perception and identification of where the threat comes from. North Korea was excluded from those multilateral coordination mechanisms; in this sense it was the Democratic People's Republic of Korea (DPRK) that was perceived as the threat to all other states involved in the mechanisms. In reality, North Korea is obviously not an economic threat to any states; it is perceived a security threat to the US, Japan, and South Korea but not in the sense of becoming a new hegemon. China, instead, was regarded and accepted as a major partner despite the voices warning of a China threat including in but not limited to the economic realm.

The Trump administration has started a shift of strategy in East Asia, as well as in other parts of the world, by, in accordance with its general emphasis on de-globalization, attempting at withdrawals from regional multilateral regimes.[39] Though actions of withdrawal taken are so far quite limited, the signal is strong, the new policy inclination is obvious, and the implications are profound. The new strategy has changed both significant features of the previous quasi-*hezong* strategy. First, it now identifies China as the major threat, primarily in the economic sense but with profound non-economic ramifications: because of this today we are here to talk about China-USA rivalry. Second, it virtually gives up any *hezong*-like effort to deal with the threat. Under Trump, the rise of the economic state in the US has now come into a mentality with which almost all other economies are, or could be, competitors of the US economy. As the US remains the largest economy in the world and the most powerful country in technologies, bilateralism, if not unilateralism

---

38. William Overholt, *The Rise of China: How Economic Reform Is Creating a New Superpower* (New York: W. W. Norton, 1994).
39. See, for example, Adam Taylor, "A Timeline of Trump's Complicated Relationship with the TPP," *The Washington Post*, April 13, 2018.

(which the relative decline of US power may not be able to support), rather than multilateralism, is preferred in dealing with each other country, as all of those countries individually are weaker in comparison and in coping with the US.

The PRC was once notorious for its propensity for bilateralism in international relations while refusing multilateralism, but it has adjusted its foreign policy since the 1990s with its deep engagement into globalization by skillfully embracing international multilateralism, especially in the economic realm.[40] In the regional international politics of East Asia, the PRC has been an active member and, in the feasible maximum, a leader country of those multilateral economic regimes such as APEC. It has also done so in global economic cooperation though to a lesser degree. Needless to say, China has enormously benefitted from its involvement in globalization in general and its participation in global and regional economic multilateral regimes in particular; thus, the rise of the Chinese economy to the current degree has experienced the successive surpassing of all other large economies next to the US, including surpassing Japan in 2010, becoming the second-largest economy in the world. In 2001, prior to its joining of the World Trade Organization (WTO), China's GDP was US$1,339 billion, roughly ten percent of US GDP ($13,262 billion); in 2017, China's GDP rose to US$12,156 billion, taking 67 percent of US GDP of US$18,051 billion.[41]

To China, however, multilateral international engagements are not contradictory, nor exclusive, to its continuous and tremendous attention to bilateral foreign-relation conduct. It is especially so in China's strategy for East Asian regional international relations in general and in East Asian economic diplomacy in particular. As a matter of fact, all of the top five trading partners of China in 2018, except Hong Kong, are on the map sketched by Figure 6.2, which include the US, ASEAN, Japan, and South Korea. Taiwan is not far away from the list, as it is the eleventh top trading partner of China in 2018.[42] In the perspective of *hezong* versus *lianheng*, it is not wrong to say that China

---

40. Guoguang Wu and Helen Lansdowne, eds., *China Turns to Multilateralism: Foreign Policy and Regional Security* (London: Routledge, 2008); John Wong and Lok Sang Ho, eds., *APEC and the Rise of China* (Singapore: World Scientific, 2011).
41. The numbers on China come from the Wikipedia entry of "Historical GDP of China," https://en.wikipedia.org/wiki/Historical_GDP_of_China. The US numbers are from The Balance, "US GDP by Year Compared to Recessions and Events: The Strange Ups and Downs of the U.S. Economy Since 1929," https://www.thebalance.com/us-gdp-by-year-3305543; both accessed March 6, 2019.
42. Daniel Workman, "China's Top Trading Partners," http://www.worldstopexports.com/chinas-top-import-partners/, accessed March 6, 2019. It could be conceptually wrong to term China-ASEAN relations bilateral, but, as implied earlier, this article takes ASEAN as an entity in a limited sense, especially according to China-ASEAN economic connections. Vietnam, Singapore, and Malaysia, all member states of ASEAN, as individual economies still take the positions of fifth, tenth, and fourteenth, respectively, among China's top trading partners in 2018.

has been practicing the strategy of *lianheng* quite successfully in the East Asian regional international political economy of the twenty-first century.

How about the smaller states' choice in their strategy coping with the emergence of the China-USA rivalry? This chapter, as emphasized, pushes traditional security considerations into the background, focusing rather on the realm of political economy in regard to the China-USA rivalry and relevant states' strategic options. It is infeasible, however, for this chapter to analyze in-depth the individual option by each of the five smaller states in Figure 6.2. Instead, the chapter intends to highlight the structural elements and the tendency these states are likely to follow as constrained by the given structure. The prominent structural element in this regard is the six states' economic connections with China. The decades of globalization have witnessed the high degree of development of economic interdependence between each of them and China, but interdependence with the asymmetry favoring China and resulting in these countries' economic vulnerability in dealing with China. Figure 6.3 tries to support this observation with statistics of their trade relationships with China, as contrasted with their much lower volume of trade with the US.

Two points can be highlighted in reading Figure 6.3, concerning, respectively, the positions of other five states in face of the China-USA rivalry, and that of the US per se in dealing with China. In the classic scenario of the ancient Chinese Warring States, each state, except Qin, the rising power and threat to the others, must take an option between *hezong* and *lianheng*. Curiously enough, Qi, the traditional, existing hegemon that could dominate the six states' cooperation against Qin's threat, is also included in this group, as it equally must make such an option rather than insisting on *hezong* while opposing *lianheng*. The historical fact is that Qi was not even the initiator of the *hezong* strategy against Qin but among the first states joining *lianheng* to cooperate with Qin. That is especially interesting, in light of Qi's experience, to read the bars in the column on the extreme left in Figure 6.3, which show the tremendous economic connections between the US and the PRC in bilateral trade relations; the latest emergence of China-USA rivalry changes them neither in substance nor tendency. In a similar vein, it is beyond imagination that Sino-American trade wars taking place since 2018 will greatly reduce such interdependence between the two economies, but, at their most effective from the US perspective, can only partially remedy the imbalance that has since the 1990s been established between them. Compared with the historical situation of the Chinese Warring States, the US seems to be repeating Qi's option in, first of all, cooperating with Qin/China and, then, giving up *hezong* against Qin/China. As lately the US perception of China as the threat began to rise, this is, still, comparable to the case of Qi, where vacillations of policy and fluctuations of perception against Qin existed for many years until it was too late to fight against Qin and the Qi state was conquered by Qin in 221 BCE.

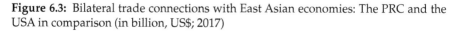

Figure 6.3: Bilateral trade connections with East Asian economies: The PRC and the USA in comparison (in billion, US$; 2017)

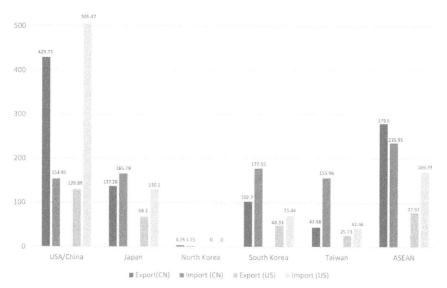

Note: The ASEAN that is regarded as one entity of statistics here includes ten member states: Brunei, Cambodia, Indonesia, Laos, Malaysia, Myanmar, Philippines, Singapore, Thailand, and Vietnam.

Sources: For data on China: National Bureau of Statistics of China, http://data.stats.gov.cn/easyquery.htm?cn=C01 (China part).

For data on the USA: United States Census Bureau, https://www.census.gov/foreign-trade/balance/index.html (USA part).

In a general consideration of international relations, especially with the China-USA rivalry as the thesis, the other five states in Figure 6.2 should be further divided into two categories, North Korea as a single-member group in a contrast to other four. This is obvious because, first of all, the DPRK has never been an ally of the US through the decades since its birth following World War II, but an enemy, while it has been a comrade, brother, and friend of the PRC. Second, North Korea is virtually not involved in post–Cold War capitalist globalization that is initially led by the US. As Figure 6.3 helps show, its foreign economic trade volume with the US is nearly zero, while its narrowly limited foreign economic connections are largely with the PRC. Among the ancient Chinese Warring States there is no state comparable to today's North Korea, which means, in its rivalry with the US it seems that China can easily gain North Korea despite recent US effort to break the ice between Washington and Pyongyang. North Korea, therefore, will have no difficulty making a choice between *hezong* and *lianheng*. Let us suppose the

US's recent diplomatic action regarding North Korea is an attempt consistent with *hezong*. Still, the PRC-DPRK relationship, despite various problems including distrust and friction, will not be a major obstacle in the foreseeable future to Beijing in its challenge to the US. The economic significance of North Korea, after all, is small; the issues surrounding it are greatly preoccupied with traditional security considerations.

South Korea, Japan, Taiwan, and, to a lesser extent, ASEAN (especially the "old members" in the south) inevitably face a difficult choice, as the US and the PRC are turning from a strategic partnership to rivalry, especially at such junctures of globalization versus de-globalization and the absence of *hezong* versus the aggressiveness of *lianheng*. They all belonged to the US-led camp in the Cold War confrontation, and their security as well as economic relationships with the US have been strong and vital. Post–Cold War globalization, however, rapidly and powerfully pushed them into economic interdependence with, or, perhaps rather dependence on, China to a degree now much higher than on the US, at least in foreign trade. As Figure 6.3 helps demonstrate, the bilateral trade volume for each of these economies with China is much higher than with the US, often by a huge gap in such a comparison. For military and security considerations, they may easily make the decision to continue their strong ties with the US; for economic interests, however, how they choose could be a serious challenge equally to these states and to observers. As it is almost impossible for a country in international relations to separate, let alone antagonize, economic interests and its own security interests, the agony of making a choice between the rivals will further zoom out.

The *Economist* recently commented that "America's allies are struggling with two bullies" from the Trump administration of the US and the Xi Jinping leadership of China, as both try hard to "frighten" them.[43] It refers to Canada, first of all, but I have found no hindrance to apply the comment to America's allies in East Asia, including Japan, South Korea, Taiwan, and ASEAN in general. More importantly, I would add that they are not only struggling with two bullies but also struggling with two lures—perhaps more with lures for East Asian economies.

Furthermore, it seems that the lure from China is larger than from the US, especially in economic terms, while also in the intent to cooperate and, as Qin did in applying its *lianheng* strategy during the Chinese Warring States period, to bribe. In fact, the trend of the rise of the economic state in these countries is always coincident with the advocacy of pro-China options by some elites in these countries. The difficulty for these East Asian states to make such a choice could be reduced because of the absence of a US-led *hezong* strategy in dealing with China, while, simultaneously, China's *lianheng* strategy is pushing

---

43. The *Economist*, "America's allies are struggling with two bullies," February 28, 2019, https://www.economist.com/china/2019/03/02/americas-allies-are-struggling-with-two-bullies, accessed March 2, 2019.

hard with attractive, ever-increasing economic lures for individual political, economic, and cultural elites and the state under their leadership. If they are not split from within between the two options of the US/security priority and the China/economic lures but lean to one side, either side, a new East Asian regional international order will emerge. If they are dubious, vague, and swinging between the two options, it seems that East Asia will experience something also new in regional international relations, but something having to be properly termed "disorder." The latter scenario, in my point of view, is more likely to occur, or, if one judges that it has occurred since late 2018, to continue in the foreseeable future.

Concluding Remarks

This chapter has attempted to combine a theory of the economic state with a historical comparison between the ancient Chinese Warring States and current East Asia, to provide an understanding of what the emergence of China-USA rivalry means for the East Asian regional international order and how it can affect the seven major states or state-like entities in their strategic options for dealing with new circumstances. The historical analogy has shifted the focus of the pertinent inter-state system from that on state survival, security, and war in the ancient Chinese Warring States period to the current one on geo-economics. But non-economic dimensions are not entirely excluded from the analysis. The fundamental similarity between the two historical cases lies in the framework within which six (or five in the current East Asian scenario if North Korea is excluded) of the major seven states (or state-like entities in international relations) are perplexed by their relations with the seventh as the rising power that poses a threat to the status quo hegemon and existing inter-state order. In the contemporary case of East Asia, the threat is multi-dimensional but practically excludes a military invasion for the purpose of territorial conquest (except in the case of Taiwan), which was the essential and the most urgent in Qin's threat to the other six states during the ancient period under comparison. This chapter focuses on the economic dimension of the current framework, which is considered one of the most prominent dimensions already starting to unfold in the China-USA rivalry in accordance with the rise of the economic state in both countries, and, perhaps, one of the most powerful dimensions in shaping the East Asian order at the historical juncture of globalization still showing its momentum, especially with China and East Asia, but the harbinger of de-globalization having already risen to the landscape of global political economy, particular in the US.

De-globalization, more importantly, also greatly contributes to the US's adoption of its international economic strategy in East Asia in general and with China in particular. Instead of making efforts to involve China in globalization as it has since the 1990s, which helped the PRC to rapidly close the economic gap with the US, the US now turns to a stance of stepping back from Sino-American interdependence, fighting trade wars and technology battles with China and hoping to claw back some advantages in the rivalry. Sino-US economic interdependence that has been deeply shaped during the high tide of globalization, however, greatly affects the US policy choice in many respects. Globalization in general and the rise of the economic state in particular have undermined American democracy, a political system in the pre-global capitalist era enjoying comprehensive advantages, including in the economic realm, over its competitors, so greatly that the US elites, including in the administration, seemingly see no value in their own political system against Chinese authoritarianism via economic competition. In the ancient Chinese Warring States period, all six states gradually come to a mentality of admiring Qin in carrying out domestic Legalist reforms in order to make them wealthy and powerful. The problem for these states lay in the lack of effectiveness of their similar efforts adopting the rationale of Qin's governance. It is too early to say that the US is repeating these states' mistakes, but President Trump has repeatedly indicated his own inclinations to do so. Meanwhile, the rise of the economic state in the US, in the essential sense that it desires for citizens' convenient acceptance of the proposition of "economics as politics," does signal a lasting, though spasmodic and often ineffective, trend in the direction of "making America great again" in the sense of greatness defined in a similar way to Chinese President Xi Jinping's "China dream."

The US economic strategy in East Asia that is dominated by the logic of de-globalization and the economic state, moreover, has featured first, the withdrawal from multilateral international regimes in the region; and second, in the best sense, decreasing attention to promoting mutual economic benefits with its allies and, in the worse sense, starting economic disputes with some of them. By contrast, China's bilateral economic connections with all of the pertinent states (or state-like entities) are extremely strong, and Beijing is also keen on participating in regional economic multilateral organizations. The historical comparison with the ancient Chinese Warring States is enlightening for understanding how these different strategies of the US and the PRC might work in shaping other states' strategic options and, accordingly, the possible picture of the new East Asian order under the China-USA rivalry. In the ancient case, the *hezong* strategy, or cooperation and coalitions among the six states against the threat from Qin, eventually failed, because the *lianheng* strategy adopted by Qin worked very well in attracting each of the six states in a row, primarily by providing benefits through bilateral connections, which also fostered the inclination toward appeasement among elites of the six states. Now in East Asia there is nothing comparable to the *hezong* strategy regarding economic cooperation aimed at balancing China, while from the China side, its bilateral *lianheng* strategy has been powerful and, so far, very successful, and it does not refuse to adopt multilateral measures as long as China itself is included in such arrangements.[44] Considering their tremendous economic interests in their connections and cooperation with China, the pertinent states in current East Asian international relations will be sorely tested by the rise of the China-USA rivalry, as that will not be so easy for them to choose the side of the US, even though the US was the leader of these states during the Cold War and post-Cold-war globalization, and underwrites their current security arrangements in world politics. In this sense, East Asia will be in disorder in regional international relations.

---

44. In the wider geographic coverage beyond the region of East Asia, it seems that a similar picture is emerging with the US trade wars with many countries including European ones and India, while China is pursuing its Belt and Road program to strengthen economic connections with a huge number of states. In this chapter's point of view, it is also the absence of *hezong* versus the powerful practice of *lianheng* if the US and the PRC are engaged in global rivalry.

7
US-China Strategic Rivalry

Great Power Competition in the Post-industrial Age

Timothy R. Heath

Introduction

Tensions between United States and China have spurred a growing literature on the possibilities of great power transition and war. Even if war is avoided, the clash between US efforts to maintain an Asia-Pacific order favorable to its interests and China's own efforts to revamp that order in its favor raise the risk of an increasingly unsettled and unstable Asia-Pacific region. By providing a "middle range" theory on the role that competition and threat perceptions play in inter-state conflict, the literature on "strategic rivalry" can potentially contribute to the study of how the emerging "Asian disorder" might evolve and the risks it might entail.

Although I will argue the concept of strategic rivalry can be useful, I will also explore some of the idea's limitations. Unique features of the current epoch, labeled here "post-industrial," raise questions about the applicability of general findings drawn primarily from studies of international politics in the industrial age. Finding ways to modify the insights of the dynamics of strategic rivalry to account for the current era will be essential if the concept is to maintain its utility as a means of analysis.

The chapter is outlined in the following manner. Section 1 will briefly survey the concept of strategic rivalry and its most important insights. This section will also explore how these concepts help predict patterns in inter-state crises and conflict. Section 2 will assess the state of the US-China rivalry in Asia through this lens. Section 3 will explore the future trajectory of the US-China rivalry. It will argue that unique features of the post-industrial age may impose hard constraints on the potential escalation of tensions to great power war. Section 4 will conclude with general observations on the future prospects for post-industrial rivalries and the risks of war.

1. Strategic Rivalry: Concept Overview

Research regarding the causes of war has advanced beyond the conclusions based on ahistorical theories on international relations, such as those proposed by realists, liberals, and constructivists.[1] In the past twenty years, scholars have gained new insights into the causes of inter-state conflict, owing in part to the availability of more data about past conflicts. Sifting through databases covering hundreds of conflicts, John Vasquez pioneered the argument that territorial disputes provided a primary cause of inter-state conflict.[2]

Since the early 2000s, however, the academic community has advanced beyond this finding to focus on conflict-prone relationships between countries—*rivalries*—as a critical driver of conflict. Brandon Valeriano describes rivalry as "a situation of long-standing, historical animosity between two countries with a high probability of serious conflict or crisis." Rivalry assumes a "zero-sum game" over incompatible goals in which one side seeks to ensure its own security at the expense of the other.[3] Vasquez defined rivalry as a "relationship characterized by extreme competition, and usually psychological hostility, in which the issue positions of contenders are governed primarily by their attitude toward each other rather than by the stakes at hand."[4] Goertz and Diehl noted that rivalries tended to feature repeated sequences of militarized inter-state disputes.[5]

Scholars have identified two key types of disputes that lie at the core of rivalries: (1) those of territory and sovereignty—which scholars call "spatial" issues. Spatial issues remain common, especially among contiguous, minor powers (countries with modest economies and limited ability to project military forces beyond the border). Among major powers (countries with more advanced, wealthier economies and militaries with some capability of deploying beyond the nation's borders), however, the disputes appear quite different. Major powers appear inclined to fight most often over (2) issues of status, influence, and hierarchy in a given order or system—also referred to as "positional" issues. Rivalries over position and status are exceptionally

---

1. Kenneth Waltz, *A Theory of International Realism* (New York: McGraw Hill, 1979); John Mearsheimer, *The Tragedy of Great Power Politics* (New York: W. W. Norton, 2001); Jack Levy and William Thompson, *Causes of War* (Oxford, UK: Wiley-Blackwell, 2010), 50.
2. Paul Senese and John A. Vasquez, "A Unified Explanation of Territorial Conflict: Testing the Impact of Sampling Bias 1912–1992, *International Studies Quarterly* 47, no. 2 (June 2003): 275–98.
3. Brandon Valeriano, "Becoming Rivals: The Process of Rivalry Development," in *What do We Know About War*, ed. John A. Vasquez (Lanham, MD: Rowman and Littlefield, 2012), 63–82.
4. John Vasquez, "Distinguishing Rivals that Go to War from Those That Do Not: A Quantitative Comparative Case Study of the Two Paths to War," *International Studies Quarterly* 40, no. 4 (December 1996): 531–58.
5. G. Goertz and P. F. Diehl, "The Empirical Importance of Enduring Rivalries," *International Interactions* 18 (1992): 151–63.

difficult to resolve. These rivalries end only when one or more rivals are forced to move down a hierarchy in a significant and permanent manner.[6]

A "strategic" rivalry may be understood as a type of inter-state hostility that primarily involves positional disputes but may also involve spatial disputes, including those involving allies. A definition offered by Rasler and Thompson provides perhaps the most concise phrasing of these ideas. They defined a strategic rivalry as two countries that view each other as: (1) *competitors*, i.e., peers or near peers that compete over unresolved, incompatible goals involving positional and possibly also spatial issues; (2) *threats*, i.e., having both the intention and the capacity of carrying out military attacks against the other.[7]

Several additional features of rivalries allow us to more fully describe the phenomenon. One is the proliferation of intractable dispute issues, which may be of both positional and spatial types. David Dreyer called this problem "issue spiral," which he defined as a "dynamic process in which tension increases as multiple issues accumulate." According to Dreyer, issue spirals "increase perceptions of fear and distrust" and can lead to the conclusion that the only way to achieve favorable issue settlement in regard to all disagreements is through "imposing one's will." Moreover, issue accumulation increases the stakes of competition and for this reason may over time make war more appealing as a course of action.[8]

Owing to the nature of competition for influence and leadership, strategic rivalries often involve other countries. Intense competition could polarize a region, adding pressure on relevant countries to "take sides." The phenomenon of "multilateralization," in which rivalries between major powers overlap with those involving other countries, is common in strategic rivalries between great powers.[9]

More broadly, studies have also noted strong linkages between arms races, alliance-building, rivalries, and war. One study concluded that arms races occur most frequently in the context of enduring strategic rivalries and that arms races are more likely in the middle and later stages of a rivalry.[10] In a separate study, Colaresi, Rasler, and Thompson found arms buildups, alliance-building, and repeated crises to be significant predictors of war.[11] Similarly,

---

6. William R. Thompson, "Principal Rivalries," *The Journal of Conflict Resolution* 39, no. 2 (June 1995): 195–223.
7. Karen A. Rasler and William R. Thompson, "Contested Territory, Strategic Rivalries, and Conflict Escalation," *International Studies Quarterly* 50 (2006): 145–67.
8. David Dreyer, "One Issue Leads to Another: Issue Spirals and the Sino-Vietnam War," *Foreign Policy Analysis* 6 (2010): 297–315.
9. Rasler and Thompson, "Contested Territory, Strategic Rivalries, and Conflict Escalation," 526.
10. Toby Rider, Michael Findley, and Paul Diehl, "Just Part of the Game? Arms Races, Rivalry, and War," *Journal of Peace Research* 48 (2011): 85–100.
11. Michael Colaresi and William R. Thompson, "Alliances, Arms Buildups and Recurrent Conflict: Testing a Steps to War Model," *The Journal of Politics* 67, no. 2 (May 2005): 345–64.

Vasquez and others have outlined patterns in an archetype "steps to war" process in which two or more rivals build strength either internally, through arms-racing-type military buildups, or externally, through alliance-building. Ironically, these steps, while ostensibly designed to improve security, exacerbate the broader problems of distrust and deepen the perceptions of threat, which raises the sense of insecurity and risk of conflict.[12]

The Cold War at its height in the 1960s may provide an archetype of the "intense" level of rivalry. During that period, both the US and the Soviet Union cooperated very little, scarcely traded, and competed intensely by building powerful militaries, organizing geostrategic "blocs" of allies, and mobilizing popular support for costly competitive policies, such as the ambitious US space program aimed at part at surpassing the Soviet Union following its launch of the spacecraft "Sputnik." The two countries depicted each other as existential threats and deployed large militaries on a persistently near-war footing. The two superpowers feuded over a complex array of issues ranging from ideology, influence in different parts of the world, and territorial disputes involving allies and partners. Both countries prioritized defense spending and built competing networks of allies, most notably that of NATO versus the Warsaw Pact. The rivalry also featured a high degree of multilateralization as proxy conflicts and parallel rivalries waxed and waned. Underscoring the connection between rivalry and conflict, the two countries came close to major war in the Cuban Missile Crisis, and their militaries clashed in proxy wars in Korea, Vietnam, Afghanistan, and others.[13]

To summarize, the concept of strategic rivalry may provide an analytic tool to help inform a more accurate assessment of the risks of crisis and conflict between two states. In general, the stronger the dynamics of competition and threat perception, the higher the risk of serial militarized crises and conflict. Several observable behaviors can help us assess the relative intensity of a strategic rivalry. These include the level of mobilization of resources against an enemy, whether a government designates a state as an enemy, and the presence of arms races, alliance-building activity, and overlapping rivalries involving other states. Table 7.1 summarizes this list of features and sorts them according to the relative intensity of the rivalry dynamic, the "strong" level based on the early Cold War as an archetype.

2. US-China Strategic Rivalry in Asia

How advanced is the strategic rivalry between China and the US and its allies? This section will attempt an assessment, using the indicators provided in Table 7.1. The indicators admittedly are broad, and greater specificity in

---

12. Paul D. Senese and John Vasquez, *The Steps to War: An Empirical Study* (Princeton, NJ: Princeton University Press, 2008), 2.
13. John Gaddis, *The Cold War: A New History* (New York: Penguin, 2016).

Table 7.1: Indicators for assessing intensity of strategic rivalry

Indicator	Weak rivalry dynamic	Strong rivalry dynamic
Level of competition	Low level of mobilization of resources against rival	High level of mobilization of resources against rival
Threat perception	Government does not identify rival as top threat	Government identifies rival as a top threat
Dispute issues	Few, manageable	Acrimonious array of intractable positional and spatial disputes
Arms racing	Defense spending within norm	Elevated levels of defense spending; capabilities clearly target rival's military
Alliance building	Little effort to build coalition aimed at rival	Intense effort to build coalition targeting rival
Multilateralization	Disputants limited to two parties	Multiple parallel, overlapping rivalries

Source: Author.

the indicators is required for a more accurate assessment. However, a basic consideration using these admittedly imprecise criteria can at least provide a thumbnail sketch of the relative intensity of the US-China strategic rivalry.

Level of competition. China is widely regarded to be a near-peer of the US in the Asia-Pacific and the only country capable of posing a long-term challenge to the leading position of the US at the global-systemic level. The two countries have intensified the competition for leadership in Asia in recent years, especially since the US announced the "Rebalance to Asia" under President Obama in 2011. Under President Trump, the competition for leadership in Asia has only intensified. The US has outlined a vision of a "Free and Open Indo-Pacific" that competes directly with China's ambitions to shape the region.[14] But the competition extends beyond Asia. The two countries compete with one another over economic issues as well as for influence around the world. China's "Made in 2025" initiative, for example, appears aimed at establishing China as a leading economy, an outcome that would necessarily relegate the US to a secondary position. The "trade war" initiated by President Trump and the bitter feud over Chinese tech companies such as Huawei underscore the importance of the economic and technological aspects of the competition. Militarily, the US retains a clear edge as a globally distributed force, but years

---

14. Department of State, "A Free and Open Indo-Pacific: Advancing a Shared Vision," November 4, 2019.

of major increases in Chinese defense spending have narrowed the gap in capability with China, especially in Asia.[15]

Yet compared to the example of the Cold War, the mobilization of resources by the US and Chinese governments against each other seems moderate. Despite efforts to reduce mutual dependence, the two countries remain among the most important trade partners of one another. The two compete for influence in Asia, but neither has organized "blocs" of aligned countries. Although the governments have outlined competing economic initiatives, the US has also abandoned some of them, such as the Trans-Pacific Partnership. China has arguably maintained a more consistent approach, but many of its initiatives, such as the Belt and Road Initiative (BRI), seem driven as much by domestic imperatives as they are by competition with the US, and the overall level of investment appears to have declined in recent years.[16] Accordingly, the level of competition may be judged as of "medium" strength.

Perceptions of threat. The US government has clearly depicted China as a primary threat. In 2017, the US National Security Strategy described China as a "revisionist power" that seeks to "displace the United States in the Indo-Pacific region."[17] In June, 2018, the FBI director called China the "broadest, most significant threat to the United States."[18] Perceptions in China of the threat posed by the US have hardened as well. Commentary in Chinese media regularly carries searing criticism of the US as immoral, unjust, and threatening. In a typical commentary published in July 2018, China's official English newspaper, *China Daily*, slammed the US for a "dictatorial bent."[19] Authorities have stepped up a harsh crackdown on Western non-government organizations, traveling scholars, and other intellectuals, due to suspicion that these individuals pose a threat to social stability and the Chinese Communist Party's (CCP) authority.[20]

Although distrust is growing, the populations of both countries show at most a "mixed" sense of threat. A Carnegie Endowment study of perceptions among the public and elite in the US and China regarding security issues

---

15. Michael Swaine et al., *China and the U.S.-Japanese Alliance in 2030: A Net Assessment*, Carnegie Endowment for International Peace (2013), accessed December 1, 2018, http://carnegieendowment.org/2013/05/03/china-s-military-and-u.s.-japan-alliance-in-2030-strategic-net-assessment.
16. Radio Free Asia, "China's Investment in Belt and Road Initiative Cools," January 17, 2020.
17. White House website, "National Security Strategy of the United States," December 2017, accessed February 1, 2019, https://www.whitehouse.gov/wp-content/uploads/2017/12/NSS-Final-12-18-2017-0905.pdf.
18. Reuters, "China Trying to Sway U.S. Vote, Poses Threat: Officials," October 10, 2018.
19. *China Daily*, "Dictatorial Bent of US Is the Real Global Threat," July 2, 2018, accessed February 10, 2019, http://www.chinadaily.com.cn/a/201807/02/WS5b3a350aa3103349141e03b0.html.
20. Reuters, "Western Governments, Rights Groups Decry China's Tough New NGO Law," April 29, 2016.

found trust had sunk to low levels in both countries.[21] According to a poll conducted by government newspaper *Global Times*, a large majority of the Chinese public believes the US intends to pursue a containment policy.[22] A 2019 Pew poll also found 60 percent of Americans viewed China negatively, a sharp increase from the previous year, when only 47 percent of people held the same view. Moreover, the number of Americans who view China as a top threat has also doubled since 2007. However, the same poll concluded that even with the increase, only 24 percent of Americans in 2019 viewed Chinas as a threat, the same percent that regarded Russia as a threat.[23] Indeed, both China and the US seem to have a limited sense of hostility towards the other. Washington and Beijing have avoided the Manichean depictions of the other country as an "evil empire" that typified the intense ideological feuding of the Cold War. The Carnegie poll similarly found only "small minorities" in either country believed the other country to be an enemy.[24] The sense of threat may thus be judged as of "medium" intensity.

Dispute issues. China and the US have experienced a proliferating array of dispute issues. At the heart of the rivalry lies a contest over who should lead the Asia-Pacific region, which is widely anticipated to become the future center of the global economy. China has promoted its vision of an interconnected region, well embodied in the BRI announced by President Xi Jinping in 2013. The BRI aims to integrate the Eurasian landmass through infrastructure and trade rules and norms led by China. China has also advanced a vision of regional security and stepped up efforts to shape the security order accordingly.[25] The US, by contrast, has proposed a vision of a "Free and Open Indo-Pacific" that better suits US interests and has similarly stepped up financial commitments and military and diplomatic engagement to shape a more favorable order accordingly.[26] Disagreements over trade, investment, and technology theft have gained prominence, especially since President Trump's

---

21. Michael Swaine, Rachel Odell, Luo Yuan, and Liu Xiangdong, "U.S.-China Security Perceptions Survey: Findings and Implications," Carnegie Endowment for International Peace, December 12, 2013, accessed February 4, 2019, http://carnegieendowment.org/2013/12/12/u.s.-china-security-perceptions-survey-findings-and-implications-pub-53820.
22. "78% Chinese Believe West Intends to Contain China," *Global Times*, December 30, 2015, accessed February 10, 2019, http://www.globaltimes.cn/content/961216.shtml.
23. Pew, "U.S. Views of China Turn Sharply Amid Trade Tensions," August 13, 2019, accessed January 2, 2020, https://www.pewresearch.org/global/2019/08/13/u-s-views-of-china-turn-sharply-negative-amid-trade-tensions/.
24. Michael Swaine, Rachel Odell, Luo Yuan, and Liu Xiangdong, "U.S.-China Security Perceptions Survey: Findings and Implications," Carnegie Endowment for International Peace, December 12, 2013, accessed February 10, 2019, http://carnegieendowment.org/2013/12/12/u.s.-china-security-perceptions-survey-findings-and-implications-pub-53820.
25. Nadege Rolland, *China's Eurasian Century? Political and Strategic Implications of the Belt and Road Initiative*, National Bureau of Asian Research, 2017.
26. Department of Defense, "Indo-Pacific Strategy Report: Preparedness, Partnerships, and Promoting a Networked Region," June 1, 2019, accessed January 2, 2020, https://media.

election.[27] Chinese officials and commentary have similarly stepped up criticism of US policies regarding such issues.[28] Even shared threats, such as the COVID-19 pandemic that emerged in late 2019, have proven to become yet another issue for dispute. As the disease spread globally, the two countries traded accusations and competed for influence.[29]

Security-related disputes have intensified in some ways. Regarding Taiwan, US officials have stepped up some diplomatic and military engagements, irritating Beijing.[30] In the South China Sea, US and Chinese officials have feuded over Beijing's construction of artificial islands.[31] In the East China Sea, US authorities criticized China's establishment of an Air Defense Identification Zone (ADIZ) in the East China Sea as provocative, charges Beijing has rejected.[32] New security-related disputes have also emerged. The two sides have argued over the US installation of missile defense systems in South Korea.[33] The decisions by both countries to build up military commands and units to operate in space and cyberspace also underscore the depth of disagreement—and sense of threat—in those domains.[34]

The trend appears towards more and different types of disputes, but compared to the level of the Cold War, these remain limited in intensity. The two sides have not engaged in the type of armed proxy conflict that typified the Cold War. Outside the important exception of Taiwan, most security-related disputes involve uninhabited reef features or waterways. Arguments have increased over rules and norms that govern cyberspace, trade, and investment, but both countries have continued to engage in negotiation to

---

defense.gov/2019/Jul/01/2002152311/-1/-1/1/DEPARTMENT-OF-DEFENSE-INDO-PACIFIC-STRATEGY-REPORT-2019.PDF.

27. *New York Times*, "For the U.S. and China, a Technology Cold War That's Freezing Over," March 23, 2018.
28. *People's Daily*, "CPC Speeds Up Modernization Drive Toward 'Great' Socialist China," October 18, 2017.
29. Thomas Christensen, "A Modern Tragedy? Covid 19 and U.S.-China Relations," Brookings Institute, May 2020.
30. "Foreign Ministry Spokesperson Hua Chunying's Regular Press Conference on December 26, 2016," Ministry of Foreign Affairs of the People's Republic of China website, December 26, 2016, accessed February 10, 2019, http://www.fmprc.gov.cn/mfa_eng/xwfw_665399/s2510_665401/t1426902.shtml.
31. David J. Firestein, "The US-China Perception Gap in the South China Sea," The *Diplomat*, August 19, 2016, accessed February 10, 2019, https://thediplomat.com/2016/08/the-us-china-perception-gap-in-the-south-china-sea/.
32. Kurt Campbell, "Maritime Territorial Disputes and Sovereignty Issues in Asia" (testimony before the Senate Foreign Relations Committee Subcommittee on East Asian and Pacific Affairs), September 20, 2012, accessed February 10, 2019, https://www.foreign.senate.gov/hearings/maritime-territorial-disputes-and-sovereignty-issues-in-asia.
33. Teng Jianqun, "Why Is China Unhappy with the Deployment of THAAD in the ROK?" China Institute of International Studies, April 21, 2015, accessed February 15, 2019, http://www.ciis.org.cn/english/2015-04/01/content_7793314.htm.
34. Ben Buchanan and Robert Williams, "A Deepening U.S.-China Cyberspace Security Dilemma," *Lawfare*, October 24, 2018, accessed February 16, 2019, https://www.lawfareblog.com/deepening-us-china-cybersecurity-dilemma.

resolve differences. This indicator may be assessed as "medium" though it does appear to trend upwards.

Arms racing. China has continued to experience significant increases in its defense budget. In 2020, China announced a 6.6 percent boost compared to the previous year, which represented the slowest rise in three decades.[35] It is difficult to estimate precisely how much of the military buildup is aimed at the US. The People's Liberation Army's (PLA) modernization efforts started from a very low base as an impoverished, backward military in the 1990s. At the very least, however, one can say that many of the PLA's acquisitions and investments in improving the quality of the force could improve its ability to fight US forces in contingencies along China's periphery. The Asia-Pacific region as a whole has also experienced a significant uptick in defense spending. Military expenditures increased 52 percent over the past decade although Chinese spending drove most of the growth.[36]

The US response to China's military buildup has been focused but restrained. The Pentagon has prioritized efforts for "great power competition" with China and Russia, and investments in relevant capabilities have increased accordingly.[37] However, US defense spending is expected to remain flat in the coming years at best, as Washington grapples with the fallout of the COVID-19 pandemic.[38] Moreover, unlike the Soviet Union, China has shown little interest in building a military capability to challenge US military dominance in geographic regions outside its immediate periphery. This indicator may thus be assessed as of "medium" intensity.

Alliance building. The activity to boost alliances has remained modest at best. China has bolstered its ties with Russia and expanded its role in multilateral security organizations such as the Shanghai Cooperation Organization (SCO). It has called for greater security cooperation with trade partners in Southeast Asia and Africa and increased the military's role in exercises, but Beijing has not formed any alliances. The US retains a formidable array of alliances and partnerships, but domestic political and economic strains have led to a loosening of those ties, in part due to trade disputes. Countries such as Japan, Australia, and India have stepped up cooperation, albeit still of a very low level, with one another to balance against China, due in part to uncertainty about the US commitment to the region. Alliance-building activity can be judged as of a "low" level.

Multilateralization. US competition with China for status and influence in Asia has overlapped with numerous rivalries involving China and its

---

35. Reuters, "China Defense Spending Rise at Three Decade Low," May 21, 2020.
36. *Los Angeles Times*, "Military Spending Is Soaring in the Asia-Pacific Region," June 7, 2019.
37. *ZDNET*, "China Aims to Narrow Cyber Warfare Gap with US," August 17, 2018; VOA, "US Prepared to Strike in Cyberspace," September 20, 2018, accessed February 1, 2019, https://www.voanews.com/a/us-prepared-to-strike-in-cyberspace/4581060.html.
38. Bloomberg, "Military Spending Will Be 'Flat' in the Near Term, Bolton Says," October 31, 2018.

neighbors. The disputes span territorial issues, such as those over the South China Sea involving Southeast Asian countries, Senkaku Islands with Japan, and the Indian border. Other disputes concern the treatment of ethnic Chinese nationals and the implementation of the BRI, as has occurred in Malaysia.[39] In June 2020, China and India engaged in a brutal brawl that left twenty Indian and an unknown number of PLA troops dead.[40] Although tensions eased slightly in 2020, China continues to compete with Japan for influence in the Asia-Pacific region and feud over history-related issues. Anxiety and concern about Chinese intentions have driven countries in Asia to boost defense spending though the increase remains modest. Tension between China and Australia and New Zealand has also increased over issues of political influence operations.[41] As apprehension over China's intensions has grown, countries have stepped up cooperation with one another to balance against China, as has occurred between India, Australia, Japan, and the US. For example, Australia and Japan have coordinated efforts with the US to counter China's BRI with competing infrastructure initiatives.[42] However, despite the limited multilateral cooperation and deepening tensions between China and its neighbors, the overlapping rivalries have remained restrained, and virtually no crises or major incidents have resulted in fatalities. Most countries seem to seek stable, profitable ties with China while increasing security ties with the US as a hedge. The level of "multilateralization" may be judged as of a "medium" level.

In sum, an assessment of the relevant indicators suggests the US-China relationship remains at a "medium" level of intensity, which suggests a worrying, but overall moderate risk of crisis (Table 7.2). Underscoring this point, there have been several near incidents involving aircraft and ships in the maritime region since then. In addition to the violent clash between China and India in 2020, Chinese maritime law enforcement forces wrested control of Scarborough Reef from the Philippines in 2012 and sustained a tense standoff with Japan following the nationalization of the Senkaku Islands the same year.[43] Chinese and US forces have nearly collided in the South China Sea on several occasions as well.[44] At the same time, the two countries have not experienced a severe militarized crisis since the collision of a US recon-

---

39. Reuters, "China, Malaysia Restart Massive 'Belt and Road' Project After Hiccups," July 25, 2019.
40. CNN, "Twenty Indian Soldiers Dead After Clash with China Along Disputed Border," June 17, 2020.
41. *Council for Foreign Relations*, "Australia, New Zealand Face China's Influence," December 13, 2017.
42. *Sydney Morning Herald*, "Australia Joins US and Japan Rival to China's Belt and Road Infrastructure Spree," July 31, 2018.
43. Congressional Research Services, "U.S.-China Strategic Competition in South and East China Seas: Background and Issues for Congress," August 6, 2020.
44. *South China Morning Post*, "U.S., Chinese Warships Within Meters of Collision in South China Sea, Leaked Pictures Show," October 3, 2018.

Table 7.2: Assessment of US-China rivalry indicators

Indicator	Assessment	Comment
Level of competition	Medium	Trending upwards with government-led initiatives but low level of popular mobilization.
Threat perception	Medium	Both sides view each other as possible threat but also necessary partner. Mixed threat perception among publics
Arms racing	Medium	Modest US military buildup; China's military continues rapid modernization
Dispute issues	Medium	Proliferating array of dispute issues, but none have involved armed conflict.
Alliance building	Low	China building partnerships but not alliances. US alliances have loosened somewhat.
Multilateralization	Medium	India, Japan, Vietnam, Australia, and others modestly step up balancing cooperation. However, disputants also maintain stable ties to gain economic benefits.

Source: Author.

naissance airplane near Hainan Island in 2001. China has also not engaged in a conflict with its maritime neighbors. Reflecting Beijing's assessment, China's 2017 white paper on "Asia-Pacific Security Cooperation" judged the maritime environment to be "stable."[45]

3. Strategic Rivalry in the Post-industrial Age

The finding that the US and China currently face a low risk of conflict is perhaps unsurprising. Most commentators would agree with such a judgment. The real challenge lies in interpreting whether the current situation represents the start of an "upswing" trend that may mature into a full-blown rivalry, or a longer-term trend with little risk of escalation. If the latter, the US-China rivalry may persist for a long time as a moderately intense competition that could see occasional crises or incidents but overall feature low risks of great power war.

It is possible that the current pacific period may be merely a lull in history between periods of great power rivalry. The factors most associated with international peace, i.e., democracy, liberal institutions, and international trade, are generally weaker in Asia than in Europe. China is not a democracy, and in fact its authoritarian tendencies have strengthened considerably under Xi Jinping. The region also has notoriously weak institutions and lacks the types

---

45. Xinhua, "Full Text: China's Policies on Asia-Pacific Security Cooperation," January 11, 2017.

of liberal, collective security arrangements typical of Europe. The region does carry out extensive intra- and inter-regional trade, but the ability of inter-state trade to restrain rivalry and war remains unclear.[46] If these are the primary restraints on great power war, the situation augurs ill for peace.

The region's security dynamics add another cause for concern. US-China competition has aggravated tensions over persistent flashpoints including Taiwan and the East and South China Seas. China has continued to insist on unification with Taiwan even though support on the island for that outcome has plummeted to well below 10 percent.[47] Under President Trump, the US government has bolstered its security relationship with Taiwan, announcing an $8 billion arms package in 2019.[48] In 2020, the US sent its highest-level official to Taiwan since 1979, when Secretary of Health and Human Services Alexander Azar visited to praise the island's handling of the coronavirus threat.[49] The US Navy has also maintained a steady pace of transits through the Taiwan Strait over the past decade, further irritating Beijing.[50] Political sparring over China's efforts to disrupt Taiwan's democracy through propaganda and disinformation have led some observers to speculate about a "proxy war" on the island.[51]

Tensions have also increased over the South China Sea, where US military forces have upheld naval exercises and freedom of navigation voyages near Chinese-held artificial islands in the Spratly Islands. In October 2018, the USS *Decatur* operating in the South China Sea nearly collided with a Chinese warship that had sought to ward off the destroyer, using unsafe and unprofessional maneuvers.[52] Although Chinese-Japanese tensions have eased in recent years, both sides maintain a tense standoff in the Senkaku Islands. The security environment in Asia is further unsettled by North Korea's provocative behavior. Deepening US-China tensions have hampered efforts by the

---

46. Katja Kleinberg, Gregory Robinson, Stewart French, "Trade Concentration and Interstate Conflict," *The Journal of Politics* 74, no. 2 (March 28, 2012): 529–40; Katherine Barbieri, "Economic Interdependence: A Path to Peace or a Source of Interstate Conflict?," *Journal of Peace Research* 33, no. 1 (1996): 29–49; Benjamin Goldsmith, "International Trade and the Onset and Escalation of Interstate Conflict: More to Fight about, or More Reasons Not to Fight?," *Defense and Peace Economics* 24, no. 6 (2013): 555–78.
47. *Taiwan News*, "Support for Taiwan KMT, Unification with China at New Lows," December 19, 2019.
48. *NPR*, "China Vows Sanctions on U.S. Firms for Arms Sales to Taiwan," August 21, 2019.
49. *Wall Street Journal*, "Health Secretary Azar Renews Swipes at China Over Coronavirus in Taiwan Visit," August 11, 2020.
50. *South China Morning Post*, "U.S. Warships Made 92 Transits through Taiwan Strait since 2007," May 3, 2019.
51. *Kyodo News*, "Competing U.S.-China Influence Sparks Talk of Taiwan Proxy War," January 3, 2020.
52. *USNI News*, "Destroyer USS Decatur Has Close Encounter with Chinese Warship," October 1, 2018, accessed January 3, 2020, https://news.usni.org/2018/10/01/37006.

two countries to coordinate efforts to restrain Pyongyang from its pursuit of nuclear weapons and destabilizing weapons tests.[53]

Despite these unsettling developments and the weakness of traditional constraints on inter-state rivalry, history may have introduced new constraints unknown in previous eras. Distinctive features of the post-industrial era raise the possibility that the US-China rivalry may persist as a tense, friction-filled competition that nevertheless carries a low risk of escalation to great power war. In particular, the current rivalry appears strongly influenced by a deepening bifurcation between elites and the public in each country that both reflects and aggravates demographic, economic, and technological factors.

The post-industrial age

The historic period that I seek to analyze is the one that has existed from the 1990s through today. This chapter will use the term "post-industrial" age, or epoch, to refer to a period of history that roughly begins with the close of the Cold War. This epoch is characterized by the rise of industries based on information technologies and the maturing of Western economies from an industrial basis to one featuring services and advanced technological manufacture. But the change in the mode of economic growth only imperfectly defines this period. After all, many countries around the world are in different stages of development, and China has only recently begun to transition into a post-industrial mode of growth. Nevertheless, this chapter will use the term "post-industrial age" as a way of emphasizing important demographic and technological changes that distinguish the current from previous eras, several of which are highlighted below.

Demographic and social trends

Among demographic and social trends, three stand out: population aging, the resurgence of social and economic inequality, and changing social values.

Population aging. In coming decades, the most powerful states in the international system will experience an aging of their populations that is unprecedented in human history. Due to steep declines in birthrates and increases in life expectancy, all of the world's great powers are expected to experience significant aging. In 2017, 13 percent of the global population was aged sixty or over, but that percentage is projected to reach 25 percent of all regions of the world, except for Africa.[54] Among the effects of demographic aging, great powers, including the US and China, will experience austere fiscal situa-

---

53. *New York Times*, "U.S. Braces for Major North Korean Weapons Test as Trump's Diplomacy Fizzles," December 21, 2019.
54. United Nations, "World Population Prospects: 2017 Revision," accessed February 13, 2019, https://esa.un.org/unpd/wpp/Publications/Files/WPP2017_KeyFindings.pdf.

tions, due to pressures arising from slow growth compounded by significant domestic demand to pay massive expenditures for elderly care. Military spending may be "crowded out" by these domestic demands. Because the US faces a slightly less severe aging problem, the same trends may well prolong America's global preeminence, as a China grappling with the enormous fiscal burden of social aging will be poorly positioned to contest that position.[55] The challenges imposed by demographic aging suggest policymakers may also struggle to mobilize domestic support for expensive competitive policies, especially among the broader public where limited incomes may result in greater dependence on government spending. The same dynamics may also constrain perceptions of threat posed by the rival country, given the strong demand for domestic spending.

Inequality and political polarization. Inequality between political and economic classes appears to be an increasingly pervasive and inescapable fact for post-industrial societies.[56] Of course, most of human history has featured deep inequality between wealthy elites and the laboring masses. However, the process of industrialization generated sustained increases in productivity and growth that in many cases dramatically increased the size of middle classes and narrowed the gap between rich and poor. The case is vividly demonstrated in China's case, which since 1978 has lifted 800 million people from poverty through rapid economic growth, according to official Chinese media.[57] However, Thomas Piketty has argued that the post–World War II boom responsible for the dramatic narrowing in inequality represented an anomaly to the historical norm of unequal societies with small middle classes.[58] The deterioration of middle classes in the developed West and the return of yawning inequality have also coincided with a widening cultural and political gap between elites and the public. The deepening divides in cultural tastes and values, education levels, health, marriage rates, and mortality have fueled political polarization and gridlock in many Western democracies. China has avoided the spectacle of widespread discontent despite slowing growth, but at the cost of a massive increase in internal security spending. According to official figures, China has spent more money on internal security than on defense since 2012.[59]

The deepening inequality and political polarization has begun to affect foreign policy. Within the US, a bifurcation between the views of foreign policy elites and the public has already emerged. Large constituencies in both the Republican and Democratic Parties have opposed costly foreign policy commitments favored by foreign policy experts in both parties. The United

---

55. Mark Haas, "A Geriatric Peace? The Future of U.S. Power in a World of Aging Populations," *International Security* 32, no. 1 (Summer 2007): 112–47.
56. Thomas Piketty, "Inequality in the Long Run," *Science*, May 23, 2014.
57. *China Daily*, "Steady Development Helped Poverty Reduction," November 6, 2011.
58. Piketty, "Inequality in the Long Run."
59. Reuters, "China Domestic Security Spending Rises to $111 Billion," March 4, 2012.

Kingdom's Brexit vote to leave the European Union similarly exposed a divide between urban elites and urban masses.[60] Coming years may see a deepening bifurcation in the perceptions of foreign policy elites, who may be more supportive of costly competitive strategies, and those of a distrustful public, which may oppose a policy that they regard as providing little benefit.

Changing social values from post industrialization. Post-industrial economic change also has coincided with significant changes in the values and outlooks of individuals in the same societies. Ronald Inglehart and his team of experts found in their survey of over forty countries that the transition of an economy into post industrialization correlated with a declining willingness on the part of citizens to fight for their countries, a greater skepticism towards authority, and an increased interest in individual pursuits.[61] The changing social values could dampen the sense of threat and competition from a rival wealthy, developed country which is both an essential trade partner and has the capacity to inflict serious harm through conventional war, and further complicate efforts by capitals to mobilize popular support for costly competitive strategies or wars (Table 7.3).

Table 7.3: Potential effects of demographic and social factors on US-China rivalry

Demographic factors		
Factor	Potential Effect	Comment
Aging population	Dampens threat, competition, especially among broader public	High resource demands to serve aging populations crowds out military spending
Rising levels of inequality and political polarization	Dampens threat, competition among broader populace	Bifurcation possible in which elites favor competitive strategies, while public resists efforts to mobilize support
Changing social values from economic transformation	Dampens competition, threat	People in post-industrial economies tend to favor individual-focused values, question authority

Source: Author.

Economic factors

Post-industrial societies are defined most notably by the structure of their economies. In general, they feature relatively larger tertiary sectors featuring services and advanced manufacturing. The US and much of Europe began to

---

60. Lubos Pastor and Pietro Veronesi, "Inequality Aversion, Populism, and the Backlash Against Globalization," Working Paper 2018-53, University of Chicago, August 2018.
61. Ronald F. Inglehart, Bi Puranen, and Christian Welzel, "Declining Willingness to Fight for One's Country," *Journal of Peace Research* 52, no. 4 (2015): 418–34.

experience such a change beginning in the 1970s, when rising wages rendered many industries uncompetitive. In recent years, China has also begun to shed some industries, as wages grow and the economy transitions into a more balanced mode of growth featuring services and advanced manufacturing.

The consequences for the US-China rivalry of the changing mode of growth may include the following. First, these economies benefit very little from the acquisition of territory. This reduces the incentive to pursue conflict for purposes of acquiring territory or resolving territorial disputes, which historically has proven one of the most salient drivers of war.[62] The importance of technological leadership does elevate the importance of competition in that domain.[63] Sparring between China and the US over issues of technology transfers underscores its salience in the contemporary rivalry. However, the contest for technological leadership is most likely to be primarily an affair of the technicians, industry executives, and decision-makers who study and understand the importance of the contest. Unlike territorial-related disputes, competitions over technology tend to resonate less emotionally with the public.

Another feature of the current situation has been the growing tendency of the technological domain to settle into broad spheres dominated by the US and China. It is possible that the spheres will overlap less and less in the future, which would undercut the imperative to dominate the other. Already, commentators have spoken of a "bifurcated" global economy defined by Chinese and US technologies, norms, and standards.[64]

Slow growth. Advanced economies tend to experience slower rates of growth as they shed industries and expand the tertiary sectors. In most industrialized countries, annual GDP growth has tended below 3 percent, especially since the 1990s. The growth has been often imbalanced, the urban centers and professional classes gaining the most, while working classes in many countries have seen stagnant incomes. GDP growth for most of the industrialized West is forecast to remain below 3 percent for the foreseeable future. In China's case, growth remains substantially higher at 6.1 percent in 2019 but is expected to fall in coming years as well, as the country transitions from an unsustainable investment-driven approach.[65]

Slower growth will exacerbate the problem of resourcing military spending to support arms- racing behavior against rival countries. The tradeoff between "guns versus butter" will be further exacerbated by the issues of demographic aging, increasing inequality and political polarization, and the extremely high costs of military warfighting technology such as stealth aircraft, submarines,

---

62. John Vasquez and Christopher S. Leskiw, "The Origins and War Proneness of Interstate Rivalries," *Annual Review of Political Science* 4 (2001): 295–316.
63. George Modelski, *Long Cycles in World Politics* (New York: MacMillan, 1987).
64. *New York*, "Why Would Google's Ex-CEO Predict a Separate Chinese Internet?" September 24, 2018, accessed March 7, 2019, http://nymag.com/intelligencer/2018/09/googles-ex-ceo-eric-schmidt-predicts-separate-chinese-web.html.
65. *New York Times*, "China's Growth Slows as Challenges Mount," October 17, 2019.

and ships. Policymakers will be hard pressed to sustain high levels of military spending amid these pressures.

To be sure, fiscal constraints hardly posed an obstacle in previous eras, such as the 1700s to 1800s, when kings bankrupted their treasuries to fight costly wars. However, in those cases, governments could gain the complicity of their citizens in furnishing troops through conscription and revenue through taxation, by offering political rights and economic opportunities. In an age of diminishing expectations within industrialized democracies, governments have fewer incentives to offer in exchange for higher taxes or conscription. Moreover, as noted, the widening cultural and political gulf between elites and the public render even more difficult the task of extracting higher taxes from the public. Virtually all major liberal Western democracies have long ago abandoned conscription, in part due to the higher demands of operating a professional military as well as the unpopularity of a draft. China continues to rely heavily on conscription, due to its inability to recruit enough volunteers. Dependence on poorly motivated draftees continues to be a major weakness for the PLA.[66] As an authoritarian state, China could offer to expand political rights for its citizens in exchange for more taxes, but the CCP has shown no indication that it is willing to do so any time soon. Government leaders and the elites who support competitive policies may have little choice but to find ways to do so with persistent resource constraints. This may dampen the competition, and could dampen threat perceptions, especially among the broader public, if domestic spending needs appear more urgent (Table 7.4).

Table 7.4: Potential effects of economic factors on US-China rivalry

Economic factors		
Factor	Potential Effect	Comment
Technological competition for growth	Dampens threat, mixed effect on competition	Elites focused on competition, but public likely less engaged
Bifurcation of global economy	Mixed effect on competition	Inability to dominate the entire global economy may encourage accommodation; competition may intensify in overlapping areas
Slow economic growth	Dampens competition, threat	Less revenue available for military buildups; domestic worries may overtake concerns about rival, especially among public

Source: Author.

---

66. Marcus Clay and Dennis Blasko, "People Win Wars: The PLA Enlisted Force and Other Related Matters," *War on the Rocks*, July 31, 2020, accessed September 2, 2020, https://warontherocks.com/2020/07/people-win-wars-the-pla-enlisted-force-and-other-related-matters/.

Civilian technological factors

The pervasiveness of digital and other technologies also distinguishes the current era from the past. Several of these technologies could affect rivalry dynamics: in particular, the technologies of cheap transportation and electronic media. Mass transportation facilitates the rapid and distant movement of peoples. It also facilitates the circulation of people and exposure to different cultures and ideas. Mass media and electronic communications have been around for over a century. However, since the 1990s, the availability of mobile communication and Internet technologies and devices has reached unprecedented levels. People have more access to information about the world than ever before. The combined effect of mass mobility and exposure to the Internet can be observed in two effects: changes in personal values and the formation of sub-national and extra-national identities.

The changes in social and personal values have already been mentioned, but the role of information technologies in accelerating this change merits a brief mention. Scholars have noted how the proliferation of information technologies and mobile devices has encouraged broad cultural changes in many countries, including individuation, relationship-building, and civic engagement.[67] Moses Naim characterized such changes a "mentality revolution" in which personal expectations have been raised and traditions questioned in many parts of the world.[68] The change in personal values and interests weakens the incentive for people to resist efforts by national leaders to depict a distant rival power as a pressing threat that must be met with costly competitive policies.

Similarly, the proliferation of sub-national identities and weakening of supranational identities such as the European Union can be seen in a number of examples. Brexit represented the most obvious example, but the EU continues to face numerous similar breakaway movements.[69] In China, the phenomenon is less pronounced, due to a greater homogeneity of the population, but Beijing's failure to win over the loyalty of people in Hong Kong, Xinjiang, and Tibet underscores a similar trend towards regionalization. In Taiwan, identity is shifting decisively in favor of the island, and support for unification continues to plummet, around 6 percent of the people identifying themselves as "Chinese" (most identify either as "Taiwanese" or "Chinese/Taiwanese").[70] These developments raise the likelihood that national leaders will face internal resistance when carrying out a large-scale mobilization of

---

67. Manuel Castells, "The Impact of the Internet on Society: A Global Perspective," *MIT Technology Review*, September 8, 2014.
68. Moses Naim, *The End of Power: From Boardrooms to Battlefields and Churches to States, Why Being in Charge Isn't What It Used to Be* (New York: Basic Books, 2014).
69. Voice of America, "Europe's Breakaway Movements Watch Catalonia's Progress with Interest," November 6, 2017.
70. *Taipei Times*, "Independence Poll Shows Widening Gap," December 31, 2019.

Table 7.5: Potential effects of civilian technologies on US-China rivalry

Civilian technological factors		
Factor	Effect	Comment
Availability of cheap mass transportation	Dampens threat, competition	Mobility facilitates formation of sub-national identities and popular resistance to national mobilization for costly competitive strategies.
Pervasiveness of electronic mass and social media	Dampens competition, mixed effect on threat	Pervasive social media may encourage formation of sub-national identities that resist national mobilization; social media also facilitates hatred and fears spreading.

Source: Author.

the people to support costly competitive strategies, as the US and the Soviet Union did during the Cold War.

The same trends of rapid mobility, rising expectations, and intensification of local identities have admittedly coincided with a surging nationalism in many industrialized countries. But in these cases, the reaction has taken an isolationist, defensive tone. There is little in the nationalism of Trump's backers, Brexiteers, and others that seek conflict with China or Russia. Viewed in another way, these movements tend to reflect in part the broader pattern of the breakdown in support for the nation-state and intensification of cultural or sub-national identities and the depth of distrust between the public and elites (Table 7.5).

Military technology factors

The advent of new technologies in computing, materials, energy, and data processing has both accelerated the potential speed of warfare and contributed to ballooning costs. The price tag for ships, aircraft, vehicles, and many weapons systems continues to escalate to astronomical levels as developers attempt to pack in more and more of the various technologies designed to give their respective militaries an edge. The US Navy's most sophisticated submarines cost over $2.7 billion each, while the US Air Force's premier F-22 fighter airplanes cost over $300 million apiece.[71] China's ambition to transform its military into a premier, joint war-fighting force has already fueled major increases in defense spending averaging over 8 percent per year since 2007.[72] The PLA plans to acquire capable platforms such as nuclear aircraft

---

71. CNN, "US Launches 'Most Advanced' Stealth Sub Amid Undersea Rivalry," October 26, 2017; *Wired*, "Buyer's Remorse: How Much Has the F-22 Really Cost?" December 14, 2011.
72. ChinaFile, "China's Military Spending," March 6, 2018.

carriers, stealth fighters, advanced surface–to-radar systems, and other expensive platforms and weapons systems. However, a slowing economy and rising domestic demands raise questions about the sustainability of this ambitious modernization program, especially given the demographic headwinds discussed previously.[73] Already, competing domestic priorities have compelled US defense officials to face the prospect of flat budgets for years to come.

The prohibitive costs of military weapons carry an additional consequence that may induce caution. Due to the precision of modern sensors and the growing range of weapons systems, conventional militaries could wreak havoc on one another in a brief amount of time. The prospect of losing billions or trillions of dollars in military capital within hours or days of the start of a war—all of which would be difficult to replace in an era of slowing growth—provides an incentive for decision-makers to act with restraint against potential rival great powers.

The deterrence afforded by expensive, advanced militaries may also be compounded by the advent of new space and cyber weapons that could inflict severe damage on the civilian populace and economy at a moment's notice. Attacks on space assets raise the prospect of an adversary undermining the satellite, timing, navigation, and communication systems that modern societies rely upon.[74] Similarly, the inherent vulnerabilities of Internet technologies have spurred experts to warn of doomsday scenarios in which adversaries knock out electric power for broad swaths of a population, which could in turn result in deaths in hospitals and traffic. Disruptions of markets through space or cyberattack could also induce financial panic.[75] The threat of space and cyberattack thus may augment the deterring effects of nuclear arsenals (Table 7.6).

4. Conclusion: US-China Strategic Rivalry in the Post-industrial Age

The literature on strategic rivalry provides insightful analytic tools for examining the risks of conflict between great powers such as China and the US. Some of the central findings regarding the linkages between interstate competition, threat perceptions, and the repeated incidences of crises and conflict can allow analysts to formulate indicators to assess the relative volatility of the bilateral relationship and estimate the risk of conflict.

---

73. John Lee, "China's Economic Slowdown: What are the Strategic Implications?" *Washington Quarterly* 38, no. 3 (2015): 123–42.
74. Brian Chow, "Stalkers in Space: Defeating the Threat," *Strategic Studies Quarterly* (Summer 2017): 82–116.
75. Jordan Robertson and Laurence Arnold, "Cyberwar, How Nations Attack Without Bullets or Bombs," *Washington Post*, May 11, 2018.

Table 7.6: Potential effects of military technologies on US-China rivalry

Military technology factors		
Factor	Effect	Comment
Advanced military technologies	Elevates threat, mixed effect for competition	High cost of advanced platforms exacerbates budget tradeoff, raising resistance among public.
Proliferation of cyber space weapons	Raises threat, mixed effect on competition	Potential destructiveness raises threat perception, but potential devastation of civilian economy also incentivizes restraint.

However, the fact that China and the US have only somewhat fulfilled the predictions of rivalry theorists raises questions about the salience of the literature's key findings. One possibility is that the rivalry is merely in its initial stages and that conflict will manifest in coming years as the competitive impulses intensify. This possibility cannot be ruled out.

Yet there are also reasons to believe that features of the post-industrial age may impose inherent limitations to the potential escalation of conflict. This feature may reflect in part broader pacific trends. Scholars have already noted the striking absence of inter-state war between the most developed economies since the end of World War II.[76] Debate has continued over the cause of the "long peace" and over its long-term prospects.[77]

But other factors unique to the current era may also be at play. The review of demographic, economic, and technological factors suggest powerful forces could be working to shape a type of rivalry characterized by long-lasting but low-intensity conflict despite economic interdependence. A striking and defining feature may be the bifurcation of audiences within each country between elites who have the most immediate interests at stake in a rivalry and a distrustful, resentful public that resists demands to pay for competitive policies. In the US, and many Western post-industrial societies, this broader political and social polarization has already unsettled politics. In China, this dynamic is less pronounced, but the driving factors of demographic aging, inequality, post-industrialized economic change, changing values, and the pursuit of civilian and military technologies are also present, and some sort of bifurcation is possible over time, if it is not already present.

Lacking a broad constituency, elites today may find themselves constrained in their ability to mobilize support for costly competitive policies.

---

76. Bruno Tetrais, "The Demise of Ares: The End of War as we Know It?" The *Washington Quarterly* 35, no. 3 (Summer 2012): 7–22.
77. Tom Szayna et al., "What Are the Trends in Interstate Conflict and What Do They Mean for U.S. Policy?" RAND Corporation, 2017, accessed October 30, 2017, https://www.rand.org/pubs/research_reports/RR1904.readonline.html.

They may instead be forced to conduct more limited, smaller-scale operations and activities to buttress their nation's position and counter the rival. Washington and Beijing could employ diplomats to scheme and outmaneuver one another in the contest for participants in their relative technological and economic spheres of dominance. They could also step up use of espionage, security contractors, paramilitary, and other proxy forces to press for advantage in the distant seas and lands of Asia, Africa, and Latin America. At the same time, the deep integration of the two economies and growing menace of transnational threats ensures considerable continuation of trade and raises the likelihood of some level of cooperation against shared concerns.

The possibility that rivalry in the post-industrial age may take a different form from that of much of the nineteenth and twentieth centuries applies most to countries that share these features, such as the US, Japan, and, over time, China. Japan's strategic rivalry with China since the flareup in tensions near the Senkaku Islands around 2010 may in fact serve as the prototype of a post-industrial rivalry. With a mature economy and one of the world's oldest populations, the conduct of tech-savvy Japan in its rivalry with China has been striking in its restraint. The country's military buildup has been modest, and Tokyo has sought opportunities to ease tensions and improve ties even as it has carried out policies to counter Chinese influence in Asia and elsewhere. Although Prime Minister Shinzo Abe supported broader efforts to bolster Japan's competitive stance against China, he struggled to gain public backing for such policies. And despite standoffs involving ships and aircraft near the Senkaku Islands and occasional crises, such as the capture of Chinese fishers in 2010, the risk of escalation to war has remained low. Both sides have preferred skirmish with paramilitary forces, primarily maritime law enforcement forces, as a way to minimize the risks of conflict.

The US rivalry with China in some ways has followed this pattern. Efforts by the Trump administration to articulate a harder line against China have resulted in a reallocation of priorities within the Pentagon and bipartisan support among intellectuals and politicians of both parties. However, polls continue to show little enthusiasm among the public for hard-line trade policies against China or for potential military contingencies against China.[78] Despite an increase in US maritime operations near Chinese-claimed territory in the South China Sea and near Taiwan, US and Chinese officials continue to behave cautiously.

In some ways, the future of the US-China rivalry may more closely resemble the rivalries of the pre-modern age than the modern European rivalries beginning in the age of Napoleon. In the Western Europe of the 1500s, for example, rulers tended to deploy small royal militaries augmented by mercenaries against their rivals. The issues of succession and influence that drove

---

78. Chicago Council on Global Affairs, "Poll: American Public Less Threatened Than White House by China," October 19, 2018.

royal courts to war likely had less salience for the impoverished peasantry who struggled to survive. Many of these conflicts were relatively limited in scale and duration and involved a small percent of the country's human resources. Another example of elite-led rivalries may be found in the Byzantine empire, which through much of its history relied heavily on small numbers of professional troops, mercenaries, and diplomats to thwart enemies—even as it traded with some of its most bitter foes.

The advent of the modern state heralded a new era of state-building, warfare, nationalism, and social mobilization. Eventually, the form of the modern state pioneered by West European countries proved so successful that it became a near universal form. Scholars have illuminated many features of this remarkable process. But as the modern state in Europe, the US, and other advanced economies strain under the burden of slow growth and political fragmentation, more attention may need to be paid to the politics and international implications of the modern system's breakdown.

Part C: Triangles

8
Bringing the Strategic Triangle Back

The Role of Small and Medium States in US-PRC Rivalry

Yu-Shan Wu

The US-PRC trade war has been in full swing since the US imposed a 25 percent tariff on all steel imports and a 10 percent tariff on all aluminum imports in March 2018.[1] It is worth noting that even though President Donald Trump began criticizing China for trying to "beat us and own our country" in his tweets years before he ran for president,[2] this trade war started with the US attempting to protect its steel industry against imports globally, of which China only took a tiny share.[3] Eventually China was singled out as the major target of US punitive tariffs, but not because China had been targeted as a geostrategic rival to the US. It was singled out because it had accumulated the largest trade surplus with the US consistently and was poised to surpass the US in key technologies. US allies were also subject to threats of economic sanctions and forced to renegotiate with Washington for a "fairer" trade deal. This shows that for the Trump administration, economic game transcends the strategic game. Even though this may change with the Biden presidency, economic competition is likely to remain the dominant concern of the US when facing a rising China.

The whole alliance system that the US so assiduously built since WWII has eroded. US allies can no longer expect to receive economic benefits by following Washington's strategic leadership. This is unprecedented. Hence, the surge of the US-PRC rivalry takes the world by surprise not only for its

---

1. This measure took place on March 23, 2018, and China retaliated on April 2 by imposing tariffs ranging from 15 to 25 percent on 128 products imported from the US (worth US$3 billion) including fruit, wine, seamless steel pipes, pork, and recycled aluminum.
2. Trump tweeted "China is neither an ally nor a friend—they want to beat us and own our country" on September 21, 2011, https://twitter.com/realdonaldtrump/status/116575636583227392.
3. US International Trade Administration, *Global Steel Trade Monitor*, September 2018, https://www.trade.gov/steel/countries/pdfs/imports-us.pdf. China was not among the top ten steel exporters to the US in 2018.

abruptness but also for its cause and the form it takes.[4] The anxiety among Asian countries that are caught in this hegemonic rivalry is unprecedentedly high. They bear the pressure from two great powers, in two games with reversed precedence. As time has gone by, the trade war has evolved into a full confrontation between the two countries, threatening to bring about a new cold war, and yet the main battleground remains on the economic front. This is a major difference between the hegemonic rivalry of today and the superpower competition between the US and the Soviet Union in the latter half of the twentieth century. The reason is that China has grown into a major economic powerhouse that rivals the US, a threat the former Soviet Union was never able to pose.

With "power transition" between the US and China imminent, and with the economic game surging to the forefront of US-PRC rivalry, the parameters of international relations in East Asia have changed. Originally, China restrained its actions in the region, as its economic reform, though highly successful, had not yet brought about a surge of economic and military prowess to rival that of the US. From the 1990s through the mid-2000s, the leaders of the Chinese Communist Party (CCP) adhered to Deng Xiaoping's admonition that China should "lie low" and avoid confrontation in foreign affairs to keep the nation focused on domestic matters. Since the global financial crisis in 2008–2009 there has been increasing assertiveness in China's policy in the region, and the US responded with its "pivot to Asia" and "Asia Rebalance" strategies. However, there were limits to the rivalry between the two countries, as they adhered (at least verbally) to the liberal international order that benefitted both. With the advent of Xi Jinping and Donald Trump, however, and with impending power parity between the hegemon and the challenger, US-PRC rivalry entered a new stage.[5] President Trump's emphasis on the economic game, sometimes at the expense of US strategic interests, further disrupts the existing structure, a development that can only be partially undone by his successor. A new age of disorder has descended on East Asia.

---

4. The trade war between the US and China looks strikingly similar to the US trade war in the 1980s with Japan, an American ally during the heyday of the Cold War. Hence, the US-PRC trade war is not derived from competition with a strategic adversary. Economic competition takes precedence.
5. Power parity is the mechanism that touches off fierce confrontation between the existing hegemon and its challenger in the "power transition theory" originally developed by A. F. K. Organski. For the theory and its later development, see A. F. K. Organski, *World Politics*, 2nd ed. (New York: Knopf, 1968); A. F. K. Organski and Jacek Kugler, *The War Ledger* (Chicago: University of Chicago Press, 1980); Jacek Kugler and Douglas Lemke, eds., *Parity and War: Evaluations and Extensions of the War Ledger* (Ann Arbor, MI: University of Michigan Press, 1996); Ronald Tammen, Jacek Kugler, Douglas Lemke et al., *Power Transitions: Strategies for the 21st Century* (New York: Chatham House, 2000); Ronald Tammen, "The Organski Legacy: A Fifty-Year Research Program," *International Interactions* 34, no. 4 (2008): 314–32. For a reformulation of the concept by reference to historical cases, see Graham Allison, *Destined for War: Can America and China Escape the Thucydides Trap?* (Boston and New York: Houghton Mifflin Harcourt, 2017).

In the literature on the surge of US-PRC rivalry, the emphasis is typically on the interaction between the two antagonists and their domestic politics. Little is said on the role played by the small and medium countries (SMCs) that find themselves on the front line of the hegemonic rivalry. How do the SMCs navigate between the two great powers? What is the response of the antagonists to their maneuvering? Without answering these questions, it would be impossible to capture the full dynamics of the US-China competition. To understand this type of trilateral relations, it is necessary to bring back the perspective of strategic triangle and adjust it for an analysis of asymmetrical power relations among the three actors.

This chapter develops a theoretical framework of "asymmetrical strategic triangle" to analyze the position of SMCs caught in great power hegemonic rivalry. Three types of options are identified for SMCs: partner, hedging partner, and pivot. In East Asia, hedging with the US against the PRC is the dominant strategy. Countries competed to take that policy under structural pressure. A calculus is developed to capture the incentive of competitive hedging. This analytical framework is then applied to Taiwan to account for its grand strategy shift towards hedging partner under President Ma Ying-Jeou. However, Ma's repositioning did not last long, as his successor, Tsai Ying-wen, swiftly brought back the old strategy of playing the role of Washington's junior partner. Throughout the process, Taiwan remains the odd one out in East Asia, as its positioning strategy between the US and the PRC is always at odds with other SMCs in the region. Two logics (internal for Taiwan and external for other Asian SMCs) are identified in three time periods (pre-2008, 2008–2016 or Shock Wave I, post 2016 or Shock Wave II) to account for the divergence. It was found that Chinese assertiveness and US mercantilist policy took turns to drive the majority of East Asian SMCs towards the other dominant power, while Taiwan's position is primarily determined by its domestic politics that centers on dueling national identities, hence the desynchronization between the two patterns. For most East Asian countries, hedging is the norm, while for Taiwan hedging is the aberration.

Asymmetric Strategic Triangle

The study of strategic triangles was in vogue when the US was exploring the possibility of involving Beijing on its side in the US-Soviet superpower rivalry from the 1960s through the 1980s.[6] This concept was then reapplied to the

---

6. Lowell Dittmer, "The Strategic Triangle: An Elementary Game-Theoretical Analysis," *World Politics* 33, no. 4 (1981): 485–516; Gerald Segal, *The Great Power Triangle* (New York: St. Martin's, 1982); Aaron L. Friedberg, "The Collapsing Triangle: U.S. and Soviet Policies toward China, 1969–1980," *Contemporary Strategy*, no. 4 (1983): 113–46; Ilpyong J. Kim, ed., *The Strategic Triangle: China, the United States, and the Soviet Union* (New York: Paragon House, 1987); Joshua S. Goldstein and John R. Freeman, "U.S.-Soviet-Chinese Relations:

study of other triangular relations, such as the US-China-Japan triangle,[7] the US-South Korea-Japan triangle,[8] and the Sino-Russian-American triangle.[9] One strategic triangle that has attracted increasing attention is Washington-Beijing-Taipei relations. This is sometimes called the "mini-triangle" as distinct from the historical US-Soviet-PRC "great triangle." Various works have sought to deepen understanding of the logic of the mini-triangle as events unfolded that testify to the interconnectedness of the actions of the trio.[10] A major difference between the traditional strategic triangle literature and its application to the Washington-Beijing-Taipei relations is power asymmetry among the three players in the "mini-triangle." This feature was noted but not theoretically explored in the literature.

The strategic triangle theory is geared toward analyzing trilateral relations. There are four ideal types of strategic triangle: ménage à trois (three amities), marriage (two enmities and one amity), romantic triangle (two amities and one enmity), and unit veto (three enmities).[11] In ménage à trois, all three players are "friends." In marriage, two "partners" act against an "outcast." In a romantic triangle, two "wings" court a "pivot." In unit veto, the players are all "foes" to one another. With the four ideal types of strategic triangle (ménage à trois, marriage, romantic triangle, unit veto), and six roles (friend, partner, outcast, wing, pivot, foe), we can begin analyzing any

---

Routine, Reciprocity, or Rational Expectations?" *American Political Science Review* 85, no. 1 (1991): 17–35.

7. See, for example, Thomas L. Wilborn, *International Politics in Northeast Asia: The China-Japan-United States Strategic Triangle* (Carlisle, PA: Strategic Studies Institute, U.S. Army War College, 1996); Ming Zhang and Ronald N. Montaperto, *A Triad of Another Kind: The United States, China, and Japan* (New York: Palgrave, 1999); Go Ito, *Alliance in Anxiety: Detente and the Sino-American-Japanese Triangle* (New York: Routledge, 2003).
8. See Victor D. Cha, *Alignment Despite Antagonism: The United States-Korea-Japan Security Triangle* (Stanford, CA: Stanford University Press, 1999).
9. Gilbert Rozman, "A New Sino-Russian-American Triangle?" *Orbis* 44, no. 4 (2000): 541–56; James C. Hsiung, "The Strategic Triangle: Dynamics between China, Russia, and the United States," *Harvard International Review* 26, no. 1 (2004): 14–17.
10. See, for instance, Wu Yu-Shan, *Kangheng huo hucong: liang'an guanxi xinquan* [Balancing or bandwagoning: Cross-Strait relations revisited] (Taipei: Cheng-chung, 1997); Bao Tzong-Ho, "Zhanlue sanjiao jiaose zhuanbian yu leixing bianhua fenxi—yi Meiguo han Taihai liang'an sanjiao hudong weili" [An analysis of role transition and type change in a strategic triangle: The case of triangular interaction between the United States and the two sides of the Taiwan Strait], in *Zhengbian zhong de liang'an guanxi lilun* [Contending theories in the study of cross-Strait relations], ed. Bao Tzong-Ho and Wu Yu-Shan (Taipei: Wunan, 1999), 337–63; Alan M. Wachman, "America's Taiwan Quandary: How Much Does Chen's Election Matter?" in *Taiwan's Presidential Politics: Democratization and Cross-Strait Relations in the Twenty-First Century*, ed. Muthiah Alagappa (Armonk, NY: M.E. Sharpe, 2001), 236–59; Alan D. Romberg, "Taiwan in U.S.-PRC Relations: A Strategic Perspective," paper presented at the conference on "U.S.-China Relations and the Bush Administration: A New Paradigm or Continuing Existing Modalities," Claremont McKenna College, Claremont, California, 2001; David Shambaugh, "The Military-Political Dimension in the U.S.-China-Taiwan Triangle," paper presented at the conference on "Taiwan and U.S. Policy: Toward Stability or Crisis?" Capitol Hill, Washington, DC, 2002.
11. Lowell Dittmer, "The Strategic Triangle: An Elementary Game—Theoretical Analysis."

Figure 8.1: Strategic triangles

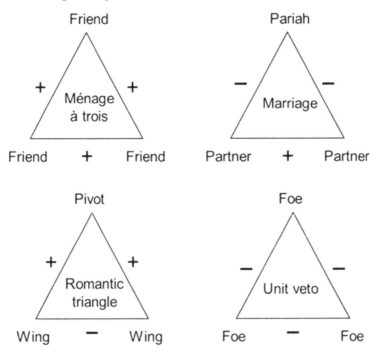

Source: Author.

triangular situation, using the strategic triangle types and roles to describe objectively the structure of the triangular game (see Figure 8.1).

In a strategic triangle, a player's amity with other players is always considered to be preferable to an enmity. However, the other two players' mutual enmity is preferable to this player than is their amity. Hence, the most preferable position is that of a pivot, which has friendly relations with the other two players while they are at odds with each other. Following this logic, it seems that if possible, an SMC caught in a hegemonic rivalry between two great powers should seek to play the pivot's role. However, the pivot's position was originally recommended for the US, i.e. for the strongest, to play in the US-Soviet-PRC triangle.[12] Is it feasible for the weakest to take that role? Obviously, we need to consider power asymmetry in the triangle.

What is the recommendation for the weak state in the international relations literature that deals with power asymmetry? The starting point is obviously the balance-of-power (BOP) paradigm. When facing a rising

---

12. For a discussion of the US role as a pivot in the Washington-Beijing-Taipei mini-triangle, see Yu-Shan Wu, "From Romantic Triangle to Marriage? Washington-Beijing-Taipei Relations in Historical Comparison," *Issues and Studies* 41, no. 1 (March 2005): 113–59.

power, BOP predicts balancing strategy of either the internal type (building up military preparedness) or the external type (forming an alliance).[13] The traditional BOP is modified by Steve Walt's "balance of threat" theory, in which perceived threat rather than capability is the criterion for the balancing behavior.[14] For weak states, "bandwagoning" is added to the toolbox, which prescribes behaviors not challenging but conforming to the core values of the rising power.[15] However, as both balancing and bandwagoning entail great costs, in the form of budgetary burden, alliance maintenance, or loss of strategic independence, yet another option presents itself: *hedging*. Hedging is a two-pronged strategy with which a country both engages and guards against the target. The "hedger" does not simply adopt a balancing or engagement strategy but rather employs a mixture of the two. The engagement prong serves to enhance a friendly relationship with the target country, bring about commercial benefits, and hopefully work to transform the values and institutions of the target so that it may stop posing a threat. The balancing prong serves to provide a security guarantee either through military buildup or alliance with another great power. Typically, the engagement prong is found in the economic area while the balancing prong is in the security realm.

From the above discussion, we find the strategic triangle lacks appreciation of a potential asymmetrical relation among actors, while policy options under BOP (balancing, bandwagoning, and hedging) are intrinsically bilateral. However, we need an analytical framework that captures both triangularity and asymmetry to understand an SMC's position in hegemonic rivalry. We can now combine the two theoretical perspectives by assuming that an SMC can play a set of roles between two rival hegemons. This will bring us a romantic triangle (in which the SMC is a pivot), unit veto (SMC

---

13. Kenneth N. Waltz, *Theory of International Politics* (Reading, MA: Addison-Wesley, 1979).
14. Stephen Walt, *The Origins of Alliances* (Ithaca, NY: Cornell University Press, 1987).
15. For the concept of bandwagoning, see Stephen Walt, "Alliance Formation and the Balance of World Power," *International Security* 9, no. 4 (1985): 3–43; Randall Schweller, "Bandwagoning for Profit: Bringing the Revisionist State Back In," *International Security* 19, no. 1 (1994): 72–107. However, bandwagoning typically is not considered a productive option in a realist world. For the limited usefulness of bandwagoning, see Walt, *The Origins of Alliances*, 33; John J. Mearsheimer, *The Tragedy of Great Power Politics* (New York: W. W. Norton, 2001), 139. For a discussion of power asymmetry in the Taiwan Strait and Taiwan's policy toward the Mainland, see Yu-Shan Wu, Kangheng Huo Hucong: Liang'an Guanxi Xinquan [Balancing or bandwagoning: Cross-strait relations revisited] (Taipei: Chengchung, 1997); Yu-Shan Wu, "Quanli Bu Duicheng Yu Liang'an Guanxi" ["Power asymmetry and cross-strait relations"], in *Chongxin Jianshi Zhengbian Zhong De Liang'an Guanxi Lilun* [Revisiting theories on cross-strait relations], ed. Tzong-Ho Bau and Yu-Shan Wu (Taipei: Wu-nan, 2009); Charles Chong-Han Wu, "Taiwan's Hedging against China: The Strategic Implications of Ma Ying-Jeou's Mainland Policy," *Asian Survey* 56, vol. 3 (2016): 466–87. For an exploration into historical cases of power asymmetry in China-centered East Asia, see Yu-Shan Wu, ed., *Zhongguo zaiqi: lishi yu guoguan de duihua* [Resurgence of China: A dialogue between history and international relations] (Taipei: Research Center for Confucianism in East Asia, Institute for Advanced Studies in Humanities and Social Sciences, National Taiwan University, 2018).

playing foe), or marriage (SMC is partner of one great power). Ménage à trois is impossible given the rivalry between the other two actors. At this point we can also dismiss unit veto, for it is an untenable position for the SMC to play that requires opposing both great powers in the game.[16] This leaves us with romantic triangle and marriage, in which an SMC either plays pivot or partner. What does that mean in relation to the BOP policy toolbox (balancing, bandwagoning, and hedging)?

Under tight bipolarity, the distances of the SMC's position to the two great power rivals are constant-sum. That means a move toward one great power will necessarily distance the SMC away from the other great power, and a shift away from a great power entails a tilt toward the other great power. If the SMC considers one great power (G1) to be its main threat, and there is power asymmetry between G1 and SMC (meaning internal balancing cannot redress asymmetry), then the latter has no choice but to embrace the other great power (G2) as a way of external balancing. Thus, balancing against G1 is tantamount to bandwagoning with G2, and vice versa. The SMC must be either a junior partner of G1 (bandwagon with it and balance against G2), or a junior partner of G2 (bandwagon with it and balance against G1), unless it stands right in the middle between G1 and G2 and plays the role of a pivot.

Now we can introduce hedging as an option. The hedger has two prongs in its strategy that are not equal in weight. If the hedger mainly tilts toward G1, then it is a hedging partner of G1 although it also flirts with G2 for economic or other benefits. The rule of constant-sum also applies here, so an SMC that is G1's hedging partner primarily bandwagons with G1 and balances against G2, and a G2 hedging partner mainly bandwagons with G2 and balances against G1. This brings us five positions on a policy continuum for a SMC to choose, as illustrated in Figure 8.2.[17]

In the post–Cold War era, East Asia is increasingly marked by the emergence of two hierarchies. One is a security hierarchy dominated by the US, and the other is an economic hierarchy dominated by the PRC.[18] The two great powers have been competing for influence and the loyalties of the SMCs between them, along a geostrategic fault line. As indicated in Figure 8.2, there are five options for an East Asian SMC to choose. They are partner of China

---

16. It is true that there was a period when communist China under Mao Zedong took a defiant position against both superpowers, the revisionist Soviet Union and the imperialist United States, in the fervor of the Cultural Revolution. Since it was an untenable position, China was forced to abandon it by improving relations with Washington in the early 1970s. Furthermore, with its revolutionary zeal and ideological appeal, China in the Cultural Revolution was a force to be reckoned with for both Washington and Moscow and thus cannot be easily dismissed as an SMC caught in superpower rivalry.
17. For a fuller derivation of the five roles, see Yu-Shan Wu, "Pivot, Hedger, or Partner: Strategies of Lesser Powers Caught between Hegemons," in *Taiwan and China: Fitful Embrace*, ed. Lowell Dittmer, 198–202 (Berkeley: University of California Press, 2017).
18. G. John Ikenberry, "Between the Eagle and the Dragon: America, China, and Middle State Strategies in East Asia," *Political Science Quarterly* 131, no. 1 (2016): 10.

Figure 8.2: SMC's choices

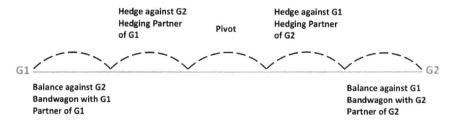

Source: Author.

Figure 8.3: Strategic fault line in East Asia

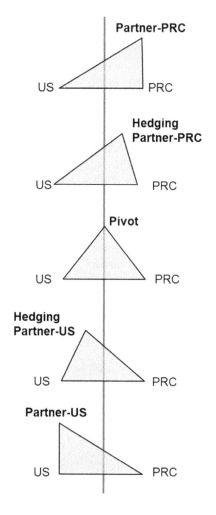

Source: Author.

(bandwagon with China, balance against the US), hedging partner of China (bandwagon with China, hedge against the US), pivot (noncommittal and tilting in between), hedging partner of the US (bandwagon with US, hedge against China), and partner of China (bandwagon with China, balance against the US). As shown in Figure 8.3, the shape of the triangles and the distances between actors indicate the relationships. Thus, a partner is fully allied with one great power and distanced from the other (the top and bottom triangles). A pivot holds equidistance with both camps, typically tilting between the two to gain benefits from them (the middle triangle). A hedging partner is committed to one camp but engaged positively with the other camp (the remaining two triangles).

Dominant Strategy: Hedging

In post–Cold War East Asia, with the US and the PRC engaged in acute competition for influence along the strategic fault line, a dominant strategy has gradually emerged for the SMCs. It is hedging.[19] More specifically, it is hedging on the US side against rising China, and the role is hedging partner of the US.[20] It is the second from the bottom in Figure 8.3. This mixed strategy reflects the multiple concerns of the SMCs and the relative threat from the competing hegemons. The SMCs want to receive the security benefits of allying with the US and the economic benefits of trading with China. At the same time, they worry about the possibility that China will use its growing economic position to dominate the region, and they worry about the credibility of the US's security commitment. In short, they worry about both their security and their economic dependency.[21]

---

19. There is a plethora of definitions of hedging. For example, Evelyn Goh defines hedging as "a set of strategies aimed at avoiding (or planning for contingencies in) a situation in which states cannot decide upon more straightforward alternatives such as balancing, bandwagoning, or neutrality. Instead they cultivate a middle position that forestalls or avoids having to choose one side at the obvious expense of another." For Evan Medeiros, hedging is "pursuing policies that, on one hand, stress engagement and integration mechanisms and, on the other, emphasize realist-style balancing in the form of external security cooperation . . . and national military modernization programs." For Cheng Chwee-Kuik, hedging is a "behavior in which a country seeks to offset risks by pursuing multiple policy options that are intended to produce mutually counteracting effects, under the situation of high-uncertainties and high-stakes." See Evelyn Goh, "Meeting the China Challenge: The U.S. in Southeast Asian Regional Security Strategies," *Policy Studies*, no. 16 (East-West Center, Washington, DC, 2005): 2; Evan S. Medeiros, "Strategic Hedging and the Future of Asia-Pacific Stability," *Washington Quarterly* 29, no. 1 (2005): 154; Cheng Chwee-Kuik, "The Essence of Hedging: Malaysia and Singapore's Response to a Rising China," *Contemporary Southeast Asia: A Journal of International and Strategic Affairs* 30, no. 2 (August 2008): 163.
20. For the prevalence of hedging in the East Asian region and its historical development, see Yu-Shan Wu, "Power Shift, Strategic Triangle, and Alliances in East Asia," *Issues & Studies* 47, no. 4 (December 2011): 1–42.
21. G. John Ikenberry, "Between the Eagle and the Dragon," 11.

Hedging always has two prongs with different weights for the SMC. The perceived major security threat from one of the great powers (typically China) determines the SMC's basic position, which is then attenuated by the need to reap benefits from engaging with that threat. The security provided by the other great power (mainly the US) acts as insurance that gives the SMC a fallback position. This arrangement makes it possible for the East Asian SMCs to both worry about the rise of China and pursue benefits offered by Beijing. It offsets multiple risks and is an instinctive human behavior.[22] It is important to grasp the different weights assigned to the security prong (US) and the economic prong (PRC) by East Asian SMCs. They want to simultaneously cultivate friendship with both great powers while retaining options for siding with one of them against the other. They are anchored on the US side. As such, hedging is but a shade away from "soft-balancing." It is an *uneven two-prong policy*.

Hedging tends to be competitive, especially when the capability of the target country rises rapidly. When a partner in an alliance (which is a marriage triangle with two partners against the outcast) decides to hedge, its payoff would immediately increase at the expense of the other partner, prompting the second partner to hedge also. The logic can be shown numerically. Take marriage triangle XYZ, for example. It is reasonable to expect a positive relation with a strong nation to be worth more than is a positive relation with a weak nation, the utilities derived from the two amities in direct proportion to the capabilities of the two countries in question. Hence, from X's point of view, if Y is two times stronger than Z, then amity with Y is worth two times amity with Z. By the same token, enmity with Y will cost X twice as much as enmity with Z would cost. Similarly, the utility for a player derived from the relation between the other two players will be weighted with the average of those players' national powers. Let F_x be the total utility of X as derived from X's position in the triangle, Y_p and Z_p the national power of Y and Z relative to X, and YX, ZX, YZ the relation between X and Y, Z and X, and Y and Z respectively, then we have:

(A.1)　　$F_x = YX^*Y_p + ZX^*Z_p + (-YZ)^*[(Y_p + Z_p)/2]$

Also we have the following:

(A.2)　　$F_y = XY^*X_p + ZY^*Z_p + (-XZ)^*[(X_p + Z_p)/2]$

(A.3)　　$F_z = XZ^*X_p + YZ^*Y_p + (-XY)^*[(X_p + Y_p)/2]$

---

22. C. C. Kuik "Great Power Uncertainties and Weak-State Hedging," paper presented at the Conference on Navigating under Hegemonic Rivalry in Asia: Intro-regional, Historical and Cross-regional Comparison, December 6–7, 2016, Academia Sinica, Taipei, Taiwan. Kuik postulates that hedging is adopted when threats are neither straightforward nor immediate and when sources of principal support are multiple, mixed, and uncertain.

Bringing the Strategic Triangle Back 177

In a marriage triangle, if the comparative power of the pariah (target) is rising, then the utility of the two partners in the triangle will decrease. Assuming in ST XYZ, Y and Z team up against X, then we have XY and XZ negative, and YZ positive. A rising X_p would reduce both F_y and F_z (see A.2 and A.3). To avert this trend, both Y and Z would have stronger incentive than before the rise of X to improve relations with X, thus bringing XY and XZ to positive. If Y makes the move of rapprochement with X first, then Z would suffer much more than before X's rise, for the weights of the two unfavorable relations (a negative XZ and a positive XY) would increase, bringing greater pressure on Z to change course too. There would then be competitive rapprochement with X, as both Y and Z becomes hedgers.

In East Asia, competitive hedging against China makes the phenomenon prevalent in the region, with only one exception: Taiwan. Because of sovereignty issues, Taiwan is the least capable of taking the role of a hedger. There was a short period of time in the early 1990s when President Lee Teng-hui and his Mainland counterpart, Jiang Zemin, were exchanging positive notes (Jiang's Eight Points and Lee's Six Articles), and the two sides reached a modus vivendi that was later called "the 1992 Consensus," but that didn't last long. Soon the missile scare brought cross-Strait relation to its nadir. With all of Taiwan's neighbors joining the hedging chorus, and mainland China's national power surging, Taipei was under increasing pressure to change course. Domestic politics and conflicting national identities on the island, however, prevented that from happening, as Chen Shui-bian of the pro-independence Democratic Progressive Party (DPP) succeeded Lee as president and cross-Strait relations remained turbulent. As the US was primarily concerned with the War on Terror in the 2000s and eager to keep a calm relation with the PRC, Washington did not want Taipei to rock the boat with sovereignty-enhancing rhetoric or surprise moves, which Chen did a lot nevertheless. Taiwan's payoff in the mini-triangle thus plummeted. If we use GDP and military expenditures as two measurements of national power and give them equal weight, then we can rewrite A.1 into A.4 as follows:

(A.4) $F_x = [YX*(G_y/G_x + M_y/M_x)/2] + [ZX*(G_z/G_x + M_z/M_x)/2] + (-YZ)* [(G_y/G_x + G_z/G_x)/2 + (M_y/M_x + M_z/M_x)/2]/2$ (where G_x stands for X's GDP, and M_x stands for X's military expenditures)

In the mini-triangle, let t stands for Taiwan, u for the US, and c for the PRC. Then we have the following:

(A.5) $F_t = [UT*(G_u/G_t + M_u/M_t)/2] + [CT*(G_c/G_t + M_c/M_t)/2] + (-UC)* [(G_u/G_t + G_c/G_t)/2 + (M_u/M_t + M_c/M_t)/2]/2$

During the turbulent years of the 1990s and 2000s, Taiwan's payoff in the mini-triangle fluctuated widely, as shown in Table 8.1 and Figure 8.4.

The ups and downs of the Ft curve in Figure 8.4 reflect the changing relations and capabilities among the players in the US-PRC-ROC triangle. Taiwan's starting point was low, as the Bush Senior administration always kept a strong tilt towards Beijing and distanced itself from Taipei. As the US was the dominant player, Washington's attitude pretty much determined Taiwan's low profile in the game. The surge of Ft in 1992 reflects the change of Washington's policy around the presidential election. Clinton's initial emphasis on human rights and revulsion against the Tiananmen crackdown meant Taiwan could benefit from the increase in tensions between Washington and Beijing. Hence, Ft rose dramatically in 1993. In 1994, a ménage à trios reappeared, and Taiwan's position declined a bit. The missile scare of 1995–1996 poisoned cross-Strait relations and yet placed the US firmly on Taiwan's side. Ft again surged, only to decline in the next two years as Washington

Table 8.1: Taiwan's overall payoff in the mini-triangle

Year	$(G_u/G_t+M_u/M_t)/2$	UT	$(G_c/G_t+M_c/M_t)/2$	CT	$(G_u/G_t+G_c/G_t+M_u/M_t+M_c/M_t)/4$	UC	F_t
1990	42.75	−1	1.91	1	22.33	1	−63.17
1991	37.72	−1	1.84	1	19.78	1	−55.65
1992	36.89	1	1.99	1	19.44	1	19.44
1993	33.18	1	2.04	1	17.61	−1	52.83
1994	31.86	1	1.80	1	16.83	1	16.83
1995	32.16	1	2.11	−1	17.13	−1	47.18
1996	31.11	1	2.35	−1	16.73	−1	45.49
1997	30.71	1	2.43	−1	16.57	1	11.71
1998	32.80	1	2.84	−1	17.82	1	12.14
1999	35.22	−1	3.10	−1	19.16	−1	−19.16
2000	37.17	−1	3.36	−1	20.26	−1	−20.26
2001	39.16	1	4.05	−1	21.61	−1	56.72
2002	44.36	1	4.72	−1	24.54	1	15.10
2003	47.90	−1	5.12	−1	26.51	1	−79.52
2004	47.77	−1	5.40	−1	26.59	1	−79.76
2005	49.90	−1	6.00	−1	27.95	1	−83.85
2006	52.70	−1	7.17	−1	29.94	1	−89.81
2007	51.55	−1	8.16	−1	29.85	1	−89.56
2008	46.72	−1	8.96	−1	27.84	1	−83.52
2009	47.53	1	9.93	1	28.73	1	28.73

Source: Calculated from International Monetary Fund, *World Economic Outlook Database*, April 2009, http://imf.org/external/ns/cs.aspx?id=28, and Stockholm International Peace Research Institute, http://milexdata.sipri.org/result.php4.

Figure 8.4: Taiwan's overall payoff curve

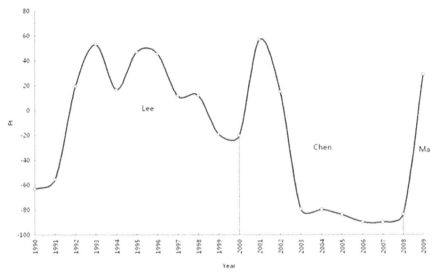

Source: Calculated from International Monetary Fund, *World Economic Outlook Database*, April 2009, http:// imf.org/external/ns/cs.aspx?id=28; and Stockholm International Peace Research Institute, http://milexdata. sipri.org/result.php4.

and Beijing reached a compromise. Lee's "two-state" theory plunged Taiwan into the abyss in 1999, as his rearguard action against US-PRC rapprochement backfired. However, the US electoral cycle kicked in, and the new Bush Junior administration demonstrated unprecedented support for Taiwan. It also showed great suspicion to Beijing, if for no other reason than a revulsion against the policy of the outgoing Democratic administration. Taiwan enjoyed a surge in its Ft score in 2001. Then from 2003 to 2008, Chen completely alienated Washington by his reckless moves toward independence that were clearly geared to domestic politics. At the same time, Beijing approached Washington to reach a modus vivendi of "co-management." Taiwan's position plummeted to a nadir. The weakest player in the triangular game antagonized the other two players to its own disadvantage. This was the international background of Ma's new course, his hedging policy.

Taiwan's rapprochement with the Mainland was dictated by the costs of balancing. By looking at the track record of Taiwan's performance in the triangle, Ma and his strategists could not but come up with the conclusion that the 2003–2008 status quo could not be sustained. The increasing power gap between Taiwan and the other two players suggests that any negative relationship with either of them, let alone both, would be amplified tremendously. The rising power of China vis-à-vis the US also suggests a negative cross-Strait relationship would bear more heavily on Taiwan's economy and defense and that a rapprochement between Washington and Beijing would prove more ominous for Taiwan as an outcast.

Even though Ma led Taiwan towards cross-Strait rapprochement, he was not interested in loosening ties with the US, particularly its defense links to the US military. Taiwan found itself in a ménage à trois in 2009. This was the best triangular mode for Taiwan, given US-PRC amity. Ma intended to recapture Taiwan's favorable position in the early 1990s. The Kuomintang (KMT) government attempted to deepen defense ties with the US and improve links with mainland China simultaneously, i.e., combining balancing with engagement, the essence of hedging.

It takes two to tango. The calculus of strategic costs and benefits led Ma to pursue rapprochement with Beijing, which had to reciprocate for cross-Strait relations to improve. In Ma's 2008 campaign, the "1992 Consensus" was re-recognized and raised as the key to cross-Strait reconciliation, which was reciprocated by Beijing ardently. The consensus then served as the foundation for cooperation in the following eight years. Thus, Taiwan was able to join its East Asian neighbors to engage with China and play hedger not simply because of cost-benefit analysis and rational decision making but also because of a compromise between the KMT and the CCP on the issue of national identity: both can accept the "one-China" principle, though expressed differently. As it turned out, when that base of identity reconciliation was gone, Taiwan would swiftly slide back to its original position as Washington's junior partner and stop playing hedger between the US and the PRC.

Fluctuations in Hedging and Taiwan as Odd One Out

The East Asian hedging chorus is premised on the two dominant powers offering security and economic services, with them in manageable relationship. Most of the SMCs anchor themselves on the US side while gaining economic benefits by doing business with China. The financial tsunami that mainly pounded the US and the West in 2008, and afterwards dramatically changed the power ratio between China and the US, set the stage for a power transition. The SMCs then found themselves in great stress: China becomes cocky, nationalistic and aggressive; and the US turns more defensive and mercantilist, and would want to restrict the SMCs' hedging behaviors. The first tendency became more prominent as Xi Jinping succeeded Hu Jintao as general secretary of the CCP; the second development came more abruptly after Donald Trump won the US presidential election in 2016. Hedging is no longer in vogue. We shall call the first development Shock Wave I (SWI), and the second Shock Wave II (SWII). The response of most SMCs to SWI was shifting away from China and getting close to the US. After all, their hedging strategy entails such a fallback position. However, SWII pushed them back a bit to their original stance, a development encouraged by Beijing.

Bringing the Strategic Triangle Back 181

Throughout the development, Taiwan remained the odd one out. It joined the hedging chorus at the beginning of SWI, conforming to the East Asian norm belatedly, when other SMCs began rethinking their relation with Beijing. It remained there when Xi turned highly assertive in his external posturing but remained amicable toward Ma, a relationship that culminated in the Xi-Ma summit in November 2015, six months before Ma stepped down. When SWII hit, Trump's mercantilist and "America first" policy estranged the US allies in Asia, who then inched back a bit toward their original hedging position. However, Taiwan, or at least its ruling DPP government, was highly encouraged by several supportive moves that the Trump administration and the US Congress took toward Taiwan, and remained close to the US. Taiwan has completely abandoned its hedging strategy under Ma and inched consistently toward Washington. The fluctuations in hedging and Taiwan as the odd one out are summarized in Table 8.2.

The contrast between the positions taken by majority Asian SMCs and Taiwan in different time periods is quite sharp. Two logics are at work here. The original hedging position for the majority of Asian SMCs is affected by the behaviors of their potential security threat and the commitment of their security provider. They prefer to stay in the original position, i.e. hedging partner of the US, but would shift because of the pressure put on them from

Table 8.2: Fluctuating strategy by SMCs

	Majority SMCs in East Asia	Taiwan	Taiwan compared with other SMCs
Pre-2008	Hedging partner of US: security reliance on US cum economic dependence on China China: tolerant	Adamantly anti-PRC China: hostile	Taiwan: Odd Man Out
2008–2016 Shock Wave I	Shifting away from Beijing toward Washington under Chinese assertiveness China: aggressive	Hedging partner of US: security reliance on US cum economic dependence on China; Xi-Ma amity China: concessionary	Taiwan: Odd Man Out
Post 2016 Shock Wave II	Estranged relation with US under Trump's "America First" policy and partial conversion toward original hedging China: embracive	Abandonment of hedging under Ma and increasingly more amicable relations with US China: hostile	Taiwan: Odd Man Out

Source: Author.

the two sides. They respond to pressure by tilting to the other side. In the following pages, I will look into the shifting positions of Japan and South Korea, to demonstrate how intensifying great power competition has an impact on major Asian SMCs, and compare that with cross-Strait relations.

Following the logic of power transition, Japan and China witnessed deteriorating relations around 2010, when China's nominal GDP surpassed that of Japan. This was the case even though at the turn of the decade Japan was ruled by the Democratic Party of Japan (DPJ) that showed unprecedented goodwill towards China compared with its predecessor, the Liberal Democratic Party (LDP). The rising Chinese power and Chinese nationalism made the territorial dispute between the two countries over Diaoyu Islands (Senkaku Islands) highly explosive. The 2010 Senkaku boat collision incident was not solved before China halted exports of rare earth minerals to Japan. The purchase of the Senkaku Islands by the Japanese government and the election of Abe Shinzo as the new Japanese prime minister in 2012 and his right-wing rhetoric added to the explosiveness of the issue. Chinese patrol boats and naval vessels began patrolling the waters around Diaoyu, clashing regularly with their Japanese counterparts.[23] Under SWI, the assertiveness of China brought about great anxiety in Japan, which accounted for the return to power by the LDP and its closer ties with the US.

The advent of the Trump administration caused a lot of adjustments on the part of the Abe government. There appear to be two major factions in the Trump administration that are both hawkish toward China but for different reasons. Former Defense Secretary Jim Mattis and his successor, Mark T. Esper, believe that the US should cooperate with its allies in the Indo-Pacific region to check the expansion of the Chinese military. In their view, alliance enhancement is of paramount importance. However, those heading the economic agencies of the government are economic nationalists who deplore the exploitative behaviors of America's allies that undermine US economic competitiveness. They are represented by US Trade Representative Robert Lighthizer and Secretary of Commerce Wilbur Ross. For the economic nationalists, China, Japan, and Europe should be treated equally, for all of them took advantage of the US. As the arguments of the latter group make more domestic political sense, Trump tilts toward that position, and Japan, as the second- largest source of US trade deficit, is under great pressure from the US.

That pressure prompted Japan to revert to a more conciliatory policy towards China, at a time when China was willing to show more accommodation.

---

23. The territorial dispute over the Diaoyu/Senkaku Islands between China and Japan has remained a flashpoint since its eruption in 2010, both sides assiduously adjusting to the shifting balance of power and new situation on the ground. See Adam P. Liff, "China, Japan, and the East China Sea: Beijing's 'Gray Zone' Coercion and Tokyo's Response," *Global China: Assessing China's Growing Role in the World*, The Brookings Institution, December 2019, https://www.brookings.edu/research/china-japan-and-the-east-china-sea-beijings-gray-zone-coercion-and-tokyos-response/.

Growing uncertainty about the role of the US created a powerful incentive for Asia's two great powers to stabilize their relationship after years in deep disrepair. Hence, the Sino-Japanese rapprochement.[24] In 2017, Japan expressed its willingness to join the Belt and Road initiative launched by China in 2013. In October 2018, Abe made a state visit to Beijing, advocating a turn from competition to cooperation.[25] This development demonstrates how Japan tilts away from the great power that pressures it and inches back to the hedging position it held prior to 2008.[26] There are bound to be further fluctuations in Japan's policy in the future, as the US-PRC rivalry unfolds, but a pattern is clear: Japan prefers to stay in the pre-2008 position as a hedging partner of the US if possible, but it would make tilts to offset the pressure put on it by the two hegemonic rivals.

Prior to SWI, South Korea reaped great economic and political benefits by nurturing close ties with China. However, Beijing still firmly sided with Pyongyang when it came to conflicts between the two Koreas, including the sinking of the *Cheonan* and the bombardment of Yeonpyeong. In the aftermath of those events, Seoul doubled its effort to court Beijing. President Park Geun-hye even attended the military parade, held in Beijing in September 2015, commemorating the seventieth anniversary of the victory over Japan and global fascism. She was the only national leader of a US ally to attend the event. At that time, Seoul seemed able to gain remarkably by forging and maintaining close ties with both Washington and Beijing.[27] However, the US insistence on deploying the Terminal High Altitude Area Defense (THAAD) system in South Korea as a response to the repeated test launches of North Korean missiles proved the most serious challenge to relations between Seoul and Beijing. Although THAAD was deployed to counter the threat from the North, it was considered by the Chinese to be a serious infringement on China's national security for its powerful surveillance radar. On this issue Seoul found itself sandwiched between Washington and Beijing. Because of an "unofficial" boycott by Chinese customers, Lotte, a Korean conglomerate that transferred its land to the government for deployment of THAAD in February 2017, was forced to sell off its supermarkets in China and shut down all its

---

24. See Mireya Solís, "China, Japan, and the Art of Economic Statecraft," *Global China: Assessing China's Growing Role in the World*, The Brookings Institution, February 2020, https://www.brookings.edu/research/china-japan-and-the-art-of-economic-statecraft/.
25. For the significance of Abe's visit to China in 2018 and the role Trump played in cementing the Sino-Japanese rapprochement, see Jonathan Pollack, "Abe in Beijing: The Quiet Accommodation in China-Japan Relations," *Trump and Asia Watch*, The Brookings Institution, October 25, 2018, https://www.brookings.edu/blog/order-from-chaos/2018/10/25/abe-in-beijing-the-quiet-accommodation-in-china-japan-relations/.
26. Such position was determined by the underlying distribution of power and wealth in East Asia. See Takashi Shiraishi, "Shinzo Abe is redefining Japan's China Policy for a Generation," *Nikkei Asia*, February 10, 2020, https://asia.nikkei.com/Opinion/Shinzo-Abe-is-redefining-Japan-s-China-policy-for-a-generation.
27. See Min-Hyung Kim, "South Korea's Strategy toward a Rising China, Security Dynamics in East Asia, and International Relations Theory," *Asian Survey* 56, no. 4 (2016): 707–30.

department stores. Obviously, South Korea also bore the brunt of surging Chinese nationalism.[28]

Then SWII struck. Like Japan, South Korea was targeted by the US in its effort to achieve "free, fair, and reciprocal trade." Seoul was forced to renegotiate its free trade agreement with the US in late 2017. Despite close collaboration by President Trump and his Korean counterpart, Moon Jae-in, in dealing with North Korea over the denuclearization issue, Korea felt great pressure from Washington on the economic front. Even joint military drills were cancelled on budgetary grounds. Under those circumstances, it is only natural that Seoul would want to revert to its previous hedging position. On October 31, 2017, China and South Korea agreed to normalize a bilateral relationship that had been undermined by the THAAD issue. Seoul was keenly aware of its position as a "middle power" in the region and eager to develop a strategy to best promote the national interest in that context. Hedging is a natural strategic choice for a "middle power."[29]

Taiwan is a different story. Cross-Strait relations are determined first and foremost by the acceptance or denial of the "1992 Consensus" by the Taiwan government. That official position is in turn determined by dueling national identities and electoral results on the island.[30] Hence, for most Asian SMCs, the position towards China and the US is a matter of foreign policy, while for Taiwan it is deeply ingrained in domestic politics and national identity. As a result, Taiwan demonstrated less policy flexibility than do other Asian SMCs when it comes to dealings with China. It responded less to international than to domestic pressure. Beijing also demonstrated less flexibility when it comes to Taiwan.[31] In dealing with a pro-unification government in Taipei, Beijing is willing to tolerate cordial Taiwan-US relations, even arms sales. However, Beijing is completely intolerant of independence-leaning government in Taipei, whether that government seeks US help or not. Hence, an independence-tilting DPP government under Chen Shui-bian prompted the passage of the Anti-Secession Law in 2005, with its stern warnings of using force against Taiwan under specific circumstances, while the inauguration of the pro-1992

---

28. For the THAAD incident and its impact on ROK-PRC relations, see Jung H. Pak, "Trying to Loosen the Linchpin: China's Approach to South Korea," *Global China: Assessing China's Growing Role in the World*, The Brookings Institution, July 2020, https://www.brookings.edu/research/trying-to-loosen-the-linchpin-chinas-approach-to-south-korea/.
29. For South Korea's "middle power" self-perception and its foreign policy implications, see Adam Cathcart, "Chinese Strategy and South Korea," in *An Emerging China-Centric Order: China's Vision for a New World Order in Practice*, ed. Nadège Rolland, NBR special report #87, August 2020.
30. Taiwan's electoral competition has centered on the identity issue, unlike most other democracies that have a left-right social and political divide. See Christopher H. Achen and T. Y. Wang, eds., *The Taiwan Voters* (Ann Arbor: University of Michigan Press, 2017).
31. For a discussion of the interactions between Beijing and Taipei and the power position of the leaders on both sides, see Yu-Shan Wu and Kuan-Wu Chen, "Domestic Politics and Cross-Strait Relation: A Synthetic Perspective," *Journal of Asian and African Studies* 55, no. 2 (March 2020): 168–86.

Consensus Ma Ying-Jeou ushered in an unprecedented thaw, a truce in diplomatic war, and bountiful economic concessions to Taiwan. Under Chen, Taiwan could not join its East Asian neighbors in their competitive hedging toward China (hence Taiwan as the odd one out during the pre-2008 period), while under Ma it could dramatically improve relations with Beijing when other East Asian countries turned away from an increasingly assertive China (again setting Taiwan apart from its neighbors under SWI). This divergent pattern continued after Xi succeeded Hu Jintao in 2012. The new Chinese leader led an aggressive policy toward China's neighbors, but he took pains to keep cross-Strait relations intact as long as Ma Ying-Jeou remained president in Taiwan. Throughout Ma's tenure, Taiwan maintained a hedging strategy toward China, attempting to court both Washington and Beijing.[32] The unprecedented Xi-Ma summit held in Singapore at a time when Ma was a lame duck president and the KMT's electoral disaster in the upcoming general election was for everyone to see and vividly demonstrates the point.

After the DPP regained political ascendancy in 2016 and refused to endorse the "1992 Consensus" with the one-China principle therein, Beijing reversed its policy toward Taiwan. The identity gap between the two sides was widened dramatically, leading to a predictable backlash. As Xi promised, "if the foundation is undermined, then the ground will move and mountains will be shaken" (*jichu bulao, didong shanyao*). As a result, the number of Mainland tourists to Taiwan was dramatically cut, semi-official ties between Taiwan's Strait Exchange Foundation (SEF) and the PRC's Association for Relations Across the Taiwan Strait (ARATS) were severed, Taiwan was denied attendance at the World Health Assembly (WHA) meeting, Panama and several other countries were taken away from Taipei's twentyish diplomatic allies, and the PLA's carrier Liaoning and military aircraft were sent on missions that circled Taiwan. Even Mainland students were discouraged from attending universities on the island.

The reversion of Beijing's policy toward Taiwan coincided with the election of Trump as US president, whose "make America great again" policy later propelled many Asian SMCs to reconsider their position between the two great powers. When China felt the need to court its neighbors back under Trump's maximum pressure and trade war (SWII), it approached Japan, Korea, and other Asian countries, but it did not reduce pressure on the DPP government in Taiwan. In 2017–2018, both Japan and South Korea tilted back toward their previous position by reaching reconciliation with China, as aforementioned. At the same time, Taiwan further moved away from Beijing and embraced the US. The inflexibility of both Taipei's and Beijing's position makes policy shift that much more difficult. Two logics of China policy are clearly at work in East Asia: the internal logic for Taiwan, and the external

---

32. For a discussion of Taiwan's hedging strategy against China, see Charles Chong-han Wu, "Taiwan's Hedging against China," *Asian Survey* 56, no. 3 (May/June 2016): 466–87.

logic for other Asian SMCs. For Taiwan, policy toward China is an innermost matter of identity choice that is at the core of domestic political contestation. For other East Asian countries, China policy is foremost a foreign policy that can be adjusted according to the circumstances. The disjuncture between these two logics is the major reason behind Taiwan's perennial status as the odd one out in the region.

This chapter deals with the role of the SMCs amid great power competition, and applies a strategic triangle perspective. It discerns five policy options for the SMCs and finds *hedging* (or hedging partner of the US) to be the dominant strategy/role for the SMCs in East Asia. The momentum for competitive hedging is provided by payoff changes for an SMC in a strategic triangle. Hedging countries may change their position in a new situation. Two logics (internal for Taiwan and external for other Asian SMCs) are explored in three periods (pre-2008, 2008–2016 or SWI, and post 2016 or SWII). It was found that for most Asian SMCs, Chinese assertiveness and US mercantilist policy tend to drive SMCs toward the other dominant power, while Taiwan's position is primarily determined by its domestic politics and dueling national identities. To grasp the full picture of hegemonic rivalry between the US and the PRC, it is necessary to understand how great powers interact with SMCs and how the SMCs' policies toward great powers are determined. The analysis of the two logics presented here is a first step toward that goal.

9
Southeast Asia among the Powers[1]

Lowell Dittmer

To a region still flailing for political coherence, Southeast Asia has brought a distinctive, one might even say creative, approach to regional integration. Since its founding in 1967, ASEAN (Association of Southeast Asian Nations) has offered its "ASEAN way" as a solution to Asia's disorder. And indeed, having brought prosperity and a loose form of unity to one of the most diverse areas on earth, it seems well qualified to do so. Insofar as the "ASEAN way" has succeeded—still contested at this point—it did so not by "iron and blood" or any form of power projection but simply by inviting countries to cooperate. Southeast Asia could be said to lead by example, as a heterogeneous (and initially querulous) hodgepodge of languages and cultures that has learned to live together peaceably. Nanyang to ancient Chinese, to their Indian contemporaries it was Savarnadvipa, and to the Arabs of antiquity it was Qumr. Geographically divided between maritime (Indonesia, the Philippines, Singapore, Brunei Darussalam, East Malaysia, Papua New Guinea, and Timor Leste) and mainland states (Laos, Vietnam, Thailand, peninsular Malaysia, Myanmar, and Cambodia), the region functions as a geographic bridge between the Indian and Pacific Oceans, overseeing the vital sea lanes that give China, Japan, and the US Pacific Coast access to the oil-rich Middle East and the east coast of Africa. Because of the region's fragmentation, it never posed the military threat to the rest of the world that sometimes emanated from Europe or Northeast Asia. This is no Shangri-La, but most strife has stayed within the region. All its constituent states are relatively small, weak, or underdeveloped, perpetually at risk from geopolitically stronger, more ambitious states—Kublai Khan tried to colonize Java, China occupied much of Vietnam for nearly a thousand years and occasionally invaded Burma, in

---

1. I wish to thank Karl Jackson for his most helpful comments on an earlier draft of this chapter. I am also grateful to the East Asian Institute (National University of Singapore) for research support.

the modern era European imperialism subjugated all but Thailand—until the area was "liberated" from Western imperialism by imperial Japan in the early 1940s, only then to be embroiled in communist-instigated "national liberation wars" over the next three decades.

ASEAN was created in 1967 to deter such threats, expanding since the end of the Cold War to include ten Southeast Asian nation-states. Though a latecomer to the modernization sweepstakes, the subregion has emerged since World War II as a center of economic dynamism, endowed with rich soil and abundant natural resources (regional GDP growth in 2018 averaged over 6 percent). It has the world's third largest labor force of more than 600 million people, behind China but ahead of the European Union and the United States—and with more than half that population under forty years old (twenty-eight median age), a demographic dividend. With a combined GDP of approximately US$2.95 trillion in 2018, Southeast Asia now boasts the third largest GDP in Asia after China and Japan and the fifth largest in the world. Although it is too soon to tell, the trade war may leave the region better off than its giant northern neighbor. The GDP of ASEAN is projected to grow by more than 5 percent per annum over the next five years, while intra-ASEAN trade is expected to exceed US$1 trillion. The latest boom has been in technology, including the region's first set of "minotaurs."[2] The number of Southeast Asian venture capital deals quadrupled from 2012 to 2017.

Southeast Asia is thus both a pivotal inter-regional choke point and a growing source of political-economic value in and for itself. The current disorder from the Southeast Asian perspective stems from the intrusion of power politics into the region, particularly since the rise of Xi Jinping and Donald Trump (in 2012 and 2016 respectively). The Southeast Asians are not historically unacquainted with power politics. But at the end of the Cold War there was a welcome interlude in which the powers withdrew from the region, leaving a power vacuum into which the Southeast Asians attempted to insert their own multilateral dream of new world order. This was done not by expanding outward but by inviting the major powers into ASEAN extended forums as "dialogue partners." A distinction thus arose between ASEAN itself, consisting of the ten full members, and a periphery of "expanded meetings" open to extra-regional powers: the ASEAN Regional Forum (ARF), the ASEAN Defense Ministers Meeting plus (ASEAN plus Japan and China, or ADMM plus), the ASEAN-EU Annual Meetings (ASEM), ASEAN plus three (China, Japan and Korea, or APT), the East Asian Summit, and finally the Regional Comprehensive Economic Partnership (RCEP), widely attributed to China but actually initiated by ASEAN.

ASEAN has always been loosely structured, but it has codified its own irenic esprit de corps, the "ASEAN way," into which it sought to socialize its

---

2. A "minotaur" is a financial term for a venture-backed private firm that has raised more than $1 billion in equity capital.

larger and more powerful neighbors as dialogue partners. This was defined by Malaysian academician Noordin Sopiee as the "Principle of seeking agreement and harmony, the principle of sensitivity, politeness, nonconfrontation and agreeability, the principle of quiet, private and elitist diplomacy versus public washing of dirty linen, and the principle of being non-Cartesian, non-legalistic." This spirit suffuses all ASEAN statements of diplomatic principles, as in the 2002 Treaty of Amity and Cooperation (TAC): (1) respect for sovereignty and territorial integrity, (2) non-interference in internal affairs, (3) settlement of disputes by peaceful means, and (4) renunciation of threat or use of force. And the transformation has been quite impressive: since 1967 no interstate wars have been fought in Southeast Asia, a respectable rate of growth has been achieved, and economic cooperation has increased, symbolized by the establishment in 1992 of an ASEAN Economic Community (AEC) with common tariffs. In 2000, China proposed (and ASEAN accepted) a gigantic free trade agreement between China and ASEAN (ACFTA), which duly came into being a decade later; in November 2020 this was expanded into the RCEP, the largest multilateral trade agreement in the world with fifteen signatories.

China's initiative was more than welcome in Southeast Asia. The creation of a multilateral FTA in the form of the ACFTA, followed by analogous FTAs with Japan and South Korea, has contributed to the rapid expansion of trade and the formation of a web of value chains that have transformed the nature of trade from international to intrafirm. ASEAN-China goods trade increased from $35.3 billion in 2000 to $644 billion in 2019 (up 76.6 percent from 2018), overtaking the US as China's largest trade partner amid the Sino-American trade war. But it has also contributed to large trade deficits for ASEAN countries with China, soaring to US$81 billion in 2016, nearly eight times higher than a decade before. The attempt to co-opt the Chinese military threat that arose in the wake of the latter's claim to sovereignty over some 90 percent of the South China Sea took the form of inviting that country to participate in negotiating a Code of Conduct for the peaceful resolution of territorial disputes. A non-binding "Declaration of Conduct of Parties in the South China Sea" (DOC) was indeed agreed in 2002, but since that date negotiations over an actual (legally binding) Code of Conduct have continued inconclusively.

What is the essential nature of "Asian disorder" insofar as Southeast Asia is concerned? Southeast Asia's bid to survive and thrive as a school of relatively small fish among whales and sharks has been to merge into a larger actor, ASEAN, designed to magnify the power of its ten constituents sufficiently to defend their interests in the international arena. We have seen how this merger appeared to succeed surprisingly well for over fifty years. China was the first great power to take ASEAN seriously as an international actor: it did so by signing TAC in 1992, the first major power to do so, also signing DOC, and by initiating the APT forum and the ACFTA and leading in the pursuit of the RCEP. All this, no less than its well-publicized restraint from devaluing the yuan and extending loans during the Asian financial crisis, was widely appreciated, breaking much of the ice left from the Cold War. Japan, Australia, and finally Russia and the US also joined ASEAN's regional forums.

Yet ASEAN's Achilles' heel all along has been its anarchic structure: any member can veto, and all members have different bottom lines. To function properly, all members (and dialogue partners) must be willing to fit into a vague but not empty political moral consensus. How shocking, then, that after a twenty-year charm campaign, beginning around 2010 China became a powerful threat to ASEAN's territorial integrity, asserting ownership of ninety percent of the South China Sea based on "ancient history," claiming therewith exclusive jurisdiction over fishing rights, subsurface hydrocarbon reserves, and above all military access, skillfully playing non-littoral states against littoral states to gut any joint resistance to its claims. Though faced with a momentous loss of resources and security by such a potential takeover, due to divisions among its members and fear of Chinese retaliation, ASEAN neither acted nor even dared speak out against these claims, and China has since strengthened its strategic position by paving over and militarizing the seven small islets it occupies (three of which are now the size of Pearl Harbor) and chasing away any vessels that approach them. While some individual nation-states, such as Vietnam and the Philippines, took steps to defend their interests, ASEAN did not.

The second regional cooperation arrangement to collapse in Southeast Asia is the US security network. The credibility of "hegemonic stability," the theory underpinning the postwar American role as "world policeman," has been in gradual decline in East Asia since American defeat in the Vietnam War, accelerated by the unhappy American experience in the Middle East since 9/11. The reasons for this are complicated, but we may point to three factors: first, there were inherent structural weaknesses in the arrangement *ab ovo*—it was bilateral rather than multilateral ("hub-and-spokes"), omitting collective security arrangements like ASEAN altogether; in fact only two Southeast Asian countries were covered (Thailand and the Philippines), and it was an exclusively military ("traditional security") arrangement. Second, there has since been a decline of the relative power of the US in the region, both economically (as a trade and investment partner) and as a security guarantor. China is now the leading trade partner of most Southeast Asian nations and the fastest-growing investor. As for the US security guarantee, the current assessment is that the US has lost its military edge and that American patronage, even formal alliance, is no longer an effective deterrent to subtle Chinese "gray zone" aggression. This was most clearly demonstrated in the Chinese takeover of Scarborough Shoal from the Philippines in 2012, which was achieved by stratagem, not military predominance. America's bilateral security alliances cover only a contingency in which the ally is directly attacked, which China carefully avoided. Third, no alternative collective organization has been conceived to replace the flawed status quo. Obama championed an American "pivot" or rebalance of forces, centered on a high-quality multilateral free-trade agreement (the Trans-Pacific

Partnership, or TPP), but he was unable to get it passed during his eight-year term, and both presidential candidates to succeed him disavowed the arrangement. Trump campaigned as a populist and has consistently focused on renegotiating relations bilaterally, but the Southeast Asians have always preferred to negotiate as a unit. Trump's November 2017 endorsement of a "Free and Open Indo-Pacific" strategy represents a dawning recognition of the need for a multilateral strategy, but it is still skeletal.

In sum, after an early post–Cold War "peace dividend" period of great power withdrawal from the region, when ASEAN began to spread its organizational wings to envelope greater Asia in a spirit of peace via an endless round of conferences, power politics is back with a vengeance. Power politics, whether practiced by Xi Jinping or Donald Trump, has in common a tendency to ignore multilateral institutions and reduce international affairs to interactions among nation-states. This places the Southeast Asian states at a distinct disadvantage, because though some are larger than others, all are small and underdeveloped relative to the powers. It is for this reason that ASEAN was founded in the first place, and the present and future autonomy of these states will depend upon its political efficacy.

In Western eyes, the major power encroaching on Southeast Asian autonomy since the evacuation of European imperialism has been the People's Republic of China. During the Maoist period this took the form of ideological and logistic support for indigenous wars of "national liberation," but since the inauguration of reform and opening, China has disavowed the export of revolution and taken a more subtle approach, mixing sticks and carrots. China is also geographically closer to Southeast Asia than any other major power is, bordering Vietnam, Laos, and Myanmar (on land), the others on water. China is the largest and fastest-growing source of trade and opportunity for economic development, and the ancestral homeland of a large (around 30 million) rich and influential ethnic Chinese minority. Southeast Asians are understandably ambivalent about China, typically seeking to "hedge"—to "bandwagon" while also "balancing"—taking advantage of the opportunities China offers while relying on continuing American engagement to deter potential threats. Those countries with no territorial issues at stake, such as Laos or Cambodia, feel free to bandwagon with China, but those bounding the South China Sea are unwilling to forfeit their stakes. As David Kang has pointed out, the Southeast Asian states have hardly been zealous internal balancers. While some spend more than others and all have escalated their arms budgets, overall regional arms spending has not kept pace with that of the PRC.[3] At the same time an external balance among ASEAN states—a pooling of forces—has not proved feasible amid the diversity of cultures, resources,

---

3. David C. Kang, "A Looming Arms Race in East Asia?" *The National Interest,* May 14, 2014, https://nationalinterest.org/feature/looming-arms-race-east-asia-10461; see also his book, *American Grand Strategy and East Asian Security in the 21st Century* (New York: Cambridge University Press, 2017).

interests, levels of development, and so forth. Not even Indonesia, the largest, can realistically hope to compete with the PRC in a bilateral standoff, so arms racing is unrealistic. Hence, the default option has been to turn to the US for support in a pinch.

In sum, the three great powers on Southeast Asia's horizon, China, Japan, and the US, have recently taken increasing interest in Southeast Asia, each offering both opportunities and risks. In this next section we look at ASEAN's bilateral relations with each of the three major regional powers. This will be followed by an analysis of how these might rationally be arranged to ASEAN's greatest strategic advantage.

ASEAN-China Relations

Following a confrontational relationship during the Cold War, China emerged as an important political and economic partner after Deng Xiaoping reoriented Chinese foreign policy from its focus on world revolution to "peace and development" in the early 1990s. China now advertised itself as an attractive economic partner and no longer a military threat (excepting the 1979 Sino-Vietnamese "pedagogic war"). The Nixon visit in 1972 made this reorientation feasible by neutralizing the US threat to China, followed by evacuation from Vietnam three years later. Soviet geopolitical ambitions died with the dissolution of the USSR in 1991. The US was pushed out of its bases in Clark Air Force Base (1991) and Subic Bay Naval Base (1992) in the Philippines, while the Russian Navy was finally evicted from Cam Ranh Bay in Vietnam in 2002.

Thus ironically commenced a period of relative regional peace and prosperity. China established full diplomatic relations with all Southeast Asian nations in the early 1990s, eliminating the "two Chinas" rivalry from the region. But China's great leap forward in its promotion of economic relations with ASEAN came during the Asian financial crisis (1997–1999), to which it responded with a loan fund of US$1 billion (never drawn upon) to Thailand and Indonesia and by refraining from devaluing its currency, to the relief of these stricken export economies. General discontent with the stringent terms of International Monetary Fund (IMF) loans awakened interest in regional financial solutions, which China encouraged, and in 1997 APT talks were initiated, from which emerged the ACFTA.

Since 2010 China has made more "assertive" claims to the islets and waters of the South China Sea as defined by the so-called nine-dash line. The legal basis of this claim is: (1) that these were Chinese waters "since ancient times", as demonstrated by the discovery of potshards and diary or logbook mentions of the islets by earlier travelers (none of whom, however, laid claim to the islands on behalf of previous Chinese dynasties); and (2) a maritime map with a then eleven-dash, now nine, or "cow's tongue" line, sketched on it by the Chinese Nationalist regime in 1947. China claims to have inherited it from the defeated Nationalists, who survived to still claim it for Taiwan though neither made determined attempts to enforce this claim until the United Nations Convention on the Law of the Sea (UNCLOS) called upon participants to stake their legal claims in 1994. Though the map overlaps the two-hundred-nautical mile exclusive economic zones (EEZs) of four littoral states as well as maritime areas previously considered high seas, China has recently attempted to enforce exclusive sovereignty by emplacing defensive military equipment on the islets it controls, by chasing away approaching vessels and aircraft, by prohibiting any further offshore oil drilling, and by proclaiming an "environmental" fishing ban. This undercuts the interests of rival ASEAN claimants to adjacent waters, some of whom have long been exploiting offshore subsurface hydrocarbon deposits and fishing in their EEZs, and they objected.

Far more disturbing in Chinese eyes was the reaction of the US. Whereas the US had previously maintained complete neutrality over ownership of the islands (and had done nothing to impede China's occupation of Mischief Reef, for example), in 2010 Secretary of State Clinton unexpectedly declared that "The United States has a national interest in freedom of navigation, open access to Asia's maritime commons and respect for international law in the South China Sea." The American offer to facilitate multilateral talks on the issue was spurned by China as "stirring up trouble" by "outsiders," and bilateral relations on this issue have since cooled.

At this point China shifted from its previous position of dealing with ASEAN as a bloc (as in the ACFTA negotiations) to insisting on negotiating territorial claims separately with each national claimant. Due to the great size and power disparity, the ASEAN claimants preferred to negotiate multilaterally. But because non-littoral ASEAN members could sometimes be persuaded to support China's position in votes requiring unanimity (and inasmuch as ASEAN per se has no legal sovereignty claims), China insisted on negotiating joint ventures with each claimant bilaterally. Although this has been awkward to arrange, China refused even to negotiate a code of conduct with ASEAN as a whole. Talks have hence proceeded with each of the ten nations, state to state. Negotiations have been ongoing since 2002 to adopt a legally binding Code of Conduct (to supersede the previous toothless DOC) that would outlaw coercion. But ASEAN has never been able to achieve an internal consensus between claimants (e.g., Vietnam, the Philippines) and non-claimants (Cambodia, Laos), let alone with China.

After the Philippines was blocked (by Cambodia) from raising the issue within ASEAN, it took its case to an UNCLOS arbitration panel (over vehement Chinese objections and refusal to participate), which finally decreed in 2016 that the nine-dash line was illegal. But because the US, the only party with the power to block China's claims, publicly supported the decision—while neither the Philippines, under newly elected Rodrigo Duterte, nor any other ASEAN state, did so—the dispute polarized not with ASEAN but between China and the US. Yet the US, having no sovereignty claim, could do no more than conduct "freedom of navigation operations" (FONOPs), defying China's territorial claims by sailing near its fortified islets (which altered neither the claims nor the islets). This has resulted in a protracted stalemate from which no one could benefit: China has succeeded in deterring other claimants from drilling new oil wells, but after a high-profile three-month episode in 2014 when it placed a drilling rig (the Haiyang Shiyou 981) within Vietnam's EEZ, it has not exploited the subsurface riches itself. The Chinese fishing fleet, now largest in the world, has, however, increasingly dominated fishing in these waters, with the backing of the Chinese Coast Guard and Maritime Militia, also the largest (and best armed) in the world.

China's launch of the vast, visionary Belt and Road Initiative (BRI), as personally announced in speeches by Xi Jinping in 2013 during visits to Kazakhstan and Indonesia, was motivated by many factors (mainly the need to offload China's industrial overcapacity), but it was advertised abroad as a great economic opportunity, hoping thereby to assuage the unease among its neighbors over China's greater assertiveness, particularly among those Southeast Asian nations whose maritime waters were claimed. This massive project consists of a network of road, rail, and port routes that will connect China to Central Asia, South Asia, the Middle East, eastern Africa, and Europe. Originally known as One Belt, One Road, namely the Silk Road Economic Belt through Central Asia and the 21st-Century Maritime Silk Road through Southeast and South Asia, it now includes six main corridors plus a planned Polar Silk Road through the Arctic. A series of high-level party documents and addresses by senior leaders make clear that this is a core part of China's efforts to achieve "national rejuvenation" and to create what the party calls a "community of common destiny" across the Indo-Pacific and beyond. It has also been a useful stimulant to China's industries: from 2013 to 2018 Chinese exports to BRI counties increased by $75 billion.

This brace of infrastructure projects will potentially create the world's largest economic corridor, covering sixty-five countries and a population of 4.4 billion with an economic output of US$21 trillion, and has already reportedly generated more than $3 trillion in trade. All Southeast Asian states have signed up with the BRI; Indonesia, Malaysia, and Vietnam consistently rank as leading recipients of Chinese capital for infrastructure development in East Asia, Indonesia leading the list at $93 billion, and Vietnam and Malaysia receiving around $70 billion and $34 billion respectively.[4] To some extent, BRI

---

4. See See Michelle Jamrisko, "China No Match for Japan in Southeast Asia Infrastructure Race," Bloomberg, June 22, 2019, https://www.bloomberg.com/news/articles/2019-06-23/china-no-match-for-japan-in-southeast-asia-infrastructure-race. Some estimates of total BRI-related capital flows into Southeast Asia run higher, Indonesia receiving as much as $171 billion, followed by Vietnam ($152 billion) and Malaysia ($98 billion). See Jinny Yan, "The BRI in Southeast Asia," in *China's Belt and Road and Southeast Asia* (Kuala Lumpur: CIMB ASEAN Research Institute and LSE Ideas, October 2018), 6–8, http://www.lse.ac.uk/ideas/Assets/Documents/reports/LSE-IDEAS-China-SEA-BRI.pdf. All as cited in Jonathan Stromseth's excellent, "Don't Make Us Choose: Southeast Asia in the throes

is a rebranding of foregoing projects. The Silk Road Economic *Belt* includes the foregoing BCIM (Bangladesh, China, India, Myanmar) economic corridor from Yunnan through Myanmar to Dhaka to Kolkata, for example, as well as plans for a Khunjerab Railway from Kashgar in Xinjiang through Kashmir to the Gwadar port that China is constructing in Pakistan. Also included is a high-speed rail line from Xi'an to Moscow and on through Belarus to Duisburg, Germany. The 21st-Century Maritime Silk *Road* will start from Fujian and link China (and Southeast Asia) to the Persian Gulf and the Mediterranean Sea through the Indian Ocean. In Southeast Asia the BRI will consist of a network of roads and railroads crisscrossing the region: the North-South Economic Corridor connects Kunming to Bangkok, while the East-West Corridor ties the Indian Ocean coast of Myanmar with the South China Sea ports of Vietnam. The Southern Economic Corridor connects Bangkok with Phnom Penh, Ho Chi Minh City, and Vung Tau.[5] In addition to roads, China is building a series of dams on the Mekong designed to greatly increase hydroelectric capacity.

Several Chinese financial instruments have stepped forward to fund this vast project. The total funding China has put on offer prospectively amounts to US$4 trillion (about $500 billion of which had been invested in fifty developing countries from 2013 to 2018, according to a 2019 World Bank report). Conceived in commercial terms, financing is negotiated bilaterally in the form of export credits and loans in "tied" projects: "no strings attached," but interest rates are high. Who benefits? The BRI has clearly been a boon to the Chinese construction industry—of the construction companies with the largest global revenue in 2019, the top five (and eight of the top twelve) were Chinese—as well as the financial sector (under pressure to recycle China's foreign exchange surplus, which peaked at $4 trillion in 2014, by lending abroad). Chinese state-owned enterprises (SOEs) needed a stream of infrastructure orders to avoid layoffs amid declining export demand and an unexpected trade dispute with their largest market, the US. The BRI was initially also welcomed by host countries, as the region-wide need for more infrastructure investment is undisputed. But the project has subsequently encountered pushback—most notably in Sri Lanka, which forfeited a ninety-nine-year renewable lease on Hambantota port as collateral for unpaid debts, but also in Malaysia, Pakistan, Nepal, and Indonesia.[6] By fall 2020, some $94

---

of US-China rivalry," *The New Geopolitics: Asia* (Brookings Institution, Washington, DC, October 2019), 5.
5. See Geoff Wade, "ASEAN Divides," *New Mandala*, December 2010, http://asiapacific.anu.edu.au/newmandala/
6. In 2016, Bangladesh opted to cancel cooperation with China on the country's first deep-water port and instead chose to work with Japan. Nepal canceled a costly hydroelectric dam project with China over concerns about cost overruns. Burma similarly canceled a dam project with China and dramatically scaled back a major port project. The Maldives asked to renegotiate Belt and Road projects after political supporters of closer economic cooperation with China were voted out of office. A similar political transition led Malaysia to canceling three Chinese pipeline projects and to re-evaluating a $20 billion rail project, again over

billion in BRI loans (about a fifth of the total) had come back for renegotiation, according to Rhodium. Although the BRI has since its advent often been depicted according to a centrally directed geostrategic scheme, more recent research indicates that projects are typically initiated from the host country and coordinated from the Chinese side quite loosely by respective SOEs and a welter of central economic agencies, and that responsibility for "white elephants" and other political, environmental, and socioeconomic externalities should be shared. Beyond the "debt trap" issue (which has not recurred since the Sri Lanka experience generated such negative publicity), concerns with BRI projects include complaints of corruption, padded contracts, and environmental damage (e.g., export of mostly coal-burning electric plants). News of China's repressive solution to Muslim unrest in Xinjiang raises tacit ethnic concerns among Muslim countries. Human rights groups object to the export of surveillance technology as featured in China's "digital silk road." BRI loans from China's Export-Import Bank or CDB typically have higher interest rates (and shorter payback periods) than the World Bank does, and loans are tied to no-bid contracts with Chinese SOEs. Borrowers must pledge existing assets as collateral and deposit significant sums in escrow accounts in China. Disputes must be taken to Chinese arbitration courts under the jurisdiction of Chinese law. After considerable publicity heralding the debut of the BRI, Chinese media have become somewhat more soft-spoken, as Beijing's access to funds available for overseas investment shrink with the decline in the pace of GDP growth and the bilateral trade war. China's outgoing foreign direct investment (FDI) reached a historic high in 2016 but has since declined steeply. China has since 2017 become more willing to renegotiate terms, seek funding from host nations, and make other concessions to keep projects afloat; China's outbound investment has dropped from US$222 billion in 2016 to around US$50 billion in 2020.

Japan and ASEAN

Japan's relationship with Southeast Asia began with Imperial Japan's 1940 declaration of a "Greater East Asian Co-prosperity Sphere" dedicated to the emancipation of Asia from Western colonialism and to the formation of a self-sufficient "bloc of Asian nations led by the Japanese and free of Western powers." It was justified in slogans of "Asia for the Asians," celebrating the spiritual values of the East in opposition to the crass materialism of the West,

---

concerns about cost overruns. Even China's closest partner, Pakistan, has canceled a $14 billion dam project as its government seeks to renegotiate the financial terms of the China Pakistan Economic Corridor (CPEC). See Christopher Balding, "Why Democracies Are Turning Against Belt and Road," *Foreign Affairs* (October 24, 2018), https://www.foreignaffairs.com/articles/china/2018-10-24/why-democracies-areturning-against-belt-and-road; and Andrew Small, "The Backlash to Belt and Road," *Foreign Affairs* (February 16, 2018), https://www.foreignaffairs.com/articles/china/2018-02-16/backlash-belt-and-road.

also in *tu quoque* terms as an Asian Monroe Doctrine with the Roosevelt corollary.[7] Originally conceived as an idealistic wish to "free" Asia from European colonialism and welcomed as such by such nationalist leaders as Sukarno in the Dutch East Indies, Aung San and Ne Win in Burma, in the course of the war it became a slogan justifying Japan's export of resources for its war machine on brutally asymmetrical terms, and although it continued to motivate diehard Japanese nationalists, it soon lost its appeal outside Japan, owing in part to the exploitative behavior of the local governments Japan installed and ultimately to avoid being caught on the wrong side as Japan was losing the war.

While this clearly attests to Japan's long-standing interest in Southeast Asia, especially as a source of raw materials, it left Japan in a rather awkward position when the Southeast Asians freed themselves from European colonialism and became sovereign nation-states after the war. Yet both the former colonized and former colonizer were equally destitute. The harsh Japanese occupation followed by the ravages of the Pacific War left these new nations economically devastated and in political turmoil, giving rise to communist insurgencies in Burma, Malaya, Vietnam, the Dutch East Indies (later Indonesia), and the Philippines. Japan was equally devastated, after two atomic bombs and the even more ruinous incendiary bombing of Japanese cities.

Blocked by the Iron Curtain and the US naval blockade from trade with China (or the USSR), Japan's postwar economic reconstruction relied heavily on access to Southeast Asian resources. As Prime Minister Yoshida Shigeru stated in November 1954, "Normal traditional trade relations with the Asian mainland are not now available to us . . . in order to be self-supporting, Japan must develop its trade with Southeast Asia." But to get there, Tokyo had to eat humble pie. Promptly after regaining sovereignty from US occupation in 1952, Tokyo undertook arrangements for war reparations agreements and the normalization of diplomatic relations. It took prolonged and hard-fought negotiations to reach agreement on the terms of reconciliation: Japan would pay reparations to the Southeast Asian countries of Burma, the Philippines, Indonesia, and South Vietnam between 1954 and 1959 in return for a peace treaty with Japan. Although these reparations were domestically referred to as magnanimous "official developmental assistance" (ODA), they also had both reciprocal economic benefits (often tied to the purchase of Japanese equipment and services) and political utility (as Japan's required contribution to the Cold War).[8]

---

7. The Roosevelt Corollary, asserted by Theodore Roosevelt in his 1904 State of the Union Address, asserted a right of the United States to intervene with "police power" in order to "stabilize" the economic affairs of small states in the Caribbean and Central America if they were unable to pay their international debts (in order to prevent European powers from doing so).
8. Both Miyagi and Kurasawa see reparations as the starting point for the political return of Japan to Southeast Asia. See Taizo Miyagi, *Sengo Ajia chitsujo no mosaku to Nihon: 'umi*

Japanese policy toward Southeast Asia was characterized by three features that were to remain consistent over time: (1) a focus on diplomacy, completely avoiding security policy (understandable in view of the constraints of Article 9); (2) an emphasis on reconciliation, avoiding taking sides whenever possible; and (3) a ready resort to foreign aid, loans, and other forms of economic statecraft (also reciprocally designed to support domestic economic interests) to facilitate peaceful solutions. The three principles of the cornerstone Fukuda Doctrine enunciated in 1977 were: first, Japan rejects any military role; second, Japan will consolidate relationships of mutual confidence and trust; and third, Japan will be an equal partner of ASEAN while fostering mutual understanding with Indochina et al. Japan was among the first to boost ASEAN as a regional forum, emulating as it did Japanese diplomatic principles of peace and conciliation.

China was from the outset an active competitor though its goals were political and transformational rather than economic. Beijing adopted a two-tier United Front strategy consisting of both traditional state-to-state diplomacy and party-to-party links to "national liberation" movements led by domestic communist parties. Chinese assistance was logistic as well as ideological, particularly in Vietnam, where China clandestinely sent troops, artillery, and jets, and suffered casualties. China also supported the Indonesian Communist Party, Sukarno's national socialism; Ne Win's Burmese socialism; and insurgencies in the Philippines, Burma, Nepal, Thailand, and Western India. Ideological and more limited material support for these insurgencies was not abandoned until the late 1980s. Chinese insurrectionary efforts, however, bore fruit only in former French Indochina, where communist parties took control of Vietnam and Laos, while an authoritarian pro-China (but non-communist) regime was established in Cambodia. The Vietnam War drew support not only from China but from the Soviet Union (then competing with China) and from the US on the opposite side. While the US tried to enlist its allies in the conflict, receiving troop support from South Korea, Australia, Turkey, Thailand, and the Philippines, Japan sent only small medical teams to Saigon and financial aid to South Vietnam. Although Japan's noncombat role was a source of increasing annoyance to the Americans (who had insisted on it in the first place), it became institutionalized as a lasting feature of Japanese foreign policy. Rather than contribute to the war effort, Japan saw its role as a mediator, maintaining cordial diplomatic relations with Hanoi, Beijing, and Moscow.

Indonesia provides a good illustration of the Japanese role. Although Sukarno maintained good relations with the Indonesian Communist Party (PKI), before 1965 the world's largest communist party outside the bloc, Japan was also happy to continue the collaboration with Sukarno that had started

---

no Ajia' no sengoshi 1957–1966 (Tokyo: Sobunsha, 2004); and Aiko Kurasawa, *Indoneshia to nihon: kirishima masaya kai sōroku* [Indonesia and Japan: Memoir of Masaya Kirshima] (Tokyo: Ronsōsha, 2011). As cited in James Llewelyn, "Japan's Cold War Diplomacy and Its Return to Southeast Asia," *Asia-Pacific Review* 21, no. 2 (2014): 86–116, fn. 37.

during the war, when Sukarno enjoyed Japanese support against the Dutch. Chinese aid to Indonesia was also quite substantial in the late 1950s and early 1960s. When Sukarno's *Konfrontasi* with Malaysia precipitated American opposition, Mao supported Sukarno, who publicly referred to Mao as his "dear friend and brother." Regularized high-level bilateral visits of political, economic, and military personnel were conducted from 1956 onward. Despite the worries of Japanese intelligence that Japan's interests might be adversely affected by Sukarno's leftward rift (e.g., would China gain control of Sumatran oil fields?), Japan continued aid and support to Jakarta while trying to defuse the Indonesian-Malayan confrontation over Borneo.[9] Prime Minister Ikeda sent the well-known political fixer and Liberal Democratic Party Vice President Kawashima Shojiro to meet with Sukarno just prior to the 1965 coup attempt, offering US$37 million in aid aimed at bringing the Indonesian and Malaysian leaders together again for talks. These efforts became extraneous when Sukarno was displaced by General Suharto's anti-communist developmental dictatorship (which settled the Kalimantan dispute fairly promptly) following an apparent abortive PKI coup attempt.

Similarly, Japan remained diplomatically and economically engaged with Burma throughout the Ne Win and SLORC (State Law and Order Restoration Council) dictatorships when the country was ostracized from the West, and was among the first to urge Burma's admission to ASEAN. When the UN's International Council of Justice in January 2020 handed down a warning to Burma (now Myanmar) to desist from "genocidal" policies against its Rohingya minority, China *and Japan* in contrast supported Myanmar's own Independent Commission of Enquiry (ICE), which referred to "clearing operations" by the Tatmadaw and denied any "genocidal intent." Japan also played a conciliatory role in Vietnam, particularly after the North Vietnamese defeat of Saigon and the evacuation of US forces from the south in 1975. While Vietnamese-American relations at this point remained embittered, Japan immediately interceded to support the rebuilding of a war-ravaged Vietnam. Tokyo made its first round of grants totaling $37.5 million to the unified Socialist Republic of Vietnam as early as 1976, informing Washington that Japan would "substitute economic assistance for military spending under the broad definition of security inherent in the notion of containment."[10]

The post–Vietnam War period (1975–1990) was characterized by two trends: the growth and regional outreach of ASEAN, and the economic (and diplomatic) coordination of Japan and ASEAN. Meanwhile, militarily victorious and unified (but economically devastated) Vietnam was ostracized by the West, particularly after its 1979 invasion of Cambodia, as was the PRC, the last international supporter of the Khmer Rouge perpetrators of the "killing fields." While China at this time viewed ASEAN askance as an anti-communist

---

9. Llewelyn, "Japan's Cold War Diplomacy and Its Return to Southeast Asia," 96.
10. R. B. St John, "Japan's Moment in Indochina," *Asian Survey* 35, no. 7 (1995): 673.

alliance, Japan continued to be guided by the Fukuda Doctrine, which deemed ASEAN the crucial element of its Asia policy. In 1977, the Japan-ASEAN forum was launched to pursue closer political coordination and diplomatic ties. From 1960 to 2011, Japan provided 34.9 percent of its ODA to ASEAN (second only to China as an ODA recipient), and Japanese ODA increased five times between 1976 and 1986. It was during this period that the Asian-Pacific value chains were established, as Japan took advantage of cheap labor to off-shore production processes after the 1985 Plaza agreement drove up domestic production costs. Japan was especially helpful during the Asian financial crisis, sponsoring a New Miyazawa Initiative and other developmental assistance totaling nearly US$80 billion up to November 1998—far more than China's $1 billion loan, which, however, gleaned more publicity, as it was the first time China had stepped forward with emergency financial assistance.[11] Yet this did not at the time incur heightened Sino-Japanese rivalry: Japan was also China's leading trade partner (and leading recipient of Japanese ODA) from 1982 to 1989. Sino-Japanese trade reached a record US$16.4 billion in 1985, ten times that of 1972. Japanese FDI continued to increase through the 1990s, accounting for 28 percent of China's technology imports in 1993.

The next several decades saw: (1) a deteriorating Sino-Japanese political and (to a lesser extent) economic relationship and (2) a vigorous (and relatively successful) Chinese "charm" campaign in Southeast Asia, encompassing economic, diplomatic, and security dimensions. The Sino-Japanese rift emerged only gradually, cumulating issues over time, especially after China's productive capacity overtook Japan's. In 1978, China's GDP was only one eighth of Japan's, but in 2004 it surpassed Japan in total trade and by 2010 in nominal GDP. The Japanese were unnerved by Chinese use of force in the Tiananmen crackdown (1989) and the Taiwan missile crisis (1995–1996)—it struck them that the missiles that bracketed Taiwan port cities also could also easily reach Japan's main islands. This gave rise to the "China threat theory" that China tried to counter with rhetoric stressing China's "peaceful rise/development" and "harmonious world."

As Western developed nations withdrew investment and imposed human rights sanctions, Beijing invoked *tao guang yang hui* (hide our brilliance and bide our time) and shifted its diplomatic focus to the developing world, particularly to its Asian neighborhood. This entailed overcoming Chinese suspicions of ASEAN (and vice versa). China launched a "smile campaign," agreeing to a Declaration on the Conduct of Parties in the South China Sea in 2002 and signing TAC in 2003 (the first non-ASEAN country to do so). The pace of Japan-ASEAN relations slackened in comparison, as Japan was distracted by its financial bubble bursting and coping with the ensuing "lost decades" of

---

11. "The Asian Economic Crisis and Japan's Contribution," Ministry of Foreign Affairs of Japan, October 2000, https://www.mofa.go.jp/policy/economy/asia/crisis0010.html. I am indebted to Karl Jackson for this reference.

economic stagnation, accompanied by electoral reform and partisan realignment. The ASEAN-Japan Comprehensive Economic Partnership Agreement (CEPA, Japan's equivalent of an FTA) was not proposed until 2002, in response to China's successful initiative negotiating the ACFTA.

Since around 2010, however, as Sino-Japanese bilateral relations flared over the Diaoyu/Senkaku dispute in the East China Sea, Japan also became more engaged in Southeast Asia, now increasingly driven by the potential Chinese threat to their supply lines. As ASEAN proceeded with its campaign to co-opt the great powers by including them in various multilateral discussion forums, a subtle competition played out between the two over how to structure regional integration. As each side proposed various multilateralization schemes, the other could reliably be predicted to be unenthusiastic. This began during the Asian financial crisis, when Japan proposed an Asian monetary fund, which was promptly debunked by both China and the US. Instead, the more modest Chiang Mai currency swap initiative was adopted, in which voting shares were allocated according to capital contributions. In 2001, Tokyo was excluded from China's Shanghai Cooperation Organization. During the creation of the East Asian Summit, China proposed to include only ASEAN plus three (China, Japan, Korea), while Japan successfully lobbied to include three (China, Japan, Korea) plus three (Australia, New Zealand, India).

Shinzo Abe placed new emphasis on Japan's commitment to ASEAN at the inauguration of his second term as prime minister in December 2012, and he unusually then visited all ten ASEAN member states, culminating in a "Vision Statement on ASEAN-Japan Friendship and Cooperation" in 2013. In addition to taking a firmer line against concessions to China's claim to the Senkaku/Diaoyu islets, Abe inserted himself into the South China Sea controversy as well, arranging for the transfer of defense equipment and technology to Vietnam, Malaysia, and the Philippines under a more liberal interpretation of Article 9 that for the first time permitted the sale of weapons. Japan declined to join China's Asian Infrastructure Investment Bank (AIIB) (which competes directly with the Tokyo-centered Asian Development Bank, ADB) as well as the BRI, which includes all other East Asian countries though it later agreed to cooperate with BRI projects on a case-by-case basis. Japan's business sector has meanwhile shifted its focus from China as factory of the world to China as market of the world, gradually shifting production facilities to the south. As Japanese FDI withdraws from China in the wake of mass anti-Japan demonstrations over Diaoyu, etc., Southeast Asia has reemerged as Japan's leading FDI destination in Asia.[12] These trends were greatly accelerated by the 2018 Sino-American trade dispute and by the ensuing 2020 coronavirus pandemic.

---

12. For a third straight year, in 2015 the amount of FDI from Japan to the ten-member ASEAN exceeded such investment in China and Hong Kong, according to figures compiled by the Japan External Trade Organization (JETRO). In 2013, Japanese corporate investment in Southeast Asia was three times that in China, and the pace has been accelerating: the outstanding amount of Japanese investment to ASEAN nations almost tripled (from $3.5

ASEAN-American Relations

American relations with Southeast Asia since World War II have been characterized by three features: (1) First, political security support, very expensive but highly inconsistent and not always effective, has been limited to select countries (and not always allies). American support has ranged from intense engagement in response to perceived ideological threats (e.g., the Vietnam war, 1955–1975), to long periods of seeming indifference.

(2) Economic relations have also varied cyclically but have been cumulatively quite massive albeit frequently underestimated. China has leaped to the forefront in trade with Southeast Asia since 2012, but the US remains second only to Japan in investment (China is third but rising fast).[13] Southeast Asia is America's fourth largest export market, recipient of about $75 billion in goods and $31 billion in services per annum. ASEAN has hosted approximately $329 billion in cumulative FDI from the US—more than the US has directed to China, India, Japan, and South Korea combined. Washington also disbursed over $800 million in foreign assistance to ASEAN countries in 2018.

(3) Political-security and economic relations have varied independently, running on separate tracks. Political-security relations are managed by government departments (mainly state and defense) and triggered by national threat perceptions, while economic relations emanate mostly from the private sector based on market vicissitudes and comparative advantage. Thus the abrupt withdrawal of portfolio investment from the region at the beginning of the Asian financial crisis had no evident political corollary, nor did the massive investment in the PRC following its entry into the World Trade Organization in 2001. These features have confused but not entirely alienated Southeast Asians, who continue to look to the US for security should relations with the PRC go south. But mistrust of American constancy is pervasive.

In the aftermath of Vietnam, and particularly during the G. W. Bush "Global War on Terror," the US made a sweeping withdrawal from the region. It gave

---

billion to $10.2 billion) from 2010 to 2018. In three of the last four years, Japanese net FDI flows to Southeast Asia have been greater than FDI to China despite China being a larger economy with a lower stock of Japanese FDI than Southeast Asia has. According to Japanese government statistics, Japanese exports to Southeast Asia increased year on year by 5.8 percent, while exports to China fell by 10.4 percent. Japanese imports from Southeast Asia grew by 4.0 percent, while those from China grew by 3.0 percent. And unlike American FDI (but like Chinese), Japan likes off-shoring personnel as well as capital: by 2017 a total of 83,000 Japanese employees were posted to offices in members of ASEAN. In interviews and surveys carried out by JETO for its 2013 Trade and Investment Report, Japanese businesses claimed they are diverting resources from China to Southeast Asia due to perceptions of growing political and commercial risks and labor problems in China. Malcolm Cook, "Southeast Asia and the Major Powers: Engagement not Entanglement," *Southeast Asian Affairs*, 2014, https://www.jstor.org/stable/44112064.

13. From 2010 to 2018 Chinese investment in Southeast Asia tripled, from $3.5 billion to $10.2 billion (outpaced, however, by Japanese and US investment). The largest investor in ASEAN is actually ASEAN, increasing from $16.3 billion to $24.5 billion.

up its two bases in the Philippines without compunction and has showed little interest in building new ones.[14] It was last of the four major Asian powers to sign TAC and (with Russia) last to be invited to participate in the East Asian Summit or in the ADMM Plus. As America's first Pacific president (raised partly in Indonesia), Obama tried to revive interest in ASEAN: many bilateral agreements were signed, including military assistance and Enhanced Defense Agreements with Indonesia, Malaysia, the Philippines, and Singapore. The Obama administration provided US$4 billion in development assistance from 2010 to 2016 and launched the Lower Mekong Initiative to support sustainable development in Indochina. Relations with Vietnam improved, and relations with Myanmar were normalized with the revival of elections in 2010 and the subsequent rise of Aung San Suu Kyi. US trade in merchandise reached US$273 billion in 2015 (tripling since the 1990s), and US cumulative direct investment reached US$226 billion.[15] American officials made it a point to attend the East Asia Summit (EAS) and other ASEAN meetings more frequently.

To counter China's perceived geopolitical assertiveness, the Obama administration announced in 2012 a "Pivot to East Asia" or "Asian Rebalance" regional strategy, which precipitated vociferous opposition from China and tended to polarize the region without noticeably impeding China's salami-slicing advances in the South China Sea.[16] Unlike China, Japan, India, South Korea, and Australia, the US has not signed an FTA with ASEAN but was the first non-ASEAN country to appoint an ambassador to ASEAN in 2008 and in June 2010 the first non-ASEAN country to establish a dedicated Mission to the ASEAN headquarters in Jakarta, with a resident ambassador appointed in 2011. Under the Obama administrations, the United States' regional trade diplomacy efforts focused on the Asia-Pacific-wide TPP, which was finally approved by twelve Asia-Pacific countries in 2016 but failed to win congressional approval before Obama's presidential term ended.

The election of Donald J. Trump in 2016 aroused fears of another American abandonment of ASEAN, leaving a strategic vacuum for China to fill, and indeed Trump rescinded the TPP just three days after taking office. Trump attended the ASEAN Summit in Manila in 2017 but left early, skipping the plenary session; he has not attended a full EAS meeting since his inauguration in January 2017. Obama's "Asian Rebalance" seems to have also been

---

14. In the aftermath of Vietnam, US military presence in Southeast Asia greatly decreased, and once the Cold War threat from the Soviet fleet ended with the collapse of the Soviet Union, strategists in the Pentagon were willing to substitute a much smaller naval and air access facility in Singapore (a "place, not a base") for the far more substantial capabilities at Clark Field and Subic Bay in the Philippines.
15. David Shambaugh, "Trends in Southeast Asia: US Relations with Southeast Asia in 2018: More Continuity than Change," Institute Southeast Asian Studies—Yusof Ishak Institute, Singapore, no. 18 (2018).
16. See Nori Katagiri, "A Critical Assessment of the Asia Rebalance," *The Chinese Journal of International Politics*, 12 (1) (Spring 2019): 36–60. https://doi.org/10.1093/poy018.

abandoned, though FONOPS have been regularized and increased in frequency.[17] Although the Trump administration's focus shifted from the South China Seas to China and North Korea, it has in various ways tried to reassure ASEAN of its continuing support. Trump welcomed the leaders of Malaysia, Singapore, Thailand, and Vietnam to the White House in 2017, and made two visits to the region in the same year. He also hosted a successful US-ASEAN summit. In place of the TPP and the Asian Rebalance, the Trump administration has increased defense budgets (and encouraged allies to increase theirs) and in 2017 adopted Shinzo Abe's "Free and Open Indo-Pacific" strategy, structured around a "quad" of democratic states (the US, Japan, Australia, and India), and emphasized private investment in "quality" infrastructure construction rather than China's reliance on state entrepreneurism. This is still more a slogan than a strategy, but the quad did hold a joint Malabar naval exercise in November 2020 although "ASEAN centrality" was therewith implicitly abandoned. ASEAN in 2019 adopted an "Outlook on the Indo-Pacific" that was essentially positive with some distinctive nuances.[18]

Dual Triangles

We envisage below two parallel triangles: an Asian triangle (on the left) consisting of ASEAN, China, and Japan, and an international triangle (on the right) consisting of ASEAN, China, and the US. Southeast Asia's relationship to China, its leading trade partner, source of economic growth, and potential security threat, is the focus ("dependent variable") of this analysis, hence the central shared fulcrum of our two composite triangles.

Some might argue that Japan, as a faithful ally of the US, so rarely strays from US foreign policy guidelines that this is a distinction without a difference. Closer examination, however, reveals that although the two might be largely complementary, there are meaningful differences. For one thing, Japan is geographically in Asia, while the US is over six thousand miles away. American school children do not know Manila from Kuala Lumpur. The fact that Japan is part of the geographical region whose fate will be affected by its decisions gives its commitment greater credibility. True, geography is partly "constructed," and Japan as the first Asian modernizer has been historically ambivalent about its Asian identity ever since Fukuzawa Yukichi's "Escape from Asia." But Japan has long had an economic interest in Southeast Asia,

---

17. According to Chinese count, US naval warships have passed within twelve nautical miles of Chinese-claimed islands twenty-one times since 2015 (once in 2015, three times in 2016, five times in 2017, five times in 2018, and seven times in 2019). Xing Guangmei and Wang Jinnan, "美国南海'航行自由行动'与军舰无害通过问题研究 [Research on the "freedom of navigation" in the South China Sea and the harmless passage of warships], 亚太安全与海洋研究 [Asia-Pacific Security and Maritime Affairs], January 2020.
18. Sc., the ASEAN Outlook dropped the "free" and emphasized an "inclusive" Indo-Pacific (potentially including China). It also sought to downplay the (US) military focus.

Figure 9.1: Dual Southeast Asian triangles

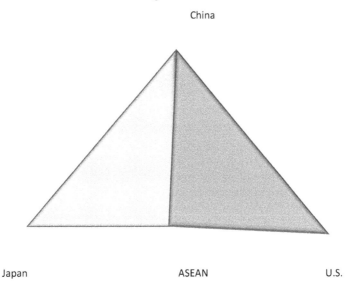

Source: Author.

and during the Cold War it became still more interested, both economically and diplomatically, having been shut out of its geographically natural market on the Chinese mainland.

Second, while Japan has been criticized for historical amnesia and not making adequate amends for wartime atrocities, in Southeast Asia it made highly persuasive efforts at redemption, backed up with generous ODA. In the 1960s, Japan negotiated peace treaties and made sizable reparation payments to all the ASEAN countries it once occupied. And while Japanese textbooks sometimes downplay Japanese wartime atrocities, the fact that Japan accepts responsibility for a very destructive experience for many Asians (in addition to Japan itself) is a lesson that endures in national consciousness—not only as formulated in Article 9 but in the form of national memorials and an electorally powerful domestic peace lobby.

Third, except perhaps when its own territorial interests are at stake (at which point its diplomatic stance tends to rigidify), Japan has been more ideologically flexible and willing to compromise than the US has, and less apt to (indeed, legally unable to) resort to force. As noted above, Japan continued to nurture diplomatic and economic intercourse with China, Indonesia, Vietnam, Burma, when this was considered politically "incorrect." Even regarding the same policy (such as the Free and Open Indo-Pacific Policy, originally proposed by Japan and then taken up by the US, India, and Australia), Japan's interpretation has focused on such aspects as disaster relief while US planning has been more in combined force exercises. Despite intense lobbying by the US to increase defense expenditures, particularly in the wake of the first Gulf War, Japan has consistently adhered to this mercantilist but pacific stance.

Faced by a growing Chinese assertiveness that does not yield to diplomatic entreaties, ASEAN tends to "hedge," not by internal balancing but by finding supplemental external support. Here it finds two options available: the US in an international context; Japan in a regional one. Each has its advantages and disadvantages. Japan has never offered military support and is unlikely to do so because of strong domestic resistance, based on Article 9 of the constitution (despite Abe's eight-year attempt to revise it). If a military confrontation should occur with China at any time for any reason, Pax Americana is ASEAN's only feasible resort. Japan cannot offer this, but as a fraternal Asian state and longtime constituent of various regional economic and political associations, it is often more useful to Southeast Asians for economic and diplomatic pursuits short of war. Japan also has seemed to have greater aptitude than the US has for multilateral organization. It was influential in putting together the EAS and the Chiang Mai Initiative, for example, and the "quad" concept is Abe's signature contribution. The Comprehensive and Progressive Trans-Pacific Partnership (CPTPP) formed after the US exit from the TPP was a singular Japanese diplomatic achievement.

China is quite cognizant of these two countries' divergent agendas, and as its ambitions have swelled its relations with both Japan and the US have grown increasingly contentious. China's coping strategy has been to employ various wedge issues to cleave the alliance. A successful wedge would split Japan from the US, for example, by charming one while threatening the other. This tactic is, however, dangerous, for unless the respective charm and threat are effective and well coordinated, they could have a boomerang effect. China's more forward stance on maritime territorial claims in its near seas (sc., the Diaoyu/Senkaku dispute) has made its situation worse, threatening Japan while at the same time challenging the American status quo. The two were thus drawn closer together. The landslide election of the Japanese Democratic Party (JDP) in 2009 might have offered a good opportunity to split the alliance, as new Prime Minister Hatoyama Yukio was intent on moving away from the US to a more "Asian" position, but the Jiang Zemin regime did not encourage him.

As for the rest of East Asia, China has taken a page from Japan's strategic history of using Western imperialism as a wedge issue, attempting to mobilize latent Asian anti-imperialism against "outside interference." Thus at the 2014 Conference on Interaction and Confidence-building Measures in Asia hosted by Shanghai in May 2014, Xi Jinping presented a "New Asian Security Concept" that postulated that "It is for the people of Asia to run the affairs of Asia, to solve the problems of Asia and uphold the security of Asia." Two of China's three basic demands in ongoing negotiations with ASEAN for a code of conduct are: "joint military exercises with countries outside the region must have the prior consent of all parties to the agreement; and no resource development should be conducted with countries outside the region." China also advocates exclusive exploitation and sharing of fish and energy resources within the region (which includes China but oddly not Japan). The implicit target of this wedge, the US, ironically used a similar tactic in renegotiating NAFTA with Mexico and Canada, writing into the document that if any party formed an FTA with a "non-market economy" the other signatories had an option to vacate the agreement. With China their leading trade partner, the ASEAN countries are unlikely to accept such a deal. But the Americans have tried analogous tactics in Southeast Asia, for example by invoking anti-communism to scare ASEAN countries away from joining the AIIB or the BRI or from contracting with Huawei to build their 5G electronic networks.

The wedge is a tactical antidote to a hedge: while the latter attempts to multiply feasible alternative options, a wedge attempts to close them. To the extent that wedge-driving works, it contributes to polarization. The target of the wedge, faced with divestiture of external support, is driven into isolation and increasing insecurity. While the purpose of the wedge is to isolate and force capitulation, it also has the potential in a fluid international environment to precipitate enhanced opposition. Mutual attempts at wedge-driving increase the market value of uncommitted third countries but also puts them under intensified pressure to take sides. The ASEAN response thus far has been to play down or even deny any contradiction with China while enhancing relations with both Japan and the US. Thus ASEAN endorsed not only the BRI but the Free and Open Indo-Pacific Policy (FOIP), ignoring the fact that neither pays deference to ASEAN Centrality.[19] Thus Singapore, a particularly agile wedge dodger, joined both CPTPP and RCEP and in 2019 even joined the free trade zone of Moscow's Eurasian Economic Union (and trains troops in Taiwan).

ASEAN's core strategy is the hedge. From the hedger's perspective the goal is to purchase reassurance by finding alternatives to a relationship that has become troublesome, possibly threatening. In triangular terms the hedger wants to supplement a positive but problematic relationship with another positive relationship that is less problematic, placing the hedger in a "pivot" position between the two wings of a "romantic triangle." In ASEAN's case it seems to have worked reasonably well. ASEAN was able to solicit assistance from both Japan and the US without alienating the PRC. The PRC complains, but vents not against ASEAN but against the US, blaming it for outside interference.

As for Japan, Beijing in 2017 warned Tokyo against participating in FONOPs in the South China Sea or it would retaliate. Like France, Canada, and

---

19. After more than a year of deliberation, ASEAN unveiled an "ASEAN Outlook on the Indo-Pacific" on June 23, 2019, which endorses "freedom of navigation" but reemphasizes "ASEAN Centrality" and the need to be "open" and "inclusive."

Great Britain, Japan nevertheless chose to accept the American invitation, and the Marine Self-Defense Force (MSDF) participated in a FONOP in September 2018. Beijing did nothing. Japan has also responded by offering constructive alternatives to China's BRI. In 2013, Abe announced a "Partnership for Quality Infrastructure," by which Japan would increase its investment in Asian infrastructure to ¥13.2 trillion (roughly $116 billion in current US dollars) between 2016 and 2020, a 30 percent increase over the previous five-year period. According to a recent Fitch survey published by CNBC, Japan's outstanding projects in the six largest countries of Southeast Asia—Indonesia, Thailand, Vietnam, Malaysia, Singapore, and the Philippines—are now valued at $367 billion, while China's projects are valued $255 billion. If one measures the stock as opposed to the flow of FDI, the differential is still greater: at the end of 2016, Japan's stock of FDI in major Asian economies (excluding China and Hong Kong) was nearly $260 billion, compared to China's $58.3 billion.[20] Japan's projects are concentrated in three of the region's largest economies—The Philippines, Singapore, and Vietnam (especially Vietnam)—while China tends to invest in the less developed economies (Cambodia, Myanmar, Laos, Indonesia). Japan's infrastructure projects target three core areas: the East-West and Southern corridors (land), the maritime ASEAN economic corridor (sea), and "soft infrastructure projects throughout the ASEAN region" (e.g., communications, IT).

Meanwhile, Chinese FDI has plunged overall since 2017, reflecting pushback against BRI as well as a slowing domestic economy: Chinese megaprojects dropped 49.7 percent in 2018 (US$19.2 billion), the lowest in four years, according to American Enterprise Institute's investment tracker. In the second half of 2018, ASEAN recorded twelve China-funded mega-projects worth $3.9 billion, vs. thirty-three projects worth $22 billion the previous year.[21] In 2019, China saw its lowest level of out-going investment (OFDI) at $41 billion, half the 2018 volume, down 80 percent from peak year 2016.

The Americans have also made a modest commitment to build infrastructure.[22] But for them the greater challenge is to prevent China from establishing de facto military hegemony over the region by deterring China's assertion

---

20. Panos Mourdoukoutas, "Japan, Not China, Is the Biggest Investor in Southeast Asia's Infrastructure," *Forbes*, June 26, 2019, https://www.forbes.com/sites/panosmourdoukoutas/2019/06/26/japan-beats-china-in-the-philippines-singapore-and-vietnam/#20af037839d8. As of 2017, the top three FDI providers in the five founding ASEAN countries (Indonesia, Malaysia, Singapore, Thailand, the Philippines) were Japan ($264 billion), Singapore ($217 billion), and the US ($134 billion).
21. See Tobias Harris, "'Quality Infrastructure': Japan's Robust Challenge to China's Belt and Road," *War on the Rocks*, April 9, 2019, https://warontherocks.com/2019/04/quality-infrastructure-japans-robust-challenge-to-chinas-belt-and-road/.
22. In December 2018, US Congress passed ARIA (Asia Reassurance Initiative Act), designed to increase US security and economic interests in Asia, for which it authorized only US$1.5 billion. But in October, the BUILD Act (Better Utilization of Investment Lending to Development) was passed, designed to create a new lending agency with capitalization of $60 billion. This agency, the US International Development Finance Corporation (DFC), was

of sovereignty over the South China Sea. This has proved frustrating partly because of the novel nature of the claim—although informally one might once have called the Mediterranean a "Roman lake" because Rome controlled all the surrounding land, no one has ever claimed legal sovereignty over an open sea, and Beijing can claim no support for its claim in international law. China has not even made clear whether its claim is to the entire sea or only to the islands within it (and their territorial waters). Parts of the sea are claimed by Taiwan, Vietnam, Malaysia, Brunei, Indonesia, and the Philippines, while China claims all. The US claims none of it yet sees an obligation to defend it on behalf of international law because ASEAN cannot.

That will not be easy. Coming late to the table, China has already established a strong position. By reclaiming and fortifying the islets it occupies, China has in effect pushed out its defense perimeter to the "first island chain." The three island chains, first prioritized by Admiral Liu Huaqing when he commanded the PLA Navy (1982–1988) and later as the sole military officer on the CCP Politburo Standing Committee, are seen by Chinese naval strategists not only as a coastal defense perimeter but as constraints on its ambition to project force into the Pacific and beyond—as "ropes" tying down the big "dragon." The East and South China Seas are both within the First Island Chain. Xi Jinping has asserted China's claim to that territory in no uncertain terms ("We cannot lose even one inch of the territory left behind by our ancestors"—June 29, 2018, to James Mattis), and China has since 2010 acquired technologically enhanced capability to defend those claims. "The US no longer enjoys military primacy in the Indo-Pacific, and its capacity to uphold a favorable balance of power is increasingly uncertain," concludes a recent Australian study.[23] From its new island bases, China has excellent surveillance of the South China Sea, and it may well boast regional superiority, having out-built the US Navy some four to one over the past decade. According to Admiral Philip Davidson, "China has made more naval deployments in the past 30 months than in the last 30 years." In his testimony to the US Senate prior to his appointment as Indo-Pacific Commander, Davidson said that "China is now capable of controlling the South China Sea in all scenarios short of war with the United States." In the light of this momentous shift in the balance of forces and the weak US legal claim to either islands or surrounding waters, Obama prudently opted to avoid confrontation when China made "salami-slicing" advances (at Scarborough for instance).

---

launched in December 2019. The DFC, with initial capitalization of $60 billion, has already reached agreements with sixteen countries to fund infrastructure partnerships.
23. Ashley Townshend, Branden Thomas-Noone, and Matilda Steward, *Averting Crisis: American Strategy, Military Spending and Collective Defense in the Indo-Pacific* (United States Studies Center, University of Sydney, August 19, 2019), https://www.ussc.edu.au/analysis/averting-crisis-american-strategy-military-spending-and-collective-defence-in-the-indo-pacific.

The Trump administration opted for a higher-risk confrontational strategy. Trump granted greater policy autonomy to the Pentagon to challenge China's claims, and since 2018 the US Navy has regularized increasingly audacious FONOPs, including double-warship deployment deep within twelve nautical miles of Chinese-occupied islands. For the first time, Scarborough Shoal is included, and the US has made clear it will come to the rescue of its treaty ally if Filipino vessels, personnel, or aircraft come under Chinese attack, including from fisher-qua-militia forces. The Pentagon, in response to China's so-called "gray zone" operations, has vowed in future to apply military rules of engagement to Chinese paramilitary forces. For the first time since the end of the Cold War, the US Coast Guard has extended its operations to the high seas to participate in FONOPs, in joint exercises with regional partners and expeditionary deployments in the Western Pacific and Taiwan Straits. This has encouraged some of the actual claimants to speak or act out. In November 2019, Vietnam threatened international arbitration against Beijing following a months-long naval standoff over the sea's energy-rich Vanguard Bank, prompting China finally to withdraw. And the following month Malaysia, ignoring Chinese protests, formally submitted its extended continental shelf claims beyond its two-hundred-nautical-mile EEZ to the United Nations' Division for Ocean Affairs and Law of the Sea.[24] In the same month, Jakarta made a "strong protest" over the trespass of sixty-three Chinese fishing boats in sovereign waters off Natuna Island, sending ships and jets to underline his concern.

Caught in a polarizing geostrategic vice, ASEAN has been reconsidering its position. In the face of the relentless advance of incremental salami tactics, a hedging strategy may be a losing one. It may be advisable at some point to draw a principled red line. In an asymmetric standoff this is only realistically feasible if external support is available. For a hedge is hardly invincible. A hedge is somewhat like an alliance in that it involves quid pro quo foreign policy coordination, but it is informal, flexible, and nonbinding—the assumed patron may simply ignore the hedger's plea for support—as the US did at Scarborough Shoal in 2012. Or, inasmuch as the transaction is implicit, the alternative patron may respond inappropriately or excessively, or demand an unaffordable price. Thus ASEAN when necessary "tilts" to either Japan or the US to hold Chinese assertiveness at bay, receiving alternative forms of assistance from each. Take, for example, the case of the Sino-American trade dispute.

The 2018–2019 trade dispute was essentially a bilateral affair having to do with a large, growing, and diplomatically intractable trade imbalance. The dispute was initiated by the US side, and the reason the "war" was then

---

24. Richard Heydarian, "China's Sea Claims to Face Stiff Test in 2020," *Asia Times*, December 30, 2019, https://www.asiatimes.com/2019/12/article/chinas-sea-claims-to-face-stiff-test-in-2020/.

stubbornly pursued for so long (about eighteen months before reaching a "first stage" truce in December 2019) is that it was based on a whole package of grievances, both implicit and explicit, which included China's intellectual property theft, industrial subsidies, alleged currency manipulation, the maritime territorial dispute, even China's support for North Korea. Trump sought to use linkage, hitting China where it was most vulnerable, in order to bring about a change in a linked area that was less vulnerable. The linkage was explicit in the case of North Korea, as Trump indicated at Mar-a-Lago in April 2017, when he promised more flexible trade terms in exchange for China's help with the North. It remained implicit regarding the South China Sea. Did it work?

From a triangular perspective, ASEAN as the hedger soliciting help from both Japan and the US would view the "trade war" as the reinforcement of one supportive leg of each of the two triangles, as both the US and Japan suddenly become more suspicious of China's intentions. The two triangles both become "romantic" as both wings compete, placing the third player (ASEAN) in a pivot position. The pivot can avoid taking sides and allow both wings to compete for its favor, as indeed they do in this case. While the US steps up FONOPs and both Japan and the US offer competing infrastructure-building programs, ASEAN does not explicitly join either in opposition to China's assertive territorial claims but quietly accepts their support while also enjoying escalating professions of benign intentions from the PRC. After all, this was all between the US and China. How was ASEAN involved?

Or does it? For many years the main Southeast Asian growth opportunity was the rapidly expanding market in China for the import of goods and services from ASEAN countries. After ACFTA came into effect in 2010, cutting tariffs below 1 percent, ASEAN trade with China rose explosively and declined commensurately elsewhere, fostering bilateral trade dependency. And China enjoyed a positive trade balance with most of its Southeast Asian partners. The reciprocal demand for ASEAN's exports was not necessarily the Chinese consumer market, however. For many years its own export sector was the leading edge of the Chinese economic miracle (about 40 percent of GDP before the global financial crisis, by 2018 down to around 20 percent), and the US was China's single largest export market (in 2019, 18 percent of the total, plus 14 percent to Hong Kong, a large share of which is transshipped or re-exported). Thus the rise in the early 2000s of the "supply chain": ASEAN produces parts and raw materials, which are exported to China, where they are assembled and exported to the US. Trump was unhappy with the Chinese surplus, which had climbed from about $83 billion in 2001 to $419.2 billion in 2018 (in goods; the US enjoys a $40 billion surplus in services). The bilateral impact of Trump's tariffs was to reduce Sino-American trade, hurting both economies. So how does that affect Southeast Asia?

The impact may be seen from three perspectives. First, tariffs negatively affect producers exporting to China, as the decline of Chinese GDP growth, in whatever sector, reduces Chinese demand. Commodity producers, for example, such as Cambodia or Australia fall into this category. The downturn could be temporary, lasting only as long as the trade war dampens demand. Second, it could disrupt supply chains by incentivizing export industries (either foreign-invested or Chinese) to relocate from China to another country to escape tariff increases. It is costly to relocate a factory, but as the dispute dragged on, leading many to assume it might last indefinitely (and even at the end of Phase I, US$380 billion in US tariffs remain in force), more and more firms (more than fifty, according to Nomura) have relocated at least parts of their production elsewhere—some "re-shore" to the US, but most to Southeast Asia or Mexico. The relocation of value chains may outlast the trade war in view of the sunk costs involved. Third, some Southeast Asian exporting countries may replace the imports into either China or US markets that have been shut out by tariffs—Brazil, for example, enjoyed a boom in soybean exports when China stopped buying American soybeans. China has encouraged such import substitution by cutting overall import tariffs while raising them for the US. In sum, while the impact of the trade war on ASEAN has been mixed, negatively affecting Singapore and Thailand while positively affecting Vietnam, Cambodia, Taiwan, and Malaysia, the overall net long-term impact may well be positive.

The main caveat is that while moderate polarization between the two wings may benefit the pivot (ASEAN), extreme polarization (as in complete decoupling, or in the worst case, war) stands to damage not only the two wings but also the pivot. And gradual decoupling has been underway even before the trade war. It began with China's "great digital firewall" to build its own impermeable internet to shield its population from Western "spiritual pollution." Since around 1995, China has ring-fenced a group of privileged "strategic" or "pillar" industries, protected from foreign competition and endowed with generous subsidies to incentivize innovation. China not only prohibited US and other foreign companies from participating in these sectors, but it also restricted procurement of telecommunications and other equipment from non-Chinese sources in its pursuit of "indigenous innovation" and greater "self-reliance" in high-tech sectors. In 2019, the government ordered all government offices and public institutions to rid themselves of foreign computers and software within three years. After trade talks temporarily broke down in May 2019, Xi gave a speech vowing a "new long march" to achieve economic self-reliance, citing as precedent China's development of an atomic bomb without Soviet assistance in 1964. Through the BRI, among other measures, Chinese economic planners hope to develop alternative sources of demand in the developing world that can help absorb the nation's exports and reduce its dependence on the US market. This policy was further advanced in the 13th Five-Year Plan as "Made in China 2025," an ambitious industrial policy designed to prepare the country for the next industrial revolution by capturing such emerging technologies as AI, quantum computing, autonomous vehicles and 3-D manufacturing (the name disappeared from the media in the light of the trade war but a similar program—"China 2035"—appeared at the 5th Plenum in 2020). By 2025, China aimed to achieve 70 percent self-sufficiency in high-tech industries, and by 2049—the hundredth anniversary of Liberation—a dominant position in global markets. International technological leadership would place the country in the industrial vanguard, setting standards and demanding rents from less technologically advanced nations. Given the emphasis on civil-military "fusion," it would also endow China with superiority in military weaponry.

Retaliatory US decoupling began in July 2018 with the unilateral imposition of tariffs, supported not by WTO rules but by an innovative interpretation of "national security." The Phase I agreement signed in January 2020 is one-sided but limited, in which the US withholds $300 billion in threatened tariffs, reduces tariffs from 15 percent to 7.5 percent on $120 billion in imports, and retains 25 percent tariffs on $250 billion. China promises to purchase an additional $200 billion of US imports in the next two years. The average American tariff on Chinese imports remains high, at nearly 19 percent, and China also retains tariffs on around 60 percent of US imports. While the impact of the "trade war" was to move toward economic decoupling, if this preliminary agreement is honored by China, bilateral trade will become more balanced and could then increase. If not (a distinct possibility, despite the safeguards written into the agreement), further economic and political alienation may be expected. More significant for decoupling is the "war" on Chinese technology, not even mentioned in the Phase I agreement. To date, two hundred Chinese technology firms, including Huawei, have been blacklisted (i.e., placed on an "entity list"). The Committee on Foreign Investment in the United States (CFIUS) has also been authorized to review incoming FDI more stringently.[25]

The trade war was started by Trump, not by Xi, who was happy with the status quo, in which China had learned to thrive.[26] The logic of the "war" has, however, been escalatory, "tit-for-tat"—to deviate from this logic is to "lose," to give way to the superior power of the other side. If this logic is consistently pursued, the trend toward partial decoupling that has been set in train is likely to continue and to spread to other dimensions—ideology, security, even health.

That trend seems to have been exacerbated by the 2020 coronavirus pandemic. This will be economically damaging to both countries, with a somewhat diluted impact on global GDP growth. Southeast Asia as pivot will be disproportionately exposed to this rivalry. Yet polarization is a double-edged sword: economically, Southeast Asia should be the beneficiary of the

---

25. The entity list ostensible rationale was to sanction contributions to the electronic surveillance of Uyghur communities in Xinjiang but has not been affected by the Phase 1 deal. The trade war and the tech war seem to run along different tracks.
26. Cf. Li Wei, "Toward Economic Decoupling: Mapping Chinese Discourse on the China-US Trade War," *Chinese Journal of International Politics* 12, no. 4 (Winter 2014): 519–56.

rerouting of global value chains. Politically, each wing will try to prevent its "loss." This has already manifested itself in the diplomatic response to the EAS, the AIIB, or the BRI. Each "pole" tries to drive wedges, to include ASEAN and induce it to exclude the other pole. The South China Sea has seen eighteen "unsafe" Sino-American naval encounters since 2016 and is likely to see more. In the incipient technology war, decoupling could damage Southeast Asians by depriving them of technological spinoff, as both powers batten down security precautions to protect their intellectual property rights. Huawei unveils 5G to the world; the US tries to block its adoption. China redoubles efforts to sell, threatening retaliation against American products. If, say, Vietnam adopts Huawei for 5G, will it then be technologically locked in? If competition intensifies to the point where one of the powers tries to punish ASEAN or one of its members for picking the "wrong" side, the game could become still more unpleasant.

In practice, decoupling is likely to be more limited. Military technology has long been "decoupled" as much as is technically feasible, and this type of securitization will no doubt continue. Civilian technology as well is typically decoupled by innovative firms hoping to retain first mover advantage. The logic of decoupling spreads its wings in the current zeitgeist of intense strategic competition. And yet competition entails not only decoupling but the mutual emulation of best practices, so even the decoupling of advanced military technology will never be perfect.

It is striking how political perspectives have changed in the light of China's rise. China was expected to emulate the advanced capitalist economies, and for the first three decades or so, it did. But as China neared the tipping point of having overtaken its capitalist models-cum-rivals, the emulation dynamic began to shift. Emulation was no longer a good thing; in fact it was dangerous. China has instead proudly reclaimed ownership of its own hybrid model of avowedly socialist development, and its own philosophical geneology. China has entered a "new era" where it will "take center stage in the world," Xi Jinping declaimed at the CCP's 19th Congress in October 2017. The Chinese experience provides "a new option for other countries and nations that want to speed up their development while preserving their independence." Not even Xi could have imagined that his recommendation would be taken seriously by none other than the US. Yet to some degree the convergence vector seems to have reversed course. The Trump trade war moves the US away from free trade and toward managed trade, while the tech war seems to be pushing the US toward adoption of some form of import-substitution industrial policy in order to regain leadership of the technological "commanding heights." Now of course "reversal" is overstated; there is still a systemic rivalry. But mutual emulation of best practices may be expected to continue even amid increasing competition (without admitting it, of course). As for ASEAN, its current strategy of commitment-shy opportunism seems likely to continue.

Conclusion

Southeast Asia has always been a meeting point. Historically, it was a meeting point between East Asia and South Asia, absorbing Hinduism, Theravada Buddhism, and Islam from the south, and Confucianism and Mahayana Buddhism from the north. Western colonialism opened the region to the West and to the winds of global modernization. Since Japan's coercive decolonization during WWII, the region has gained independence and, after a protracted period of domestic turmoil, grown economically prosperous and more integrated. It remains politically divided, but the advent of ASEAN alleviated that fragmentation somewhat and instilled an ideology of peaceful coexistence and non-interference in internal affairs. After the Cold War, ASEAN aspired to expand its membership to all Southeast Asia and more than that, to reach out to and embrace the whole of Asia in a vague and toothless but well-meaning ecumenical institution-building effort.

During the two decades or so since the end of the Cold War, the region benefited from benign neglect by the great powers. The US had learned its lesson from Vietnam; China after the 1989 Tiananmen Incident, ostracized by much of the world, was "hiding and biding"; while Japan in the early 1990s lurched into its "lost" economic decade, amid electoral reform and partisan realignment. Left on its own, the region began to thrive economically.

But since the late 1990s, for the first time since the era of national liberation wars, China took marked new interest in the region. China pursued a successful "charm" campaign, joined and actively participated in ASEAN meetings, and negotiated FTAs. ACFTA came into full effect in 2010, and Sino-ASEAN trade took off, surpassing all other trade partners. Meanwhile, however, China's increasingly insistent attempts to enforce its maritime claims sparked resentment, exacerbated since 2013 by the "reclamation" and militarization of the seven islets it occupied. The Maritime Silk Road only partially allayed that concern for many, after reading the fine print. ASEAN, the organizational instrument contrived to maximize the international influence of these smaller powers, proved unavailing. ASEAN had invited China to be part of the ASEAN ecosystem, and it skillfully used its access to defend its interests.

We have conceived the new set of relationships since the floundering of multilateral solutions and the return of power politics in the form of a composite triangle. The emergent main axis is between China and ASEAN (AC). The AC relationship is net positive but problematic, harboring both opportunity and risk. As risk becomes salient, ASEAN tends to hedge. ASEAN has built "hedging" relationships with the United States (AU) and Japan (AJ). While the "international" triangle (AUC) can be manipulated for hard power deterrence, the "regional" triangle (AJC) may be more useful in a regional diplomatic and economic context. In triangular terms, as AC becomes perceived as threatening, this leads to the reinforcement of AJ and AU. Given that the CJ and CU relationships had meanwhile also become more attenuated for related but distinct reasons, the "hedgee" in both cases has been responsive. In both triangles, a problematic CA relationship /reinforces negative CU and CJ relationships; that is, as ASEAN-China relations deteriorate, ASEAN strengthens relations with both the US and Japan, whose relations with China have meanwhile deteriorated for analogous but not identical reasons. In the regional triangle, Japan responds by offering different, competing (but not incompatible) infrastructure-building projects, in which it has long professional experience, with attendant financing from the ADB. In the international triangle, the US response includes both security augmentations and a modest but perhaps more financially sound infrastructure-building program. More consequential than either of these in the long run may well be the shift of supply chains to Southeast Asia in the course of the trade war.[27]

The potential for transformation of this dynamic lies in the resolution of any leg of the composite triangle. If China, for example, reaches a compromise in its maritime territorial claims to share subsurface resources with ASEAN that is mutually acceptable, then ASEAN no longer needs its hedges and can drift further into China's orbit, where its economic future seems to lie. Given Xi Jinping's adamant reaffirmation of China's claims, however, that does not seem likely at present. If China-US relations should improve markedly, that would lessen their value as a hedge, putting pressure on ASEAN to accommodate China's demands. Indeed, inasmuch as the US is the most powerful member of the two triangles, it would also in that case put pressure on Japan to reach an accommodation with China. But in view of unresolved bilateral economic and political issues, and the underlying insecurity over power transition, this too seems unrealistic. A more likely resolution would be a China-Japan reconciliation, as Japan has defied its superpower ally in the past in favor of an improved Asian economic position. Yet again the territorial issue seems intractable, and China has offered no tempting compromise, still sending daily patrols into Japanese waters.

It is also conceivable (though hardly inevitable) that Sino-American relations continue to deteriorate, as advocates of "decoupling" would like.[28] This would be seriously risky for that bilateral relationship, in view of the potential for issue-linkage and escalation. It would also jeopardize ASEAN's advantageous position as pivot, enjoying good relations with China while maintaining leverage with Japan and the US. This will become increasingly difficult to maintain if and when Sino-American relations polarize, as both

---

27. Cf. Finbarr Bermingham, "China's manufacturing exodus set to continue in 2020, despite prospect of trade war deal," *South China Morning Post*, January 12, 2020, https://www.scmp.com/economy/china-economy/article/3045141/chinas-manufacturing-exodus-set-continue-2020.
28. A *partial* decoupling is advocated by Charles W. Boustany and Aaron L. Friedberg, *Partial Disengagement: A New US Strategy for Economic Competition with China* (National Bureau of Asian Research, Special Report No. 82) (November 4, 2019), https://www.nbr.org/publication/partial-disengagement-a-new-u-s-strategy-for-economic-competition-with-china/.

will pressure ASEAN to choose sides. This would be very painful, but given ASEAN's economic ties to the PRC, a China choice would not be unlikely. That, of course, would be contrary to the interests of both the US and Japan, and ultimately to ASEAN as well.

10
A Moderate Phase Transition from Order to Disorder in Asia

The Political Economy of the US-China-Japan Strategic Triangle

Ming Wan[1]

Introduction

To answer questions about the new Asian disorder from a political economy perspective, this chapter begins by defining and measuring international order by drawing from existing literature in the field of international relations and beyond. Order can be understood as a stable and predictable state of affairs or a social and political arrangement serving embedded larger purposes. Moreover, international order should be viewed as only one element of the international system competing and interacting with other elements in the system. Order is seldom all-encompassing or deeply entrenched. Conceptually, the modern notion of international order has evolved from and is intricately linked to an array of modern conceptions of imperialism, sovereignty, nationalism, human rights, and capitalism.

Second, this chapter examines Asia's empirical record to determine whether and what type of order has existed in Asia and if it has changed or is changing. If stability is used as the principal criterion for order, then it can be said that Asia is doing well from both the historical and comparative perspectives. But tensions in the region have increased as a result of a more assertive China, which has caused security concerns for the immediate and mid-term future of the region. Meanwhile, if we define order by the embedded social and political purposes, then the current Asian order is being challenged by the "America First" approach of the Trump administration, which rejects the free-trade, immigration-friendly, multilateralist postwar bipartisan consensus in the United States that sustains the US-led liberal international order.

---

1. I thank Caroline Wesson for able research assistance. I am also grateful for useful comments provided by Yu-Shan Wu, Suisheng Zhao, and other participants at the conference "The New Asian Disorder: Diagnosis and Prognosis," University of California at Berkeley, Berkeley, March 15, 2019.

Third, this chapter focuses on one specific component of the Asian international system, the US-China-Japan strategic triangle. The US may return to the "norm" now that Trump lost the 2020 election to a veteran politician, Joe Biden, but it is increasingly clear that US domestic politics have changed profoundly in response to globalization. The US shift in policy is also a reaction to the manner in which Asian economies have interacted within the liberal international order in the past. Put simply, the Asian nations have never been as liberal or free-market-oriented as desired by the US within Pax Americana. Japan and China, the two legs of the strategic triangle studied in this chapter, have had to adapt profoundly to the prevailing international conditions in which the US dominates. Not surprisingly, they selectively emulate the US to fit their own conditions while maintaining their own national identities and systems of political economy. The US itself has been a moving target, choosing a variety of tools at its disposal and changing purposes and objectives whenever it sees fit. The Asian order is indeed experiencing serious challenges.

It is difficult to predict what will happen to the Asian order now that the balance of power and underlying liberal purposes are in flux. If I have to, I forecast that it will be difficult to go back to the pre-Trump status quo, due to nationalist reactions to the evolving political economy within and between the countries in the region. The course of action each government chooses to take now and in the future will shape the Asian order. Judging by what has happened, Asia is likely to become less orderly and less liberal than before but still more stable than other regions in the world. Put simply, I argue that Asia is experiencing a moderate-phase transition—defined as a qualitative change of the system.

Theorizing International Order

The concept and theory of international order used in this chapter primarily comes from the English School of International Relations. Hedley Bull defines international order as "a pattern of activity that sustains the elementary or primary goals of the society of states, or international society."[2] Bull treats international order as a variable that may or may not exist and may be present to different degrees. He argues that "order is not the only value in relation to which international conduct may be shaped, and is not necessarily an overriding value."[3] Put differently, international order may be viewed as one element in international relations that competes or interacts with other elements. The conception of order as coexisting with other forms of international arrangements is important for practical analysis of order's existence and type.

---

2. Hedley Bull, *The Anarchical Society: A Study of Order in World Politics* (New York: Columbia University Press, 1977), 8.
3. Bull, *Anarchical Society*, xii.

International order may be achieved through great power politics and related balance of power, international law, diplomacy, and war.

International order as both a concept and in practice draws heavily from Western traditions. Thus, international order should not be viewed in isolation but as part of a package of ideas and practices from the same source, which includes sovereignty, imperialism, colonialism, democracy, liberalism, racism, human rights, nationalism, and capitalism.[4]

Since we are studying whether Asia is shifting from order to disorder, we can think about this issue as one of "phase transitions" that are evident in the history of life and society. Asian international systems are complex and should "potentially display a number of different patterns of qualitative behavior or *phases*" that "correspond to different forms of internal organization . . . usually separated by a sharp boundary, and crossing such a frontier implies a change in system-level behavior."[5] Particular attention is paid to a critical point defined as "the presence of a very narrow transition domain separating two well-defined phases, which are characterized by distinct macroscopic properties that are ultimately linked to changes in the nature of microscopic interactions among the basic units."[6] The phase transition literature is thus relevant, for our discussion of if the Asian order is at a critical point to tip to disorder or a different order. Interactions between countries in the region are linked to changes of order parameters.

Phase transitions may result from either sudden external shocks or gradual changes within the system. It is easy to see how an external shock such as the European arrival in the New World can lead to phase transition. But phase transitions can take place when gradual changes approach a critical point. The concept of "bifurcation" describes "a qualitative change in the dynamics of a given system that takes place under continuous variation (tuning) of a given parameter."[7] This bifurcation phenomenon naturally leads to a question of resilience, "the ability of a system to recover to the original state upon a disturbance."[8] We readily observe that something at a tipping point does not require much to collapse, but it requires far more energy to restore that something to its original state. Stability in a dynamic complex system depends on "a balance between internal order (which needs to be preserved) and flexibility (adaptability)."[9]

---

4. Anthony Pagden, *Lords of All the World: Ideologies of Empire in Spain, Britain, and France, c. 1500–c. 1800* (New Haven, CT: Yale University Press, 1995); Heather Streets-Salter and Trevor R. Getz, *Empires and Colonies in the Modern World: A Global Perspective* (New York: Oxford University Press, 2016); Emanuele Saccarelli and Latha Varadarajan, *Imperialism Past and Present* (New York: Oxford University Press, 2015).
5. Ricard V. Solé, *Phase Transitions* (Princeton, NJ: Princeton University Press, 2011), xi.
6. Solé, *Phase Transitions*, 11.
7. Solé, *Phase Transitions*, 37–38.
8. Marten Scheffer, *Critical Transitions in Nature and Society* (Princeton, NJ: Princeton University Press, 2009), 11.
9. Solé, *Phase Transitions*, 25.

International order is structural in that it imposes constraints and offers opportunities for the countries in it, thus shaping state behavior. But behavior also shapes structure in a feedback loop. As Edward Wilson argues, structure and behavior co-vary, but behavior changes before structure.[10] Thus, we should focus on behavior as a pacemaker for political evolution.

Measuring Asian Order

To understand the current state of the Asian order, we need to trace the orders experienced in the past. This short chapter does not allow a thorough discussion of how Asian international relations have been ordered. But East Asia experienced the Chinese world order for two millennia, European colonialism for the modern era, Japan's failed attempt at a pan-Asian order for less than two decades, and US-led liberal international order after World War II. All of these orders were contested and incomplete, but it is possible to identify the prevailing ordering projects at any historical moment.[11]

The US-led postwar international order has always had limited coverage. The start of the Cold War and the Chinese Communist Party's victory created a divided Asia between the free world, the communist world and the non-aligned movement countries during the Cold War. The end of the Cold War led to a US-dominated world order. Serious studies of Asian order reveal a rich diversity of international arrangements, different pathways to order, and different methods of managing security issues in Asia. Asian security order became largely predictable and stable by the early 2000s.[12] International order also requires institutional design. In the case of Asia, institutions vary in different issue areas and maturity when compared to European institutions.[13]

Where are we now? I argue that we should examine the Asian order under challenge from a complex systems perspective. The US is more of a game changer than is China in how a great power affects international order as we speak. The Trump administration advocates an America First policy in both rhetoric and actions. The US has withdrawn from or expressed public disdain for multilateral institutions such as the Trans-Pacific Partnership Agreement (TPP), the Paris Climate Change Agreement, the Iranian nuclear deal, the

---

10. Edward O. Wilson, *Sociobiology: The New Synthesis* (Cambridge, MA: Harvard University Press, 2000), 13–14.
11. Ming Wan, *The Political Economy of East Asia: Wealth and Power*, 2nd ed. (Northampton, MA: Edward Elgar, 2020), 56–139; G. John Ikenberry, *Liberal Leviathan: The Origins, Crisis, and Transformation of the American World Order* (Princeton, NJ: Princeton University Press, 2012); G. John Ikenberry, *After Victory: Institutions, Strategic Restraint, and the Rebuilding of Order after Major Wars* (Princeton, NJ: Princeton University Press, 2001).
12. Muthiah Alagappa, ed., *Asian Security Order: Instrumental and Normative Features* (Stanford, CA: Stanford University Press, 2003).
13. Saadia M. Pekkanen, ed., *Asian Designs: Governance in the Contemporary World Order* (Ithaca, NY: Cornell University Press, 2016).

International Criminal Court, and the World Trade Organization. Trump also repeatedly questions the value of America's traditional alliances.

By contrast, China has not declared war on the existing international order and is indeed portraying itself as a defender of the postwar order. In some areas, Beijing has stepped up. On climate change, China did not take the helm of global leadership because it did not want to shoulder the costs, but it did seek to be part of the solution rather than the problem. The Chinese government remains committed to the Paris Agreement. China's carbon dioxide emissions increased by 5 percent in 2017, among the highest in the world, but its carbon intensity (carbon dioxide emissions per unit of GDP) has decreased 46 percent from 2005 levels, exceeding its promised target for 2020.[14] Of all the countries in the G-20 Group, only Brazil, China, and Japan are on emissions target. But Brazil's new president has vowed to speed up deforestation of the Amazon rainforests. Japan has largely shirked its leadership role. The European Union is off track on pledges to cut emissions although the EU countries pledged far more aggressive targets than China did.[15] China has also sharply increased financial contributions to international organizations such as the United Nations. However, China is regressing on the human rights front, but democracy is in retreat worldwide, including in the US and the West.[16]

The main challenge to Asian security is Beijing's increasing assertion over its territorial disputes in the East China Sea and the South China Sea. Asia has a whole range of territorial disputes which have long complicated Asian security.[17] A rising China using heavy-handed measures is currently one of the main sources of Asian instability and is a challenge to the primary institution of territoriality. China has not acted as recklessly as Russia through its seizure and annexation of Crimea, but neighbors worry that a powerful China may behave in this manner in the future.

Postwar US foreign policy has not been all about liberal order, and liberal ordering has not been the only game in Asia for the past seven decades. At the same time, it is incorrect to suggest that liberal order has not been truly in practice or that pursuit of liberty has not been part of the motivations for American diplomacy. It is illogical to conclude that liberal order must never have been sound, based on its current troubles. All things end at some point,

---

14. Brady Dennis and Chris Mooney, "Global Carbon Reaches Record," *Washington Post*, December 6, 2018, A1.
15. United Nations Environment Program (UNEP), *Emissions Gap Report 2018* (Nairobi: UNEP, 2018).
16. See Freedom House, *Freedom in the World 2019: Democracy in Retreat* (Washington, DC: Freedom House, 2019).
17. Much has been written about these disputes. For theoretical discussion, see Jean-Marc F. Blanchard, "Maritime Issues in Asia: The Problem of Adolescence," in *Asian Security Order*, ed. Muthiah Alagappa, 424–57; and Jianwei Wang, "Territorial Disputes and Asian Security: Sources, Management, and Prospects," in *Asian Security Order*, ed. Muthiah Alagappa, 380–423.

which does not negate their presence or value before collapse. Alternative international arrangements such as alliance politics also experience periodic challenges. Moreover, while liberalism is suffering a setback, it may yet come back stronger.[18] I will not engage in a debate about the saliency of different belief systems in this chapter. Rather, I will adopt the phase transitions perspective discussed earlier in the chapter. Order transition may be viewed as a type of phase transition.

Asian order defined as stability results from an equilibrium of several international arrangements on different dimensions. Some countries in the Asia Pacific such as Australia, India, and Japan share similar democratic values. But great power diplomacy has always been an important part of regional security. When it comes to political economy systems, most Asian countries follow some form of state-guided or state capitalism. Sovereignty has always been a dominant feature of Asian international relations although it has often been violated.

Empirically, we readily observe how governments conduct their foreign policy, taking into consideration bilateral diplomacy, regional diplomacy, global diplomacy, economic diplomacy, security diplomacy, and so on. These divisions of labor are organizationally structured. Status quo governments seek some general balance between their goals on all of these fronts. Disruptive governments prefer to see chaos to advance their objectives that are incompatible with the status quo. Governments also have to consider a balance between domestic politics and international relations and normally prioritize domestic considerations. If a liberal order includes human rights and free market, we know that the American promotion of human rights and free market is a reality to which Asian countries have had to respond, more enthusiastically by some Asian citizens than others in the domestic context. But governments also know the saliency of American pressure on those fronts depends on interactions with other pressing concerns. Not surprisingly, governments prefer certainty and have their tested ways to handle relations with the US or China or any other countries in the region.

The Asian international system is going through a transition. The equilibrium is breaking down. The order component of the Asian system is shifting, reflecting and reinforcing changes in other components. From a complex systems perspective, the sudden change in US policy can be viewed as "bifurcation," a qualitative change of behavior in response to cumulative gradual change domestically and internationally.

The Anglo-Saxon capitalist system has led to a great divide in income and wealth in the US.[19] It is not just a result of the free market either. Government

---

18. Daniel Deudney and G. John Ikenberry, "Liberal World: The Resilient Order," *Foreign Affairs* 97, no. 4 (July/August 2018): 16–24.
19. Steven Pearlstein, *Can American Capitalism Survive? Why Greed Is Not Good, Opportunity is Not Equal and Fairness Won't Make us Poor* (New York: St. Martin's Press, 2018).

regulations and policies also favor the advantaged.[20] The US is now polarized. Donald Trump's election highlighted the claim that the liberal order had been rigged in favor of self-serving elites.[21] That is why the Trump administration is turning against the liberal order the US helped to create and why other countries increasingly expect Trumpian policy to continue in some form, given his support base in the country.

The free-trade international order the US championed has had a profound impact on the Asian economy. Close ties with the US were not a sufficient condition for economic success but seemed to be a necessary condition. Not every country that had a close relationship with the US succeeded economically. At the same time, few countries succeeded without being part of the American economic system. The Asian allies and friends of the US mostly prospered during the Cold War and afterwards.[22] That is why they want to maintain the status quo.

The Asian miracle of rapid growth with relative equity was a virtuous cycle. The miracle countries believed prosperity and security were associated with American leadership, not the liberal order per se. China has been different. It grew rapidly with an enlarging gap in income, wealth, and opportunities, as development economists used to expect a catch-up economy to experience in its early stage of development. Different from America's allies in the region, the Chinese government views the US as a threat to its regime security but has adapted to take advantage of globalization while minimizing liberal and democratic pressure on regime change. I doubt that China can logically hold out forever, but the party government seems secure for now and the immediate future.

The US began to pressure East Asia in trade as early as the 1960s. The Asian development model was both praised and criticized in the US. In retrospect, if the US had chosen to adapt its own system to incorporate a deliberate attempt at a fairer distribution of income, wealth, and opportunities, the political support for a liberal order could conceivably be stronger and more sustainable. But that is not how the American political economy system works. It is easier to force less powerful partner countries to change. The Asian countries played an asymmetrical game with the US and constantly frustrated American officials who sought to achieve immediate results. This is an important reason that many in the policy community in the US initially accepted and even cheered for Trump's unorthodox methods to address trade imbalances. The trade disputes, serious though they were at the time, were adjustments in retrospect. The attractiveness to participate in the US-led system did not diminish. That is partly the reason that China chose opening and reform. It

---

20. Jacob S. Hacker and Paul Pierson, *Winner-Take-All Politics: How Washington Made the Rich Richer—and Turned Its Back on the Middle Class* (New York: Simon & Schuster, 2010).
21. Jeff D. Colgan and Robert O. Keohane, "The Liberal Order Is Rigged: Fix It Now or Watch It Wither," *Foreign Affairs* 96, no. 3 (May/June 2017): 36–44.
22. Wan, *Political Economy of East Asia*, 109–11.

was not possible to have reform without opening, which meant opening to the US-led world economic system.

Are we seeing a phase transition in Asian order? Evidence suggests that we are experiencing a moderate phase transition of the Asian order that results from gradual changes within the system rather than from sudden external shocks, if defined by the embedded purposes. While the US surprisingly is turning its back on its international liberal order project, the US itself is not experiencing a major phase transition. Despite much claim about the unprecedented nature of the Trump presidency, we can see similar changes before in a cyclical view of American politics.[23] The US is going through another cycle of evolving political ideals and backlash although Trump's challenge to American democracy is arguably far more consequential than that of previous populist leaders.

The anti-globalization wave in Western democracies has not gained traction in East Asia. This is not because there has not been an urban-rural divide, cosmopolitan versus non-cosmopolitan, or elites versus masses. Rather, immigration has not been as salient in Asia simply because Asian countries have tight immigration controls.

If we define order as stability, the Asian international system will become less orderly due to China's rise, US-China tensions, and greater uncertainties. The US-China rivalry is now rocking East Asian international relations. The US-China rivalry prevented APEC (Asia Pacific Economic Cooperation) leaders from issuing a joint statement, for the first time in the organization's history, paralyzing APEC. But other regional organizations are moving forward. The TPP, renamed the Comprehensive and Progressive Agreement of Trans-Pacific Partnership (CPTPP), and minus the US, entered into effect on December 30, 2018. The Regional Comprehensive Economic Partnership (RCEP) that includes China and fifteen countries, but not the US, did not make the deadline at the ASEAN meeting in November 2018, but the negotiating countries still aim at conclusion in November 2020 although India opted out in November 2019. RCEP was indeed concluded in November 2020 as planned.

A US-China-Japan Triangle

As Lowell Dittmer argued in the early 1980s, a strategic triangle is formed when all three involved countries treat their relations with the other two as central and when all three are autonomous even if they are not equally powerful.[24] The focus at the time was on a strategic triangle between Washington, Moscow, and Beijing. I provided discussion of the US-China-Japan triangle in my 2006 book on Sino-Japanese relations. That triangle was no repeat of the

---

23. Samuel P. Huntington, *American Politics: The Promise of Disharmony* (Cambridge, MA: Belknap Press, 1981).
24. Lowell Dittmer, "The Strategic Triangle: An Elementary Game—Theoretical Analysis," *World Politics* 33, no. 4 (July 1981): 485–515.

US-Soviet Union-China triangle. The US dominated the alliance with Japan. The trilateral relationship was also asymmetrical with the US as a crucial factor in Sino-Japanese relations. At the same time, triangular tendencies did exist between Washington, Beijing, and Tokyo.[25] Those triangular tendencies have now strengthened. The US, China, and Japan as the world's three largest economies necessarily view the other two as central for their foreign relations, more so for Japan than for China and the US. The US and Japan remain strong allies. The Japanese want to keep the US as a close ally and fully engaged in Asia even more strongly than before. But this is a case of a more autonomous Japan making a conscious choice for an alliance due to its fear of a more threatening China, consistent with a typical triangular dynamic. Simultaneously, a more autonomous Japan seeks to improve relations with China at present, which would put the country in a more advantageous position vis-à-vis the US and China, which are now in open rivalry. Conversely, Beijing is also moving to reduce tensions with Japan, to avoid fighting against both the US and Japan.

The US-China-Japan strategic triangle plays out on the security, economic, and values dimensions, which are all connected. This chapter focuses on the political economy dimension. In some way, we may approach the triangle from any dimension and may end up with similar conclusions. Goldsworthy Lowes Dickinson, an early adopter of anarchy as an analytical tool, reasons that "It matters little, in this analysis, at what point we begin, for all the points are connected; so that, metaphorically, we shall be describing a circle, and shall complete the same figure wherever we start."[26] He was thinking of how the state of international anarchy in Europe had always led to war. He chose to start with the fact that the states were armed.

The US has experienced the most drastic change at present. It is now deeply divided along two intertwined fault lines of identity politics and economic fortunes. Trump was elected because of popular resentment toward coastal urban and suburban elites. US-led globalization has left many Americans behind, particularly in rural areas. Paul Collier, for example, has recently criticized Anglo-American capitalism as a root cause of "anxiety, anger and despair" that "have shredded people's political allegiances, their trust in government, even their trust in each other."[27] The capitalism practiced

---

25. Ming Wan, *Sino-Japanese Relations: Interaction, Logic, and Transformation* (Stanford, CA: Stanford University Press, 2006), 168–78. See also Ming Wan, *Understanding Japan-China Relations: Theories and Issues* (Singapore: World Scientific, 2016), 77–98; and Ming Wan, "Japan-China Relations and the Changing East Asian Regional Order," in *Japan and Asia's Contested Order: The Interplay of Security, Economics, and Identity*, ed. Yul Sohn and T. J. Pempel (New York: Palgrave Macmillan, 2019), 221–37.
26. Goldsworthy Lowes Dickinson, *The International Anarchy, 1904–1914* (New York: Century Co., 1926), 4.
27. Paul Collier, *The Future of Capitalism: Facing the New Anxieties* (New York: Harper, 2018), 5. For a defense of American capitalism, see Alan Greenspan and Adrian Wooldridge, *Capitalism in America: A History* (New York: Penguin Press, 2018).

in the US and Great Britain ruthlessly pursues profits at the expense of more equal income and opportunity distribution. Collier cites Japanese firms more favorably in their shared purpose and trust. The Japanese-style capitalism was actually assaulted by the US in the late 1980s and the early 1990s and has since gone through a painful process of transformation due to both US pressure and internal dynamics.

President Trump represents a different worldview from that of the mainstream American policy community. So much ink has been spilled on the causes and consequences of Trump's election and presidency, with much theoretical insight and empirical vigor. There is no need to belabor that topic in this chapter. I will add two comments directly related to the theme of this chapter. First, I do not view Trump's election as representing a regime shift in US politics even though this is surely more than a typical presidential transition, and one has to worry whether this is the beginning of the end for American democracy.[28] Trump was elected from the US electoral system although one may debate whether Russian interference affected the results. US politics has experienced periodic swings in one direction or another, partly due to voter backlash against existing policies. American democracy may be weakened, but the US democratic system is robust enough to rebound. Trump's unilateralist, isolationist, and nationalist tendencies in foreign policy are not unprecedented in American diplomatic history. It seems clear that domestic change in the US is leading to a bigger shift in foreign policy, not uncommon for the US or any other countries. But a shift in a superpower's foreign policy ripples throughout the system; the bigger the shift, the more violent the effect. Asian countries are all adapting to the changed American policy, and how they respond is partly constituting the change in the international system we see.

Second, the Trump administration is responding in important ways to the past practices from Asia as well. The US has initiated trade disputes with Asian exporting countries since the 1960s, to address what it views as unfair trading practices and to level the playing field. The last big battle was waged against Japan in the early 1990s.[29] The American policy community viewed Japan, ally though it was, as having taken advantage of the US. In response, anti-American sentiment also grew in Japan. Starting from Japan, the East Asian countries adopted a range of policy measures to fend off American pressure, including protracted negotiations, lobbying, conciliatory gestures,

28. Michael Abramowitz, "Trump Strains Democracy—Everywhere," *Washington Post*, February 5, 2019, A19. He is the president of Freedom House, which had just issued its annual report on freedom in the world that traces the decline of American democracy to earlier administrations but concludes that Trump's election has hastened the downward process. See also Steven Levitsky and Daniel Ziblatt, *How Democracies Die* (New York: Crown, 2018); and Michael Tomasky, *If We Can Keep It: How the Republic Collapsed and How it Might be Saved* (New York: Liverlight, 2019).
29. Ming Wan, *Japan Between Asia and the West: Economic Power and Strategic Balance* (Armonk, NY: M.E. Sharpe, 2001), 22–63.

concessions, and tough rhetoric and actions at times while not adopting structural reforms desired by the Americans. The trade disputes were frustrating for both sides. For the Americans, there was a strong resentment and desire to try something new. That is why even though much of the business community and policy community would not do what Trump has done they still view his unorthodox measures initially as worth a try, since nothing conventional has seemed to have worked.

However, the haphazard and reckless way the Trump administration has been pursuing its America First policy could potentially weaken globalization, which has slowed down since the 2008 great recession. Globalization continues but is becoming more fragmented along regional lines. The US absence from regional free trade agreements other than a revised North American Free Trade Agreement could potentially yield regional leadership to other countries such as China. Globalization is now being decimated by the COVID-19 pandemic with growing economic nationalist policies to reduce reliance on global supply chains.

During the 2016 presidential election, the Chinese seemed to prefer Trump over Hillary Clinton mainly because they did not like Clinton's past strong criticism of China's human rights record and her recent push for a "rebalancing" strategy to shift focus on China as a competitor. They also thought that they knew how to handle an erratic business tycoon and could take advantage of his vanity and inexperience. Most saw the Trump phenomenon as a daily reality show that was hurting the US, not China. Trump used stronger words for China during the election campaign, but the Chinese thought they had seen this before. Presidential candidates tended to be tough on China but would gradually shift to a more cooperative policy once in the White House. Additionally, Trump was critical of America's alliances, which would suit Beijing's interest in weakening America's position in Asia.

Things were working in China's favor initially. On the first full working day, Trump announced US withdrawal from the TPP, which the Obama administration had concluded with eleven partner countries meant partly to create strong rules to counter China's economic advance. As China was excluded from the group and was indeed an implicit target of the group, Beijing scored. Trump also took aim at America's traditional allies over trade and burden sharing. China believed this would make it more difficult for a coalition of like-minded countries to put collective pressure on it, which normally was quite successful.

Then Trump turned to China over trade in March 2018, starting a massive trade war that has resulted in a partial truce ("phase one"). The Chinese government apparently did not expect Trump to walk the walk when it came to tariffs on China, based on their experiences dealing with previous American presidential transitions. Trump's aggressive, sweeping tariffs on Chinese exports to the US aggravated the difficult internal rebalancing the government had started before Trump. While Beijing seemed to be confident that it could weather this fight better than the US could, by the end of the year it became obvious that China was getting hurt more than the US was. In 2018, China saw its lowest annual growth rate since 1990, at 6.6 percent, and the real number might be even lower. Tariffs are blunt instruments which also hurt American firms and the global economy, as one would expect from disruption of an interdependent world economy.

It would be difficult for China to achieve an agreement with the US to remedy this situation. Trump often focuses on trade deficits with China and others, but the American government as a whole has a broad range of grievances against China. Whether it was intentional or not, the US Justice Department announced charges against Huawei just when China's chief trade negotiator, Liu He, was landing in Washington, DC, for a new round of trade talks on January 30–31, 2019. Despite apparent willingness by Trump and Xi to reach a compromise, the gap between the two sides is wide. The hawks on the US side want to force structural change in the Chinese political economy and set up a mechanism to hold the Chinese government accountable for any promises made. The Chinese side seems willing to compromise by promising to purchase more American products and improve intellectual property rights (IPR) protection for foreign firms. By the end of 2018, the Chinese government announced a new law to punish IPR violations.

The Chinese government is unlikely to change their system under American pressure. Fundamentally, they believe their system has been working well for them, and for pride and regime security they would probably accept no more than cosmetic changes. After all, China is not a defeated country. Even defeated, occupied, democratized, and allied countries like Japan and Germany maintain their distinct systems of political economy that allow them to be chronic surplus countries, even more so than China in recent years if measured by current account balances as shares of GDP. China, Japan, and Germany have all followed "China First," "Japan First," and "Germany First" strategies even though the government leaders in all three nations never explicitly say so. These approaches are a factor in laying the ground for the America First response.

Unlike the Russians, the Chinese prefer the status quo when it comes to economics because they have benefited massively from an open global economy although one may argue that China's intensifying development initiatives may position the country to challenge the status quo over time. In fact, the Chinese economy began to take off after the Cold War ended, when globalization was the talk of the day. Not every country has grown, given the same international environment. Governments have to make a choice to formulate and implement policy to take advantage of the opportunities presented and minimize the risks perceived by them. The Chinese government frequently characterized the international environment as presenting a "strategic opportunity." The rise of China is a familiar story that need not be repeated here. The Chinese government continues to be interested in promoting globalization.

That is why Xi gave a well-publicized speech championing free trade and globalization at Davos in 2017. That speech could be viewed as cynical, since China is not nearly as market-friendly as the US is, and its own trading practices were part of the reason for the backlash.

To be sure, China's rapid economic growth and exposure to the global economy could lead to domestic backlash as well. Unlike the Asian tigers before it, China has seen an enlarging gap in income, wealth, and opportunities. One recent study shows that China's income gap is worse than Europe's is but slightly better than that of the US. The wealth gap is bigger than the income gap in China, which is now worse than in France but still better than in the US.[30] One should expect troubles from these expanding gaps that look worse because of better communications technologies. The principle of relative deprivation indeed applies. The social unrest and protests in China partly result from this perceived unfairness of the system. One should predict a more heated ideological debate in the country. Indeed, China has seen waves of ideological debates since reform and opening in the late 1970s, often heated and in full public view.[31] Debates of a similar nature are also taking place in the US, as revealed by the tax-on-the-wealthy proposals by some Democratic presidential candidates. The Democratic Party is leaning more to the left, with redistributive ideas that would be unthinkable in the US even a few years ago. The political scene is changing in the US. In comparison, there is far more fertile ground for leftist ideas in China, as the nation has practiced a socialist system. There has been nostalgia for an "egalitarian" past in China, particularly among those who did not have first-hand experience of the intolerable suffering of a planned economy. The Chinese government has itself to blame because it has always been tougher on the "extreme" right than the "extreme" left. The leftist and nationalist resentment, which share some common ground, can combine into a populist wave.

One key reason that we are not seeing current pressure for regime change in China is that while the gap is getting larger, the rising tide did lift most boats. Put simply, as Branko Milanovic has shown in his now famous "elephant curve" graph, the working class and the middle class in China may not be doing nearly as well as the super-rich and powerful are in their country, but they are doing better than their counterparts in the US.[32] Globalization is a process that has an uneven impact at a given historical moment, and it is not a zero-sum game. The gains in China's working class and middle class do not have to come at the expense of the working class and middle class in the US. American firms have clearly benefited from globalization, which is

---

30. Thomas Piketty, Li Yang, and Gabriel Zuckman, "Capital Accumulation, Private Property and Rising Inequality in China, 1978–2015," NBER Working Paper No. 23368, April 2017.
31. Ming Wan, *The China Model and Global Political Economy: Comparison, Impact, and Interaction* (New York: Routledge, 2014), 29–36.
32. Branko Milanovic, "Global Income Inequality by the Numbers: In History and Now," World Bank Policy Research Working Paper 6259, November 2012.

why they have promoted it in the first place. A key issue lies with America's own system of political economy. At the same time, there is strong empirical evidence that some manufacturing job loss in the US may be caused by competition from Chinese imports. An often-cited study by David H. Autor, David Dorn, and Gordon H. Hanson shows the US lost 2.0 to 2.4 million manufacturing jobs due to Chinese competition from 2000 to 2007.[33] In another National Bureau of Economic Research study, Katharine Abraham and Melissa Kearney have estimated that the employment-to-population ratio decreased by 4.5 percent from 1999 to 2016. Most could be attributed to the aging population. Chinese competition was a key factor, explaining a 1.04 percent decrease (2.65 million job loss) ahead of automation (0.55 percent decrease).[34] The general public arguably ignores all of these empirical publications, but they can make a mental connection between loss of jobs around them and the presence of Chinese products in Walmart stores. The charge of China's unfair trading practices thus resonates. The charges of forced technology transfers and IPR theft are more important for much of the US government and business community. A US-China technological rivalry is becoming a defining feature of the current global political economy.

In China's political system, repression plays a key role along with social and economic bargains. I do not see Xi's government as representing a phase change in Chinese politics. Xi has gone backward in collective leadership, social and media control, as well as market reform, but is still within the larger framework of the Chinese system. He is not a revolutionary leader. From a prominent political family that founded the People's Republic, Xi is not going to burn down his own house. He very much wants predictability and stability. He has a populist streak in him, as he uses media to portray himself as a leader who cares about people and as he has conducted a high-profile anti-corruption campaign to much applause by the public, which coincides with his consolidation of power. Xi has been successful so far, but the future of China's political development remains uncertain. A regime is strong until it is not. Bifurcation may result from cumulative gradual changes.

The Chinese government should be worried about the Trump administration and the trade disputes with the US. Even though the Chinese government is viewed as in a stronger position because of suppression of domestic opposition, the Chinese system is fundamentally more fragile than the American system is. Poor economic performance in the US may contribute to the demise

---

33. David H. Autor, David Dorn, and Gordon H. Hanson, "The China Shock: Learning from Labor Market Adjustment to Large Change in Trade," NBER Working Paper 21906, January 2016; David H. Autor, David Dorn, and Gordon H. Hanson, "The China Syndrome: Local Labor Market Effects of Import Competition in the United States," *American Economic Review* 103, no. 6 (2013): 2121–68.
34. Katharine Abraham and Melissa Kearney, "Explaining the Decline in the U.S. Employment-to-Population Ratio: A Review of the Evidence," National Bureau of Economic Research, Working Paper 24333, February 2018.

of a president's administration, but it has not damaged the whole political system, at least for now. By contrast, the Chinese government is now heavily dependent on performance legitimacy, which is far more to worry about. At the same time, if the Chinese government panics, it would make things worse. Sometimes, solutions are more damaging than the initial problems. The Chinese Communist Party leaders attended a four-day study session to toughen the fighting spirit against challenges, without naming the trade war with the US.[35] As it is well understood, regime security is paramount for the Chinese government. Beijing faces serious challenges. At the same time, the Chinese government is now touting the advantages of its political institutions as measured by its relative success in keeping the COVID-19 pandemic under control despite its initial mishaps, as contrasted to the poor performance of the US, an assessment apparently echoed by much of Chinese society.

Of the three countries studied in this chapter, Japan is the most status quo conscious. This does not mean that Japanese politics has been boring. If one follows Japanese politics, one would know all the dramas and back-stabbing intrigues. There have also been sudden changes in the political scene. But in the scheme of things, Japan has been relatively stable from a historical and comparative perspective. Most Japanese citizens want it that way.

Japan is also in a different political cycle from that of the US and much of Western Europe. The country experienced a populist backlash and opposition victory starting in the late 2000s. Things did not quite work out as hoped under the Democratic Party of Japan in power. A conservative backlash put the conservative Liberal Democratic Party (LDP) back in power at the end of 2012. Abe Shinzo became the longest-serving Japanese prime minister. Like Xi, Abe hails from a prominent political family. Abe is everything that Trump is not. But no other world leader has tried as hard as Abe to forge a close personal relationship with Trump. Abe is merely doing what is expected of a postwar Japanese prime minister who is supposed to maintain a strong alliance with the US for the country's security and to gain access to the global market for its prosperity. Trump's election rhetoric posed a potential threat to Japan's fundamental interests. Abe's early outreach efforts were largely applauded in Japan.

The Japanese government prefers the postwar American bipartisan consensus. They prefer to contain China through the strength of a coalition led by the US. Ryan Avent, a senior economics columnist with the *Economist*, writes that China's future "is anything but assured" and that "It is in the world's interest to see China become prosperous and free. The best way to get there is to be firm with China, generous with friends and patient."[36] Avent is not counting on Trump to act strategically and rationally. The Japanese would agree with that assessment. At the same time, like other allies, they cannot

---

35. Anna Fifield, "Chinese Leaders Call on 'Tenacious Spirit' to Battle Challenges," *Washington Post*, January 26, 2019, A8.
36. Ryan Avent, "Why It's Important to Wait China Out," *Washington Post*, December 23, 2018, G5.

count on Trumpism being "generous with friends and patient." That is why the Japanese are exploring other options while fighting hard to maintain their traditional alliance with the US.

The basic international imperative for Japan is now clear. As observed insightfully by Yoichi Funabashi, a former editor-in-chief of *Asahi Shimbun*, Japan and China are moving closer now partly because of the "Trump factor." He concludes: "It is impossible for Japan to choose unequivocally between the US and China. Or between national security and the economy. Or between alliances and autonomy. These are no straight either-or choices."[37] The Japanese resent both American protectionism and Chinese hegemonism. They note that the international forums such as the G-20 summit in October 2018 and the G-7 summit have become an empty shell. It was a challenge for Japan to exercise leadership as host of the G-20 summit in 2019.

The Japanese government has adopted a strategy of proceeding with free trade agreements as a hedge against American protectionism and a check on Chinese influence. Japan signed the TPP-11, entering into effect on December 30, 2018, and the Japan-EU Economic Partnership Agreement, which entered into effect on February 1, 2019, and concluding RCEP in November 2020. Abe's longevity results from the Japanese voters' view that they now want a more decisive leader, given the severe challenges the country is facing. Japan under Abe and now his successor, Yoshihide Suga, is doing its best so far in the US-China-Japan triangle thanks partly to its own strategic moves and partly to Trump's handling of foreign policy. Abe moved his country toward a middle ground, which is desirable in any triangular relationship. Suga appears to be following Abe's approach.

This chapter does not focus on the security aspect of the Asian order, but suffice it to say that the Abe government is seeking to strengthen the alliance for its own defense. As a case in point, the Japanese government is now seeking to extend Article 5 of the US-Japan Security Treaty to cover cyberattacks.[38] Japan has expanded defense cooperation with other countries as well. Japan is also increasing its defense spending and upgrading its weapons and defense infrastructure. For example, the Self-Defense Forces began to use Japan's own GPS in November 2018, with four satellites in place. Japan expects to have seven satellites by the 2023 fiscal year, which could allow Japan to use its own system rather than America's GPS around Japan.[39] Japan needs a Plan B just in

---

37. Yoichi Funabashi, "Normalizing Japan-China Ties Poses Risks," *Japan Times*, December 11, 2018, accessed on December 11, 2018, https://www.japantimes.co.jp/opinion/2018/12/11/commentary/japan-commentary/normalizing-japan-china-ties-poses-risks/#.XA_xICBOns0.
38. "Japan Seeking to Extend U.S. Security Treaty to Cyberattacks," *Kyodo News*, January 5, 2019, accessed on January 5, 2019, https://www.japantimes.co.jp/news/2019/01/05/national/politics-diplomacy/japan-seeking-extend-u-s-security-treaty-cyberattacks/#.XDCWSMIo5Zc.
39. *Yomiuri Shimbun*, January 16, 2019, accessed on January 16, 2019, https://www.yomiuri.co.jp/politics/20190116-OYT1T50016.html?from=ytop_ylist.

case the US reduces protection of Japan. Trump's focus on burden sharing and trade imbalance and his unpredictable leadership style have caused concern in Tokyo as in other capitals around the world.

At the same time, Japan is also seeking to improve relations with China and Russia, diverging from the US government, if not Trump himself, that has repeatedly identified China and Russia as the greatest strategic threats to the US. The contrast cannot be sharper if one reads Abe's own version of the "state of the union" given on January 28, 2019. Abe views the Japan-China relationship as returning to normalcy, an assessment shared by the Chinese side. Abe also reiterates his strong desire to resolve the territorial dispute and conclude a peace treaty with Russia.

Japan and China have been improving relations since 2017. The Trump factor has facilitated this normalization. The US-China trade war is affecting Japan negatively. China's exports to the US include parts and materials from other countries, like Japan. The trade tensions between the world's two largest economies are beginning to bring down the global economy, a double hit on export-dependent Japan. Polls have shown the negative impact on the business environment. As an example, a joint poll of owners and managers in Japan, China, and South Korea between November 27 and December 13, 2018 shows that 79 percent of the Japanese surveyed think the US-China trade war will have a negative impact on their business, compared to 81 percent in South Korea and 73 percent in China.[40]

The Japanese government also needs China in dealing with North Korea. China does not control North Korea but has greater influence than other countries do, as testified by Kim Jong-un's three visits to China in 2018 and fourth in early January 2019. Japan also knows that there is only so much it can do to play ASEAN against China, knowing full well that the Southeast Asian countries want to chart their own course and avoid being caught in the crossfire between China and the US. To reduce China's suspicion of the "Indo-Pacific Strategy," the Abe government has recently replaced it with the word "vision," which would also make the initiative more palatable for the Asian countries close to China.[41]

Abe courted Russia partly to prevent a coalition between Beijing and Moscow. Trump has not objected, but much of the American policy community is fiercely anti-Russia. Therefore, the Japanese know that they have to move with caution. Any success with Russia would be a personal victory for Abe and his political family. This is yet another sign of Japan seeking greater autonomy in foreign policy. The Abe government warmed to the idea of seeking the return of only two of the four islands Tokyo disputes, in order

---

40. *Nikkei Shimbun*, January 7, 2019, accessed on January 26, 2019, https://www.nikkei.com/article/DGXMZO39699860X00C19A1SHA000/.
41. *Nikkei Shimbun*, November 13, 2018, accessed on November 12, 2018, https://www.nikkei.com/article/DGXMZO37648990S8A111C1PP8000/.

to achieve a peace treaty with Russia. But it is always doubtful whether Putin would be willing to give up what he views as legitimate Russian territories.

Meanwhile, China and Russia want to improve relations with Japan to create some distance between Japan and the US even though neither has any illusion that they can drive the two allies apart. China wants to avoid taking on too many enemies at the same time. Russia continues to dangle a possible peace treaty. Both Beijing and Moscow are driven by geopolitical and geo-economic considerations.

The conservative LDP government is also driven by geopolitical and geo-economic calculations. Japan is currently in serious disputes with South Korea, another ally of the US, over forced labor and comfort women during World War II, a territorial dispute, and the radar lock-in controversy. Japan is also retreating from its former commitment to multilateral institutions when they contravene national interests. The Japanese government decided on December 26, 2018 to withdraw from the International Whaling Commission (IWC), thus restarting commercial whaling from July 2019 restricted to Japan's territorial waters and Exclusive Economic Zone. Japan's proposal for partial commercial whaling was rejected at the IWC meeting in September 2018, by a vote of forty-one to twenty-seven. Another recent case is the International Coffee Agreement from which Japan withdrew in 2009 but rejoined in 2015. Japan also withdrew from the Common Fund for Commodities (CFC) in 2012. Japan's aim was to reduce its financial contributions in the two cases.[42] Japan also criticized UNESCO in 2016 over what it viewed as lack of transparency in its decision-making process for the Memory of the World Register and decided to withhold contributions temporarily over the organization's decision to include documents regarding the 1937 Nanjing Massacre submitted by the Chinese government. Japan has not been and will not be a champion of a liberal international order.

Different from the US and some European countries, Japan is not making a dramatic shift from multilateralism. As discussed, Japan continues to promote multilateral trade, which is in its fundamental interest. Moreover, Japan does not want to go against China alone. Last but not least, Japan has not faced an immigration "crisis" like in the US and Europe. Immigration has been extremely sensitive for the Japanese. Like almost all other Asian countries, Japan has followed a highly restrictive policy toward immigrants and refugees, which explains the absence of a backlash, shown consistently in polls. In fact, some anti-immigration activists cite Japan as a good example to maintain its culture and way of life. At the same time, some Japanese politicians that repeatedly employ hate speech against the Koreans and other minorities in Japan have recently gained some ground among voters.

---

42. *Nihon Keizai Shimbun*, December 26, 2018, accessed on December 26, 2018, https://www.nikkei.com/article/DGXMZO39409090W8A221C1EA2000/?nf=1.

Looking into the Future

It is hard to predict what will happen in Asia. For one thing, leaders change from time to time, adding uncertainties about a country's future policy. While Xi's position seems stable, the US will either reelect Trump or elect Joe Biden in the November 2020 presidential election. Either administration is expected to take a tough stand on China, but a Biden government would seek to strengthen ties with traditional allies like Japan. While I was revising this chapter, Abe made a somewhat surprising announcement on August 28, 2020, that he would resign due to illness, only a few days after he became the longest-serving prime minister in Japan's history. Unlike in the US, a successor to Abe will not be selected based on ideology or policy choice. Indeed, it took only a few days for Abe's right-hand man, Yoshihide Suga, to emerge as a sure successor when key LDP factions expressed support, a clear indication of preference for continuity and stability. Suga then announced his candidacy on September 2 and won the September 14 election, limited to only LDP parliamentarians and limited representatives of LDP prefectural chapters. He was formally elected prime minister on September 16.

Suga is expected to continue Abe's domestic policy if not his leadership style and to strengthen the alliance with the US while maintaining a cordial relationship with China. Indeed, Nikai Toshihiro, the LDP secretary-general who was instrumental in Suga's electoral victory, said on September 17 that he hoped the thaw in Japan-China relations would continue and that President Xi's postponed state visit to Japan would take place. In fact, Nikai indicated that a fifth political document that emphasizes "co-creation" for achieving world peace and prosperity centered on Japan and China.[43] In a phone conversation on September 25, Suga and Xi talked about strengthening bilateral cooperation. It was reported in Japanese media that the conservative wing of the LDP visited the prime minister's office before the scheduled phone talk, to express strong opposition to Xi's visit.[44] There exists a strong anti-China sentiment in the government and the public in Japan, which will restrict the extent to which the two countries can cooperate or even maintain a normal relationship.

The best we can do is to forecast some scenarios. We observe that globalization started with the introduction of America's liberal international order and was unleashed after the end of the Cold War but has slowed down since the 2008 great recession, judging by the flow of goods, money, ideas, and people. The only indicator that has seen a dramatic increase is the volume of data.[45] But if one considers the increasing state control over data, the cross-

---

43. *Asahi Shimbun*, September 18, 2020, accessed on September 18, 2020, https://www.asahi.com/articles/ASN9L567BN9KUTFK017.html?iref=comtop_list_pol_n07.
44. *Asahi Shimbun*, September 25, 2020, accessed on September 25, 2020, https://www.asahi.com/articles/ASN9T6FM3N9TUTFK018.html?iref=comtop_8_04.
45. "The 'Global List'," *The Economist*, January 26, 2019, pp. 19–22.

border volume should have been much bigger. Anti-globalization sentiment, aggravated by the COVID-19 pandemic, is so strong that it is difficult to see a renewed globalization wave anytime soon. Globalization is likely to continue but become more fragmented along regional lines or between the US and China.

We are moving toward a more managed globalization or simply more managed trade. Whether governments can accomplish this is another matter, but they are trying. If that is the case, both the US and China would survive and even thrive relative to other countries. Both have the size and the comprehensive industrial and technological basis. The US is still in the lead, but China is catching up fast, with a far larger population and soon a larger retail market. The Asian order will be less orderly, and the Asian international system will become polarized between Washington and Beijing. A US-China rivalry will provide both constraints and opportunities for other countries in the region. The Asian nations, large or small, may potentially benefit from shifting supply chains.[46] But a less liberal and less open regional economy may also mean less opportunity for them to climb the development ladder the way Japan, the Asian tiger economies, and China have done. At the same time, Asia, particularly East Asia, is likely to continue to be more peaceful than the Middle East is and more stable than most other regions in the world are.

---

46. A recent United Nations Conference on Trade and Development (UNCTAD) report estimates that trade diversion from the US-China trade tensions would benefit developed countries more than it would benefit developing nations. The European Union is estimated to capture $70 billion from diversion of bilateral trade between the US and China. Mexico, Japan, and Canada would capture above $20 billion. Australia, Brazil, India, the Philippines, Pakistan, and Vietnam would a capture small amount although significant relative to the size of their exports. But the report warns that the trade diversion effects could be offset by the overall negative effect from the trade tensions between the US and China. UNCTAD, *Key Statistics and Trends in Trade Policy 2018* (Geneva: United Nations, 2019), 3–4.

Conclusion

Lowell Dittmer

The central thesis of this book has been that East Asia, the successful modernizing core of the emerging world, is afflicted by disorder, a disorder that has been steadily escalating without any visible exit ramp. The leading source of the disorder is growing polarization between China and those countries loosely affiliated with it and the American-led rules-based order that was emerging in the wake of the superseded Cold War order. Disorder is no anomaly in East Asia—in the world's fastest-growing region change is constant. Yet this is more disorienting than previous disorders, which took place within relatively clearly structured parameters. But since the Cold War framework fell apart in the early 1990s, no new one has yet generated consensus. We appear now to be moving toward a new bifurcated framework of "Cold War II," but while public opinion has certainly hardened in both China and the United States, there is no consensus in favor of a new cold war. Public opinion in East Asia is even more averse. The economic ties that bind us are thick, mutually functional, and would be costly to sever.

This helps account for the sense of befuddlement that has greeted China's "rise." That rise has been perhaps the most swift and momentous shift in the Asian balance of power since the rise of Genghis Khan in the thirteenth century.[1] China has now moved to consolidate its status, extending sovereignty claims into the East China Sea and South China Sea, introducing a massive new intercontinental infrastructure building project undergirded by new financial and security institutions while at the same time maximizing its role within the existing ones. Pointing to a swift, efficient recovery from the

---

1. China seeks "Asia for Asians," says Xi Jinping, and intends to build "a future where we will win the initiative and have the dominant position." Huawei founder and CEO Ren Zhengfei puts it starkly: "our goal is to stand on top of the world. To achieve this goal, a conflict with the US is inevitable."

coronavirus pandemic, Xi Jinping advertises Chinese socialism as a superior alternative to liberal democracy.

Still, the China challenge is an ambiguous one. China is the most conspicuous beneficiary of the liberal rules-based global order that it challenges. Since its entry into the WTO in December 2001, China's rate of GDP growth reached its peak, becoming the world's second largest economy and largest trading nation, since 2012 the leading trade partner of 124 countries, including most of Asia. China's leaders are thus quite aware of their objective interest in maintaining the global status quo.[2] China is an active (and increasingly influential) participant in the United Nations, the IMF, and World Bank, the WTO, the Group of 20, and many other multinational organizations (while staying out of those like the Organisation for Economic Co-operation and Development that require statistical reports).

The American response has been no less ironic. After years of disappointing "constructive engagement," the 2016 election brought forth a populist sharply critical of the globalizing order America had helped build, leaving a leadership vacuum in forsaken institutions such as the UNHRC or the WHO for China to fill. Yet although "America first" is hardly its most appealing foreign policy advertisement, the West has awakened to China's challenges. The major political response has been the Japan-initiated Free and Open Indo-Pacific Initiative (FOIP), centered on the "Quad" of democratic countries (the US, Japan, Australia, and India). FONOPS have become more frequent and multilateralized, including France, Britain, and Japan. Despite withdrawal from the TPP, in 2018 the US Congress passed the Asia Reassurance Initiative Act (ARIA) and Better Utilization of Investment Lending and Development (BUILD) programs to counter the Belt and Road Initiative (BRI), and in 2019 the Blue Dot Network and International Development Finance Corporation were launched to finance infrastructure investment with largely private funding. The trade and tech war has certainly been mutually damaging but eventually resulted in a promising "first stage" deal designed to rectify the trade imbalance. In brief, the American response to China's rise, after initial ambivalence, has been competitive.

Thus great power politics returns to East Asia. The Cold War's international and regional structures are gone, and ASEAN's attempt to construct a new one has proved strategically impotent. China and the US have emerged as competing architects of the emerging new Asian order. China steps forward with its own set of institutional alternatives, which have been greeted with

---

2. "Economic globalization has powered global growth and facilitated movement of goods and capital, advances in science, technology and civilization, and interactions among peoples," Xi Jinping declared at Davos. "Whether you like it or not, the global economy is the big ocean we cannot escape from, any attempt to cut off the flow of capital, technology, products, industries and people between economies . . . is not possible." Full Text of Xi Jinping keynote at the World Economic Forum, *CGTN America*, January 17, 2017, https://america.cgtn.com/2017/01/17/full-text-of-xi-jinping-keynote-at-the-world-economic-forum.

initial enthusiasm but may have reached their fiscal limits. The US responded with a trade and tech war against China, polarizing the region, offering its own set of (fiscally more modest) initiatives. The competition has now been further aggravated by a global pandemic.

Analyzing Asian Disorder

The Asian "rules-based order" is a slightly modified transplant of the Westphalian Peace that ended the Thirty Years' War. It is in considerable disarray at the moment; the most we can say is that this is now widely acknowledged as a serious problem warranting serious remedial efforts. It would be premature to prescribe a "new world order," a task that will in any case fall to power-political actors rather than scholars; our goal is to analyze the disorder that inhibits its emergence. In a series of insightful chapters by our international panel of distinguished scholars, the Asian disorder comes into focus from three perspectives: identity, strategy, and triangulation.

Identities

National identity has in political science been considered a core constituent of nation-building, engendering the necessary loyalty to raise revenue and political support for the state to pursue public interests. The concept was introduced into the study of international relations literature in the 1990s, after the collapse of such established entities as the Soviet Union raised awareness of how fragile they were. Identities were reconceived as "constructed" entities, requiring foundations, architectures, hard work to build and maintain.[3] The Cold War structures had been built at great public expense; their disappearance resulted in a perceived vacuum, precipitating a rush by both states and international organizations to fill it. Thus we deal here with two aspects of identity: the reconstruction of China's *national* identity as a "great power," and the attempt to redefine *Asian* identity. Asian identity is recast as distinct and autonomous from Western identity, sharing some Western values (such as economic modernization) while also prizing its own distinct values.[4] In the context of rising nationalism throughout East Asia, these two projects coexist uneasily.

As accelerated communication and transportation integrated the region economically, a number of institutions arose to regulate the process; but the

---
3. See Y. Lapid and F. Kratochwil, eds., *The Return of Culture and Identity to International Relations Theory* (Boulder, CO: Lynne Rienner, 1996); Alexander Wendt, "Anarchy Is What States Make of It: The Social Construction of Political Identity," *International Organization*, no. 46 (1992): 391–425.
4. See Gilbert Rozman, ed., *East Asian National Identities: Common Roots and Chinese Exceptionalism* (Stanford, CA: Stanford University Press, 2012).

only one to articulate a persuasive unifying vision of Asian identity has been ASEAN, with its "ASEAN way" of peaceful development, mutual respect, sovereignty, noninterference, and compromise, arranged through innumerable meetings. Loosely related to this has been the more controversial formulation of "Asian values" by such leaders as Mahathir Mohamad and Lee Kuan Yew, advocating a regionally distinctive idea system substituting a form of authoritative communalism for Western competitive individualism. ASEAN found early support from Japan, compromised as it was by its history from any attempt to exert national ideological leadership.

China's ideological commitment to revolutionary class struggle and wars of national liberation initially inhibited any attempt to facilitate intra-regional cooperation, but since the advent of "reform and opening" China has become an active advocate of Asian values as well. In 2017, the Chinese government announced its plan to increase soft power significantly by 2035, declaring that China's modernization "offers a new option for other countries and nations who want to speed up their development while preserving their independence; and it offers Chinese wisdom and a Chinese approach to solving the problems facing mankind."[5] China would teach Asia to embrace "Chinese wisdom," and the Chinese public too would be embraced as part of the "community of common destiny for mankind." As Xi put it in a 2013 speech, "The more China grows the more it will create development opportunities for the rest of Asia."[6] In short, "win-win." As for the content of these values, they are virtually indistinguishable from those put forth in the ASEAN Charter.[7]

Inasmuch as China, ASEAN, and Japan, all the major Asian actors profess to be on the same page with respect to core values, how could there be any disputes among them? While values and identities may be shared, interests tend to diverge. As Yun-han Chu, Hsin-Che Wu, and Min-Hua Huang point out in Chapter 2, China's basic dilemma is that the more China's hard power grows, the more it is perceived not as a benign example but as a "threat." As noted, China has become the chief trade partner and fastest-growing investor of nearly all Asian nations, but it has also tripled military spending in less than

---

5. Xi Jinping, "Juesheng quanmian jiancheng xiaokang shehui, duoqu xin shidai Zhongguo tese shehuizhuyi weida shengli" [Secure a decisive victory in building a moderately prosperous society in all respects and strive for the great success of socialism with Chinese characteristics for a new era], *Renmin ribao* [People's Daily], October 28, 2017, 2.
6. Full text of Xi Jinping's speech at the opening ceremony of the Boao Forum for Asia AC 2013, April 7, 2013, http://english.boaoforum.org/mtzxxwzxen/7379.html.
7. "Throughout its five thousand-year history, the Chinese nation has developed the humanistic-oriented concept of loving all creatures as if they were of your species and all people as if they were your brothers, the political philosophy of valuing virtue and balance, the peaceful approach of love, non-aggression and good-neighborliness, the idea of peace as of paramount importance and harmony without uniformity, as well as the personal conduct of treating others in a way that you would like to be treated, and helping others succeed in the same spirit as you would want to succeed yourself." Wang Yi, "Exploring the Path of Major-Country Diplomacy with Chinese Characteristics," *Foreign Affairs Journal* 10 (2013): 14.

a decade. Donald Trump has been publicly explicit in his claim that China's continued rise threatens the national interest of the US, effectively weaponizing this fear as a foreign policy rallying call. Deng Xiaoping previously tried to assuage such anxieties with his famous "24-character admonition," in which the most often cited characters were *tao guang yang hui* ("keep a low profile and bide our time"). Hu Jintao revised "China's peaceful rise" to "China's peaceful development" for the same reason. But the Chinese leadership began to chafe at such self-abnegation as early as 2007, and Xi Jinping has since candidly articulated China's great power ambitions, no longer mentioning Deng's watchwords. This represented a subtle shift from seeking to blend into the Asian identity as defined by ASEAN to a proud assertion of Chinese national identity coupled with an offer to lead by example. To assuage anxieties, China has at the same time paid much more heed to "soft power." Shambaugh estimates that the PRC now spends over US$10 billion per year on what Chu, Wu, and Huang call public diplomacy.[8] Xi's drive to enhance China's soft power has focused on controlling the discussion of China-related issues throughout the world, often paired with economic statecraft to punish slow learners.

Despite hopes to enhance regional cooperation by crafting a set of distinct "Asian values," social scientists search in vain for the emergence of a coherent Asian identity. The PRC leadership has attempted to midwife such an identity by rhetorically conflating Chinese interests with Asian values. How successful have they been? In a sophisticated data analysis of the three waves of the Asian Barometer Survey (ABS) administered by the Hu Fu Center for the Study of East Asian Democracy, Yun-han Chu et al. are able to measure the causal impact of this charm campaign on Asian attitudes. They find widespread support for the assumption that China has displaced the US as the region's main growth locomotive and future economic hegemon, though whether public opinion favors that depends on other factors. Although those who positively value globalization and growth tend to have positive perceptions of China as a role model, there is surprisingly little correlation between economic ties and favorable public perceptions. China's image is lowest in Vietnam, scoring 2.1 on a range of 1 to 6, although bilateral trade and investment has been high. Cambodia has the most favorable perception, and it has enjoyed generous Chinese FDI (foreign direct investment) (and foreign aid), but the rating has slipped from 4.5 in round 3 (2010–2012) to 4.1 in round 4 (2014–2016). In Myanmar, also a major Chinese FDI recipient but with historically ambivalent China ties, China scored only 2.7 in round 4. Even in friendly Indonesia it scores 4.1 in round 4, down from 4.3 in round 3.

Far more significant than BRI funding is positioning in the South China Sea dispute: the frontline claimant states (Vietnam, Philippines) are more

---

8. David Shambaugh, "China's Soft-Power Push: The Search for Respect," *Foreign Affairs*, July/August 2015, https://www.foreignaffairs.com/articles/china/2015-06-16/china-s-soft-power-push.

anti-China, and the authors find China's positive ratings plunged dramatically following the commencement of "reclamation" (island-building) in December 2013. The critical value indicator is democracy: those who value democracy tend to have more critical views of China.[9] Their findings provide some support for the efficacy of Chinese public diplomacy, but that effect can be eclipsed by a hard power drive like the fortification of China's South China Sea islets.

The regime did not really need soft power during the Deng Xiaoping era because Deng's "reform and opening up" policies were widely popular and spoke for themselves, representing as they did a repudiation of the chaotic Cultural Revolution foreign policy of world revolution. Deng's "opening up," however, culminated within a decade in the Tiananmen protests and their sanguinary suppression, tarnishing China's international reputation. So in the 1990s, the regime turned to soft power as its salvation, a topic on which Jing Sun is an acknowledged authority.[10] Soft power is more than public diplomacy, more than the strategic use of language and culture to persuade other states of one's benign intentions.[11] As the concept's originator, Joseph Nye, makes clear, soft power includes admiration for the whole nation, not just the political regime, and that necessarily includes the relationship between domestic and foreign policy, between civil society and the state. The Chinese party-state has contrariwise preferred to keep the two separate, for example advocating *nei jin, wai song* (strict domestically but internationally liberal), or "international democracy" (not advisable for internal use). While China has not visibly democratized in a structural sense, Sun concedes, the role of the public in Chinese politics has expanded considerably since Liberation in 1949. In the early Maoist period the regime used the masses quite effectively as diplomatic props, even in some cases choreographing their positions in public displays of commitment. The regime built solidarity by mobilizing enthusiastic masses to greet visiting delegations from Russia or Cuba or other fraternal socialist republics, or "spontaneously" appearing to shovel snow in Beijing to make way for Richard Nixon's icebreaking 1972 visit.[12] All that was important was their vast number.

Since reform and opening gave birth to an educated Chinese middle class along the eastern seaboard, however, public opinion has begun to evince some autonomy, for which the foreign policy apparatus was ill prepared. True, China ranks 177th of 180 nations in freedom of the press (according to the 2020

---

9. For a more comprehensive analysis, see Yun-han Chu et al., eds., *How East Asians View Democracy* (New York: Columbia University Press, 2008).
10. See *China and Japan as Charm Rivals: Soft Power in Regional Diplomacy* (Ann Arbor, MI: University of Michigan Press, 2012); also "Charmless Offensive: The Fate of Soft Power in East Asia," *Current History: A Journal of Contemporary World Affairs* 112, no. 755 (September 2013): 217–23.
11. Joseph Nye, "Soft Power," *Foreign Policy*, no. 80 (Autumn 1990): 153–71.
12. See Alan P. L. Liu, *Mass Politics in the People's Republic: State and Society in Contemporary China* (Boulder, CO: Westview Press, 1996).

rankings of Reporters sans frontières), and any public expression that flatly contravenes the party "line" is likely to be suppressed. But activists can still find space between censors to cause considerable mischief in foreign affairs. Resourceful grassroots activists have three options: first, they can introduce a new meme if it is generally consistent with party sentiments and the state has not explicitly ruled it out, and they may then push it too far for diplomatic comfort.[13] Second, even when the leadership has taken a position on an issue, what Sun calls "patriotic vigilantes" can co-opt the issue and exaggerate or bend it. Third, when the state is undecided or has no stated position on an issue, the field is wide open for mass innovation. A classic example is the vacuum left by the death of Hu Yaobang on April 15, 1989, when the leadership initially declined to hold a state funeral for the (unofficially) disgraced leader. This left space for activists to launch a public demonstration of appreciation for the former general party secretary, and the embarrassed indecision of the leadership over what to do eventually led to Tiananmen.

The "patriotic education campaign" institutionalized in China's socialization media since the collapse of European communism has been quite successful, but it has also provided a legitimating vocabulary for spontaneous protest. Local protests can be aimed at domestic or foreign policy targets or repressed—or both, sequentially. The cadre fear of the masses as dangerous "wild horses" implanted during the Cultural Revolution has been repeatedly reinforced. And as Sun notes, there has been a decline in officially sponsored mass campaigns since then and indeed a growing gulf between elite and masses.[14] (True, Xi Jinping revived Mao's "mass line." But this is not really about the masses at all but about rectifying the behavior of party cadres. Xi's anti-corruption campaign has similarly been tightly controlled from the top down.)

Canadian professor Jeremy Paltiel analyzes East Asian ideological disorder according to the Chinese challenge to American leadership relying on the theory of symbolic interactionism, with particular attention to China's relations with Commonwealth countries Canada and Australia.[15] Despite rhetorical efforts to drape Chinese foreign policy in a an Asian collective identity, the Xi leadership in its focus on "rejuvenation of the Chinese nation" has

---

13. After Chinese protesters trashed the US embassy in Beijing in spontaneous demonstrations after the US bombing of the Chinese embassy in Belgrade in 1999, China agreed to pay $2.87 million in compensation (while the US agreed to pay $4.5 million to compensate for the three Chinese killed in the bombing).
14. As Sun notes, mass spontaneity does not always deviate from the political status quo; in fact the opposite has been far more frequent. But even pro-regime spontaneous mass protests can be troublesome, inasmuch as observers tend to assume the regime is pulling the strings. The anti-Japan demonstrations in 2015, for example, seem to have been organized via grassroots cell phone, inflicting serious damage on Sino-Japanese relations, yet the regime let them run for weeks because they echoed official propaganda.
15. See also Jeremy Paltiel, *The Emperor's New Clothes: Cultural Particularism and Universal Values in China's Quest for Global Status* (New York: Palgrave Macmillan, 2007).

signaled an implicit departure from the universal values underpinning the American-led rules-based order, more boldly articulated by Xi than by any of his predecessors since Mao.[16] Xi thus dismisses the pentagonal American bloc system of bilateral defense alliances with Japan, Australia, South Korea, Thailand, and the Philippines as an outmoded relic of "Cold War thinking," proffering in its place a "new Asian security concept" bereft of alliances, conceptualized by Xi as "common, comprehensive, cooperative and sustainable" security. By introducing the BRI, "ASEAN centrality" is meant to give way to a new norm of Chinese centrality in Asia. Taking advantage of Trump's increasing withdrawal from multilateral diplomacy in favor of discrete bilateral "deals," Xi steps forward (at Davos, CICA, and other fora) to headline Chinese support for globalization and international cooperation against climate change.[17] Giving sedulous attention to opportunities for democratic personnel nominations in the UN, the World Bank, and other global institutions, China is indeed becoming not only a global stakeholder but a leader, offering a "Beijing consensus" of rapid, orderly economic development in place of the pluralistic ("chaotic") Washington consensus.[18] CICA (Conference on Interaction and Confidence-Building Measures in Asia) which Xi Jinping chaired in 2014–2018) is touted as a new cooperative security dialogue for all of Asia.[19]

Although Asia's prosperity has become economically dependent on China, not all Asian states are sure they can trust it. What is the quid pro quo? According to Paltiel there are at least three distinct discourses in China's vision of a new Asian order: (1) "national rejuvenation" of the "China dream"; i.e., the China model has been extraordinarily successful; we should follow China.

---

16. See Michael J. Mazarr, Jonathan Blake, Abigail Casey, Tim McDonald, Stephanie Pezard, and Michael Spirtas, *Understanding the Emerging Era of International Competition: Historical and Theoretical Perspectives* (Santa Monica, CA: RAND Corp, Research Report, 2018), https://www.rand.org/pubs/research_reports/RR2726.html; and Xuetong Yan, "Chinese Values vs. Liberalism: What Ideology Will Shape the International Normative Order?" *The Chinese Journal of International Politics* 11, no. 1 (Spring 2018): 1–22, https://doi.org/10.1093/cjip/poy001.
17. Xi Jinping, "President Xi's Speech to Davos in Full," *World Economic Forum*, January 17, 2017, https://www.weforum.org/agenda/2017/01/full-text-of-xi-jinping-keynote-at-the-world-economic-forum/.
18. Although China continues to borrow about $2 billion per year in subsidized loans from the World Bank's International Bank for Reconstruction and Development (IBRD), China's outstanding loans, mainly to poorer countries, have gone from almost nothing in 2000 to more than $700 billion in 2019, making it the world's largest official creditor, more than twice as big as the World Bank and IMF combined. For fifty developing countries that have borrowed from China, that debt has reportedly increased on average from less than 1 percent of their GDP in 2015, to more than 15 percent in 2017—but documentation of these loans has been at best opaque. Vide supra, note 18. See also Emily S. Chen, "Is China Challenging the Global State of Democracy?" *Issues and Insights* (Working Paper) 19, no. 5 (June 2019), Honolulu, Pacific Forum.
19. Full text (oral only, in Chinese) of Xi's keynote speech to the 4th CICA (May 20–21, 2014), http://www.china.org.cn/world/node_7206254.htm.

(2) The "democratization" of international relations, defined as multipolarity among the great powers. What about smaller powers? They "need not and should not take sides among big countries."[20] (3) Multilateral institutions, the UN in particular, should be relied on to maintain global order and progress. In addition to these three there is Zhou Enlai's old "Five Principles of Peaceful Coexistence," echoing Westphalian principles of sovereignty and non-interference. And finally China's "New Asian Security Concept" (replacing the old "Asian Security Concept") envisions progressively displacing the US-led security order by offering economic incentives to invite an open Asia structured only by bilateral "partnerships" with the PRC. Common to all is an invitation to a serenely peaceful world relieved of any need for common defense.

Strategies

By rough count, twenty books were published in 2020 (by August) on "China" and "strategy," seven in 2019, more than thirty in 2018. As intra-Asian relations become fraught, small wonder more energy has been invested in trying to find ways to survive and prevail. Strategy becomes particularly relevant when the two sides are evenly matched, as is increasingly the case in the China-America standoff.[21] The modern Asian strategic ecology, though not a radical departure from the Western experience (advanced literate civilizations in complex interweaving rivalries and intermittent strife), does have one distinguishing feature. It is far more diverse, lacking any shared religious or linguistic background. The Westphalian system is a relative newcomer, a superficial overlay over ancient cultures and political orders.

One unifying feature of today's Asia is the laser focus on economic modernization. Since 1960 East Asia has grown faster than any other region in the world, with an estimated (nominal) GDP of US$20.8 trillion in 2018. The region is site of some of the world's longest economic booms, starting from the Japanese economic miracle (1950–1990), South Korea's Miracle on the Han River (1961–1996), the Taiwan miracle (1960–1996), and, biggest of all, China's economic boom (1978–2012). All the successful modernizers have followed a similar blueprint consisting of state control of finance, direct support of state-owned industries or private "national champions," export-oriented growth, a high rate of savings and investment (and low consumption), and authoritarian but relatively efficient governance. By dint of its size and population, China's economic miracle since 1978 has been the most consequential, lifting

---

20. China's Policies on Asia-Pacific Security Cooperation (January 2017), Section I, http://www.fmprc.gov.cn/mfa_eng/zxxx_662805/t1429771.shtml.
21. See Office of the Secretary of Defense, *Military and Security Developments Involving the People's Republic of China, 2020: Annual Report to Congress*, https://media.defense.gov/2020/Sep/01/2002488689/-1/-1/1/2020-DOD-CHINA-MILITARY-POWER-REPORT-FINAL.PDF; also Eric Hegenbotham et al., *The U.S.-China Military Scorecard: Forces, Geography, and the Evolving Balance of Power, 1996–2017* (Santa Monica, CA: RAND Corp, 2015).

billions from poverty and replacing a now stagnating Japan as economic locomotive for the region. In Asia the focus on successful economic development seems to have supplanted a shared religious creed or ideology as the basis for discussions of regional cooperation. And in the event of inter-state conflict, economics becomes weaponized as "economic statecraft." Whenever conflict occurs, whether hard or soft, political or economic, strategy comes into play.

World systems theory, as insightfully applied by Ho-fung Hung, is a more advanced form of Marxist theory that integrates market economics with political science and international relations. Hung begins with a review of the rise and fall of the "New World Order" in the immediate aftermath of the Cold War. The fall of the Communist Bloc in the early 1990s inspired hope for a globalized world of democracy and market capitalism. The collapse of the Iron Curtain opened vast new labor and commodities markets, and the US sought to capitalize by opening its market to imports and encouraging trade partners to open theirs to American FDI. There were three justifications for this neoliberal approach. The first was that trade would be mutually beneficial, economically based on Ricardian comparative advantage (for the US, enabling it to offload its industrial overcapacity during the post–Cold War "peace dividend" of slackened military expenditure). The second was the "trickle down" theory that labor would ultimately enjoy the benefits of globalization (which, Hung makes clear, turned out to be a cruel illusion). The third was that democratization would inevitably follow baptism into the capitalist world market. The latter assumption legitimated including authoritarian and even communist states into a now truly global marketplace.

The evolution of this division of labor, however, did not redound to the long-term advantage of the US. Falling profitability in the developed countries necessitated a "new division of labor" in which manufacturing was offshored to developing countries with large pools of cheap labor. The American role was to supply financial services (the "exorbitant privilege" of the dollar as global reserve currency gave it almost unlimited lending capacity) and to serve as consumer of last resort. Inasmuch as the Asian developing countries typically resorted to a combination of export-oriented growth and import substitution, the US was ultimately able to export little more than agricultural commodities and advanced weaponry, and a negative balance of trade quickly cumulated. This was temporarily alleviated in the case of Japan and the small tigers by the Plaza agreement, whereby the latter revalued their currencies, making exports more expensive and imports cheaper. While the Asian tigers still drew sufficient benefit from this trade and security protection tradeoff to accede to US pressure to balance bilateral trade, the PRC was big enough to resist, retaining a communist political system and semi-marketized economy in which the state occupies the "commanding heights," maintaining control of the financial sector and upstream state-owned enterprises.

The trend toward market reform that began in 1978 and gained subsequent momentum has had two consolidation phases, the first after Tiananmen in 1989–1992 and the second beginning in 2012 with the rise of Xi Jinping. During these consolidation phases the emphasis shifts back to centralized party control and nationalist foreign policy. It is not yet clear how prolonged the current, already more sustained, retrenchment will last; that will probably depend on how successful it is. As globalization loses legitimacy in the US (and to some extent even in China, though not rhetorically) due to a combination of distributive inequality, environmental externalities, and recurrent financial crises, Chinamerica gives way to inter-imperial competition between two mega-economies with increasingly similar industrial policies and a (first phase) planned trade agreement. We now see a post–Cold War bipolarity emerging, as the balance of military power is still (marginally) on the Western shores of the Asia-Pacific while economic dynamism migrates to the East.

Wu Guoguang begins his chapter with an innovative geostrategic analysis of the logic of China's rise. Wu sees China's grand strategy as analogous to that successfully pursued by the Qin dynasty under China's first emperor, Qin Shihuang, who brought the Warring States period (*zhanguo shidai*) to a close by unifying China in 221 BCE. While the analogy may seem stretched, the Warring States period, cradle of Chinese civilization (Confucius, Mencius, Legalism) was also a fertile field for military strategizing (Sun Tzu, the seven military classics), quite familiar to all literate Chinese. The strategy pursued by Qin against six rival states was amoral and highly flexible ("Machiavellian"). In this loosely bipolar competition, one group of kingdoms advocated a "vertical" or north-south alliance called *hezong*, in which the weaker states would ally with each other to repel Qin. The other side advocated a "horizontal" or east-west alliance called *lianheng*, in which a state would ally with Qin to participate in its ascendancy. Qin, the successful aggressor, pursued bilateral alliances with each successive rival state to subdue and ultimately incorporate it, moving from the relatively small and weak to the more powerful, culminating in the first unification of China under Qin Shihuang. In so doing, Qin was the strategic innovator, using successive bilateral alliances to prize apart a defensive bandwagon. In the analogous contemporary confrontation, the PRC sees itself as Qin and the US in the role of Qi, the last and most powerful state to be conquered by Qin. And like Qi, the US has endeavored to form a coalition among smaller neighboring states to contain China.

The historical analogy is not perfect, of course. The Warring States period extends over a longer time span than the current post–Cold War era. Territorial conquest is no longer an option for China (except in the case of Taiwan), and soft power and weaponized economics largely replace armed force. Here, Wu shifts from geostrategic to geo-economic analysis: globalization has turned both powers into "economic states" in which the business sector becomes fused to the state ("China, Inc."), and ideology is subsumed by strategic-economic competition. China thus fights tooth and nail in defense of the ostensibly private Huawei Corporation as a "national champion" for instance, while the US upholds the interests of the American multinational corporations that are off-shoring American jobs. The US is at a disadvantage in this competition because the pluralistic democratic state is less focused and the market more autonomous, giving China the opportunity to divide and conquer. While the US initially succeeded in forming a successful *hezong* of smaller countries "containing" China, China's economic rise has enabled it to displace the US as the main economic partner of most of the states in this containment perimeter. Trump's deglobalization à la "America first" severely weakens the *lianheng* option by disavowing multilateralism and alienating erstwhile allies with pressure to assume the financial burden of hosting American bases. Wu concludes his historical analogy with a critique of Trumpism: US grand strategy forms a close parallel to that pursued by Qi against Qin, dithering and equivocating while failing to recognize the nature of the threat. Despite having pulled much of Asia into supply-chain dependencies, China's *hezong* political victories remain few and tenuous, scaring off potential allies with expansive territorial claims and pointed demonstrations of hard power.

But why can these two great states not just get along? What is the basis of the antipathy that divides them? In a classic strategic policy analysis, Timothy Heath begins his chapter with a review of the theoretical literature on interstate rivalry. Sustained strategic rivalries, he finds, fall into two categories: those concerning spatial issues (contested sovereignty over territory), and positional disputes (over rank order in a hypothetical international hierarchy). The famed "Thucydides' trap" thesis (rivalry ignited by the power transition dynamic) falls into the latter category.[22] Ideological and economic disputes are deemphasized on the assumption that China has already adopted a form of state-led capitalism.[23] Rivalry is dangerous: it can easily escalate to arms racing and from there to armed conflict. Yet the Cold War shows that polarization can be sustained indefinitely without war between the two poles.[24] Regarding spatial issues there is no territorial dispute (even in the South China Sea the

---

22. Graham Allison, *Destined for War: Can America and China Escape Thucydides' Trap?* (Boston, MA: Houghton-Mifflin, 2017).
23. The preclusion of ideological/identity factors (a defining feature of mainstream realist analysis) is questionable in this case. Ideology according to Marx was a mere "opiate" offering wish fulfillment for unmet material needs, but the CCP attributes far greater importance to it as a master plan for identifying friends and enemies and prescribing future socioeconomic development with illocutionary force. The late discovery that China was on an avowed non-democratic ideological trajectory (Article 9, footnote 5) was a shock to American public opinion, for example, causing China's favorability ratings to drop eighteen points from 2017 to 2019 (according to Pew: "American Views of China Plummet Amid Coronavirus Crisis"; a later (2020) Gallup poll found a steeper drop, https://www.duihuahrjournal.org/2020/03/american-views-of-china-plummet-amid.html. The best synthesis of realism and identity analysis is (in my view) found in Gilbert Rozman's recent work.
24. See John Lewis Gaddis, *The Long Peace: Inquiries into the History of the Cold War* (New York: Oxford University Press, 1987).

US stakes no territorial claims).²⁵ Thus, Heath views the Sino-US standoff as a relatively manageable form of positional rivalry. Compared to the Cold War, a zero-sum conflict between two economically integrated, mutually exclusive blocs that included a strategic nuclear arms race and proxy wars over territory, the Sino-US rivalry has been offset by several mutually beneficial components, including extensive social interaction and still one of the largest bilateral trade and investment regimes in the world.

It is a positive-sum game, a growing pie with benefits for both—but not proportionately: since joining the WTO, China has enjoyed relative gains, precipitating Trump's tariffs. The real question, to Heath, is the trend line: Will the rivalry spiral up, or down? Although no one knows the future, Heath points to a number of leading indicators. First, demographic change: The future looks brighter here for the US than for the PRC, which due to its thirty-six-year-long one-child policy may well get old before it gets rich. As the population ages, social welfare expenses eat into the budget, crowding out fixed asset investment and arms acquisitions. And with the growth of the middle class there may well be a shift of social values toward greater individualism and environmental concerns.²⁶ Second, he anticipates developmental inertia: as China's economy matures economically and technologically (a top priority for Xi Jinping) and the population growth rate declines, the quest for additional territory or raw materials becomes less relevant, while consumption and welfare claim larger budget shares. Third, the military still matters: while China is gaining on the US in quality, the cost of sophisticated modern weaponry has increased exponentially—the dollar cost of China's military budget has grown more than 8 percent per year since 2007. Both rivals may eventually see the need to negotiate an arms limitation deal. In sum, Heath judges the Sino-US rivalry to be essentially positional, of sustained but low intensity, with minimal probability of a major bilateral conflagration. The economically warm but politically cool Sino-Japanese relationship may be a harbinger of the future.

Triangles

Triangulation involves geopolitics, i.e., a certain geographic proximity as well as overlapping geopolitical interests, among three actors. Whether we say "Asia-Pacific" or "Indo-Pacific," the US has since World War II seen itself

---

25. The US Navy may question this regarding the South China Sea, one of the busiest waterways of the world, shipping US$3.4 trillion in trade in 2016, supplying 90 percent of the petroleum consumed by China, Japan, and Korea. Although the US has no territorial stake, if China makes good its own claim and thereby denies access to American warships, this has obvious strategic implications for both the US and ASEAN.
26. Cf. Lowell Dittmer, "On the Sixth Generation: Preliminary Speculations about Chinese Politics after Xi," *Journal of Contemporary China* 29, no. 122: 253–65, https://www.tandfonline.com/doi/full/10.1080/10670564.2019.1637569.

as very much a part of the Asian region and intends to remain so. American national interests must hence be factored in. Triangulation has hitherto most frequently been applied to great power relations, but Yu-Shan Wu reasonably asks whether the model can help clarify the options of "small and medium countries" (SMCs) as well. The obvious problem is asymmetry: the SMCs are smaller and weaker than the great powers. How can they possibly hope to defend their interests? Take, for example, the tiny island of Melos in the Peloponnesian War, as recounted by Thucydides.[27] Threatened with invasion by the more powerful Athens, Melos relied on two defenses: the first and main defense was to appeal to the Athenians' sense of justice, and the second was to hope for support from Sparta, with which Melos had been loosely allied. But the Athenians spurned the appeal to justice—justice only applies among equals, they retorted with brutal realism—and the Spartans would not come to their rescue. Indeed, Melos was crushed by Athens, all the men slain, women and children cast into slavery.

The plight of small powers facing big ones in a triangular context is not easy. A small or medium country has three options, according to Wu: it can try to play pivot, it can be junior partner in a marriage, or it can become a pariah. Pariah is the worst option and pivot is the best, but it is hard for an SMC to play pivot because it lacks the leverage to withstand pressure by both "wings" to take sides. Wu concludes that the optimal strategy for an SMC is to "hedge," as Taiwan's president Ma Ying-Jeou sought to do in 2008–2016, moving toward China while maintaining an insurance policy with the US. This seems to have worked, insofar as trade and diplomacy with the Mainland thrived and Taipei negotiated a "diplomatic truce" with Beijing that let it retain formal diplomatic ties with twenty-three allies, attain observer status in the World Health Assembly (WHA), and establish free trade agreements (FTAs) with New Zealand and Singapore and a form of FTA (the Economic Cooperation Framework Agreement, or ECFA) with Beijing. For this Taipei was obliged only to agree to mouth the "one China principle" and adhere to certain Chinese linguistic self-effacements ("Chinese Taipei" etc.).

Yet these symbolic concessions were not without cost: Ma's presidency was followed by a crushing defeat of his Nationalist Party and the rise of the Tsai Ying-wen of the Democratic Progressive Party, historically rooted in the Taiwan independence movement. The DPP has since endured a quasi-Melos in the international arena, losing eight diplomatic allies to Beijing and getting kicked out of the WHA. Nevertheless, in 2018 and again in 2020, the DPP was overwhelmingly reelected, for the first time capturing a legislative majority as well. True, this was primarily due to the exogenous factor of China's hard-line response to the protests in Hong Kong. Altogether the experience illustrates the risk of playing pivot: trying to balance between two giant, demanding

---

27. Thucydides, *History of the Peloponnesian War*, trans. Rex Warner (Baltimore, MD: Penguin Books, 1954), 358–66.

rivals demands a high tolerance of ambiguity, even humiliation, which a domestic electorate may not sustain. Taiwan has perforce shifted from pivot to junior partner of the US (and potential victim of an increasingly hostile PRC) as the Sino-US rivalry escalates to full power transition.

My own chapter relates the plight of ASEAN, a much larger and geopolitically significant actor of some 650 million people, in trying to balance between China, the US, and Japan. Visualize a composite triangle with one side (sc., Sino-ASEAN relations) in common, as hedged by ASEAN's relations with Japan on the one side and the US on the other. While the relationship with the US is the only one that offers deterrent support in the event of a hard power assault by the PRC, Japan remains an economically still consequential Asian power that has offered a more diplomatically supple and ideologically resonant form of support to ASEAN. While the US has been prone to use the stick, Japan favors carrots. The game is still in play: this analysis is admittedly based on the rather heroic assumption that ASEAN is the consequential actor that it aspires to be. Still, the region's geopolitical future depends on that assumption's credibility. China's spendthrift BRI has made a seductive impression on the ASEAN economies, but China's fiscal capacity is finite,[28] and the PRC is diplomatically encumbered by its island-building claim to some 90 percent of the South China Sea. Meanwhile, the US maintains its network of mutual defense alliances and sends military signals designed to keep China's advances at bay, and both Japan and the US have countered the BRI with financial and infrastructure-building initiatives of their own.

Ming Wan's focus is on the larger triangle of Japan, China, and the US, which he sees making a "phase transition" from liberal rules-based order to moderate disorder. "Order" he defines in relation to stability. Ironically, China claims to be a major supporter of the global order and a leader on climate change and continuing globalization, yet it continues to operate under Chinese rules that incur global financial imbalances. Xi's initiatives since 2012—harder territorial claims, the BRI, the construction of a set of alternative multilateral financial institutions, the "China 2025" drive toward technological supremacy (followed by a similar fifteen-year plan broached at the 5th Plenum in October 2020), an arms budget consistently outpacing GDP growth—boldly challenge American leadership, precipitating a backlash. Japan and other Asian states find themselves caught in the middle, neither as liberal as the US nor as authoritarian as the PRC, with vital economic links to both. Challenged by both Xi's "assertiveness" and Trump's "America first" policies, neither of which it can wholly accept, Asia according to Wan finds itself in a "moderate phase transition" from order to greater (but still manageable) disorder. Though global trade has been declining of late, globalization will continue, though it

---

28. For example, Beijing cut its foreign aid from a high of $338 million in 2018 to $169 million in 2019 to just $5.62 million in new commitment in 2020 (as of October). Some of its BRI loan commitments (in the Philippines and Pakistan) have been quietly shelved.

is likely to fragment along regional lines. Following the lead of the Phase I Sino-US trade agreement, the world will, upon recovering from the coronavirus pandemic, move toward more managed trade and a stronger government role in the international economy.

Conclusion

East Asia currently finds itself in considerable disorder. It is thriving economically but is politically and ideologically disorganized, and nascent order is ineffectively defended. Asia is not unacquainted with disorder—amid rapid economic growth, it has been a region of constant turmoil, from the Korean War to the Asian financial crisis. But this is now a new kind of disorder. Previous disorders occurred within the clear and stable ideological framework of the Cold War. But the Cold War is no more, and though some nostalgically yearn to return via "decoupling," that would be a difficult and costly undertaking, in both sunk costs and opportunity costs. And there is no consensus on a framework to take us beyond globalization.[29] Like it or not, we are one world.

The economic dimension has been China's trump card, enabling it to rise from around 3 percent of global GDP in 1980 to about 16 percent in 2019. The Chinese global locomotive powered one-third of the world's GDP in the decade since the global financial crisis. And China has more recently begun to use its economic heft in pursuit of geopolitical goals—as in its boycott of Korean tourism and bankrupting Lotte markets following emplacement of the THAAD (Terminal High Altitude Defense) anti-missile system, or the cutoff of rare earth exports to Japan after the arrest of a Japanese fishing boat skipper in 2010, or the 2020 tariffs or bans on over a dozen Australian exports as punishment for calling for an independent investigation of the origins of the coronavirus (all unofficial, the leadership disclaimed any responsibility). China's ambitious BRI promises to transform the region, stimulating connectivity and growth and further extending Chinese influence.

It is too early to limn the outlines of the future order toward which the system is moving. The Chinese vision of a "community with shared future for mankind," or "win-win" is vaguely attractive but confronts a credibility gap in view of China's expansive territorial claims, the opaque terms of Chinese loans, and overall "promise fatigue." The ASEAN Charter is an appealing

---

29. For a cogent defense of decoupling, see Charles W. Boustany, Jr. and Aaron L. Friedberg, *Partial Decoupling: A New U.S. Strategy for Economic Competition with China*, National Bureau of Asian Research, NBR Special Report No. 82 (November 2019); see also Friedberg, "Competing with China," *Survival* 60, no. 3 (June 2018): 7–64, httpds://doi.org/10.108 0/00396338.2018.147055. For a Chinese perspective on decoupling, see Li Wei, "Towards Economic Decoupling? Mapping Chinese Discourse on the China-US Trade War," *The Chinese Journal on International Politics* (2019): 519–56, https://academic.oup.com/cjip/article-abstract/12/4/519/5650490.

model for the new Asian order, but ASEAN lacks the teeth to enforce either internal consensus or external security. The "Free and Open Asia-Pacific" framework, anchored in the Quad, is likewise a promising concept but not yet much more than that, and risks being abandoned by American electoral turnover or caught up in regional polarization. Economic "decoupling" is an American threat and certainly a risk going forward, but full realization faces insuperable interest group resistance. What is most likely in the near term? Globalization will continue to recede amid a nationalist quest for security, resulting in a reshuffling of global value chains (though China will fight to keep them). Polarization will also continue (albeit perhaps at a lower decibel level), shrinking the maneuvering room of the smaller countries. In my view, the most plausible emergent order is, however, not "Cold War II" but triangulation: Sino-US rivalry remains, while much of the rest of Asia tries to profit from both sides for as long as possible without taking sides.

Index

AAAD (anti-access, area denial) technologies, 82
Abe, Shinzo, 162, 182–83, 201, 204, 206, 208, 232–34
Abraham, Katharine, 231
ABS (Asian Barometer Survey), 32–54, 34n46, 242
Acemoglu, Daron, 107–8, 113
ACFTA (ASEAN-China Free Trade Agreement), 9, 189, 192, 201, 211
activist intervention, 94, 103, 115, 116, 243–44, 244n13
ADB (Asian Development Bank), 2
ADIZ (Air Defense Identification Zone), 148
ADMM-plus (ASEAN Defense Ministers Meeting Plus), 7, 188, 203
advanced capitalist economies, 94–95, 97, 99, 112, 156, 214
AEC (ASEAN Economic Community), 189
Aecon Construction, 85
AEI (American Enterprise Institute) investment tracker, 16n31, 208
AIIB (Asian Infrastructure Investment Bank), 7, 27, 201, 214
Air Defense Identification Zone (ADIZ), 148
alliances: and alliance-building, 84, 143–45, 149, 151, 172, 182; and Asia-Pacific, 76, 82, 84; bilateral, 5, 190, 245, 248; and East Asian security, 120; and economic competition, 167; and hedging, 176, 210; mutual defense, 10–11; and US-China-Japan triangle, 226, 232–33; and wedging, 206

America First policies, 181, 218, 221–22, 228–29, 239, 249
American empire, 103–6, 112
American Enterprise Institute, 208
American Enterprise Institute (AEI) investment tracker, 16n31, 208
anarchy, 226
Anglo-American capitalism, 226–27
Anglo-Saxon capitalism, 223–24
Anglo-Saxon culture, 104
anti-access, area denial (AAAD) technologies, 82
anti-corruption, 17, 231
anti-globalization, 114, 225
anti-immigration activists, 235
anti-imperialism, 206
anti-Japan demonstrations, 201, 244n14
anti-Japan TV, 67–71
anti-labor policy, 95–96
Anti-Secession Law, 184
anti-Taiwan independence, 62–67
anti-WTO protests, 113
APEC (Asia Pacific Economic Cooperation), 60, 133–34, 225
APT (ASEAN plus three), 9, 83, 188, 189, 192, 201
ARATS (Association for Relations Across the Taiwan Strait), 185
ARF (ASEAN Regional Forum), 10n20, 13, 188
ARIA (Asia Reassurance Initiative Act), 208n22, 239
arms races, 16, 143–44, 149, 156–57, 191–92
ASEAN. *See* Association of Southeast Asian Nations

ASEAN-China Free Trade Agreement (ACFTA), 9, 189, 192, 201, 211
ASEAN Defense Ministers Meeting Plus (ADMM-plus), 7, 188, 203
ASEAN Economic Community (AEC), 189
ASEAN-EU Annual Meetings (ASEM), 188
ASEAN plus three (APT), 9, 12, 83, 188, 189, 192, 201
ASEAN Regional Forum (ARF), 10n20, 13, 188
ASEM (ASEAN-EU Annual Meetings), 188
Asia for the Asians, 83, 196–97, 238n1
Asian Barometer Survey (ABS), 32–54, 34n46, 242
Asian century, 1–4
Asian Development Bank (ADB), 2
Asian disorder, 9–20, 141, 187–92, 220, 240
Asian Drama (Myrdal), 1
Asian financial crisis, 93, 104, 109, 189–90, 192, 200–201, 202
Asian Infrastructure Investment Bank (AIIB), 7, 27, 201, 214
Asian monetary fund, 201
Asian order, 8, 9, 75, 218–25
Asian Rebalance, 78, 145, 168, 190–91, 203–4
Asia-Pacific, 75–90, 141, 145, 147, 149–51, 200, 203
Asia Pacific Economic Cooperation (APEC), 60, 133–34, 225
"Asia-Pacific Security Cooperation," 79, 151
Asia Reassurance Initiative Act (ARIA), 208n22, 239
Asia Society report, 84, 88
Association for Relations Across the Taiwan Strait (ARATS), 185
Association of Southeast Asian Nations (ASEAN): and ASEAN-American relations, 202–4; and ASEAN-China relations, 192–96; and ASEAN-Japan relations, 196–201, 234; and the ASEAN way, 87–88, 187–89, 241; and Asian disorder, 187–92; and Asian identity, 241–42; bilateral trade, 136–37; and centrality, 204, 207, 245; and charm campaign, 9; and dual triangles, 204–14; and East Asia under China-USA rivalry, 122n9, 123, 134, 137; and peripheral diplomacy, 87–88; and retreat framework, 12n22; and rules-based order, 8; and Sino-American rivalry, 87; and South China Sea, 11–12
asymmetric strategic triangles, 169–75, 210, 226
Australia, 5, 84–87, 150, 244–45
authoritarian allies, 101–2, 115
authoritarian regimes, 93–94, 100, 102, 112, 115, 117, 119, 127, 198
authoritarian value orientations, 31, 41
authority, 4, 20, 31n39, 120, 155
automation, 231
autonomy, 3, 10, 110, 191, 210, 234, 243
Autor, David H., 231
Avent, Ryan, 232
Awami League, 4
Azar, Alexander, 152

bailout policy, 93, 105, 109
balance-of-power (BOP), 171–73
balance of threat theory, 172
balancing, 172–73
bandwagoning, 172–73
Bangladesh, 4, 195, 195n6
Bangladesh, China, India, Myanmar (BCIM), 195
Bank of China Foreign Exchange Certificate (*waihui quan*), 59
BCIM (Bangladesh, China, India, Myanmar), 195
Beijing Olympics, 60, 80
Belgrade, 93, 244n13
Belt and Road Initiative (BRI): and AEI investment tracker, 16n31; and ASEAN centrality, 245; and ASEAN-China relations, 194–96; and Asian century, 3; and Asian order, 13, 16–17; and canceled cooperation with China, 195–96n6; and Chinese assertiveness, 81; and competition, 146; and dispute issues, 147, 150; and domestic economic crisis of China, 116; and FONOPS, 239; and global affairs, 27–28; and innovation, 212; and

Japan, 183, 201; in Pakistan, 3n6; and perceptions of China, 29–30; and public diplomacy, 24–25
Berlin, Isaiah, 129–30
Better Utilization of Investment Lending and Development (BUILD), 208n22, 239
bide and hide strategy, 24
Biden, Joseph, 114, 219
bifurcation, 154–57, 161, 220, 223, 231
bilateral alliances, 5, 190, 245, 248
bilateralism, 80, 87, 133–34
bilateral negotiations, 11, 97
bilateral relationships, 11, 20, 119, 121, 184, 201
bilateral trade, 17–18, 134–37, 196, 211, 213, 237n46, 242, 247, 250
bipolarity, 4, 173, 248
black markets, 59
BOP (balance-of-power), 171–73
boycotts, 63–64, 183–84
Brady, Anne-Marie, 86
Brazil, Russia, India, China, South Africa (BRICS group), 7
Bretton Woods, 5, 7
Brexit, 113, 155, 158
BRI. *See* Belt and Road Initiative (BRI)
BRICS group (Brazil, Russia, India, China, South Africa), 7
BUILD (Better Utilization of Investment Lending and Development), 208n22, 239
Bull, Hedley, 219
Burma. *See* Myanmar
Bush, George H. W., 93, 178
Bush, George W., 105, 179
Buzan, Barry, 79

Cambodia, 4, 11, 13, 49–50, 193, 198–99, 208, 212, 242
Canada, 85–87, 137
capital accumulation, 106
capital export, 99
capital flight, 17, 109, 112
capitalism, 7, 14, 93–94, 98, 103, 125, 223–24, 226–27
Carnegie Endowment study, 146–47
CCCI (China Communications Construction Corporation International), 85

CCP. *See* Chinese Communist Party
CDB (China Development Bank), 16–17, 196
censorship, 3, 243–44
centralization, 15
CEPA (Comprehensive Economic Partnership Agreement), 201
CFC (Common Fund for Commodities), 235
CFIUS (Committee on Foreign Investment in the United States), 213
charm campaign, 8–9, 18, 49, 190, 200, 242
Chen Shui-bian, 177, 179, 184–85
Chiang Ching-kuo, 62–63
Chiang Mai Initiative, 201, 206
Chiba University, 73
Chimerica, 3n8, 109, 112, 122
China: and anti-Japan TV, 67–71; and ASEAN-American relations, 202–4; and ASEAN-China relations, 192–96; and ASEAN-Japan relations, 198–201; and Asian century, 1–4; and Asian disorder, 9–19; and Asian identity, 89–90; and Asian order, 222–25; assertiveness of, 79, 81–82, 87–88, 168–69, 181–82, 192–94, 203, 206, 210; and Australia, 85; authoritarian system of, 23, 30–31, 51, 112, 115, 116–17, 127, 131, 151–52, 157; and Canada, 85–87; Chinese Warring States, 118–24, 118n2, *121*, 131–38, 248–49; and competition with US, 167–69; and crisis management, 55–56; and the Cultural Revolution, 173n16; and dual triangles, 204–14; and East Asia international relations, 131–38; and economic hierarchy, 173–75; and economic state, 123–27, 129–31; and foreign policy, 27–32, 57–58; GDP of, 19n38; and global economy, 46–48, 106–12; and globalization, 51, 119, 127; and globalization-democratization project, 96, 105–6, 112–17; Great National Rejuvenation, 75, 77, 81, 194; and hedging, 175–77; and human rights, 6–7, 7n15, 25–26, 107, 114, 196, 222; and identities,

240–46; influence of, 7, 23–24, 26–27, 29–38, 40–46, 48, 51–52, 115–17, 233–34; and inter-imperial rivalry, 116–17; and international relations, 52; and Japan, 162, 182–83, 185; and liberal values, 51–52; and loans, 245n18; media, 15, 56, 62, 146, 154, 196, 231, 244; military, 28, 182, 189, 250; and New Zealand, 86–87; and one-China principle, 180, 185, 251; and open-door policies, 58–60; and patriotic industry, 68–74; and patriotic vigilantes, 62–67; and perceptions of influence in Asia, 32–46; and peripheral diplomacy, 87–90; post-cold War era, 6–9; and power transition, 182; and public diplomacy, 23–27, 48–49; and regime evaluation, 51; role in the Asia-Pacific, 75–84; and Sino-American naval encounters, 214; and Sino-American rivalry, 86–87, 120–23, 127–31, 133–37, 144–63, 167–69, 225, 249–50; and Sino-Soviet dispute, 5–6; and socialism, 79–81; and socioeconomic perception, 51; and Southeast Asia, 189–92; and South Korea, 183–84; and strategic rivalry, 144–63; and strategies, 246–50; and Taiwan, 62–67, 123–25, 179–81, 184–86; and trade war, 167–68, 168n4, 234; and US-China-Japan triangle, 225–35; variable information, 53–54
China Communications Construction Corporation International (CCCI), 85
China Daily (newspaper), 146
China Development Bank (CDB), 16–17, 196
China Pakistan Economic Corridor (CPEC), 3n6, 196n6
Chinese Coast Guard, 194
Chinese Communist Party (CCP): and Asian order, 221; and the Asia-Pacific, 82, 88; and cross-Strait relations, 180; and economic development, 131; and the GFC, 10; and ideology, 249n23; and international payments, 112; and international relations, 168; and leadership, 15; and market reform, 107; and multilateral trading order, 77; and overseas organizing, 72–73; and perceptions of China, 30; and public diplomacy, 25; and taxation, 157; and threat perceptions, 146; and trade war, 232
Chinese Dream, 69, 88
Chinese Solution, 81
Chinese Warring States, 118–24, 118n2, *121*, 131–38, 248–49
Chou Tsu-yu, 66–67
Chunxiao field, 11
Chu (state), 121
CICA (Conference on International Confidence Building Measures in Asia), 7, 206, 245
citizenship, 61–62
civilian technologies, 158–59, 214
Clark Air Force Base, 192
Clash of Civilizations (Huntington), 103
clash of civilizations thesis, 103–5
climate change, 222
Clinton, Bill, 104–5, 107, 128, 178
Clinton, Hillary, 13, 113–14, 193, 228
code of conduct, 12, 189, 193, 206–7
coercion, 3, 130–31, 193
Colaresi, Michael, 143
Cold War, 4–9, 76, 95, 100, 125–30, 144, 205, 221, 224
collective identity, 19–20, 244–45
collectivism, 31
Collier, Paul, 226–27
colonialism, 1, 11, 196–97
COMECON (Committee on Mutual Economic Assistance), 5
commercial patriotism, 68–74
Committee on Foreign Investment in the United States (CFIUS), 213
Committee on Mutual Economic Assistance (COMECON), 5
Common Fund for Commodities (CFC), 235
communism, 5, 8–9, 14–15, 94–95, 103
community of common destiny, 82–83, 88–89, 194, 241
competition. *See also* hedging: and American hegemony, 82, 94; and arms racing, 149; and coercion, 131;

Index 259

and collapse of Soviet Union, 103–4; and decoupling, 214; and dual triangles, 211–12; and economic security, 124; hard-power, 46–48; and inter-imperial rivalry, 116–17, 248; and inter-state politics, 132; and manufacturing jobs, 231; and multilateralization, 149–50; and post-Cold War globalization, 129; Sino-US, 1–2, 23–24, 33, 48, 151–61; and strategic rivalry, 141–46, 151–61; and trade wars, 167–68, 168n4
complex bilateralism, 80
complex systems perspective, 221–23
Comprehensive and Progressive Agreement for Trans-Pacific Partnership (CPTPP), 2, 87, 206–7, 225
Comprehensive Economic Partnership Agreement (CEPA), 201
Conference on Dialogue of Asian Civilizations, 89
Conference on International Confidence Building Measures in Asia (CICA), 7, 206, 245
Confucian culture, 89–90
Confucius Institutes, 25
conscription, 157
constant-sum, 173
constant war mode, 124
consumer markets, 96–99
consumption, 97–101, 107, 109
containment policy, 88, 147, 199
"Course Correction: Toward an effective and sustainable China Policy" (Asia Society), 88
COVID-19 pandemic, 15, 19, 55–56, 90, 114, 148, 149, 201, 213, 228, 232
cow's tongue line. *See* nine-dash line
CPEC (China Pakistan Economic Corridor), 3n6, 196n6
CPTPP (Comprehensive and Progressive Agreement for Trans-Pacific Partnership), 2, 87, 206–7, 225
cross-Strait relationships, 177–80, 184–85
Cross-Strait Service Trade Agreement, 29
crotch bomb hero, 68
Cuban Missile Crisis, 144
cultural diplomacy, 24–25

cultural identities, 159
cultural particularism, 80
cultural resources, 79
Cultural Revolution, 173n16
cultural superiority, 63
culture, 31
currency, 7, 59, 98–99, 101, 110–11, 247. *See also* renminbi (RMB); USD (US dollars)
cyberattacks, 233
cyber weapons, 160–61

Davidson, Philip, 209
Davos, 230
Declaration on Conduct of Parties in the South China Sea (DOC), 9, 11, 189
Declaration on the Conduct of Parties, 200
decoupling, 212–14
defense spending, 144–46, 149–50, 159–60. *See also* weaponry
defensive weapons systems, 12
defined order, 4
de-globalization, 119, 127–28, 130–31, 133, 137
democracy, 17, 30, 31n39, 41, 43–48, 51–52, 54, 93, 103–5, 116, 128–31, 151–52, 227, 239, 243
democracy promotion project, 100–101, 115
Democratic Party, 114, 230
Democratic Party of Japan (DPJ), 182, 232
Democratic People's Republic of Korea (DPRK). *See* North Korea
Democratic Progressive Party (DPP), 66, 181, 184–86
democratic regimes, 102
Democratic Republic of Vietnam (DRV). *See* North Vietnam
democratization, 77, 101–2, 106
demographic and social trends, 2, 153–55
Deng Xiaoping, 6, 8, 10, 14, 24, 58–59, 80, 106–7, 168, 192, 242–43
Deng Yuwen, 82
developing countries, 14, 28n25, 100, 102, 107, 113, 115–17, 245n18, 247
DFC (US International Development Finance Corporation), 208–9n22

dialogue partners, 188–90
Diaoyu Islands. *See* Senkaku Islands
Dickinson, Goldsworthy Lowes, 226
Diehl, P. F., 142–43
digital silk road, 196
diplomatic relations, 85, 106, 192, 197–98, 223
disruptive governments, 223
Dittmer, Lowell, 225
DOC (Declaration on Conduct of Parties in the South China Sea), 9, 11, 189
domestic politics, 30, 85, 169, 177, 179, 184, 219, 223
Dorn, David, 231
DPJ (Democratic Party of Japan), 182, 232
DPP (Democratic Progressive Party), 66, 181, 184–86
DPRK. *See* North Korea
Dreyer, David, 143
DRV. *See* North Vietnam
dual citizenship, 61–62
dual hierarchy, 76
dual triangles, 204–12
Duterte, Rodrigo, 4, 13, 193

EAS (East Asian Summit), 188, 201, 203, 214
East Asia: and Asian order, 221; and COVID-19 pandemic, 19; economies, 1–2, 82, 136–38, 208, 219, 224–25; economy-predominance, 125; globalization, 119–20; and hedging, 177; identities, 19–20; international relations in, 131–38, 168; under PRC-USA rivalry, 120–23; regional international relations, 118, 138; and rules-based order, 8; security environment, 76; strategic triangles, 169, 173–75; strategies, 20; territorial disputes, 124; triangles, 20
East Asian Summit (EAS), 188, 201, 203, 214
East China Sea, 10–11, 34, 36, 41, 148, 201, 209, 222
East Coast Rail Link, 29–30
East-West Corridor, 195
economics. *See also* global economy: and ASEAN-American relations, 202; and ASEAN-China relations, 192–96; and Canada, 85–86; and Chinese Warring States, 118–38; and decoupling, 212–14; and economic globalization, 40–46; and economic growth, 6–7, 27–28, 46, 106, 112, 130–31, 153–54, 157, 204, 230; and economic hierarchy, 173; and economic state, 125–32; and economic threat, 132–35; and free-trade international order, 224; and hedging, 175–76, 180; and interdependence, 119, 133, 135, 137, 139, 161; and Japan, 197; and market reform, 100–101; and modernization, 246; and neoliberalism, 129, 129n30; and political economy, 7, 97, 120, 132, 135, 219, 224, 231; and postwar boom, 94–95, 154; and reform, 10, 15, 168; and security, 124–25; and Trump, 182; and US-China-Japan triangle, 226–35; and US-China rivalry, 155–57, 167–69
Economist (magazine), 137
EEZ (exclusive economic zone), 10–11, 13, 87, 193, 194, 210, 235
electronic communications, 158–59
elephant curve (Milanovic), 112, 230
elites, 58–60, 119, 137–38, 153, 154–55, 157, 159, 161–63, 224, 226, 244
emergent order, 4
The End of History and the Last Man (Fukuyama), 103
end of history thesis, 80, 103–4
engagement, 172
English School, 79, 219
"Escape from Asia" (Yukichi), 204
Esper, Mark T., 182
ethnic Chinese nationals, 150
EU (European Union), 155, 158, 222, 237n46
Eurasian Economic Union, 207
European communism, 8, 15, 244
European imperialism, 4–5, 188, 191, 206
European Union (EU), 155, 158, 222, 237n46
exclusive economic zone (EEZ), 10–11, 13, 87, 193, 194, 210, 235
exorbitant privilege, 98, 247

Export-Import Bank, 16–17, 196
export-oriented growth, 1–2, 8, 95–97, 107, 246–47
exports, 95–103, 107, 109, 114
extra-national identities, 158

farcical anti-Japan TV (*kangri shenju*), 67–68, 70–71
FDI (foreign direct investment), 15, 19, 27, 100, 196, 200, 201–2n12, 202, 208, 213, 242, 247
Ferguson, Niall, 3n8, 109
5th Central Committee Plenum of the CPC, 12–13
financial crises, 115–16
First Island Chain, 75, 209
fiscal constraints, 157
fiscal crises, 95, 115–16
fishing, 193–94
Fitch survey, 208
five do-not-adopts, 72
"Five Principles of Peaceful Coexistence," 77, 246
fixed asset investment, 108, 116, 250
FOIP (Free and Open Indo-Pacific Policy), 145, 147, 191, 204, 207, 239
FONOPs (freedom of navigation operations), 13, 87, 152, 193–94, 204, 207–8, 210–11, 239
forced technology transfers, 231
Foreign Affairs (magazine), 103
foreign-bound personnel (*chuguo renyuan*), 59
foreign contacts, 59
foreign direct investment (FDI), 15, 19, 27, 100, 196, 200, 201–2n12, 202, 208, 213, 242, 247
foreign exchange reserves, 98–99, 108–9, 115, 195
foreign intervention, 58
foreign-oriented system (*duiwai xitong*), 59
foreign permanent residence, 61
foreign policy: and ASEAN-China relations, 87–88, 192; and Asian order, 223; and bide and hide strategy, 24; and China's favorability, 36–38; and ideological and cultural frames, 77–79; and inequality and political polarization, 154–55; and international multilateralism, 134; Japanese autonomy in, 234–35; and liberal order, 222–23; Mao's interventionist, 57–58; and open-door policies, 58–59; and organized labor, 95–96; and Sino-US relations, 32–33; and Taiwan, 184–86; and Trump, 17–18, 227; and US interventionism, 104; under Xi's leadership, 27–33
Free and Open Indo-Pacific Policy (FOIP), 145, 147, 191, 204, 207, 239
freedom of navigation operations (FONOPs), 13, 87, 152, 193–94, 204, 207–8, 210–11, 239
free flow of capital, 93, 101
free markets, 101, 103–4, 130
free trade, 18, 29, 85–87, 101–2, 105, 108, 113–15. *See also* global free trade
free trade agreement (FTA), 184, 189, 203, 207, 228, 233
FTA (free trade agreement), 184, 189, 203, 207, 228, 233
Fukuda Doctrine, 198, 200
Fukuyama, Francis, 103–4
Funabashi, Yoichi, 233

G-20, 222
GDP (gross domestic product): and the Asian century, 1–3; and BRI loans, 196; and China's economic performance, 16; and China's foreign policy, 27; and China's political economy, 229; and COVID-19 pandemic, 19, 213; and export-oriented growth, 8; and globalization, 134; and great power politics, 10; and hedging, 177; per capita of China, *108*; and power transition, 182; and Sino-Japanese relations, 200; and slow growth, 156; and Southeast Asia, 2, 188; and tariffs, 211–12; and wages, 107
geo-economics, 119, 120, 129, 132
Germany, 229
Ge Tian, 67–68, 71
GFC (global financial crisis), 2–3, 10, 12, 15, 105, 109, 116, 168, 211
global capitalist system, 106, 116
global competition, 129, 131
global dollar standard, 98–99, 109–10

global economy, 29, 40–41, 46–47, 51, 58, 90, 96–97, 99, 105–12, 134, 156–57, 229–30, 234, 239n2
global exceptionalism, 83
global financial crisis (GFC), 2, 10, 12, 15, 105, 109, 116, 168, 211
global free trade, 15, 27, 97, 99–100, 102, 104, 107, 112–14
globalism, 15, 17, 93, 116
globalization. *See also* de-globalization; global economy: and Asian economy, 224; and BRI, 24; China-led, 132–35, 229–31; economic dimension of, 40–46; explanatory accounts, 35, 51; and free markets, 103–4; and geo-economics, 119; globalization-democratization project, 93–103, 105–6, 112–17; in post-Cold War era, 6, 125–31; and rules-based order, 8, 17; and Trump, 228; US-led, 96–103, 226–27
global markets, 107, 213, 232
Global North, 112–13
global order, 4–5, 76–77, 84, 105, 239, 246
global public goods, 49, 80–81
global reserve currency, 7, 98, 247
global role, 77
Global South, 24, 100, 115
global supply chains, 96, 228
Global Times (newspaper), 63–64, 147
global value chains, 18–19, 214
Goertz, G., 142
Goh, Evelyn, 175n19
gold standard, 95, 98
government spending, 154
gray zone, 190, 210
Great Britain, 227
great digital firewall, 212
Greater East Asia Co-Prosperity Sphere, 82, 196–97
great leap forward, 14, 192
great power politics, 10, 10n20, 13, 17, 24, 78–79, 142–44, 149, 151–53, 168–69, 171–73, 176, 183, 191–92, 220, 223
Great Proletarian Cultural Revolution, 14
Great Recession, 80, 82

Great Rejuvenation of the Chinese Nation, 15, 24, 75, 77, 81, 194, 244–45
Group of 20, 7, 239

Han Kuo-yu, 125
Hanson, Gordon H., 231
hard power, 24, 26, 27, 32–33, 34, 36–37, 40, 46–47
harmonious world, 9, 78, 80, 200
harmony without sameness, 76, 83–84, 241n7
Harper, Stephen, 85
hedging, 169, 172–81, 175n19, 176n22, 183–86, 206–7, 210, 251
hegemonic rivalry, 168–69, 171–72
hegemonic stability, 190
hegemony, 82, 94–95
Hengdian, China, 71
hezong, 118–21, 118n2, 120–21n6, 132–37
hierarchies, 31, 142–43, 173
Hong Kong, 3, 14, 64–65, 106–7, 110–12, 122n9, 158
household registration (*hukou*), 61–62
Huang, Michael, 66–67
Huawei Corporation, 33, 86, 145, 207, 213–14, 229, 248–49
Hu Jintao, 24, 32, 78, 80, 180, 185, 242
hukou (household registration), 61–62
humanitarian intervention, 104–6
human rights, 6–7, 7n15, 10, 25–26, 107, 114, 178, 196, 222, 223
human wave strategy, 58–60
Hun Sen, 4
Huntington, Samuel, 103–5
Hu-Wen regime, 24
hybrid democracy, 3

IBRD (International Bank for Reconstruction and Development), 245n18
ICCPR (International Covenant on Civil and Political Rights), 9
ICE (Independent Commission of Enquiry), 199
ICESCR (International Covenant on Economic, Social and Cultural Rights), 9

identities, 19–20, 75–84, 89–90, 158–59, 177, 180, 184–86, 204, 240–46, 249n23
identity gap, 9, 185
ideology, 249n23
IGOs (international governmental organizations), 6–7
Ikeda, 199
Ikenberry, G. John, 9, 76, 87
IMF (International Monetary Fund), 5, 6–7, 16, 27, 100–101, 102, 105, 192
immigrants, 129
immigration, 225, 235
immobilization, 60
imperialism, 4–5, 188, 191, 206
imports, 18n36, 167, 213, 231
import-substitution industrialization, 100, 102, 212–14
income gap, 230
Independent Commission of Enquiry (ICE), 199
India, 4, 7, 28, 149–50, 195, 202–4, 225, 239
individualism, 31, 90, 104, 241
Indonesia, 4, 38, 49, 50, 192, 194–95, 197–99, 203, 205, 208–9, 242
Indonesian Communist Party (PKI), 198–99
Indo-Pacific. *See* Asia-Pacific
Indo-Pacific Strategy, 234
industrialization, 100, 102, 154, 212–14
industrialized democracies, 128–29, 157
industrialized economies, 94–96
industrial policies, 129, 212–14, 248
inequality, 154–55
inflation, 16, 95, 100
information acquisition, 40, 51
information technologies, 153, 158
infrastructure, 13, 16, 57–58, 194–96, 204, 208
Inglehart, Ronald, 155
innovation, 212
intellectual property rights (IPR), 229, 231
inter-imperial rivalry, 115–17, 248
internal security spending, 154
International Bank for Reconstruction and Development (IBRD), 245n18
International Coffee Agreement, 235
international contacts, 59

International Covenant on Civil and Political Rights (ICCPR), 9
International Covenant on Economic, Social and Cultural Rights (ICESCR), 9
International Crisis Group, 86
international debt crisis, 100
international governmental organizations (IGOs), 6–7
international law, 10, 13, 209
International Monetary Fund (IMF), 5, 6–7, 16, 27, 100–101, 102, 105, 192
international multilateralism, 134
international order, 4, 6, 8, 138, 168, 218–22, 224, 235
international payments, 110–12
international peace, 151
international political economy, 24, 132–38
international relations, 35, 52, 119, 122–23, 131–38, 168, 223
international society, 79
international system, 120, 223–25, 227
international tourism, 27
international transaction currency, 98, 110
International Tribunal on the Law of the Sea (ITLOS), 13
International Whaling Commission (IWC), 235
Internet, 10, 14, 158, 160, 212
inter-state conflict, 132, 141, 142–43, 161, 247
inter-state relations, 124–25, 152
investment, 3n6, 15–17, 27–29, 96, 102, 104, 109, 116, 195–96, 201–2n12, 202–4, 208, 239, 250. *See also* foreign direct investment (FDI)
IPR (intellectual property rights), 229, 231
island building, 29, 32, 34
isolationism, 159
issue spirals, 143
ITLOS (International Tribunal on the Law of the Sea), 13
IWC (International Whaling Commission), 235

Japan: and anti-Japan TV, 67–71; and ASEAN-Japan relations, 196–201;

and Asian century, 2; and Asian order, 5, 221–22; and bilateral trade relations, 134–37; and capitalism, 227; and China, 162, 182–83, 185; and cohort observations, 34, 36–38; and dual triangles, 204–8, 210–11; and multilateralization, 150; and political economy, 229; and Senkaku islands, 10–11; and strategic rivalry, 162; and trade disputes, 227; and US-China-Japan triangle, 225–37
Japanese Democratic Party (JDP), 206
Japan-EU Economic Partnership Agreement, 233
Japan External Trade Organization (JETRO), 201n12
JDP (Japanese Democratic Party), 206
Jeju Air, 64
JETRO (Japan External Trade Organization), 201n12
Jiang Zemin, 80, 177, 206
Jin Canrong, 69, 71
Jin Yinan, 69
joint development, 11, 83
Justice Pao (TV series), 66
JYP Entertainment, 66

Kang, David, 191
kangri shenju (farcical anti-Japan TV series), 67–71
Kearney, Melissa, 231
Kennedy, John F., 55
Kim Jong-un, 234
Kissinger, Henry, 4
KMT (Kuomintang) government, 180, 185
Konfrontasi, 199
Kovrig, Michael, 86
Ko Wen-je, 125
Kuik, C. C., 175n19, 176n22
Kuomintang (KMT) government, 180, 185

labor, 16, 94–96, 99–100, 102, 107–9, 112–13, 188, 223, 247
land reclamation, 38
Laos, 8, 9, 187, 191, 193, 198, 208
LDP (Liberal Democratic Party), 182, 232, 235
Lee Kuan-yew, 4, 63, 179

Lee Teng-hui, 177
legal relativism, 14
legitimacy, 20, 84, 112–13, 232
level of competition, 145–46, 151
lianheng, 118–21, 118n2, 120–21n6, 132, 134–38
liberal democracy, 3, 30, 41–48, 54, 103–5, 239
Liberal Democratic Party (LDP), 182, 232, 235
liberal internationalism, 89
liberalism, 80–82
liberal order, 8–10, 84–90, 222–25
liberal values, 31, 35, 41–46, 51–52, 81
Liberation, 213
Lighthizer, Robert, 182
Li Keqiang, 3
Lin, Ruby, 65–66
Little Red Book (Mao Zedong), 58
Liu He, 229
Liu Huaqing, 209
Liu Xiang, 67–68
Liu Xiaobo, 69
living standard, 112
Li Yi, 56
local governments, 71
Lotte markets, 183–84
Lower Mekong Initiative, 203
low wage regime, 107
Luo Yuan, 59, 68

Made in China 2025, 145, 212–13
MAGA (Make America Great Again), 83, 128, 185
Mair, Victor, 55
major powers, 142–43, 188
Make America Great Again (MAGA), 83, 128, 185
Malaysia, 4, 30, 38, 49, 50, 150, 194–95, 199, 201, 203–4, 208–10, 212
Manila, Philippines, 13
manufacturing jobs, 16, 18n36, 96, 99, 107–10, 113, 129, 231, 247
manufacturing profits, 94–95
Maoism, 82
Mao Xinyu, 70
Mao Zedong, 57–58, 62–64, 173n16, 199
Marine Self-Defense Force (MSDF), 208
maritime disputes, 10, 124, 150–51, 162, 206

Maritime East Asia, 82
maritime militia, 12, 194
market capitalism, 7, 247
market economy status, 23
marketization, 14, 17
market reform, 101, 106–7, 231, 247–48
MAR (missing-at-random) hypothesis, 35
marriage, 170–71, 173, 176–77
Marshall Plan, 5
Marxism-Leninism, 6, 77–80, 249n23
masses, 57–62, 243–44, 244n14. *See also* One China Policy
mass immobilization, 60
mass media, 25, 158
mass mobilization, 58–60, 158–59
mass transportation, 158–59
Mastanduno, Michael, 78
materialistic privileges, 59
Mattis, Jim, 182
Ma Ying-Jeou, 169, 179–81, 185, 251
Memory of the World Register, 235
ménage à trois, 170–71, 173, 178–80
Meng Wanzhou, 86
mentality revolution, 158
Mercedes Benz, 64
Mexican peso crisis of 1994, 93, 104–5, 116
middle classes, 2, 10, 112, 154, 230, 243–44, 250
middle power, 184
Middle Powers and China's Rise (Ikenberry), 87
Milanovic, Branko, 112, 230
military: and American empire, 105; and arms racing, 149, 151; Chinese, 28, 182, 189; and competition, 145–46; and economic security, 124; expenditures, 28, 149, 154, 156–57, 160, 177; and security-related disputes, 147–48; and South China Sea, 29, 32, 34, 47, 152; and strategic rivalries, 144; technologies, 159–60, 214; and US supremacy, 98–99
mini-triangle, 170, 177–78
minotaurs, 188, 188n2
Minowa Yasufumi, 70
miracle of rapid growth, 211, 224, 246–47
missile scare of 1995–1996, 177–78, 200

missing-at-random (MAR) hypothesis, 35
modernization, 2, 15, 149, 159–60, 241, 246
modern state, 130, 163
monetary tightening campaign, 95, 100–101
Moon Jae-in, 184
morality, 14
Most Favored Nation status, 106
MSDF (Marine Self-Defense Force), 208
multilateral diplomacy, 17, 245
multilateralism, 78–80, 133–34, 235
multilateralization, 143–44, 149–50, 201, 206
multilateral trading order, 76–77
multinational defense alliances, 5
Muslim unrest, 196
mutual defense alliances, 10–11
Myanmar, 3, 29, 34, 49, 187, 191, 195, 199, 203, 208, 242
My Boy (TV drama), 65–66
Myrdal, Gunnar, 1

Naim, Moses, 158
Nanjing Massacre, 235
National Bureau of Economic Research study, 231
National Defense Strategy, 23, 117
national identities, 177, 180, 184, 219
nationalism, 15, 17, 68, 159, 182, 184
Nationalist Chinese, 11
national liberation movements, 198
national liberation wars, 5, 188, 191, 241
national security, 23, 183–84, 213
National Security Strategy, 23, 146
national self-determination, 5, 83
nation-building, 11, 19, 240
nation-states, 4, 19, 159, 191, 197
NATO (North Atlantic Treaty Organization), 5, 93, 104, 144
Natuna Island, 210
naval warships, 204n17
neoliberalism, 129, 129n30
neoliberalization, 130n31
Nepal, 195, 195n6
"New Asian Security Concept," 206–7, 245–46
new great power relationship, 24, 75, 78, 81, 84

Ne Win, 199
new international division of labor, 95, 247
New Miyazawa Initiative, 200
new world order, 8, 9, 93, 102, 104, 115–17, 188, 240, 247
New Zealand, 84–87, 150
nine-dash line, 11, 13, 32, 87, 192–93
1992 Consensus, 177, 180, 184–85
9/11 terrorist attack, 105
Nixon, Richard, 5, 57, 95, 98, 106, 192
non-interference, 6, 12n22, 77, 189
non-market economy, 86, 207
North American Free Trade Agreement, 228
North Atlantic Treaty Organization (NATO), 5, 93, 104, 144
North Korea, 4, 9, 75, 125n14, 133, 136–37, 152, 183–84, 211, 234
North-South Economic Corridor, 195
North Vietnam, 5, 11

Obama, Barack, 78, 81, 114, 145, 190–91, 203–4, 209, 228
ODA ("official developmental assistance"), 197, 200, 205
OFDI (out-going investment), 208
"official developmental assistance" (ODA), 197, 200, 205
off-shoring, 16, 107, 113, 200, 202n12, 247, 249
Okinawa, Japan, 68
One China Policy, 63–67
one-China principle, 180, 185, 251
open-door policies, 58–60
open regionalism, 83
Operation Red Sea (film), 74
organized labor, 94–96, 99–100, 108, 112–13
out-going investment (OFDI), 208
Outlook on the Indo-Pacific, 204, 204n18, 207n19

Pacific War, 76, 197
Pakistan, 3n6, 28, 195, 196n6
Paris Agreement, 222
Park Geun-hye, 183
"Partnership for Quality Infrastructure," 208
patriotic education campaign, 15, 244

patriotic industry, 68–74
patriotic vigilantes, 62–67, 244
Pax Americana, 206, 219
payoff, 176–79
peacekeeping organizations, 8
Peace of Westphalia, 4
peasant economy, 106
People's Liberation Army Navy (PLAN), 12n23
People's Liberation Army (PLA), 25, 69, 82, 149–50, 157, 159–60
People's Republic of China (PRC). *See* China
People's Revolution, 102
peripheral diplomacy, 87–88
Permanent Court of Arbitration, 13
personalization, 15
personal values, 158
Pew Survey, 33, 147
phase transitions, 220, 223–25
Philippines, 4, 5, 12–13, 25, 32, 38, 87, 150, 190, 192–94, 197, 201, 203, 208–9, 245. *See also* Scarborough Shoal
Piketty, Thomas, 154
pivot, 175, 190–91, 207, 212
Pivot to East Asia. *See* Asian Rebalance
PKI (Indonesian Communist Party), 198–99
PLA Military Academy, 69–70
PLA Navy, 209
PLAN (People's Liberation Army Navy), 12n23
PLA (People's Liberation Army), 25, 69, 82, 149–50, 157, 159–60
Plaza agreement, 200, 247
polarization, 4, 23–24, 154–55, 207, 212–14
Polar Silk Road, 194
policy blunders, 61–62
Politburo Standing Committee, 209
political crisis management, 55–56
political economy, 7, 97, 120, 132, 135, 219, 224, 231
political identity, 19
political polarization, 154–55
population aging, 153–55, 231, 250
populist politics, 113–14
positional disputes, 142–43, 249–50
post–Cold War era, 6–9, 125–31, 136–37

post-industrial age, 141, 151–63
post–Vietnam War period, 199–200
postwar economic boom, 94–95, 154
postwar order, 75, 222
power asymmetry, 170–73
power parity, 168, 168n5
power politics, 10, 17, 188, 191, 220, 239–40
power transition, 168, 168n5, 180, 182–83
PRC. *See* China
private consumption, 109
profitability crisis, 95, 96, 100
propaganda, 23–24, 152
protectionism, 233
proxy war, 152
pseudo-panel method, 33–35, 50
public diplomacy, 23–27, 40, 46–49, 243
punitive tariffs, 167

Qin empire, 119, 120–22, 132, 135, 137
Qing empire, 83
Qi (state), 121–22, 135

Rasler, Karen A., 143
RCEP (Regional Comprehensive Economic Partnership), 2, 83, 87, 188–89, 207, 225, 233
Reagan, Ronald, 95, 100, 101
reconciliation, 180, 185, 197–98
redemption, 205
Red Flag (journal), 72
reform and opening, 6, 14, 191, 224–25, 230, 241, 243
reform(s), 7–8, 10, 14–15, 30, 48, 100–102, 106–7, 224–25, 228, 243, 247–48
regime change, 105, 115–16, 224, 230–32
regime evaluation, 30–31, 35, 41–47, 51
regional arms spending, 191–92
Regional Comprehensive Economic Partnership (RCEP), 2, 83, 87, 188–89, 207, 225, 233
regional identity, 90
regional integration, 82, 187, 201
regional international politics, 125, 133–34, 138
regionalization, 158
regional security, 147, 223
regional trade, 152, 203
relative deprivation, 230
religious minorities, 3, 25–26

renminbi (RMB), 107–12
repression, 231
repression of dissent, 3
reserve labor, 107, 113
resilience, 220
retreat framework, 12n22
revisionist powers, 117, 146
Rhodium, 196
rights defense movement, 10
rivalries. *See also* strategic rivalries: Sino-American, 86–87, 120–23, 127–31, 133–37, 144–63, 167–69, 225, 249–50; Sino-Japanese, 200; strategic, 141–63; US-Soviet, 144, 169–70
RMB (renminbi), 107–12
role models, 31–32
romantic triangle, 170–73, 207, 211
Roosevelt corollary, 197, 197n7
Ross, Wilbur, 182
Rozman, Gilbert, 9, 249n23
rules-based order, 8, 9–10, 14, 17–18, 77–84, 88–89, 239, 240, 245
rural surplus labor, 107
Russia, 4, 5, 9, 33, 104, 117, 147, 149, 190, 234–35
Russian Navy, 192
Rwanda genocide of 1994, 104

salami tactics, 12, 203, 209–10
Sanders, Bernie, 113–14
Scarborough Shoal, 12, 150, 190, 210
SCO (Shanghai Cooperation Organization), 7, 27–28, 201
SDR (Special Drawing Rights), 7
SEATO (Southeast Asia Treaty Organization), 5
Second Persian Gulf War, 93
security: and alliances, 120; and ASEAN-American relations, 202; and Asia-Pacific, 82, 85; and China, 7; and Cold War order, 5–6; and disputes, 147–48, 152, 222; and economics, 124–25; and hedging, 175–76; and hegemonic stability, 190; hierarchy, 173; and international relations, 137–38; and security threat, 40–46, 49, 133, 146–47, 176, 181; and Taiwan, 152
SEF (Strait Exchange Foundation), 185

Senkaku Islands, 10–11, 150, 152, 162, 182, 201
seven do-not-talks, 71–72
Shanghai, 61–63
Shanghai Cooperation Organization (SCO), 7, 27–28, 201
Shangri-La Dialogue, 7, 25, 25n9
shared prosperity, 81
Sheik Hasina, 4
Shigeru, Yoshida, 197
Shinawatra, Thaksin, 3
Shi Tianjian, 31n39
Shi Zhongpeng, 71
Shojiro, Kawashima, 199
Sichuan TV, 67–68
Silk Road Economic Belt, 194–95
Singapore, 4, 25, 63, 87, 185, 207, 208
Sino-American naval encounters, 214
Sino-American rivalry, 86–87, 120–23, 127–31, 133–37, 144–63, 167–69, 225, 249–50
Sino-American trade, 15–16, 18, 135–36, 167, 168n4, 189, 201, 210–11, 237n46
Sino-Canadian relations, 85–87
Sino-Japanese relations, 182–83, 201, 225
Sino-Japanese rivalry, 200
Sino-Soviet dispute, 5–6
Sino-US relations, 32–34
SLORC (State Law and Order Restoration Council), 199
slow growth, 154, 156–57, 163
SMCs (small and medium countries), 169, 171–73, 175–76, 180–86, 251
smile campaign, 11, 200
social contagion model, 32n40
social democratic policies, 94
social globalization, 40
socialism, 79–81
social values, 155
socioeconomic perception, 35, 40, 51
SOEs (state-owned enterprises), 15–16, 106, 195–96
soft-balancing, 176
soft power, 26, 27, 29, 32–33, 47–48
Sopiee, Noordin, 189
South China Sea: and ASEAN-Japan relations, 201; and Asian disorder, 10–12, 190; and claimants, 41–47; and dual triangles, 214; and FONOPs, 207–8; nine-dash line, 11, 32, 192–93; and perceptions of China's influence, 34–36, 41; and security-related disputes, 148, 152, 222; and Sino-American rivalry, 87; and smile campaign, 200; and sovereignty, 10–13, 29, 32–33, 65–66, 189, 193–94, 209; and US Navy, 250n25
Southeast Asia. See also Association of Southeast Asian Nations (ASEAN): and ASEAN-American relations, 202–4; and Asian disorder, 187–92; and charm campaign, 200; Chinese investment in, 202n13; and democratic recession, 3; and dual triangles, 205, 207; and GDP (gross domestic product), 2; and Japan, 196–98, 201–2n12, 205; and polarization, 213–14; and South China Sea, 11; US military presence in, 203n14
Southeast Asia Treaty Organization (SEATO), 5
Southern Economic Corridor, 195
southern tour (*nanxun*) speeches, 8
Southern Tour of 1991–1992, 80
South Korea, 4, 134, 137, 148, 183–85, 189, 234–35
South Vietnam, 11, 197–98
sovereignty: and Asian disorder, 9–14, 19–20; and Chinese narrative of identity, 83; and international order, 4; and international relations, 223; and international society, 79; and Japan's postwar economic reconstruction, 197; national, 4, 6; and new Asian order, 246; South China Sea, 10–13, 29, 32–33, 65–66, 189, 193–94, 209; and spatial issues, 142; and Taiwan, 122n9, 124
Soviet Bloc, 5, 128
Soviet Union, 5–6, 102–3, 106, 144, 169–70, 198
space technology, 28
space weapons, 160–61
spatial issues, 142–43, 249–50
Spavor, Michael, 86
Special Drawing Rights (SDR), 7
Special Friendship Stores, 59
spiritual pollution, 63
Spratly Islands, 152

Sri Lanka, 195–96
stability, 220, 223–25
stability maintenance, 131
state bank lending, 116
state capitalist system, 106, 112
state coercion, 127, 130–31
State Law and Order Restoration Council (SLORC), 199
state-market dichotomy, 130
state-owned enterprises (SOEs), 15–16, 106, 195–96
state survival, 118, 123–24
status quo, 23–24, 179, 190, 206, 213, 219, 223–24, 229, 232, 244n14
steps to war process, 144
Strait Exchange Foundation (SEF), 185
strategic fault line, 173–75
strategic rivalries: concept overview, 142–44; indicators for assessing intensity, 145; literature on, 141, 160; policy analysis, 249–50; post-industrial age, 151–63; Sino-American, 144–63
strategic triangles, 169–75, 225–26
strategies, 19–20, 246–50. See also *hezong*; *lianheng*
structural reforms, 30, 48, 100–102, 228
Subic Bay Naval Base, 192
sub-national identities, 158–59
Suga, Yoshihide, 233, 236
Su Hao, 89–90
Sukarno, 198–99
Sunflower Movement, 29
Sun Jianguo, 25, 25n9
Sunnylands, 81
supply chains, 96, 211–12, 228
surveillance, 3, 183, 196, 209, 213n25
Suu Kyi, Aung San, 3–4, 11–12, 203

TAC (Treaty of Amity and Cooperation), 8–9, 189, 200, 203
Taipei, 177–79, 184–85
Taiwan, 6, 29, 34, 35–40, 62–67, 122n9, 123–25, 134, 137, 148, 152, 158, 177–86, 251–52
Taiwan missile crisis, 177–78, 200
tao guang yang hui, 200, 242
tariffs, 18, 18n36, 97, 114, 167, 167n1, 211–12, 213, 228–29
Tatmadaw, 3–4, 199

taxation, 157
tax systems, 97
technologies: civilian, 158–59, 214; and decoupling, 213; and forced technology transfers, 231; and imports, 200; and industrial policy, 212–13; and leadership, 156, 213; military, 159–60, 214; surveillance, 196; and tech war, 18, 213n25, 214, 239–40
Terminal High Altitude Area Defense (THAAD), 49, 183–84
territorial claims, 3, 10, 13, 16, 87–89, 193–94, 206, 209, 211, 216, 249–50
territorial disputes, 49, 123–24, 142–44, 156, 182n23, 189, 211, 222, 234–35. See also nine-dash line; South China Sea
territorial integrity, 4–5, 189–90
Tesla, 65
THAAD (Terminal High Altitude Area Defense), 49, 183–84
Thailand, 3–4, 5, 49, 188, 192, 208, 212, 245
Thatcher, Margaret, 95
3rd Plenum of the 18th Party Congress, 15
Third World, 57–59
13th Five-Year Plan, 212
13th Party Congress, 8
Thirty Years' War, 4, 240
Thompson, William R., 143
threat perceptions, 25–26, 124–25, 135, 143–48, 151, 154–55, 157, 202
Tiananmen, 6, 8, 10, 18, 68, 80, 107, 130–31, 178, 200, 243–44, 247–48
Tibet, 18, 158
tied projects, 195
Tin-bor Hui, Victoria, 120–21n6
Together We Fight the Devils (TV drama), 67–68
Toshihiro, Nikai, 236
township and village enterprises (TVEs), 107
TPP-11, 233
TPP (Trans-Pacific Partnership), 2, 83, 87, 114, 133, 146, 190–91, 203, 228
trade: and ASEAN-American relations, 202–3; bilateral, 17–18, 134–37, 196, 211, 213, 237n46, 242, 247, 250; deficit, 96–99, 182; diversion,

237n46; and multilateral trading order, 76–77; Sino-American, 15–16, 18, 135–36, 167, 168n4, 189, 201, 210–11, 237n46; Sino-Japanese, 200; and trade disputes, 1–4, 18, 114, 210–11, 224–25, 227–28; trade surplus, 97, 109, 167, 211; and trade wars, 1–4, 16, 19, 114, 131, 145, 167–68, 168n4, 188–89, 211–14, 228–29, 231–32
transactional bilateralism, 87
Transatlantic Trade and Investment Partnership (TTIP), 114
transnational capital, 106
Trans-Pacific Partnership (TPP), 2, 83, 87, 114, 133, 146, 190–91, 203, 228
Treaty of Amity and Cooperation (TAC), 8–9, 189, 200, 203
triangles, 19–20, 169–80, 204–14, 225–33, 250–53
"trickle down" theory, 112, 247
Trudeau, Justin, 85
Trump, Donald J.: and alliance-building, 84, 182; and anti-China campaign, 16; and ASEAN-American relations, 203–4; and Asian order, 221–25; and China's foreign policy, 27; and China's rise, 25–26, 81, 242; and competition, 145; and COVID-19 pandemic, 55; and de-globalization, 119, 133, 249; and dual triangles, 210–11; and foreign policy, 17–18, 227; and Free and Open Indo-Pacific strategy, 191; and globalization-democratization project, 113–14; and hedging, 180–81; and identities, 159; and international relations, 137; and Japan, 232, 234; and Korea, 184; and multilateral trading order, 76–77; and neoliberalization, 130n31; and perception of China, 29–30, 37–38; and rise of economic state, 128–29; and Sino-US relations, 33–35; and strategic confrontation with China, 23; and Taiwan, 181; and trade wars, 3, 117, 131, 213–14; and transactional bilateralism, 87; and US-China-Japan Triangle, 226–29; and US-China rivalry, 162, 167–68; and value conflict, 48

Tsai Ying-wen, 66, 169, 251
TTIP (Transatlantic Trade and Investment Partnership), 114
TV dramas, 65–71
TVEs (township and village enterprises), 107
21st-Century Maritime Silk Road, 194–95
Twin Centenaries, 81
two Chinas rivalry, 192
"two-state" theory (Lee), 179
2008 financial crisis. *See* global financial crisis

UNCLOS (United Nations Convention on the Law of the Sea), 6, 10–11, 13, 18, 193–94
UNCTAD (United Nations Conference on Trade and Development), 237n46
UNESCO, 235
UN Human Rights Council (UNHRC), 6
unilateralism, 27, 133–34
unions, 95–96
United Front strategy, 198
United Kingdom, 154–55
United Nations Conference on Trade and Development (UNCTAD), 237n46
United Nations Convention on the Law of the Sea (UNCLOS), 6, 10–11, 13, 18, 193–94
United Nations' Division for Ocean Affairs and Law of the Sea, 210
United Nations (UN), 5, 6–8, 77, 79, 239, 245–46
United States: and American Empire in the 2000s, 103–6; and ASEAN-American relations, 202–4; and ASEAN-China relations, 192–93; and Asian order, 218–19, 221–25; and the Asia-Pacific, 75–90; and Australia, 84–87; and China's foreign policy, 27–33; and China's reincorporation into the global economy, 106–12; and China's rise, 26, 88–90; and dual triangles, 204–14; and East Asia international relations, 122–23, 131–38; and economic state, 127–31; and globalization-democratization

Index

project, 95–103, 105–6, 112–17; global military supremacy of, 98–99; and global order, 4–5; and hard-power competition, 46–48; and hedging, 175–82; hegemonic status, 82, 94–95, 190–91; and Korea, 183–84; and New Zealand, 84–87; and post-industrial age, 153–63; and public diplomacy, 23–27; and the Roosevelt corollary, 197, 197n7; and rules-based order, 17–18, 77; and Sino-American rivalry, 86–87, 120–23, 127–31, 133–37; and Sino-American trade, 15–16, 18, 135–36, 167, 168n4, 189, 201, 210–11, 237n46; and Sino-Japanese relations, 182–83; and Sino-US relations, 32–34; and strategic triangles, 169–75; and Taiwan, 177–80, 184–86; and territorial claims, 13; and US-China-Japan triangle, 225–37; and US-Soviet rivalry, 144–63; and the Vietnam War, 198
United States-Mexico-Canada Trade Agreement (USMCA), 85–86
unit veto, 170–73
University of California, Davis, 72–73
University of Illinois, 73
UN's International Council of Justice, 199
UN (United Nations), 5, 6–8, 77, 79, 239, 245–46
US Air Force, 159
USA Today (newspaper), 60
US Coast Guard, 210
USD (US dollars), 98, 109–12
US Federal Reserve, 109–10
US Foreign Agents Registration Act, 72
US International Development Finance Corporation (DFC), 208–9n22
US-Japan Security Treaty, 233
US Justice Department, 72, 229
USMCA (United States-Mexico-Canada Trade Agreement), 85–86
US Navy, 152, 159, 210, 250n25
USS *Decatur*, 152
US Treasuries, 93, 105, 109–10, 115
Uyghurs, 3

Valeriano, Brandon, 142

value chains, 18–19, 189, 200, 212, 214
value conflict, 48
value foundation, 89–90
Vanguard Bank, 210
Vasquez, John, 142–44
Vietnam, 5, 8–9, 11, 32, 38, 50, 87, 194, 197, 203–4, 208–10, 212, 242
Vietnam War, 95, 106, 192, 198–99
"Vision Statement on ASEAN-Japan Friendship and Cooperation," 201
Volcker, Paul, 95, 100

wage growth, 96, 99–100
wage level, 107
wage-price spiral, 94–96
waihui quan (Bank of China Foreign Exchange Certificate), 59
Walt, Steve, 172
war-related stories, 73–74
war reparations, 197
Warsaw Pact Organization (WPO), 5
wealth gap, 62–63, 230
weaponry, 20, 159–61, 213, 247, 250
Weber, Max, 130
wedge issues, 206–7, 214
weiji (crisis), 55
Westphalian Peace, 240
Westphalian system, 4–5, 8, 9, 246
whaling, 235
WHA (World Health Assembly), 185, 251
Who Are We? (Huntington), 104
Wilson, Edward, 221
Wolf Warrior 2 (film), 73–74
working classes, 112, 117, 156, 230
World Bank, 3n6, 5, 6–7, 16, 100–102, 196, 239, 245, 245n18
World Health Assembly (WHA), 185, 251
World Trade Organization (WTO), 7–8, 18, 80, 107–8, 113, 202, 239, 250
WPO (Warsaw Pact Organization), 5
WTO (World Trade Organization), 7–8, 18, 80, 107–8, 113, 202, 239, 250
Wu Bangguo, 72
Wu Po-hsiung, 62–63

Xi Jinping: and Asian identity, 89; and Belt and Road Initiative (BRI), 24, 147, 194; and challenge to American

leadership, 244–45; and China's rise, 2, 88–89, 214, 239, 241–42; and communist leadership, 15; and cross-Strait relationships, 185; and decoupling, 212; and foreign policy, 27–33; and globalization, 230; and hedging, 180–81; and international relations, 137; and Japan-China relations, 236; and market reform, 248; and mass mobilization, 60; and "New Asian Security Concept," 206–7; and perceptions of China's influence, 35–47; and peripheral diplomacy, 87–88; and repression, 231; and rules-based order, 17–18, 77–84; and Sino-US relations, 32–34; and the South China Sea, 209; and trade wars, 18, 213–14; and US-China rivalry, 151
Xi-Ma summit, 181, 185
Xinhua News Agency, 74
Xinjiang, China, 14, 26, 158, 195–96, 213n25
Xinjingbao (newspaper), 56

Yukichi, Fukuzawa, 204
Yukio, Hatoyama, 206

zero-sum game, 81, 142, 230, 250
Zhang Weiwei, 69
Zhang Yimou, 80
Zhang Zhaozhong, 69
Zhao Ziyang, 8
Zhonghua Minzu, 83
Zhou Enlai, 77, 246
Zhu Chenghu, 68–69
Zhu Rongji, 15

Lightning Source UK Ltd.
Milton Keynes UK
UKHW022334111221
395455UK00003B/305